# A
# Cultural
# DICTIONARY
# of
# PUNK
## 1974 – 1982

# Acknowledgments

Thank you to those who answered questions or pointed me in the right direction, including David Bowler, Norman Durkee, Howard Fields, Richard Hell, Craig Leon, Paul Marotta, Joe Rees, David Scharff, and David Thomas. And also to Ann E. Butler, senior archivist at the Fales Library and Special Collections at New York University.

To my colleagues and students at the University of Detroit Mercy: Your mix of curiosity, wonderment, and resistance to the world is a blessing to me.

I am thankful to David Barker, who first approached me about writing this book several years ago with the e-mail subject line "An odd suggestion." He and the designers, editors, and everyone else at Continuum have been wonderful to work with especially Max Novick and Claire Heitlinger.

To my mom and dad, Diane and Nick, who have always encouraged me to ask questions: This book is an answer to some of them. The ever-changing Maumee River shaped me more than you can know. My sisters, Andrea and Lisa: We made songs out of everything, even Risk. And for Kori: Never forgotten, always loved.

Niko and Maddy: You have grown so much, and so beautifully, during the writing of this book.

Finally and at last and forever, Lisa:

You, to me, are what love is.

# A Cultural DICTIONARY of PUNK

## 1974 – 1982

NICHOLAS ROMBES

continuum

NEW YORK • LONDON

2009

The Continuum International Publishing Group Inc
80 Maiden Lane, New York, NY 10038

The Continuum International Publishing Group Ltd
The Tower Building, 11 York Road, London SE1 7NX

www.continuumbooks.com

Copyright © 2009 by Nicholas Rombes

Library of Congress Cataloging-in-Publication Data

A catalog record for this book is available from the Library of Congress.

Printed in the United States of America

9780826427793

# Opening Shot

**This book is arranged as a series of entries,** of investigations really, into the raw materials of punk. Some entries offer facts, analysis, commentary. Some are accumulations and catalogs of evidence from primary-source materials: speeches, interviews, movies, novels, letters, lyrics, advertisements. A very few are stories. They are arranged alphabetically, out of deference to the reader. Ephraim P. Noble appears occasionally, when I could bear it no longer. (You'll see what I mean.) All in all, I have allowed the content of the entries to determine their shape, format, and tone. The book is neither a plea nor an apology for punk, which has always had its legions of fans. It is not a debunking of punk, either, for, at its best, punk demythologized itself. There are omissions, yes, because at the end of the day this book has a story to tell, and the entries in the pages before you *are* that story, shaped in no small part by punk's own methods of short and fast assaults.

When at all possible, I have gone back to primary-source materials, especially to original vinyl, newspapers, magazines, and fanzines. Walter Benjamin's *Arcades Project*, with its montage and passageways of quotes, provided a model.

Punk was such a radical, absurd, and dangerous phenomenon not just for what it was but for how it emerged in the context of its historical time. Like a weed, punk emerged during the parched decade between the sixties and the eighties, when the compass was spinning out of control, when the captain seemed to have abandoned the ship. Rather than limit the entries to facts about the songs, the bands, and the personalities, I have attempted to cast a wider net, illuminating some of the cultural undercurrents and codes that gave rise to punk. "Standing in the line we're aberrations / Defects in a defect's mirror / And we've been here all the time" go the opening lines from the Germs song "What We Do Is Secret." In your dream, there is the nighttime sound of crickets, and nothing else. In your dream, punk stayed a secret forever: It never became a trend, it never caught on, there was never a backlash against it, it never became the object of nostalgia, it never had any of its songs used in commercials or Guitar Hero or Rock Band, and it was never the subject of a book called *A Cultural Dictionary of Punk 1974–1982*, whose words you are reading at this moment, whoever you are, wherever you are.

N.R.
*Detroit, 2008*

"My overall situation is a black X on a black wall."

—Hunter S. Thompson (from a letter to Paul Semonin, June 6, 1962)

"He was, he knew, an anankastic, a person for whom reality had shrunk to the dimension of compulsion; everything he did was forced on him—there was for him nothing voluntary, spontaneous or free."

—Philip K. Dick, *The Simulacra* (1964)

"When my belly's going bad vodka soothes me and my belly's always going bad."

—Charles Bukowski (quoted in *Creem*, January 1976, p. 9)

"You can hear me for a million miles / I'm surrounded by a thousand dials / And what I want to see / Is a million more of me."

—Avengers, "Thin White Line" (1978)

"At least we weren't hippies."

—Mike Hudson, The Pagans

"Here the full nightmare of the hippie generation in control is laid out for all to see."

—Jon Savage (from a Screamers article, *Melody Maker*, 1979)

The new wave before the New Wave

## 400 Blows, The

**A French New Wave film** directed by François Truffaut, released in 1959. The movie centers on the everyday life of an alienated child, Antoine Doinel, played by Jean-Pierre Léaud. Richard Hell has cited *The 400 Blows* as one of the visual sources for his tattered clothes and cropped hair: "There were some artists that I admired who looked like that. Rimbaud looked like that. Artaud looked like that. And it also looked like the kid in *The 400 Blows*, the Truffaut movie. I remember I had a picture of those three guys. I really thought all this stuff out in '73 and '74."

But there is a moment of deeper alienation in the film, disguised as a sort of sweet and funny and nostalgic scene. Like all really subversive art, it doesn't seem subversive at first. The amusement park sequence, where Antoine is pinned to the wall in the rotating ride, is both thrilling and terrifying in its black-and-white glory. By allowing the scene to play out with natural sound, Truffaut ensures that we come to identify so closely with the boy that his alienation becomes ours. In a 1959 article on the French New Wave directors, Bosley Crowther noted the "brutal realism embraced in their attitudes." Whereas Warhol and others turned that realism and delinquency into camp as the sixties sputtered to nothing, punk—as imagined by Richard Hell and others—took it seriously and extended it into a brutality of sound, creating extended sonic landscapes in which characters like Antoine could, like us, become lost.

[Bosley Crowther, "New Wave in France," *The New York Times*, November 29, 1959, p. X1; Richard Hell, quoted in Clinton Heylin, *From the Velvets to the Voidoids: A Pre-Punk History for a Post-Punk World*, New York: Penguin, 1993, p. 121.]

# a

## *Adolescents*

**Released on Frontier Records in 1981,** the debut album by the Orange County punk/hardcore band the Adolescents is, for all its fierceness, an at times beautifully wrought, progressive work. This isn't obvious until the fourth track, "L.A. Girl," written by Tony Cadena when he was a student at Magnolia High, and specifically the tempo change that occurs at the forty-second mark, between the lines "You didn't create our scene" and "We don't care." In some ways, the song is, as Cadena has noted, a response to the Doors' "L.A. Woman," whose lines are ripe with a sort of mellow breeziness: "L.A. woman Sunday afternoon / Drive through your suburbs / Into your blues, into your blues, yeah." Featuring Tony Cadena on vocals, Frank and Rikk Agnew on guitar, Steve Soto on bass, and Casey Royer on drums.

"We did the first Adolescents show in a Boy Scout house up in Yorba Linda," Steve Soto has said, and you can imagine some of the songs on the album being played with acoustic guitar at night around a campfire as the dark is coming on and the forest creatures are stirring. Like the Ramones and the Sex Pistols before them, and Sonic Youth and Nirvana after them, the Adolescents wrote songs that, sometimes, moved beyond a mere reflection of their particular subculture and into the terrain of critique. "Kids of the Black Hole"—one of the best songs on the album and among the most brilliant of any punk/hardcore song—offers a searing portrait of "kids":

> Kids in the fast lane living for today
> No rules to abide by and no rules to obey
> Sex, drugs and fun is their only thought and care
> Another swig of brew another overnight affair
>
> Messages and slogans are the primary décor
> History's recorded on a clutter on the floor
> Inhabitants that searched the grounds for roaches or spare change
> Another night of chaos is so easy to arrange.

The lyrics are both a proclamation and an indictment—later on, Tony Cadena will sing, "Carefree in their actions as for morals they had none," and sound not too different from conservative social commentators of the time. But the song is of

The Adolescents in *New York Rocker*, 1981

course more than its lyrics, and this is the shattering paradox of rock and roll, and punk especially: The sound of the song and its lyrics are sometimes, beautifully, at odds with each other. You could listen to "Kids of the Black Hole" casually, knowing nothing about the band or the lyrics, and come away thinking that the snarling voice, the volume, the violence of the music suggest the morally bankrupt world that the song itself indicts.

The sheer force and speed of "Word Attack"—which lasts just over one minute—suggestthatitshouldbewrittenaboutinablurofwordswithnopause andnowaytocatchyourbreathinbetweenwordsbecausehumanbeingscanonlyplay instrumentsandsingsofastandthenitisuptoyourimaginationtogofasterand"Word Attack"pushesrightuptotheimaginationandifyouwantafastersongitwillhavetoexist onlyinyourmind.

The violence of hardcore—both in its performance and on vinyl—is such an obvious fact, now romanticized as "the good old days," that you are likely to see it either as the End of Something or the Beginning of Something. This is what Richard Meltzer said about the scene, and a 1981 concert featuring Black Flag and the Adolescents in particular, looking back on it from 1989: "After the cops closed down the joint, the kids (who the heroin addict Peter Townshend used to claim were alright) went out and trashed the ghetto, pissing and puking in doorways, hurling bottles through the window glass of fried-chicken stands, ripping wipers and antennas off old Buicks. Loathsome dogfood: Fuck 'em. I never went back."

[Richard Meltzer, "A Hermit's Tale" (1989), in *A Whore Just Like the Rest*; New York: Da Capo Press, 2000; Steve Soto interviewed by Marcia Taylor, www.skratchmagazine.com.]

## Adverts

**The Adverts, formed in 1976,** made one of the most deconstructive songs in punk with "One Chord Wonders," released in April 1977 on Stiff Records. Around that time, they consisted of T.V. Smith, Gaye Advert, Howard Pickup, and Laurie Driver. "There was no strange reason for the name Adverts," Smith has said. "It seemed like something that everybody could relate to, that was ironic." "One Chord Wonders" is just a catchy pop song, and it is just a form of radical theory:

I wonder what we'll play for you tonight
Something heavy or something light
Something to set your soul alight
I wonder how we'll answer when you say
"We don't like you—go away
Come back when you've learned to play."

I wonder what we'll do when things go wrong
When we're halfway through our favourite song
We look up and the audience has gone
Will we feel a little bit obscure?
Think "we're not needed here
We must be new wave—
They'll like us next year."
The Wonders don't care
We don't give a damn.

The entire song turns on the line "Will we feel a little bit obscure," which is both a lament and a badge of honor. But it is also a paradox—especially in punk, where obscurity was for many fans the mark of a band's authenticity. In a survey of U.K. New Wave bands in the May–June issue of *New York Rocker*, Kris Needs wrote that the single was "fast and rocky, but melodic." It is that melody that masks the song's rough sentiments. At their best, on songs like "One Chord Wonders," "Bored Teenagers," and "Television's Over," they barely keep up with themselves; the beauty of the Adverts was that, on several of their recordings, remarkably, the anarchy of their sound was not refined away.

Of course, the band eventually disintegrated. The former members are, I am sure, doing productive and equally fascinating work today.

[Kris Needs, "And the Best of the Rest," *New York Rocker*, May–June, p. 22; T.V. Smith quoted in Jon Savage, *England's Dreaming: Anarchy, Sex Pistols, Punk Rock, and Beyond*; New York: St. Martin's Press, 1992, p. 293.]

## Against Method

Insomuch as seventies punk was part of a larger cultural crisis that saw deep economic recession in the United Kingdom and the United States, the catastrophe of the Vietnam War, the Watergate scandal, etc., books like *Against Method*, published in 1975 by the philosopher Paul Feyerabend, are a ghostly backdrop. Is this an optional entry in this big book? No, and if you skip it, something very bad will happen to you. In *Against Method*, Feyerabend suggests that although we tend to think of science and progress as rationalist, it is precisely an anarchist spirit that underlies our most cherished and significant scientific developments. The most radical thinkers—and, paradoxically, those thinkers whose radical ideas eventually become accepted into the mainstream—are those who accept a big dose of chaos and anarchy into their thinking and methods. The most revolutionary scientists, Feyerabend suggests, have not followed the methodologies, traditions, and paradigms set out before them, but rather have abandoned the prison house of order and reason.

Punk's method was remarkably similar, as it shattered the conventions of music at the time. Here are some things that Feyerabend wrote, describing science in the same spirit that animated punk's rule-breaking spirit:

More specifically, one can show the following: given any rule, however "fundamental" or "rational," there are always circumstances when it is advisable not only to ignore the rule, but to adopt its opposite.

Allegiance to the new ideas will have to be brought about by irrational means such as propaganda, emotion, ad hoc hypotheses and appeal to prejudices of all kinds. We need these "irrational means" in order to uphold what is nothing but a blind faith.

In all these cases we have a practice, or a tradition, we have certain influences upon it, emerging from another practice or tradition and we observe a change. The change may lead to a slight modification of the original practice, it may eliminate it, it may result in a tradition that barely resembles either of the interacting elements.

Punk's relation to tradition was deeply contradictory: It returned to the fun, simple music of the fifties and early sixties only to destroy it. Punk was irrational, but only for a brief time. By late 1977, it had become notorious enough to cease being notorious. The final Sex Pistols concert, in San Francisco on January 14, 1978, effectively put an end to the notoriety of punk's *method* of provocation. Punk worked best in secret, as a rumor, an expectation. In confirming the public's expectations, the Sex Pistols also destroyed them. They were *against method*. Which meant they had no choice but to destroy themselves.

[Paul Feyerabend, *Against Method*, 3rd ed., 1975; repr., New York: Verso, 1993, pp. 14, 114, 215.]

# Agnew, Spiro

See *Sixties, punk as a rejection of*

# "Alternative Ulster"

**A single by Belfast's Stiff Little Fingers**, released in 1978.

Nothin' for us in Belfast
The Pound's so old it's a pity
OK, there's the trident in Bangor
Then walk back to the city.

Take a look where you're livin'
You got the Army on your street
And the RUC dog of repression
Is barking at your feet.

The music is relentless and only hints at fun. "Growing up in Belfast means death, a murder rate almost as high as Detroit's, bombings, detention camps, kneecappings and a sectarian divide so wide that at times you might as well consider Northern

Ireland as two separate countries," Peter Silverton wrote in *Sounds* in 1978. Four months later, these words appeared in *The New York Times*, under the headline BOMB IN RESTAURANT KILLS 14 IN ULSTER; MANY CHILDREN ARE AMONG DEAD—I.R.A. IS SUSPECTED:

> A bomb exploded last night in a restaurant where more than 400 people had gone for dinner and dancing, killing at least 14 persons, many of them children, the police said.

The previous year, the *Green Book*—the IRA training manual issued to new volunteers—was revised from its 1956 version. The *Green Book* said many things, including:

> Volunteers are expected to wage a military war of liberation against a numerically superior force. This involves the use of arms and explosives. Firstly the use of arms. When volunteers are trained in the use of arms they must fully understand that guns are dangerous, and their main purpose is to take human life, in other words to kill people, and volunteers are trained to kill people. It is not an easy thing to take up a gun and go out to kill some person without strong convictions or justification.
>
> The strategy is:
>
> 1. A war of attrition against enemy personnel which is aimed at causing as many casualties and deaths as possible so as to create a demand from their people at home for their withdrawal.
>
> 2. A bombing campaign aimed at making the enemy's financial interest in our country unprofitable while at the same time curbing long term financial investment in our country.

They say that U.S. punk was—until hardcore—basically nonpolitical. This is because everything was already political in the United States during the Watergate period, which ended, mercifully, in the hot summer of 1974. But in the United Kingdom it was bombs and bullets. "If punk rock is a class war in England," wrote Marylou Luther in *The Los Angeles Times*, "as the Sex Pistols' manager Malcolm McLaren claims, or a new subculture of second- and third-generation welfare kids bent on terrifying the middle class, it seems definitely less threatening here in the U.S."

And Stiff Little Fingers made a song that you are reading about now, and that you should go listen to now.

["Bomb in Restaurant Kills 14 in Ulster; Many Children Among Dead-I.R.A. Is Suspected," *The New York Times*, February 18, 1978; Irish Republican Army, *Green Book*, available at http://uk.geocities.com/oglaigh_na_heireann3Z/THE_GREEN_BOOK.html; Marylou Luther, "Shock Chic: The Punk Persuasion," *Los Angeles Times*, July 31, 1977, p. E1; Peter Silverton, "Stiff Little Fingers," *Sounds*, October 7, 1978.]

## "Anarchy Is Dead"

**A song by Government Issue (the G.I.s)** that lasts half a minute. And yet you get the feeling that if the band could have made it even shorter, they would have. Technically, it's probably not the fastest punk song, but in your mind it is. John Stabb on vocals, with John Barry, Brian Gay, and Mark Alberstadt. Recorded in July 1981, and released in September on the *Legless Bull* EP.

## Angry Young Men

**In the fifties, a group of writers—**John Osborne, Philip Larkin, Kingsley Amis, Alan Sillitoe, and others—came to be known by this name. The critic Edgar Wind wrote that "Brecht's famous technique of 'alienation' sought to break up the inertia of empathy; and it is well known how Angry Young Men have tried to shock their public into attention—but these effects have little chance of lasting." In its rejection of sentimentality, punk shared some characteristics with this movement.

[Edgar Wind, *Art and Anarchy: The Reith Lectures, 1960*, London: Faber and Faber, 1963, p. 10.]

## *Art and Fear*

**The title of a book published in France in 2000** under the title *La procédure silence*, and in its translated form in the United States and the United Kingdom in 2003. The book is by Paul Virilio, and it is not about punk, but the pitiful destruction of the human form in art and in science:

Remember what Friedrich Nietzsche advised: "*Simplify your life: die!*" This extremist simplification in which "ornament is a crime," has stayed with us throughout the history of the twentieth century, from the pointlessly repeated assault on the peaks of the Chemin des Dames in 1917 to the genocide perpetuated by the Khmer Rouge in Cambodia in the Seventies.

Avant-garde artists, like many political agitators, propagandists and demagogues, have long understood what TERRORISM would soon popularize: if you want a place in "revolutionary history" there is nothing easier than provoking a riot, an assault on propriety, in the guise of art.

Punk's dictum—DESTROY!—has been rendered harmless by the passage of time; no one today takes pop music seriously as philosophy. But during the seventies, there were serious discussions about the "meaning" of punk, and not in academic journals but in the pages of fanzines and music-press publications. In 1978, Tom Carson wrote this in *New York Rocker*:

> What had always bothered me about punk was that its vision was completely negative. It foresaw no possibility of redemption. Worse, its audience—which needs redemption like you wouldn't believe—didn't seem to want any. They were perfectly willing to get off on destruction, but they didn't give a damn about what they were going to replace it with.

The reason punk became a mainstream commodity, made safe enough for easy consumption by listeners who themselves knew or cared little about the punk scene, had less to do with money and greed and more to do with the way that the dominant order (whatever that may be, or mean, at specific moments in history) incorporated punk in order to negate or weaken its "negativity." Raymond Williams has written about how the dominant culture "selects" what it deems significant from the past in order to shape the present, "the way in which from a whole possible area of past and present, certain meanings and practices are chosen for emphasis, certain other meanings and practices are neglected and excluded." As early as the late seventies, the most violent, negative tendencies in punk were being redirected into the emerging California hardcore scene, which magnified punk's dark side, even as power pop evolved out of the more melodic, sunny side of punk. The potentially destructive, anarchic elements of punk never became a threat because the scene fragmented into competing micro-scenes and independent labels.

Near the end of *Art and Fear*, Virilio writes that "contemporary art can't quite shake off the accusation of passivity, indeed, of pointlessness." Punk's greatest achievement was—for a brief, glimmering time—transforming its own pointlessness into something unforgettable.

[Tom Carson, "Truth & Beauty Etcetera," *New York Rocker*, February–March 1977 [1978], p. 60; Paul Virilio, *Art and Fear*, translated by Julie Rose, London: Continuum, 2003, pp. 31, 93; Raymond Williams, *The Raymond Williams Reader*, ed. John Higgins, 1973; repr., Oxford, United Kingdom: Blackwell Publishers, 2001, p. 169.]

## "Art of Noises, The" futurist manifesto

**In her essay "Futurism: Proto-Punk,"** Karen Pinkus examines the relationship between Italian Futurism and punk, much like Greil Marcus explored the secret affinities between the Situationist Internationale and punk in *Lipstick Traces*. Here is one of the things she says:

> Futurism created an immediate mass scandal, and the members of the movement began to organize "evenings" (happenings) that combined drama, music, politics,

provocation, and assault on the audience. The performances were violent, and as the Futurists gained notoriety throughout Italy, they were stalked by a sizeable police presence which only helped to further arouse the curiosity of the spectators.

In particular, Pinkus looks to the 1913 "Art of Noises" manifesto, written by Luigi Russolo, which argues for the deformation and destruction of traditional musical methods and the creation of a new form of musical noise that harnesses the chaos of everyday sounds. Here are a few quotes:

- "Nowadays musical art aims at the shrillest, strangest and most dissonant amalgams of sound. Thus we are approaching noise-sound. This revolution of music is paralleled by the increasing proliferation of machinery sharing in human labor."

- "But our ears, far from being satisfied, keep asking for bigger acoustic sensations."

- "It is hardly possible to consider the enormous mobilization of energy that a modern orchestra represents without concluding that the acoustic results are pitiful. Is there anything more ridiculous in the world than twenty men slaving to increase the plaintive meowing of violins?"

- "I can't repress much longer the intense desire to create a true musical reality finally by distributing big loud slaps right and left, stepping and pushing over violins and pianos, bassoons and moaning organs! Let's go out!"

If punk channeled noise into short, confined outbursts of melody, then the building blocks of that noise were to be found in many proto-punk bands from the 1974–75 period. The work of the Futurists and other members of the avant-garde was frequently discussed in even the most mainstream music publications (see *Theory, punk as a form of*). Lest you think that this entry on *futurism* is something concocted by some hare-brained academic with too much time on his hands (and too much beer at his side) consider this statement by Vale, the publisher of *Search and Destroy*:

Punk rock started as a kind of rebellion against rock, what rock music & pop music had turned into. This kind of rebellion had happened before; at the beginning of the century the Dadaists and Futurists had tried to completely overturn every musical value and oppose noise to it, as in Luigi Russolo's essay "The Art of Noises." I was always interested in extending my critique of culture and society further.

In the United States, Cleveland, Ohio, was an especially fertile ground for sonic experimentation. Just listen to "Now" by the Electric Eels, three minutes and eighteen seconds of melody-less clatter from a clarinet, two guitars, and drums recorded in September 1975. Paul Marotta has said that "noise was a big part of the Eels . . .

We really believe that mainstream FM radio in Cleveland would embrace the Eels as another part of the local scene."

[Paul Marotta, liner notes to *Those Were Different Times: Cleveland 1972–1976*, Scat Records.; Vale quoted in James Stark, *Punk, '77*, San Francisco: Stark Grafix, 1992, p. 27.]

## "Art Rock"

**An article by Tony Rocco** from the fanzine *Damage*, published in 1980. In retrospect, it is startling how quickly punk was dismissed even within the punk community.

Perhaps the strength of punk is in its limitations, in spite of the fact that those limitations make it difficult to be original and easy to repeat worn clichés. Punk rock is pretty much a cliché now. The suburbanites are catching up with it and that, based on past experience, means it's at least two years past being worthwhile.

But of course the suburbanites had always been a part of punk. And yet by 1980, when a lot of the fun and absurdity of punk and the seventies had faded, the grubby paradoxes of the time were giving way to the new, clean, coherent ideology of the conservative movement. Nostalgia for the fifties—which had been an important part of punk's appeal—had become literal with the election of Ronald Reagan.

[Tony Rocco, "Art Rock," *Damage* vol. 1, no. 5, 1980, p. 25.]

## Ashbery, John

**Although not as obviously associated** with the New York underground/punk scene that developed in the early and mid-seventies as writers like William Burroughs, the poet John Ashbery (b. 1927) was an influence on Richard Hell, Patti Smith, and others. His 1977 book *Houseboat Days* has lines and fragments that you imagine as being from distant, buried songs from that era, recorded and then locked away forever—like these, for instance:

They all came, some wore sentiments / Emblazoned on T-shirts
(from "The Other Tradition")

That will someday paste a black, bleeding label / In the sky
(from "Variant")

The time of all forgotten / things is at hand
(from "Collective Dawns")

Our behavior was anarchically / Correct, at least by New Brutalism
standards

(from "Daffy Duck in Hollywood")

They live with us. And we understand them when they sing

(from "All Kinds of Carresses")

[John Ashbery, *Houseboat Days*, 1977; repr., New York: Farrar, Straus and Giroux, 1999.]

## Ask the Dust

**In 2006, Thomas Pynchon** published a long novel called *Against the Day*, which is not
nearly as good as John Fante's novel *Ask the Dust*, published in 1939. Long before I
discovered punk, I discovered Charles Bukowski, who led me to John Fante and the
book that is the subject of this brief entry. So, when I finally discovered punk in the
records spread out on the bedroom floor of the girl whose sister I would eventually
fall in love with and marry, I was prepared for its humor and truthfulness by passages
like this one from *Ask the Dust*. Here is the setup: The narrator, Arturo Bandini, is
a struggling Los Angeles writer. In this scene, he visits a Catholic Church because
he is having some problems with women and with writing. Recently, and to his
delight and pride, he has had a story of his, "The Little Dog Laughed," published in
a literary magazine edited by a man named J. C. Hackmuth:

> The priest came to the door. He was stocky, powerful, smoking a cigar, a man in
> his fifties. "What is is?" he asked.
>
> I told him I wanted to see him alone. I had some trouble on my mind. . . . The
> priest opened the door and led me to his study. It was a small room crammed with
> books and magazines. My eyes bulged. There in one corner was a huge stack of
> Hackmuth's magazine. I walked to it at once and pulled out the issue containing
> *The Little Dog Laughed*. The priest had seated himself. "This is a great magazine,"
> I said. "The greatest of them all."
>
> The priest crossed his legs, shifted his cigar.
>
> "It's rotten," he said, "Rotten to the core."
>
> "I disagree," I said. "I happen to be one of its leading contributors."
>
> "You?" the priest asked. "And what did you contribute?"
>
> I spread *The Little Dog Laughed* before him on the desk. He glanced at it,
> pushed it aside. "I read that story," he said. "It's a piece of hogwash."

The punk imagination is alive and well in passages like this, where the weight of
authority is rendered with such exaggerated humor that you can't help but love the
underdog—in this case a writer. Forty-some years later, the underdog would be a

musician. When told his music was "rotten," he would take the term and wear it as a badge of honor. In fact, he would take it as his name and make music even more catastrophic than he thought possible.

[John Fante, *Ask the Dust*, 1939; repr., New York: HarperPerennial, 2006, pp. 73–74.]


# Avengers

**In 1967, Joan Didion published an essay,** "Slouching Towards Bethlehem," about San Francisco and Haight Street that began, "The center was not holding." Ten years later, a San Francisco band, Avengers, formed. Their first recordings feature Penelope Houston, Danny "Furious" O'brien, Greg Ingraham, and James Wilsey, some of whom attended the San Francisco Art Institute. There is a catastrophe and beauty in their music that bridges the gap between the melodic, almost nostalgic East Coast punk of the Ramones and what would become the darker, more serious hardcore punk of West Coast groups like Black Flag. Although they never released a full album, their influence is deep and wide, in part because they played with the Sex Pistols at their last show at the Winterland Ballroom in January 1978. Looking at pictures of the band today, it is difficult to imagine how unusual their short hair was. As V. Vale has noted, "[U]nlike in England, most of the people who started Punk in San Francisco were still under the stylistic influence of the Sixties Hippie youth movement—consequently they sported long, or at least longish, hair. . . . The first band to sport very short hair was the Avengers." But that is not why you should know about them.

Their best songs always stake out ambivalent territories and work as a form of radioactive theory. "Open Your Eyes," from early 1978, is built on a relentless roar, as if the Ramones were to meet heavy metal. The first verse goes like this:

At first I thought you were dead
but now I see you're one of the rest
they drugged you with musak and TV sedation
you're one of the blank generation

A seven-inch featuring "Blank Generation" was released in 1976 by Richard Hell & the Voidoids, and the phrase "blank generation" had, by 1978, circulated widely. Out of Richard Hell's mouth, the term was wildly unstable, hovering somewhere between a bold new proclamation and generational self-condemnation. But coming out of Penelope Houston's mouth, the phrase turned back in on itself in an almost didactic manner. It was as if all the junky things the New York bands celebrated—TV and comics and TV dinners and war movies—were suddenly the drugs of the masses. As you listened to groups like Avengers and Gang of Four, you wondered: Did you want your music to tell you how you ought to feel, or did you want it to confirm for you the way you really felt? When you listened to groups like the Dictators and the Ramones you thought, "Yeah, that's me!" But when you listened to groups like Avengers or Gang of Four, with their relentless critique of pop culture and social norms, you thought, "Maybe that *should* be me!"

"The American in Me," produced in 1978 by Steve Jones and Avengers, confirms and renounces the stereotypically ugly, shallow American: "It's the American in me that makes me watch the blood / running out of the bullethole in his head. / It's the American in me that makes me watch TV." And later, "It's the American in me says it's an honor to die / in a war that's just a politician's lie." In truth, links between the sixties and the seventies are everywhere in Avengers songs, from their remake of the Stones' 1966 "Paint It Black" to songs like "The American in Me" with its references to Kennedy. It was as if the sixties were a nightmare that punk could not disavow precisely because it *was* a nightmare and provided a sort of black well of information that could be reconstituted under the banner of punk. Avengers, like so many later bands, ranging from Hole to Nirvana, wrote lyrics that were wildly unstable, veering back and forth between sincerity and mockery. In "Thin White Line," Penelope Houston sang, "You can hear me for a million miles / I'm surrounded by a thousand dials / And what I want to see / Is a million more of me." The lyrics are both ironic and affirmative: In some ways, punk *did* want to level the world with a sonic boom, even as it mocked the self-serious full-soundedness of arena bands.

James Stark has written that bands like Avengers emerged out of the need young people felt to create something of their own: "Young people felt they were not part of nor did they want to be part of the culture of the Sixties and Seventies. They wanted to be part of something *they* created." By the mid seventies—as Hollywood was discovering the blockbuster in movies like *Jaws* and *Star Wars*—punk was rejecting overproduced spectacle, but not spectacle. Looking back on it, the frantic pace of punk, as bands raced through songs and through history, was a bold, doomed attempt to escape the void, the center that was not holding. Or, truer yet: doomed because, by 1977, there was no center.

[James Stark, *Punk '77: An Inside Look at the San Francisco Rock n' Roll Scene, 1977*, Stark Grafix, 1992, p. 56; V. Vale, "What Is Punk Rock and How Did It Begin?" RE/Search Publications, www.researchpubs.com/features/whatispunk.php.]

**b**

# Bad Brains

**"Bad Brains are *perhaps* the most important** hardcore band ever . . . but they are definitely the most *interesting* one," James Porter and Jake Austen have written. Over the years, more than a few people have suggested that punk was essentially a reactionary movement against "black" rhythm-and-blues-based rock and roll. As with all Grand Narrative theories, this is a gross oversimplification, and yet . . . Isn't there a grain of truth in the claim? Bad Brains is a counterexample: a black band that, sometimes, played punk. "By becoming punks," Mark Andersen and Mark Jenkins have written, "Bad Brains had entered a largely white world. The band members were often harassed in the black community, where 'punk' was an anti-gay slur, but some of their initial experiences in the white rock scene were scarcely more encouraging. While distributing fliers at a heavy metal show at the Keg, McCray says, they were harassed and called 'nigger' by some in the crowd."

Bad Brains' members were HR (Paul Hudson), Dr. Know (Gary Miller), Darryl Jenifer, Earl Hudson, and (briefly) Sid McCray. Originally founded in 1975 as a jazz band (called Mindpower), the band was changed once McCray played HR *Never Mind the Bollocks, Here's the Sex Pistols* and *No New York* in 1979. Most of all, they played very, very fast, and skillfully; footage of them from 1979 and 1980 show them tearing through songs in ways that made the Ramones look like balladeers at a home for the aging just before it is shuttered by health inspectors. However the real power of the band was not in simply playing the fastest, but in slowing everything down on the reggae/dub tracks; the result was like flooring the accelerator and then slamming on the breaks, over and over again.

Bad Brains are sometimes glossed over as a Reagan-era "political" band, as if they merely sloganeered their way through their songs. But the truth is more radically disturbing. Some of the band's songs contain a sort of mystical-political critique. Babylon—as a place and as the idea of a place—figures in interviews and songs as the United States, especially as HR became more deeply involved with Rastafari.

    **a.** Babylon, in the Bible, from Revelations 18:

        1  "And after these things I saw another angel come down from heaven, having great power; and the earth was lighted with his glory.

        2  "And he cried mightily with a strong voice, saying, Babylon the great is fallen, is fallen, and is become the habitation of devils, and the hold of every foul spirit, and a cage of every unclean and hateful bird.

3 "For all nations have drunk of the wine of the wrath of her fornication, and the kings of the earth have committed fornication with her, and the merchants of the earth are waxed rich through the abundance of her delicacies."

b. "Leaving Babylon," from the first album (released originally as cassette only) in 1982: "Say I'm leaving this Babylon / It will not be too long / It will not be too long now / I said my people are starving but your money's runnin / Your dollar, dollar drop down real low."

c. "Destroy Babylon," from their second album, *Rock for Light* (1983): "How many days do we sit around / while they keep on burying all our leaders in the ground / Organize, centralize / It's time for us to fight for our lives / Destroy Babylon / Oh there is a way."

d. From a 1981 interview in *Now What*: "HR: They [youth] know that things are really messed up in the U.S. . . . these cats are trying to fool us and they just think everything is rosy and dandy here in America; it's just not true. How long do we keep our eyes closed to the fact?"

e. From a 1982 interview in *Flipside*:

> **FS:** How'd it go in SF?
>
> **HR:** Well, it's ok but too many faggots.
>
> **FS:** Oh Yeah! Welcome to California! How do they bother you?
>
> **HR:** Well because they act confused . . .
>
> **FS:** They act confused?
>
> **HR:** They act confused.
>
> **FS:** They act confused or are confused?
>
> **HR:** They act confused.
>
> **FS:** You don't think they are?
>
> **HR:** Well that goes along with it but mostly if they just act sensible they wouldn't be so bad, most of them act so crazy even out in public, it disturbs me, makes me want to go out and shoot one of them.

[Mark Andersen and Mark Jenkins, *Dance of Days: Two Decades of Punk in the Nation's Capital*, New York: Akashic, 2003, p. 37; David Byers, Sarah Woodell, and Tom Bizarre, "Bad Brains: An Update," *Now What*, October 25, 1981, www.30underdc.com; "Bad Brains Interview," *Flipside* no. 31, April 1982, www.30underdc.com; James Porter and Jake Austen, "Black Punk Time: Blacks in Punk, New Wave and Hardcore 1976–1983," *Roctober* no. 32, 2002, p. 43.]

*Pink Flamingos*: The Tyranny of Incoherence

# Bad Taste in 1974

**An advertisement from *The Village Voice*,** August 1974. Nixon had just resigned. Television's and the Ramones' first public performances had occurred several months earlier. The ad is for a midnight showing of John Waters's *Pink Flamingos* (1972), proclaiming it as "an exercise in poor taste" and it is just that: the revenge of real, terrible, funny, absurdity—completely politically incorrect—in the face of the orthodoxies of the counterculture and the seriousness of women's liberation, proper eating, pacifism, brotherhood and sisterhood, self-actualization. *Pink Flamingos* breaks all sorts of rules in ways that are both shocking and mundane: When the police arrive to answer a complaint about an out-of-control birthday party at Babs's trailer, they are promptly beaten to death and then—of course—eaten. The cannibals are not the zombies of *Night of the Living Dead*. They are zombies of a different sort, brought back to life.

In the same year that saw the release of *Pink Flamingos*, Joan Didion said this about the Women's Movement:

> The idea that fiction has certain irreducible ambiguities seemed never to occur
> to these women [the feminist theorists], nor should it have, for fiction is in most

ways hostile to ideology. They have invented a class; now they had only to make that class conscious. They seized as a political technique a kind of shared testimony at first called a "rap session," then called "consciousness-raising" . . . They purged and regrouped and purged again, worried out one another's errors and deviations, the "elitism" here, the "careerism" there. It would have been merely sententious to call some of their thinking Stalinist: of course it was.

"The relation between boredom and Camp taste cannot be overestimated," Susan Sontag wrote. "Camp taste is by its nature possible only in affluent societies or circles capable of experiencing the psychopathology of affluence." Excess without meaning; that was *Pink Flamingos*, and that was the seventies, which was a decade of exaggeration in fashion, in music, in movies. The sudden zoom shot in movies found its equivalent in the suddenness of the New York Dolls or Alice Cooper or early punk. The incoherence of the early part of the decade was the triumph of bad taste over ordered aesthetics, as the excesses and the remainders of the counterculture floated freely, unanchored to any larger social "meaning."

Early punk was both the last expression of bad taste linked to the sixties and the first expression of the coming reformation and order of the conservative era, which in the early 1980s began to "correct" the avant-garde elements of the counterculture, in part by absorbing them into safer pop cultural forms. Movies like *Beyond the Valley of the Dolls* (1970), *Pink Flamingos, Coffy* (1973) *Phantom of the Paradise* (1974), and *The Rocky Horror Picture Show* (1975) were so oversaturated with meaning that there was no meaning at all. Their extravagance in terms of camera movement, split screens, music, acting, plot, and genre conflation made it impossible to accept them on any terms except those imposed by the films themselves. The result was an audience tyrannized by the films: You either were "in on" them or you were not. Strangely, punk achieved the same effects through the opposite of extravagance—minimalism. And while, at first, punk's outrageousness seemed to be just another confirmation of bad taste, it quickly became apparent that punk was coherent. Like the "bad taste" movies and musicals of previous years, it too pillaged different styles (the Phil Spector Sound, mod rock, etc.) but with a difference: In punk, everything sounded the same. The musical styles collapsed in a sort of pastiche that transcended camp, for there was nothing campy about punk. It may have been, by turns, absurd, satirical, self-deprecating, and mocking, but its orientation was not camp because, in spite of its hostility, the music did not hold you at a distance.

[Joan Didion, "The Women's Movement," in *The White Album*, New York: Farrar, Straus and Giroux, 1979, p. 112; Susan Sontag, "Notes on 'Camp,'" in *Against Interpretation and Other Essays*, New York: Farrar, Strauss and Giroux, p. 289.]

## Balm, Trixie A.

**You probably don't know her name** (she was really Lauren Agnelli, a rock-crit writer who made, for a while, nearly perfect music in the band Nervus Rex), but she wrote a prophetic review of the Dictators' album *The Dictators Go Girl Crazy!* (1975) with lines that explained punk before it had entered the public imagination. "Basically a vocal group using rudimentary riffs and instrumentals—frenetic and fuzzed-out guitar, strong emphasis on beat, adherence to 4-4 tempo—the Dictators aren't much bothered by having a facsimile sound or with taking tedious breaks." Plus, she used the word "punk" twice: "The Dictators parody the California Dream in *Go Girl Crazy*, eternally on the cruise for burgers, the perfect wave, and monkeyshines ooh la la—with punk aplomb," and, a little later, "braggarts and rowdies, the vinylized punk menace, they're a slice of Deco-American life: casualties of Coca Cola Drain." The amazing thing is not that Trixie A. Balm attached her name to these lines, but that she wrote them in such proximity to ground zero, and that she was right.

[Trixie A. Balm, review of *The Dictators Go Girl Crazy!*, *Creem*, June 1975, p. 64.]

## Bangs, Lester

**Lester Bangs was born in Escondido, California,** in December 1948. His first published work was a 1969 review of the MC5's *Kick Out the Jams* for *Rolling Stone*, the magazine for which he continued writing until 1973, and then again beginning in 1979. He moved to Detroit and wrote for *Creem* from 1971 until 1976, when he left Detroit for New York City, where he wrote for *The Village Voice*, *New York Rocker*, *New Musical Express*, *Gig Magazine*, the *Los Angeles Times*, and other outlets.

More than any other writer, Bangs captured the menace, the absurdity, the end-of-the-world glory of punk rock. His writing played like a form of expressionistic conversation. Bangs's strategy was to lure you in through a slangy banter that read like a cross between the hard-boiled dialogue of classic film noir and the everyday chatter of a street-corner conversation, such as these lines from his 1971 essay "James Taylor Marked for Death": "You can talk about yer MC5 and yer Stooges and even yer Grand Funk and Led Zep, yep, alla them badasses've carved out a hunka turf in this town, but I tell you there was once a gang that was so bitchin' *bad* that they woulda cut them dudes down to snotnose crybabies and in less than three minutes too." Bangs had a habit of incorporating his own myth (even before there was a myth) into his writing in a way that suggested *Mad* magazine crosswired with Theodor Adorno. In a 1975 review of Kraftwerk's *Autobahn*, he says that he received a letter in the mail that went like this: "DEAR LESTER—YOU BIG PHONY. WHY DON'T YOU DROP YOUR PRETENSE. YOU DON'T LIKE ROCK ANYMORE, DO YOU? YOURS TRULY, HAPPY JACK."

But eventually Bangs's essays (well, most of them) would move into more serious territory. Like Hunter S. Thompson and the film critic Pauline Kael, Bangs was deeply disaffected and even alienated from the trends, scenes, and movements about which he wrote.

His essays, for all their humorous and deeply humane camaraderies, were really pessimistic critiques and even moralistic indictments of the world he was documenting. In his notorious essay "The White Noise Supremacists," for instance, Bangs cut straight into the dark heart of punk: "So many of the people around the CBGB's and Max's scene have always seemed emotionally if not outright physically crippled—you see speech impediments, hunchbacks, limps, but most of all an overwhelming spiritual flatness. You take parental indifference, a crappy educational system, lots of drugs, media overload, a society with no values left except the hysterical emphasis on physical perfection, and you end up with these little nubbins."

Bangs's writing was a form of critique, of theory, in disguise. Like punk itself—especially the work of Patti Smith, John Cale, Richard Hell, the Ramones, the Sex Pistols, and Wire—Bangs was avant-garde, a writer whose influence, ironically, has made possible the worst possible sort of personal-essay-criticism that substitutes the author's own "personal life story" for skeptical criticism. Of course, Bangs showed that all criticism is, at its heart, autobiographical. The sweet sadness for us today of Bangs's writing is that it illuminated a path not taken; it showed how criticism could find a middleway between arid academicism ("theory") and populist sentiment. In his James Taylor piece, when he asked, "Am I a crank? I feel somewhat like the Uncle Scrooge of pop top journalism; except that twenty-two seems like no age to wear the persona of cantankerous koot so naturally," he was really acknowledging the impossibility of writing about culture—of pop music specifically—in a serious and unforgiving way without coming across as too serious, too critical. If one of the nagging questions that informed his work was, *Does the stuff that I'm writing about really deserve to be written about?*, the answer was *yes*, because his writing did more than simply inform on what was happening—it actually gave beautiful shape and form to the disparate threads that constituted punk. Like all good critics and theorists, Bangs cultivated a stance and created a story that demanded response.

His professional writing span—from 1969 to 1982—encapsulated the great transitional period in the United States between the comfortable, largely white, middle-class hope and idealism of the sixties and the vicious reality of the 1980s. For the seventies really were a sort of threshold era, an undefined decade, epitomized by loser, underdog, anti-heroes like Walter Matthau in *The Bad News Bears*, Bill Murray in *Meatballs*, or the unlikely presidency of the peanut farmer Jimmy Carter.

Although he was not the first to use the word "punk" in relation to music, the word shows up in a lot of his columns in the years before "punk rock" came to mean what it does today. In a 1973 review of *Buddy Guy and Junior Wells Play the Blues*,

Bangs made a blues-to-heavy-metal-to-punk family tree that is important but largely forgotten. He noted that "metal heavies like Stooges and Black Sabbath build their songs on two or three notes as identical as the stock riffs of the most lame rib joint bluesman." And then he wrote of "this new era of Blues as More Punk Rock."

Bangs was a punk writer because he created the conditions of his own acceptance. He concocted a stance and then proceeded to destroy it at every possible opportunity. Bangs managed to efface and hide the strict rules that governed the loose, colloquial vibe of his writing, and in the process he disguised the fact that he was, at heart, an old-fashioned moralist. When Bangs wrote in 1977 that "realizing life is precious the natural tendency is to trample on it," he was specifically addressing the punk movement, which had elevated destruction to an art form. Bangs was one of the few writers from that era who dared to ask, "[B]ut at what cost?" And it is upon this very question that the best of his writing turns.

[Lester Bangs quoted in "James Taylor Marked for Death," 1971, *Who Put the Bomp*, 1971, "The White Noise Supremacists" (1979, *The Village Voice*), and "Peter Laughner" (1977, *New York Rocker*) collected in *Psychotic Reactions and Carburetor Dung*, ed. Greil Marcus, New York: Vintage, 1988; Lester Bangs, review of *Buddy Guy and Junior Wells Play the Blues*, *Creem*, January 1973, p. 73; Lester Bangs, review of *Autobahn*, *Creem*, June 1975, p. 63.]

## "Biafra: 6,591 votes (3%)!!"

A headline from the punk fanzine *Damage* regarding Jello Biafra's (born Eric Reed Boucher in 1958, the lead singer for the Dead Kennedys; I don't need to tell you this) run for mayor of San Francisco in 1979 (Dianne Feinstein was eventually declared the winner; Biafra finished fourth out of ten). "Jello Biafra was not elected mayor of San Francisco for reasons everyone knows," Tony Rocco declared in *Damage*. "But a campaign that produces 6,591 votes for a cash outlay of about $400 (averaging less than 6.5 cents per capita), and gets 3% of the vote, means something. San Francisco may not have to grapple with the question, 'What if he wins?' but it will have to endure further confrontations with a man whose sizeable constituency consists of cynics, malcontents, and sundry other concerned deviants." One of his campaign promises? To "create a Board of Bribery to set standard government influence rates such as building code exemptions and vice squad insurance." He also proposed banning cars from San Francisco and abolishing the vice squad.

Although in many ways Biafra's run was absurd, its very spectacle raised a serious point: Were Biafra's campaign stunts and promises any more absurd than those of mainstream politicians, like Cleveland's Ralph Perk (mayor from 1971 to 1977), who accidentally set his hair on fire at a campaign event while attempting to use a blowtorch, and who suggested that sanitation workers conduct a pornography study? But beyond this, Biafra's mayoral run suggests an affinity with sixties radicalism that complicates the notion that punk was a reaction against the soft, easygoing pieties of the counterculture. He has said that "Spiritually, I think that punk was in tune with the *early* hippies . . . I'd once had so much belief in everything 'hippie' being so great: the Diggers with their free store concept and serving free dinners in the park; watching the Vietnam War being brought down; watching Nixon leave Washington in disgrace." Of course, once punk's politics (whatever and however contradictory those were) began to become explicit, punk as an aesthetic force and power began to fade. True enough, all art is political, but once those politics surface into the bright light of day, many people are likely to say, *No thanks, not for me.* Because politics always suggests "right ideas," doesn't it? And punk, at its dirty heart, was always about escaping the tyranny of authority, the tyranny of right ideas, the tyranny of those who would say, *Here is how you are supposed to think.* Once people like Biafra and others in the California scene began proclaiming their ideas, and once the political "meaning" of their songs became important, punk died a little more.

BIAFRA FOR MAYOR CAMPAIGN COMMITTEE WOULD LIKE TO THANK:

campaign staff:

| | |
|---|---|
| DIRK DIRKSEN | BARBARA HELLBENT |
| CHI CHI | GINGER COYOTE |
| BRAD L. | MICKEY CREEP |
| LENORE REALCOOLCHICK | MERCEDES MORA |

and:

| | |
|---|---|
| MARK BERLIN | JOE TARGET |
| THERESA | BILL ADAIR |
| TRACY | STAN FLORIDE |
| JEAN TARGET | KLAUS FLORIDE |
| ANNE MILLER | SAM EDWARDS |
| JEANINE RICHARDSON | PAULA & JULIE |
| CYNTHIA STRAND | JONATHAN FORMULA |
| TONY ROCCO | STEPHANO |
| MARK PAULINE | CURTIS GRAY |
| JONITHIN POWERS | STEVE TAYLOR |

special thanks:

| | |
|---|---|
| JEANINE YEOMAN | KRON- TV |
| HERB CAEN | S. F. CHRONICLE |
| BILL SCHECKNER | KPIX- TV |
| JOEL SELVIN | S. F. EXAMINER |
| MIKE HENNESSEY | |
| ACME CAFE | |
| MABUHAY STAFF | |

and of course:

DEAD KENNEDYS     **And**
Last, but not least

**6,591 VOTERS!**

Post-election thanks regarding Jello Biafra's run for mayor of San Francisco, from *Damage*, 1980

[Jello Biafra quoted in Stacy Thompson, *Punk Productions: Unfinished Business*, Albany: State University of New York Press, 2004, p. 38; Tony Rocco, "Biafra: 6,591 votes (3%)," *Damage* no. 4, Jan 1980, pp. 18–19.]

# Blank (1)

*Continued . . .*

# Blank (1) *Continued . . .*

# Blank (2)

**A word that haunted the mid-seventies** and that is closely associated with the subsequent No Wave movement. In the February–March 1979 issue of *New York Rocker*, there is a contest that asks readers to submit material to fill actual blank pages in the fanzine. Strangely, one such entry (by Steve Lombardi) includes a photograph of a page from what appears to be *New York Rocker* with nothing but the words "My Blank Pages" at the top. Of course, the page is blank, although the photograph of it fills part of the space in the blank page of the real-life—not the represented—issue of *New York Rocker* for February–March 1979.

In Walter Tevis's bleak and beautiful 1963 novel *The Man Who Fell to Earth*:

> Bryce's gaze met this sullen disarray: the scattered paper sheets like a fallen, bombed-out city of card houses, the endless, frighteningly neat student solutions of oxidation-reduction equations and of the industrial preparations of unlovely acids; the equally dull, dull paper on polyester resins. He stared at these things, his hands in the pocket of his coat, for a full thirty seconds, in blank dismay.

In a 1976 article in *Creem*, Tony Glover wrote that "Patti [Smith] snuck me into the booth that night, a haunted warp time of day. On the first take Patti did the singing part fine but when it came time to do the poetry Patti went blank and just threw out occasional words." In 1977, in *Zigzag*, Colin Newman of Wire said this about the band's early performances at the Roxy: "When we first started the general reaction of audiences was almost absolute blank nothingness. They wouldn't react, didn't know how to react."

Blank. Belief in nothing. Not one way or the other. Pessimistic? Yes, but also strangely hopeful. Tabula rasa—the blank slate. Awaiting your imprint. It's no surprise that punk's blankness could survive for only a few short years (1974 to '77) before being filled in with competing visions of what "punk" really was (rockabilly, ironic, arty, minimalist, hardcore, funny, serious, apolitical, politically engaged, etc.).

"I turned on the T.V. and watched a bag of doctors and nurses spew their love-troubles. They never touched. No wonder they were in trouble. All they did was talk, argue, bitch, search. I went to sleep." So says the narrator in a Charles Bukowski short story "No Neck and Bad as Hell," from 1973.

[Charles Bukowski, "No Neck and Bad as Hell," in *South of No North: Stories of the Buried Life*, Santa Barbara: Black Sparrow Press, 1973, p. 136; Tony Glover, "Patti Smith: Sweet Howling Fire," *Creem*, January 1976, p. 74; Colin Newman quoted in Kris Needs, "Wire," *ZigZag*, March 1978, p. 19; Walter Tevis, *The Man Who Fell to Earth*, London: BFI, 1976, p. 23]

# Blank (3)

**The following scene, from Philip K. Dick's novel** *Flow My Tears, the Policeman Said*, published in 1974. On the cusp of everything. Near the end of the novel. Jason Taverner's life is being erased. He can't even get his thirty-three-and-a-third records to play:

> Loud noise of the needle hitting the lead-in groove. Crackles of dust, clicks. Typical of old quad records. Easily misused and damaged; all you had to do was breathe on them. Background his. More crackles.
>
> No music.
>
> Lifting the tone arm, he set it farther in. Great roaring crash as the stylus struck the surface; he winced, sought the volume control to turn it down. Still no music. No sound of himself singing.
>
> The strength the mescaline had over him began now to waver; he felt coldly, keenly sober. The other record. Swiftly he got it from its jacket and sleeve, placed it on the spindle, rejected the first record.
>
> Sound of the needle touching plastic surface. Background hiss and the inevitable crackles and clicks. Still no music.
>
> The records were blank.

[Philip K. Dick, *Flow My Tears, the Policeman Said*, 1974; repr., New York: Vintage, 1993, pp. 160–61.]

## *Blank Generation*

**An album by Richard Hell and the Voidoids,** released on Sire in 1977, whose energy, bitterness, and humor helped set the tone for an entire generation of punk. Taken individually, the songs are good enough, but the album as an entire document rises above any one song and stands as a strangely coherent new genre of music that really captures the power of music that would come to be canonized as "punk." In some ways, this is not an easy album to like, and this is precisely why it is a great album. Many critics—including Hell himself—have expressed reservations about the album. For one thing, as Clinton Heylin has noted, by the time it was completed, Hell had "recorded most of the songs for between two and four separate 'projects.' Several songs had already been recorded prior to any Sire sessions." Large portions of *Blank Generation* were rerecorded as the result of a nearly yearlong delay in the album's distribution that gave Hell too much time to secondguess the results of the first sessions. But Hell's distance from the songs only makes them sound more alienated from any sort of music that had come before.

[Clinton Heylin, *From the Velvets to the Voidoids: A Pre-Punk History for a Post-Punk World*, New York: Penguin, 1993, p. 282.]

# "Blank Generation" / "Beat Generation"

**"Blank Generation" was written by Richard Hell in 1975** when he was playing with Television but was never officially recorded as a Television song. Recorded as a demo in January 1976 with the Heartbreakers, released as an EP on Ork Records in November 1976 with the newly formed Voidoids, and rereleased on the 1977 *Blank Generation* LP the song captured and gave voice to the emptiness that made punk possible. The song begins like this:

> I was sayin let me out of here before I was
> even born—it's such a gamble when you get a face
> ‚it's fascinatin to observe what the mirror does
> but when I dine it's for the wall that I set a place.

> I belong to the blank generation and
> I can take it or leave it each time
> I belong to the _____ generation but
> I can take it or leave it each time.

That pause—that blank—in the chorus, where the listener stumbles ahead and fills in the missing word, is, as Hell has suggested, an opportunity as well as a void. Which is to say, Hell's work in Television, the Heartbreakers, the Voidoids, and subsequently has always been informed by a sly, resigned humor. "Blank Generation" was, in part, a riff on the 1959 Rod McKuen (using the pseudonym "Dor") and Bob McFadden single "The Beat Generation," which parodied the emerging "beat" community. While this fact is often relegated to a footnote or an aside, the relationship between the punks and the beats is significant. For, in their rejection of the hippies, the punks—in the United States especially—had turned to the fifties, to the detached cool of Marlon Brando (the subject of an article in the very first issue of Holmstrom's and McNeil's *Punk* fanzine) and the films of Nicholas Ray (like *Rebel Without a Cause*—and Ray had provided a blurb for Television in 1974: "Four cats with a passion"). In a *New York Times Magazine* article (titled "This Is the Beat Generation") that helped popularize the term, John Clellon Holmes wrote:

> The origins of the word "beat" are obscure, but the meaning is only too clear to most Americans. More than mere weariness, it implies the feeling of having been used, of being raw. It involves a sort of nakedness of mind, and, ultimately, of soul; a feeling of being reduced to the bedrock of consciousness. In short, it means being undramatically pushed up against the wall of oneself . . .
> But the wild boys of today are not lost. Their flushed, often scoffing, always intent faces elude the world, and it would sound phony to them. For this generation lacks that eloquent air of bereavement which made so many of the exploits of the

Lost Generation symbolic actions. Furthermore, the repeated inventory of shattered ideals, and the laments about the mud in moral currents, which so obsessed the Lost Generation, do not concern young people today. They take these things frighteningly for granted. They were brought up in these ruins and no longer notice them . . .

So it is a generation with a greater facility for entertaining ideas than for believing them.

Holmes was also a novelist. His 1952 book *Go* was published in England as *The Beat Boys*, with these words branded on its cover: "America's Teen-Age Jungle and a Searing Story of Youth in Search of Kicks." In a 1978 conversation with Victor Bockris and Susan Sontag, Hell said that "I want to encourage in my songs . . . that feeling of being an adolescent throughout your whole life, of rejecting the whole idea of having a self, a personality." This rejection—which denied the hippie idea of finding yourself—drew on the Beats' cool detachment and seemingly apolitical rejection of social mores. And the beat sensibility informed how many of the rock critics approached punk, as well. "Wire dredges up images of Kerouac and Ginsberg—beat poetry," Ira Robbins wrote in 1978, "short fragments of impressions set to music. In 1953 the accompanying instrument would be bongos. 1978 bongos have six strings and make lots of noise. They have volume. They have lots of loose ends and rough edges. They be Wire."

But what motivated the "blank generation" more than anything was the desire to make something new, and the most significant difference between punk in America and punk in England was the starting point. The British impulse, epitomized by the Sex Pistols, was to destroy, and indeed punk became notorious in America largely because of the Sex Pistols' antics. The American impulse, on the contrary, was to assume simply that the slate was clean: a tabula rasa. There was less fury—at least until hardcore—in part because America had already destroyed itself. Nixon had resigned, the war in Vietnam was over, major cities had pockets of ruin and were on the verge of bankruptcy. There was nothing to destroy because there was nothing to destroy.

[Richard Hell quoted in Victor Bockris, "Susan Sontag Meets Richard Hell," in *Beat Punks*, New York: Da Capo, 1998 [1978], p. 198; John Clellon Holmes, "This Is the Beat Generation," *The New York Times Magazine*, November 16, 1952, pp. 10–11; Ira Robbins, Wire: *Pink Flag, Trouser Press*, April 1978.]

## Bloody Chamber, The

**A collection of short stories by Angela Carter** published in 1979. The stories took as their starting point the old myths, fairy tales like Little Red Riding Hood, Beauty and the Beast, and Bluebeard. They are shocking and beautifully told; far more than feminist "corrections" to the originals, they suggest deeper levels of terror that were dormant in the first tellings. You can't help but think of the all-girl punk-era bands that emerged at the same time as this book: the Slits, the Raincoats, the Mo-dettes, as well as bands with strong women members, like Au Pairs or Patti Smith, and then the later riot grrrl movement. There are stories in the collection that seem to describe, in secret code, images from the punk imagination. This from "Wolf-Alice":

> Her panting tongue hangs out; her red lips are thick and fresh. Her legs are long, lean and muscular.
>
> Wide shoulders, long arms and she sleeps succinctly curled up into a ball . . .
>
> Like the wild beasts, she lives without a future. She inhabits only the present tense, a fugue of the continuous, a world of sensual immediacy as without hope as it is without despair.
>
> Mutilation is her lot . . .

In 1976, three years before the publication of "Wolf-Alice" in *The Bloody Chamber*, Patti Smith gave an interview to Nick Tosches in *Penthouse* called "Patti Smith: A Baby Wolf with Neon Bones" in which she noted that Rimbaud had predicted that the "next great crop of writers would be women" writing with "new rhythms, new poetries, new horrors, new beauties."

> [Angela Carter, "Wolf-Alice," in *The Bloody Chamber*, 1979; repr., New York: Penguin, 1993, pp. 119, 121; Patti Smith, interview with Nick Tosches, "Patti Smith: A Baby Wolf with Neon Bones," *Penthouse*, April 1976.]

## Boredom

**Was it out of the boredom** of the early seventies that punk was born? In 1972, *National Lampoon* did a whole issue on boredom, featuring Bonnie Boredom on the cover, staring out at readers like a demented Betty Crocker and wearing a pin that proclaimed I'M BORED. In the opening editorial, George W. S. Trow considered the boredom of self-criticism sessions, Grateful Dead concerts, organic vitamins, Yoko Ono, Woodstock, and "your tedious Multi-Media in the Third World Studies program." Later in the issue there is a list of boring topics that include air-pollution statistics, bussing issue, cancer research, counterculture, cult murders, disarmament talks, economic sanctions, emerging nations, famines, gay liberation, generation gap, goodwill missions, holiday-death-toll predictions, juntas, labor unrest, nonviolent protest, nuclear holocaust, penal reform, police brutality, population explosion, poverty programs, race riots, sexual revolution, skyjacking, Third World struggle, urban renewal, wage and price controls, and welfare cases.

The sheer weight of "issues" had become too much; the utopian idealism of the sixties had been drained off, leaving a bitter residue of guilt, narcissism, and boredom—a vacuum that punk filled. In 1976, the Buzzcocks wrote a song, "Boredom": "You know me—I'm acting dumb / you know the scene—very humdrum / boredom—boredom." These lines had the ringing endorsement of truth, and that was punk's solution: to transform boredom into the very premise of modern life. When the Ramones sang "I wanna have something to do," they weren't complaining so much as stating a fact.

In *SCUM Manifesto*, the radical-feminist-crazyperson-Andy

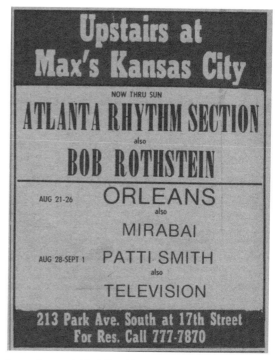

Laissez-faire punk: *The Village Voice* ad for Television, August 1974

Warhol–shooter Valerie Solanas included an entry on boredom that read: "Life in a society made by and for creatures who, when they are not grim and depressing are utter bores, when not grim and depressing, an utter bore." It was as if the Great Society had produced nothing so much as boredom, as if the idealism of the sixties deflated into the realization that, even though Nixon was on his way out and the Vietnam War was over, not that much had changed after all. THE GREAT AMERICAN SOAP OPERA, declared the cover of *The Village Voice* in August 1974, a week after Nixon resigned the presidency on August 9. The Fords replacing the Nixons. Alexander Cockburn wrote: "Now we're talking here strictly about iconography: the new images, not the new political realities. And alas the new iconography is, at first sight, not encouraging. In the great American soap opera we've gone from grand guignol to family charades in a couple of days, from Key Biscayne and San Clemente to the boring good cheer of a Washington suburb."

In that same issue there was an advertisement for an upcoming show at Max's Kansas City by Television (who had been performing live since only March) and Patti Smith. An even earlier ad for Television had appeared in March with a blurb from the director Nicholas Ray (*Rebel Without a Cause*) that read "Four cats with a passion." Passion, yes, but a sort of bored, detached passion. Laissez-faire punk. The boredom of the seventies had become more than a cultural phenomenon,

Bonnie Boredom on the cover of *National Lampoon* in 1972: waiting for punk, with a smile

covered in all the major newspapers and magazines (*Harper's Magazine, Playboy, Newsweek, The Village Voice*, etc.). It had become an aesthetic that would soon be transformed by punk into a disregard for order. It was true, the great crises of the sixties and early seventies were over (the assassinations, war in Vietnam, race riots, campus shootings, etc.). Punk filled that vacuum with a sound so terrifying and disordered that you knew—from the first moment you heard it—that it couldn't last.

[Alexander Cockburn, "Press Clips," *The Village Voice*, August 15, 1974, p. 8; George W. S. Trow, "*National Lampoon*, September 1972, p. 4.]

## Brando, Marlon

**American actor born in 1924, died in 2004.** On stage and in films like *A Streetcar Named Desire* (1951), *Viva Zapata!* (1952), *The Wild One* (1953), and *On the Waterfront* (1954), he worked within the constraints of the fifties to suggest that, just beneath the tight surface of things, there was a raw and primitive violence that could not be papered over forever with shiny cars, hoop skirts, bubblegum, milkshakes, paved streets, blue swimming pools, fishing and camping, and the crooning from juke boxes on Eisenhower summer nights. "What are you rebelling against?" "What have you got?" goes the dialogue in *The Wild One*, a prophecy of the end of square society.

But not really. Brando's presence in *The Wild One* casts a weird sadness over the film. He plays Johnny (not Rotten), a member of the Black Rebel Motorcycle Club. Yet during the teasing and harassing of some of the town's regular folks, you detect a reluctance in his face. He sees both sides, and this acknowledgment charges the film with a secret knowledge, as if he knew that in the not too distant future, his type of subcultural outcast would become just another commodity, as blue jeans, black leather jackets, and then ripped-and-safety-pinned clothes and spiky hair became acceptable soon after being incorporated into the realm of fashion. "What comes alive in *Last Tango in Paris* is Brando's own iconography and his conclusions about the punk character he created," wrote Joe Koch in the very first issue of John Holmstrom's *Punk* fanzine in 1976. "So twenty years after *The Wild One*, with cycle and road movies in full swing, nostalgia on the rise, and Bruce Springsteen eulogies to today's street people just around the corner, Brando put himself in a film that showed what it all came out to: nothing." By the early seventies, Brando's image was scrambled and had become incoherent. His movies from the fifties (the angry young man with NO FUTURE before him) were available on television, and the power and controversy of *Last Tango in Paris* gave audiences a fresh chance to see what the rebel had become. He was a street punk in 1953 who had grown up into a different sort of narcissist, withdrawn and inward-looking. Most of all, by the seventies he exuded boredom, which punk transformed into art by proclaiming it over and over again. Of the many references to Marlon Brando from the punk era, here, to end this entry, are four:

1. Richard Hell: "I should read Artuad and Stanislavsky and go see Brando and James Dean movies (they did very vulgar and vulnerable things with their voices and bodies and their physical appeal just increased)."

2. Caroline Coon: "The arrogant, aggressive, rebellious stance that characterizes the musicians who have played the most vital rock and roll has always been glamorized. In the 'Fifties it was the rebel without a cause exemplified by Elvis and Gene Vincent, the Marlon Brando and James Dean of rock. In the 'Sixties it was the Rock 'n' Roll Gypsy Outlaw image of Mick Jagger, Keith Richards and Jimi Hendrix. In the 'Seventies the word 'rebel' has been superseded by the word 'punk.' Although initially derogatory, it now contains all the glamorous connotations once implied by the overused word 'rebel.'"

3. Mitchell Cohen: "Patti Smith is not Marlon Brando by any means, but she has some of his instinct."

4. Patti Smith: "A good writer can get into any gender, can get into any mouth. When I write I may be a Brando creep, or a girl laying on the floor, or a Japanese tourist, or a slob like Richard Speck."

[Mitchell Cohen, "Patti Smith: Avery Fisher Hall, NYC," *Phonograph Record*, May 1976; Caroline Coon, "Punk Rock: Rebels Against the System," *Melody Maker*, August 7, 1976; Richard Hell, *Artifact: Notebooks from Hell, 1974–80*, Madras and New York: Hanuman, 1992, pp. 72–73; Joe Koch, "Marlon Brando: The Original Punk," *Punk* vol. 1, no. 1., January 1976, p. 2; Nick Tosches, "Patti Smith: A Baby Wolf with Neon Bones," *Penthouse*, April 1976.]

# British National Front

**Formed in the sixties,** this extremist group opposed immigration and multiculturalism in general, and took to the streets in several well-publicized clashes with antifascist groups. Their relationship to punk is complicated, as the punk hostility to the free-and-open-and-easy-and-peace-and-love sixties seemed, to some, in sync with the restrictive ideology of the National Front. There were important early disavowals of the National Front from Johnny Rotten and others. In 1976, Joe Strummer told an interviewer that "we're hoping to educate any kid who comes to listen to us, right, just to keep 'em from joining the National Front when things get really tough in a couple of years. I mean, we just really don't want the National Front stepping in and saying, Things are bad—it's the Blacks . . . We want to prevent that somehow, you know?"

By the late seventies, as Simon Reynolds notes, the National Front was "running candidates in every single parliamentary seat in the impending May 1979 election," and the backlash against the swinging sixties was taking full and brutal shape. It's easy to make too much of the connection between punk and xenophobia and racism, just as it's easy to make too little of it. Punk was an aesthetic rejection of the myth that the sixties had become, and because the rejection was aesthetic, it was ambiguous. Mark Perry, the founder and editor of the seminal punk fanzine *Sniffin' Glue*, wrote of the Sex Pistols that "Britain is going downhill and it'll take more than memories of glory to save it. The Pistols are here because this country's so pathetic, they're a reaction against all the stupid apathy and ignorance."

In its insistence on sharp lines of division and clean breaks with the hippies, punk found itself aligned with the manifesto-like spirit of groups like the National Front, for whom the "soft" sixties had dulled Great Britain into the sort of place that no longer seemed to mind that it was an Empire No Longer. For groups like the Sex Pistols, the response was an anarchy of noise so fierce you knew it couldn't last. For groups like the British National Front, the response was anarchy that you suspected of being the pathway to tyranny.

[Miles, "The Clash: Eighteen Flight Rock . . . And the Sound of the Westway," *New Musical Express*, December 11, 1976; Mark Perry, "The Sex Pistols," *Sniffin' Glue*, January 1977, p. 4; Simon Reynolds, *Rip It Up and Start Again: Postpunk 1978–1984*, New York: Penguin, 2005, p. 64.]

## Buffalo, New York

**A place where many things relevant to punk** have happened, including a 1974 "Rock Critics' Symposium" organized by Billy Altman and others at Buffalo State College. Lester Bangs, Patti Smith, Lenny Kaye, Richard Meltzer, Nick Tosches, and Rob Tyner went. Bangs and Tyner stayed at a girls' dorm on campus. By all accounts the symposium was a disaster. "Well, the whole thing was pretty much NOTHING," Meltzer has said. "It wasn't even really that much fun, it was more like three days of a hangover. Nobody came close to getting laid." In *Let It Blurt*, Jim DeRogatis reproduces some of the actual content of the symposium, based on an audio recording. Here is Bangs, telling the college audience:

> I used to be in college . . . I was going to be a college teacher until I discovered that I hated academic people and I couldn't stand college students because it's totally insular. And then I realized that when I got into *this* bullshit [rock criticism] that it's even more insular than that is! My feeling about rock 'n' roll is that it's a bunch of garbage! Everything your parents ever said it was, it's in one ear it's out the other, it's trash—here today and gone tomorrow—so what? The only people who are more unnecessary than rock musicians, who are totally interchangeable, is rock *critics*, because who gives a fuck, right? I think this whole thing is ridiculous, but I'm glad I'm here.

It's fitting that this shambling caravan of rock critics, who were as critical of themselves as they were of the bands they wrote about, would end up in Buffalo, a so-called rust-belt city, a city of blight (but we, as northern United States kids growing up in the seventies who knew no better, thought the whole world was blighted) whose population was declining rapidly by the seventies, and whose enormous factories resembled deserted cities and fueled the imagination of disaster.

Four months before the symposium, the newly elected mayor of Buffalo, Stanley M. Makowski, delivered his inaugural address, punctuated by moments that sounded like a prophecy of Jimmy Carter's infamous 1979 "Crisis of Confidence" speech mixed with a warped, New Age version of the transcendentalist critiques of American culture from the 1830s and '40s. A rusty Emerson, a rusty Thoreau, before there were rust belts:

> The clear truth . . . has taught . . . that state and federal administrations cannot be relied upon to solve our problems. We are heading into bad times and we know it.

It is more—and deeper—than an energy crisis of any other of the crises in this troubled world. We can choose to strip off the irrelevant, the artificial, the spoiled and soft and luxurious and over-indulged life-style and attitudes that are choking the spirit out of us. We can choose to find our real selves again, to learn who we really are and what we really want for ourselves and our kids.

[Lester Bangs quoted in Jim DeRogatis, *Let It Blurt: The Life & Times of Lester Bangs, America's Greatest Rock Critic*, New York: Broadway, 2000, p. 97; Richard Meltzer, June 2000 e-mail, www.slippytown.com; Stanley M. Makowski, "Inaugural Address: January 1, 1974," in Michael Rizzo, ed., "Through the Mayor's Eyes," www.buffalonian.com/history/industry/mayors.]

## C

# Callaghan, James, Prime Minister of Great Britain (1)

**In a 2002 essay in *The New York Times*,** Ed Ward wrote that when "the Sex Pistols' Johnny Rotten, draped on his microphone, intoned, 'No future,' it was the cry of youth coming out of school to discover that there were no jobs in Margaret Thatcher's Britain and refusing to accept that as reality." At the end of the article there was this correction: "An article last Sunday about the legacy of the Clash and other punk rock bands in the 1970's referred incorrectly to the social climate from which the Sex Pistols emerged. It was not the Britain of Margaret Thatcher: she became prime minister in 1979, and the Sex Pistols disbanded in 1978."

Does Ward's mistake reflect the broader tendency of many (certainly not all) rock critics and historians to interpret, reflexively, punk's nihilism as a street-level reaction against conservatism? Perhaps. But the facts tell a different story, as it was James Callaghan, not Margaret Thatcher, who was prime minister from 1976 to 1979, during punk's initial and most fertile period. Like his American counterpart, Jimmy Carter, Callaghan frequently and openly spoke of the economic crisis, helping to doom himself for speaking the truth: "You and I, Mr. President," he told Carter in March 1977, on the same day that the Sex Pistols "officially" signed with A&M Records, "will be holding our discussions in a world which has now experienced 4 years of recession, the deepest since the 1930's." Callaghan's public comments and speeches about Great Britain's tail-spinning economy were a mix of doomy, almost apocalyptic warning ("No one group of nations," he told Carter, "and no one nation can survive permanently as an island of prosperity if the remainder of the world is in recession") and hollow-sounding optimism. "Your future will be as distinguished," he told an audience at Ruskin College in 1976, "as your past and your present."

By 1979, what came to be known as "the Winter of Discontent" had practically secured Labour's defeat. With inflation hovering around 10 percent, Callaghan placed limits on pay raises, resulting in a series of crippling strikes, most notably by lorry drivers and oil tanker drivers, who secured higher raises, resulting in subsequent strikes by trash collectors, ambulance drivers, and even grave diggers. "The lasting images of the time," notes BBC News, "are of rubbish in the streets and reports of bodies lying unburied in mortuaries." Making matters worse, at an airport in January 1979, upon returning from an economic conference in Guadeloupe in the sunny West Indies, Callaghan told reporters, in response to a question about the chaos in Great Britain, "I don't think other people in the world share the view that there is mounting chaos." Of course, at that moment he was not speaking to "other people in the world" so much as he was speaking to his fellow citizens. Whether or not "other people in the world" thought that there was chaos in England was perhaps irrelevant to those whose social fabric was being torn asunder.

Ed Ward's recollection that the Sex Pistols were a response to "Margaret Thatcher's Britain" is really a function of nostalgia, a dream of punk as giving the middle finger to the conservative ideology of shrinking government, tradition, and dwindling social services. And yet, as Momus (Nick Currie) has suggested, punk can be looked at from another angle: as the flowering expression of a deeper cultural conservatism. "In retrospect," Momus argues, "we can see punk rock's no future nihilism as one of the factors contributing to the triumph of Margaret Thatcher in 1979. If you refuse to believe in—and therefore start building—a positive future, you prepare the way for a politics of fear, which usually means authoritarian leaders. Punk was simply the sexy face of Britain's innate conservatism, its fear of the future."

By 1981, when the fun of deconstructing the sixties had passed and various fragmentations (post-punk, power pop, industrial, hardcore, goth) had emerged, there were sober reassessments of punk's larger meaning in social life. In *New Musical Express*, Ray Lowry, in a far cry from "No Future!," wrote that we "must believe that we can affect the shape of our future if we try hard enough" and asked, "Has John Lydon anything more important to contribute than a sneer?" That sneer was fun and thrillingly menacing in 1977 because the social and economic crisis in the United States and the United Kingdom coming on full throttle—there was an air of, *Let's make music fast, before it's too late.* But by the early 1980s, when Reagan and Thatcher were overseeing the Restoration of Order, those punk sneers took on a different meaning. They would now find expression in the joylessness of hardcore and its offspring.

[BBC News, "Crisis? What Crisis?" September 12, 2000, http://news.bbc.co.uk/2/hi/uk_news/; James Callaghan, "Visit of Prime Minister James Callaghan of Great Britain: Remarks of the President and the Prime Minister at the Welcoming Ceremony: March 10, 1977," The American Presidency Project, www.presidency.ucsb.edu; James Callaghan, "Towards a National Debate," speech delivered at Ruskin College on October 18, 1976, http://education.guardian.co.uk/thegreatdebate/story/0,9860,57465,00.html; Ray Lowry, "Titanic Refloated," *New Musical Express*, June 20, 1981, p. 11; Momus, "On Punk," October 1999, http://imomus.com/onpunk.html; Ed Ward, "No Second Act in Punk? Says Who?" *The New York Times*, December 29, 2002.]

# Callaghan, James: Prime Minister of Great Britain (2)

**From the House of Commons** PQs, May 2, 1978:

*Mr. Fairbairn:*

For once, my question relates to the Prime Minister's engagements today. Could he fit in one further engagement today and listen to the regional election results tonight on the radio from Scotland and note the profound defeat that the Labour Party will have at the hands of the Conservatives?

*The Prime Minister:*

Unfortunately I cannot get Scotland on my set. When I tried to listen to the news on the set in my hotel in Glasgow early this morning, all I could get was punk rock music.

["House of Commons PQs," Margaret Thatcher Foundation, www.margaretthatcher.org/speeches.]

# Captain and Tennille

**One of the most orthodox myths** about punk concerns is the uniqueness of its do-it-yourself method of creating music and image. And yet, a profile of the pop duo Captain and Tennille from *Melody Maker* in 1975 begins:

> In September 1973, two Chatsworth residents recorded a song, "The Way I Want to Touch You." Subscribing to the Phil Spector school of self-distribution, they pressed 500 copies and without the aid of a major record label or formal distribution, achieved success in the Los Angeles area. Two years later the Captain (Daryl Dragon) and Tennille (Toni Tennille) have the definitive summer record of 1975, "Love Will Keep Us Together."
>
> [Harvey Kubernik, "The Captain and Tennille: Captain Fantastic," *Melody Maker*, July 26, 1975.]

# Carter, Jimmy

**On January 20, 1977—the day he took the presidential oath—**Jimmy Carter got out of his limousine and walked down Pennsylvania Avenue to the White House. These and other populist gestures during his first few years in office have been overshadowed by the perceived failure of his presidency. And yet they capture the spirit of the times, the spirit of punk. For the rejection of pomp and overproduced spectacle animated Carter and punk alike: Both offered a return to a simpler, more basic time and tone. In other words, they were both nostalgic. CROWD DELIGHTED AS

CARTERS SHUN LIMOUSINE AND WALK TO NEW HOME read the headline in *The New York Times*: "To the astonishment and delight of hundreds of thousands of jubilant Inauguration Day celebrants, President Carter got out of his bullet-proof limousine this afternoon to march, grinning and ebullient, the mile and a half from the Capitol Hill site of his oath-taking to the White House . . . It seemed, at times, a celebration of the natural. Mr. Carter eschewed the formal attire of his predecessors for his "people's inaugural." Two months earlier, the Ramones released their third and last great album, *Rocket to Russia* (other, lesser ones would follow), signaling the end of the first, absurdly fun phase of punk. The album featured "Sheena Is a Punk Rocker" near the end of side one, so perfect a pop song that it's no wonder hardcore had to reject the easy camaraderie of the Ramones. Several months earlier, in June 1977, William V. Shannon had written about how Carter had "slashed encumbering ritual." So many of the great punk-era albums also functioned this way, revealing in the spaces between their sounds the evidence of real human beings doing work. [For more on Carter, see *Down-and-Out during the punk era, the fun of being*]

[James M. Naughton, "Crowd Delighted as Carters Shun Limousine and Walk to New Home," *The New York Times*, January 21, 1977, p. A1; William V. Shannon, "The Style of the 70's: Politics," *The New York Times*, June 5, 1977, p. 11.]

## Carter, Jimmy, and the New Wave

**This entry begins with Blondie** and ends with Carter. Blondie was the fullest expression of pop pleasure. Approximately ten years before Blondie, Lionel Trilling wrote that, according to psychoanalysts, "the very existence of civilization is threatened unless society can give credence to the principle of pleasure and learn how to implement it." But he was skeptical: "Yet secretly we know that the formula does not satisfy the condition it addresses itself to—it leaves out of account those psychic energies which press beyond the pleasure principle and even deny it." Pleasure, and the denial of pleasure.

In 1978, Chris Stein (the cofounder of and a guitar player in Blondie), who was perhaps not as paranoid as Richard M. Nixon, said in an interview with *New Musical Express*, "There is no new wave in America. I was told by a pretty heavy rock person that Jimmy Carter has actually put a stop to the new wave 'cos he considers it politically dangerous."

[Paul Morley, "Blondie and the Beast," *New Musical Express*, September 2, 1978; Lionel Trilling, "The Fate of Pleasure," in *Beyond Culture*, 1963; repr., New York: Harcourt, Brace, Jonavovich, 1965, p. 75.]

## Cassidy and Bangs in 1977

**A page from *Creem*, 1977.** Ted Nugent is on the cover, glaring at you with wide open, maniacal eyes. (Was he the true punk? That is another history.) On page twenty-two, there are three short articles that, taken together, convey the incoherence and absurdity of the times. The first article, "Crash Course in Punk Rock," begins, "Like a pack of nervous wieners looking at the world through hotdog colored glasses, Britain's 'new wave' punk bands are now demanding protection from their more ardent fans." The second article, "Shaun Cassidy Sticks Out His Lips," is about Cassidy's hit show, *The Hardy Boys*, and his remake of "Da Do Run Run." The third piece, "Is the World Ready for This?," describes Lester Bangs's band performing at CBGB in June: "Besides dancing and lying down," one sentence begins. You get the idea. Shaun Cassidy and Lester Bangs represented two sides of the same coin: Both were extreme versions of a vision of America's darkness and lightness. *The Hardy Boys* could have been a missing link between the fifties and the Reagan era, with Cassidy and other "teenagers" solving crimes in the dark, in abandoned warehouses, old mills, and deep forests. Order is always restored. For Lester Bangs, that order was just as necessary, for without it his anarchy, expressed in words, would not have been possible. Was there a predatory darkness there beneath the smooth surfaces of Shaun Cassidy's face? And was there a sweetness and light that sometimes showed itself in between the many words of Lester Bangs? That both punk rock and Shaun Cassidy were popular in the mid-seventies is not a contradiction so much as an affirmation that the old, bipolar culture was still alive and kicking.

## "Cindy" (1)

**A song by the Revelons,** produced by Jimmy Destri. A forgotten gem of the late seventies. The sort of messy perfection that reminds you that, in all honesty, hard-core forever ruined the ambiguous, earnest innocence of punk's pre-1980s phase. A cross between Television (the guitar solo from 1:31 to 1:52), the Dictators, and maybe even Blue Oyster Cult. Punk was incoherent in the seventies, when there was, as late as 1975, nothing to rebel against. The sixties had burned out. Watergate and Vietnam were over. So were the race riots and the assassinations. For five whole years—between 1975 and 1980—there was a once-in-a-lifetime breathing space, a long, disorganized exhale before Reagan and Thatcher reorganized ideologies along the familiar lines. If you didn't live through this time and don't believe me, simply go back to a few newspapers from the era and read for yourself the radical incoherence in the pages of daily life. Just try to find meaning.

The pop music from this time is so hard to categorize because the era itself was incoherent—the signals were all mixed up. Punk gave voice to a dangerous idea that briefly broke the surface and then disappeared again. You have to fight hard to remember context, I know. You are jaded because punk had become myth, and myth exists to be destroyed.

The song's first seconds deliver a promise that is thwarted by the angular, jerky sounds that so-called greater bands like Gang of Four perfected. "I might not cry / I might just look in your eyes," the song goes, briefly surfacing in the long history of rock, and then going under again.

## Cindy (2)

**But that is only a sliver** of the story about Cindy.

Yes, a song by the Only Ones. Yes, yes, of course, obviously.

In retrospect, the story of how the girl Cindy from far away put my hand on her heart that night sounds unbelievable, yet at the time is seemed the most natural, truest thing in the world. Was 1978 a special year? Not at all. Of course not. In those early days I considered everything she did miraculous. I remember spending one entire day walking the campus in a kind of daze, my head completely filled with her. When I didn't hear from her for two or three days in a row, I'd go into a kind of withdrawal, lose my appetite, develop the shakes.

I didn't know where she lived. She never told me.

Did she fear me? I think not.

So I went out walking and searched for two days, up and down the streets, peering in windows, checking names on mailboxes. I walked and walked, hung out at donut shops and record stores, poster shops and coffee joints, movie theater lobbies, and busy street corners. I watched the busses, the cars, the bicycles. I followed groups of college students to their classes and scanned the rows for her face. I stood on the busiest street corner, Main and Ashley, and spent four hours watching the faces of the people who crossed the street. I forgot to eat. To shave. To comb my hair. I slept curled up on the grass beneath a tree outside Old Main and listened to the crickets and stray night birds. I awoke in dew.

I ran into Ephraim P. Noble, in his seventy-eight-year-old-fuck-the-world-and-everybody-in-it glory, in the English department mailroom on what would turn out to be his last day ever on university property. He was busy emptying out each and every mailbox, throwing everything into a pile on the floor in the middle of the room. His hair was spiked and wild—he had cut it shorter and, despite his age, it made him look a little like Johnny Rotten. He was pitching all the mail on the ground with great fanfare and exaggeration, mumbling to himself something about "crucibles of untruth."

"Boy!" he said when he saw me. "Get in here!" He sprung to the door, grabbed me by the collar, and yanked me in.

"Quick, boy, before they come!" he said, and shoved me toward the mailboxes. He was wearing his typical white suit with white shoes. He may have been seventy-eight but on this day he looked more like eighteen.

I just stood there, but he kept going. A few people, students mostly, had gathered at the doorway, but nobody said or did anything.

"Mendacity, boy, mendacity! I have seen *dullness* in my day. Lies. *Liars!* A butchery of lies by dimwits and halfwits! The perseverance of sheer *stupidity*, boy, as foul as a turd! Yet persevering! *A clean sweep!* Starting fresh! This girl Cindy. You've fallen in love with her because her name's in a song?"

"No, sir. She's *in* the song."

"In it, boy? Not possible. You know it's not. You know better."

He was clearly out of his mind. There had been hints of this before, in our graduate seminars, as he would get going on some hobbyhorse usually involving William Faulkner or Flannery O'Connor or George Lippard or the dismal pitching of the Detroit Tigers. One day, to illustrate a proper forkball, he threw a baseball at the window and cracked it. He then immediately cancelled class, out of shame that he hadn't actually broken the window, we suspected.

But this was different. This was full-on. Once all the mailboxes had been emptied out, Ephraim reached into the breast pocket of his jacket, plucked out a book of matches (bright red, with the letters "K.G.B." embossed in white on them), and lit the mail on fire.

"It's *all* junk mail now!" he whooped. One of the graduate students—a pathetic hunchback who was as petty and mean as he looked—turned and ran down the hall, but it was too late, the mail was already aflame, the gray smoke collecting near the ceiling like a fog. Without saying another word, Ephraim grabbed me by the collar, tugged me toward a window, and pointed to it. I opened it, pushed out the screen, and helped him climb up onto the sill. By the time he was halfway out, the English department chair—a broken little man with a missing tooth and a glass eye and a perpetually sweaty brow—had appeared at the doorway and, as if on cue in a movie, said, "What the . . . ?"

Ephraim scampered out the window and into the bushes and I quickly followed, the department chair coming at me in the smoke with one arm outstretched and the other clasping a ridiculous white handkerchief to his face. He leaned through the window after me and yelled feebly, "Come back here! Don't wait for Cindy. There is no such person for you."

By this time Ephraim was out of the bushes and making his way in a mad zigzag across campus. It was cold out so he shoved his hands in his pant pockets; with each step he looked as if he would topple over. I caught up with him quickly and, glancing back over my shoulder, noticed smoke coming from the Burrowes Building. The distant wail of sirens, warped by the wind, drifted into our ears. Exhausted, Ephraim finally collapsed onto a park bench beneath the beautiful, towering elms that lined the mall.

"Well, boy," he said, rasping. "Didn't expect that, did you?"

"No, sir," I said.

"Don't sir me! No need for that now. That's all done."

"We've got to go back. We've got to explain . . ."

"Explain what? The event explains itself. It doesn't need me. Or you. The past is done. Over. Caput. That's the very nature of your problem, boy. What in the hell has this D. Barker gotten you into?"

"It wasn't his fault. I agreed to write . . ."

"No excuses, boy. You've lost track of the difference between songs and the real world. Don't ever do that . . ."

He leaned forward and hung his head low, practically between his knees, and for a moment I thought he was crying.

"No harm done back there. Just junk mail and a little smoke."

"And fire," I said.

He sat up, straightened his tie at his collar, cleared his throat, and looked at me. His eyes were bloodshot, probably from the smoke. There was a formality to him, an elegance that marked him as a man not of my generation.

"Tell me why you're really here," he said, his voice lowered. Even though I knew what he meant, I didn't want to say.

"What do you mean, sir? I wanted to help . . ."

"Don't *fuck* with me boy. It's a direct enough question. Indulge the old man with the new haircut. Like one of those silly punks you always write about. Who knows, maybe I can be of some help. I'm offering now but I may not offer again."

The campus had quieted down. The fire was contained. Birds flew to and fro in the high branches above us. Ephraim's hands were large and waxy.

"The only reason I'm here," I said, "is because of her."

"The one you call Cindy."

"That's right."

"So you came here to find her? The one from the song."

"I did. It's beyond reason, I know," I said.

"Not really. In fact, it makes some sense. I suppose you read my book? *A Cultural Dictionary* of whatever?"

"I did. That's why I chose this university, of course. Your story was my story, in so many ways. Even your narrator, Nick, and the girl, Cindy. The first time I read it, I kept checking the date, but it was published when I was only five. So you couldn't have known."

"Of course not. Don't get supernatural on me. In fact, I wrote that book before you were even born. Don't trust the publication date, either. It had nothing to do with you."

"But it had everything to do with me. It was my story, in so many ways."

"I understand. Yes, it makes sense that you would come. I'm sure I've disappointed you," he said.

"Not at all. In fact, you've been of great help."

"How so?"

The sun was setting, and everything took on an impossible orange glow.

"Well, just seeing that you're real, for one thing."

"Real? Of course I'm real. God, boy, what kind of thing is that to say?"

"You know what I mean. So much today turns out not to be what it appears."

"True. Lamentable, but true. I suppose I don't blame you for not trusting me."

"But that's just it. I did trust you. I trusted the voice in your book. More than anything, I trusted that voice. It seemed to describe the world precisely the way I saw it."

"And how is that?"

I paused. The campus had fallen into twilight. The shadows were deepening and widening.

"As untrustworthy."

"Is that all?" he asked.

"No. As beautiful, too. In fact, its beauty is what makes it untrustworthy."

"Precisely."

"People make the mistake of not trusting the world because of its flaws, its ugliness, its violence and brutality," I said. "But it's the beauty that's dangerous. That's why punk is the only true form."

"Why do you think that is, boy?"

"I don't know. That's why I'm here. To find out."

"I thought you were here to find Cindy."

I sensed a tiredness in Ephraim's voice. This talk was wearying. It was getting dark fast.

"Later," I said. "We've got to get home."

Ephraim didn't argue. In fact, I sensed he was relieved. In the shadows, he looked old again. We sat there a while longer, until it went dark. Then I heard him get up and shuffle away.

I didn't follow him, because he had led me as far as he could. From now on, I was on my own.

# Cities, decay and beauty of

In 2006, *The New York Times* ran an article—NEW YORK CITY AS FILM SET: FROM MEAN STREETS TO CLEAN STREETS—that noted that "Times Square, once home to drug dealers, prostitutes and beleaguered theaters, has morphed into a Mickey Mouse Mall." Perhaps this is so much nostalgia—after all, those of us who lived through the economic gloom of the seventies must surely remember those times with a mixture of fondness and nausea. But it's undeniable that there was something about the disintegration, the sense of everything falling apart, that gave pre-punk and punk the breathing room it needed to grow and thrive. The sense of almost magical urban despair is captured in passages like this from Samuel Delany's 1975 novel *Dhalgren*:

> He stepped off the sidewalk and kept along the loose line of old cars—nothing parked on this block later than 1968—thinking: What makes it terrible is that in this timeless city, in this spaceless preserve where any slippage can occur, these closing walls, laced with fire-escapes, gates, and crenellations, are too unfixed to hold it in, so that, from me as a moving node, it seems to spread, by flood and seepage, over the whole uneasy scape. He had a momentary image of all these walls on pivots controlled by subterranean machines, so that, after he had passed, they might suddenly swing to face another direction, parting at this corner, joining at that one, like a great maze—forever adjustable, therefore unlearnable.

In a 1976 article on Patti Smith in *New Musical Express*, Lisa Robinson wrote, "Cleveland is beyond belief, it looks like it's been evacuated. Perhaps that's why it's such a great rock-and-roll town; there's nothing else to do." And in 2001, John Morton of the Electric Eels said, "Cleveland, the best location in the nation to get the fuck out of."

In her 1980 review of the band Human Switchboard, Charlotte Pressler—one of the great unsung writers from that period, famous for being the wife of Peter Laughner—wrote that "[N]obody's listening: This is Cleveland, where you can do anything you want precisely because nobody cares . . . The freedom of Cleveland cuts both ways. Because nobody cares, you can do what you want, but equally certain, it will never get you anywhere. After a while, it starts getting hard to face your high school buddies." In 1980, Pressler could say what could not have been said in 1975: that the dark side to the desperate, romantic allure of a place like Cleveland was that you might not get recognized.

In fact, Cleveland, in all its down-and-out, abandoned, flaming river glory, took on a special sort of place in the imagination of disaster. Tom Carson, writing about Human Switchboard in *New York Rocker* in 1979, recognized the strange, almost romantic allure of fallen cities like Cleveland:

> Most of the other Ohio bands work in terms of black humor, sociological irony, and musical complexity; the Switchboard, though they use all those elements to some extent, have a much narrower and more private version, and home in directly on your emotions . . . The Human Switchboard are the only real romantics the scene has yet produced, combining the grinding urban bleakness of the Cleveland sound with the gaunt-cheeked alienation and haunting intensity of feeling of the New York art-rock sensibility.

Cities of the American Midwest, the heart of the auto and steel industries, approached postapocalyptic dimensions in your imagination. In downtown Toledo, the boarded up buildings offered a visual contradiction that verged on mystery: Here were beautiful buildings with ornate architectural details but whose windows were covered over with warped plywood. On one level, you understood perfectly well what had happened: The perils of the economy were on the news every night. And yet, it still didn't make sense; you wanted to solve the contradiction of ruined beauty, either by restoring the beauty or pushing things further into ruin. Only later would it become clear that while disco had tried to push things back into decadent beauty, punk had tried to push them deeper into ruin. Whether you lived in these cities or not, you knew that what was happening there was a large-scale version of the same disaster that was playing out in small towns. In 1972, before the sound of the Stooges had been rematerialized as punk, Lester Bangs wrote:

> Detroit's a nice place to be from. If you teethed in this burgh and made it out at a reasonable age you can cop a degree of macho charisma, because Detroit still means that to a lot of people. If you're still stuck here, though, you just have to bear with it. Because it's no place to live in. San Francisco is still running on the myth of its mid Sixties rock 'n' roll renaissance, which is only one of the things that makes it a constant pain in the ass, but Detroit, even though it went through something similar a couple of years later, doesn't even try to justify itself with those crippled nostalgias. Because everybody in Detroit knows this is nowhere. There's some people who'll actually claim that they're proud of this muck, even defend these lousy below zero winters against the Coast state of constant spring, as if endless ice was some kind of forge you proved yourself on. But they're only justifying themselves. Why did you sit in the pit so long? Because I didn't know how to move.

Two years earlier, in his 1970 State of the Union address, President Nixon said that "street litter, rundown parking strips and yards, dilapidated fences, broken windows, dingy working places, all should be the object of our fresh view." He also said, "The violent and decayed central cities of our great metropolitan complexes are the most conspicuous area of failure in American life today."

[Lester Bangs, "Detroit's Rock Culture," *Phonograph Record*, December 1972; Tom Carson, "Live Delivery," *New York Rocker*, October 1979, p. 46; Samuel R. Delaney, *Dhalgren*, 1975; repr., New York: Vintage, 1996, pp. 382–83; John Morton, liner notes to *The Electric Eels: The Eyeball of Hell*, Scat Records, 2001; Richard Nixon, "Annual Message to the Congress on the State of the Union," January 22, 1970, The American Presidency Project, www.presidency.ucsb.edu; Charlotte Pressler, "Human Switchboard," *New York Rocker*, March 1980, p. 21; Lisa Robinson, "So What Do You Park in an Intellectual Garage?" *New Musical Express*, February 21, 1976, pp. 22–23.]

# Clash

**At some point, summer came.** All at once, it was warm. You could literally smell the sun. School was out. You were bored. You slept with your window open at night for the first time all year, and the next afternoon you rode your bike down the dry dirt paths and through the weeds and up the steep hill to visit the girl whose sister you would marry someday. You must have been in her bedroom, sitting on the floor, thumbing through her record collection, when you came across *Combat Rock*. Of course, you had heard of the Clash—"Rock the Casbah" was on the radio all the time—but you had never really *heard* the Clash. You wondered at their picture on the album cover; they reminded you of kids from a fifties musical, and you couldn't square that with the music. You thought that somehow the Clash wanted you to become *devoted* to them to understand their music. Unlike other punk-type music that made you feel free, the Clash made you feel like you didn't belong. Even though you liked their music—and would grow to like it even more as you grew older—you somehow felt excluded in a way you never did with the Ramones or Sex Pistols.

For one thing, there were the politics. Of course now you have learned that all music is "political"; absurdly, a song like "I Want to Hold Your Hand" might be said to inscribe hetero-normative ideologies, and thus be more insidiously political than the most bitter Joni Mitchell song. The difference is that the Clash staked out a conscious stance, and you believed that unless you truly felt that stance—truly and deeply *felt* and *sympathized* with that stance—you were a hypocrite for liking their music.

Some people have said some simple things about the Clash, and some have said some complicated things. Here is a complicated thing, by Fredric Jameson, from his book on postmodernism:

The shorthand language of co-optation is for this reason omnipresent on the left, but would now seem to offer a most inadequate theoretical basis for understanding

a situation in which we all, in one way or another, dimly feel that not only punc-
tual and local countercultural forms of cultural resistance and guerrilla warfare but
also even overtly political interventions like those of *The Clash* are all somehow
secretly disarmed and reabsorbed by a system of which they themselves might well
be considered a part, since they can achieve no distance from it.

Here is something else, by Robert Christgau, from 1978:

> There are two essential albums in English punk: *Never Mind the Bollocks, Here's
> the Sex Pistols*, available on American Warner, and *The Clash*, a CBS import that
> may well never be released here. Hard rock fans should pick up one and seek out
> the other. I know no one who was bowled over by The Clash on first listen, and I
> know a lot of people who love it now; it's one of my favorite records of the decade.
> Give it some time.

There are so many words surrounding the mention of the Clash. Why are there
so many words? Because the Clash promoted themselves as an idea and as a band.
The force of this idea—progressive, anti-reactionary, sincere, bitter—weighs upon
you even now, after the idea has grown stale.

But has the music grown stale? Their first album, released in England in 1977
(not until 1979 in the United States), is like a loaded shotgun that misfires. Which
is to say, it is dangerous. "Remote Control" is almost a parody of U.K. punk ("Who
needs the Parliament / Sitting making laws all day," but you don't believe there is
any sincerity behind those lines for one minute: You believe that the Clash understand perfectly well why laws are needed) and literal lyrics like that make clear what
an obvious band the Clash were compared to the Sex Pistols, whose lyrics are so
bitterly funny and vicious that they range into the abstract. And yet, for about seventeen seconds—from 1:45 to 2:02—"Remote Control" bursts open in wordless-
ness that surpasses almost all music from the era. Earlier in the song, the lyrics "You
got no money / So you got no power" presented themselves as more dispiriting
than Pink Floyd's "us and them"—except that where Pink Floyd's narrators seemed
resigned to this fact of separation, the Clash seemed pissed about it. In your heart
of hearts, you preferred Pink Floyd's stance. There was something about how the
Clash seemed determined to *speak for you* that rubbed you the wrong way. You
realized, in a half-dim-witted way, that the Clash were as sincere as the hippies they
mocked. The fact that the Clash were becoming rich (you assumed) and famous
(you knew) made you wonder how long they could keep up the stance. Worse, you
wondered if they were just giving the punk kids what they wanted: a version of
rebellion in sporting shorter hair. At least the Sex Pistols had the decency to destroy
themselves before they became total hypocrites.

"I'm So Bored with the U.S.A." presents a litany of failures, from Watergate
("Let's print the Watergate tapes") to Vietnam ("Yankee soldier / He wanna shoot

some skag / He met in Cambodia"). The problem was that in 1977 Americans were as bored with the U.S.A. as the rest of the world, the Brits included, and so the Clash's lyrics seemed like an obvious confirmation rather than radical sentiment. There were all sorts of rumors about how the song was originally about a girl ("I'm So Bored with You") but you never believed these stories. The conspiracy theorist in you (you are an American after all) believed, in fact, that certain members of the Clash, embarrassed by the obviousness of the song, invented the story about the song's "original" title out of sheer air. By the terrific end of the song, the Clash are making fun of Starsky and Kojak. "Yankee detectives / Are always on the TV / 'Cos killers in America / Work seven days a week." But who cares about the lyrics, which you could barely understand anyway? The music came on like a roar.

Whereas American punks like the Ramones and the Dictators used pop culture references to suggest, *Hey, we're all in it together, and it's sort of absurd and funny at the same time*, bands like the Clash and, later, Gang of Four were *serious*, man. "[Rock and roll] has impact," the Clash's Paul Simonon told Caroline Coon in 1976, a few months after their first live show, "and, if we do our job properly then we're making people aware of a situation they'd otherwise tend to ignore. We can have a vast effect!" For those of us who hated overt political sentiment in music, the Clash were difficult to endure, and we were thankful for the songs where the lyrics were hard to hear or decipher. There was nothing more disappointing than reading in some fanzine or music magazine that the Clash were anti-this or anti-that, or that they were against racism, or that they were against war, or that they were against imperialism. Now, get in line behind all the other righteous people. In 1979, Johnny 1980's wrote in the Austin, Texas, fanzine *Sluggo!* about seeing the Clash perform in L.A.: "The Clash was really good but not apocalyptically so. Partly because I no longer believe in them since the second album. Get this—they made $26,000 the night I was there! (I read it in *Billboard*). The Zeros told me that the Dils, who opened, only made $300. They've got a lot of anger for members of the grand-bourgeoisie. I feel cheated in retrospect, but—what a great show!"

The Clash embodied one of punk's great dangers: They were always in peril of "selling out." Of course so were other bands like the Ramones and the Sex Pistols, except that the Ramones never positioned themselves as outside the mainstream and the Sex Pistols were too cynical to believe that being "authentic" was somehow superior to selling out. In this regard, the Clash were more of a sixties band than groups like the Ramones or the Sex Pistols or even Blondie because, despite their persistent critiques of economic conditions, apathy, corrupt government policies, etc., they were, aesthetically, idealists.

This is especially clear on their song "Magnificent Seven" (released in April 1981), from their album *Sandinista!* Inspired by the Grand Master Flash and the Furious Five, the song is a rap-infused, kaleidoscopic narrative, looking backward to Bob Dylan's "Subterranean Homesick Blues" and forward to R.E.M.'s "It's the End of the World as We Know It (And I Feel Fine)." In June 1981, the Clash performed the song on *The Tomorrow Show with Tom Snyder* in what is one of the great live pop performances captured on video. The song is cinematic in its sound; it is the sound of a new decade being tuned in. "Gimme Honda, Gimme Sony / so cheap and real phony" sings Joe Strummer, as a prophet.

[Robert Christgau, "Punk Guide: A Consumer Manual to New Wave Wax," *Creem*, April 1978, p. 40; Caroline Coon, "The Clash: Down and Out and Proud," *Melody Maker*, November 13, 1976; Fredric Jameson, *Postmodernism, or, The Cultural Logic of Late Capitalism*, 1984; repr., Durham, North Carolina: Duke University Press, 1991, p. 49; Johnny 1980's, "L.A. Trip," *Sluggo!* March 1979.]

# Class

**Perhaps it was inevitable** that one measure of punk's authenticity would come to be class. As in, "British punk was more authentic than American because it was made by outsiders, not well-to-do kids from suburbia." Here is one formula:

New York Punk  ⟶  U.K. Punk  ⟶  California Hardcore

(avant-garde; arty)     (class anger, but not militant)     (destructive; extreme)

Now, objections abound, but brush those aside and consider this: What the Brits heard in New York underground and punk was an anger that made sense in the context of class, and what the California hardcore bands heard in U.K. punk was a fury that made sense in the context of a society that permitted all.

The contours of class difference—or perceived difference—became clear early on, illuminated by writers like Simon Frith and Dick Hebdige. In *Creem* in 1977, Frith wrote from England on the differences between American and British punk: "There was too much space between the Ramones and their music." The Ramones were "Pop artists, New York style, of course, but still with an air of care and what I missed in comparison with the British new wave was the edginess, the tension, the squalor of poor musicians who aren't at all sure of what they're doing as they thrash around seeking success from sneers, riding the streets and the record companies in uneasy tandem." At graduate school, you felt the tremendous chasm opening up: You became a critic of everything, and wondered if this would kill the passionate, irrational side of you that attracted you to music and literature in the first place. There was a bit of *Mad* magazine in American punk from the mid-seventies, the kind of self-deprecating humor that comes from the confidence of empire. I should put my cards on the table now and say this: It boils down to nationalism. As bad as things were economically in the mid-seventies in New York (and things were bad; the city teetered on bankruptcy) there was still a deeper assurance that the empire would not collapse. No matter what. Something like 9/11 was unimaginable. Simon Frith was right in noticing that there was too much "space between the Ramones and their music." That space was the confidence that *everything was going to be okay.* That's why the true, secret connection between American and U.K. punk has nothing to do with New York and everything to do with Cleveland and bands like the Electric Eels, Rocket from the Tombs, and, later, the Pagans.

That's why Frith dismisses Television as "cold, cutting, and about as cutting as Peter Frampton" and refers to Tom Verlaine as a "white faced robot of the guitar." How can you really care and be pissed off about things and be as cold and calculating as Television? Of course, it's a sort of old-fashioned Marxism (politely called "cultural theory") that wants to see revolution first and art second. The problem is that it doesn't matter. Art is always representation: It's a vision of the way we experience the world, not the way the world really is. To claim that the Clash or Sex Pistols were somehow more authentic than the Ramones or Television says a lot about your intentions as a listener, but probably not too much about the music itself.

[Simon Frith, "Letter from Britain: Queen of the Silver Squalor," *Creem*, September 1977, p. 36.]

## Cleveland, Ohio

**Throughout this book,** there is much about Cleveland, the Cleveland area, and its punk-era bands and personalities, such as Rocket from the Tombs, Pere Ubu, Electric Eels, the Pagans, Peter Laughner, David Thomas, Mike Hudson, and others. Here are ten quotes about Cleveland:

1. "In mid-November 1974, after [the] election, the situation in fragmented, divided, polarized Cleveland was about as depressing as it was possible to be . . . The mayor announced that he would have to lay off 1,200 employees at once, and cut the budget drastically for 1975. He said 150 policemen and 100 firemen would be among those laid off. Garbage and rubbish could be collected only fortnightly, not every week." (Porter 272)

2. "As the population continues to decline and industry and jobs flee to the suburbs, new wastelands of vandalized, abandoned neighborhoods spread amoeba-like through the city." (Whelan)

3. "Corporate America's domination of the news media eclipses the meaning of a free press doctrine. Mainstream America has been presented a false social, political and economic reality supported by a consensus among the self-serving

elite. However, big business, big government and big media are all out of touch with mainstream America, so they do not know how thoroughly disappointed, how utterly disgusted, how fed up, but how perceptive ordinary people are. This power elite is unaware how readily the myths can be toppled by the emerging new urban populism." (Mayor Kucinich)

4. "The events in Ohio [possible public-school shutdowns] apparently constitute the only dramatic expression this fall of the fiscal difficulties that have affected school systems throughout the nation during the 1970's, a decade of deteriorating tax bases in many older cities and of taxpayer revolts in city, suburb and small towns alike. The difficulties appear particularly acute in the older northern industrial cities like Cleveland and Toledo, where the flight of industry to the countryside and the Sunbelt." (Stevens)

5. "On 15 December 1978, Cleveland became the first American major city to default since the Depression. The city could not repay $15.5 million in short-term notes that came due, and city officials were unable to agree with local banks on a program to avert default." (Miller and Wheeler, 178)

6. "The early Seventies were sad, tumultuous years for Cleveland, years when the city seemed to be in the midst of its own Great Depression, years of physical and psychological erosion. The parks were, once again, dumping grounds. The transit system was approaching financial disaster. The downtown, offering little to attract people, was largely dead at night." (Miller and Wheeler)

7. "If environment really does determine musical styles, then Cleveland, Ohio, must be a very weird place indeed. Over the past year a steady flow of vinyl esoterica has made its way to Britain. The garage explosion seems to have taken special hold in that town and prompted all sorts of social outcasts and other vermin to congregate, form bands, and seek ways of captivating the more curious punter." (Rambali)

8. "Between 1958 and 1977, Cleveland lost an estimated 130,000 jobs, while the suburbs of Cuyahoga County gained almost 210,000." (Miller and Wheeler)

9. In CB lingo, Cleveland is the Dirty City, where sulfur dioxide permeates human pores." (Hull)

10. "[During the 1830s] many of the poor lived in the Flats, the floodplain on either side of the river, 'under the hill.' Here the thriving economy spawned numerous 'groceries,' which appeared on every wharf to dispense alcohol. A racecourse destabled in 1835 encouraged 'a flood of imported depravity, strengthened by all the canaille [rabble] that could be mustered from groceries and other dens of pollution.'" (*Whig*, October 14, 1835, in Miller and Wheeler)

[Robot A. Hull, "The World According to Pere Ubu," *Creem*, November 1979; Dennis J. Kucinich, speech before National Press Club in Washington, reprinted in the *Cleveland*

*Press*, October 3, 1978; Carol Poe Miller and Robert Wheeler, *Cleveland: A Concise History, 1796–1990*, Bloomington: Indiana University Press, 1990; Philip W. Porter, *Cleveland: Confused City on a Seesaw*, Columbus: Ohio State University Press, 1976; Paul Rambali, "Pere Ubu: Weird City Robomen," *New Musical Express*, January 7, 1978; William K. Stevens, "Cleveland Schools Face Shutdown on Friday for a Lack of Money," *The New York Times*, October 17, 1977; Edward P. Whelan, "Mayor Ralph J. Perk and the Politics of Decay," *Cleveland Magazine*, September 1975.]

## Compact Audio Cassette

**The Compact Audio Cassette—the cassette tape—**was first introduced in Berlin by Philips in 1963, but it wasn't until the late seventies and early eighties that the quality (metal and chrome tape) increased to the point where it rivaled the vinyl album as a playback medium for music. By the mid- to late seventies, most major record labels advertised their music as available on "records and tapes." The Sony Walkman (one of its earlier names was the "Soundabout") was introduced in 1979 and caught on in 1980. An early *New York Times* article on the Walkman in July 1980 profiled it as a fashion accessory and as a way to block out the ugly sounds of the city. "'I couldn't even lift one of those monstrous box things but I love this,' said Karen Meyers, who was listening to 'Pavoratti's Greatest Hits' on her Walkman as she strolled along East 57th Street. Miss Meyers said she had bought the set because 'its sound is so fantastic and it shuts out the awful sounds of the city.'" For a short while, the Walkman was associated with, as Andrew Pollack put it, "joggers and

A copy of a copy of a copy: mechanical reproduction in the punk era, from *New York Rocker* in 1981

bicyclists"—a sort of urban, nerdy, exercise-as-style crowd. "That's the stereotype—
two ferny-looking, quiche-eating people jogging down the street."

As the popularity of the Walkman and its many imitators (the Walkie, the Solo,
the Sportster, the Sportmate, the Hip Pocket Stereo, etc.) spread, the very idea of
the idea of pop music changed. For a recorded song is never heard or listened to
from nowhere; it always eminates from some place, some physical, material place.
Marshall McLuhan's aphorism "the medium is the message" applies not only to
visual media but to sonic ones, as well. The idea of a song in our heads—its shape,
its connections to other things—is often very clearly attached to its medium: the
record player, the stereo, the car radio, the boom box, the Walkman, the iPod, the
computer. Not to get too metaphysical, but the circularity of the LP, or the seven
inch, or the 45, with their slow, steady, relentless turning, meant something different than the barely perceptible or invisible movement of tape winding its way
through the plastic cassette. "Will cassettes eventually replace albums?" asked Robert Palmer in 1981. "Most record-industry insiders doubt it . . . one can put the
phonograph needle down on a favorite selection, for example, instead of having to
speed through a tape looking for it." The cassette was yet another step in the disap-
pearance of the *idea* of music as a physical object. It was also the end of the idea of
music as circular, following the grooves in concentric circles on a side of vinyl.

With the advent of cassettes came mix tapes, which allowed for the creation
of personalized, easily portable anthologies of music, taken from the radio, vinyl,
or other cassettes. Thurston Moore recalls the explosion of singles by bands such
as Minor Threat, Necros, Youth Brigade, and others in the early eighties, singles
that could not always afford to buy. "I also felt I needed to hear these records in a
more time-fluid way, and it hit me that I could make a killer mix tape of all the best
songs from these records," he has said. Divorced from the medium of their original
recording, the songs took on a new life next to other songs on these tapes. Others
have waxed nostalgic about the mix tape and its romance, or the mix tape as an
aesthetic expression in its own right. A dissenting view: It is not the best songs, but
the worst ones, that are most worthy of attention. The totalitarianism of the LP,
with its inevitable inclusion of weak or just plain bad tracks, encouraged a sort of
close listening, a hostility that was well suited to punk. Bad music made the good
music even better.

Buying an album was a commitment to the idea of a band and its vision. To
take just the best songs was to ignore a central mystery: Whose album was it, really?
Who decided that these songs belonged on this album in this particular sequence
with this particular cover? The band itself? The producer? The know-nothing
executives at the record company? Of course the answers varied from band to band,
and from album to album. The rise of independent labels and mix tapes made this

question irrelevant, as control over the sequencing of material rested with the band or, increasingly, the listener, whose imposition of her own taste on the material rendered the world more and more and more like her.

[Ron Alexander, "Stereo-to-Go—and Only You Can Hear It," *The New York Times*, July 7, 1980, p. B12; Thurston Moore, *Mix Tape: The Art of Cassette Culture*. New York: Universe, p. 12; Robert Palmer, "Cassettes Now Have Material Not Available on Disks," *The New York Times*, July 29, 1981; Andrew Pollack, "Personal Stereo Market Swells," *The New York Times*, June 5, 1981.]

## Cooper, Alice

**Alice Cooper was the missing link** between glam rock and what came to be known as punk rock. He also prompted Grace Lichtenstein, in *The New York Times*, to use the phrase "punk rock" in 1972, after Dave Marsh had used it in *Creem* in 1971 but before it had entered the mainstream. Like the best rock writing of the era, Lichtenstein's article verged on the hostile; she saw the truth behind Cooper's act as only an outsider could.

> Alice (the name of the lead singer as well as the group) plays archetypal punk rock—the pimply music the fifties rock and rollers so excelled in, which the Stones brought to fruition in the sixties. Any kid who ever threw up from too many beers at a basement party, any kid who was ever dragged into the dean's office for disrupting a class, any kid who ever dreamed of breaking loose while slinging Big Whoppers in the local Burger King can relate to Alice's songs. Nasty, yes. Juveline, yes. But they have touched the nerve center of teen-age malaise.

Alice Cooper was born Vincent Furnier in Detroit in 1948, the same year as Alan Vega and William Gibson. In a strange way, it makes sense that Lester Bangs would eventually do his best writing in Detroit, and that he would call Alice Cooper's first album "a tragic waste of plastic." His theatrics on stage veered absurdly and ominously between camp, horror, and high art, and although it seems as if punk, with its minimalism, and the sheer excess of Alice Cooper could not be further apart, in truth they are kissing cousins, for both depended on tightly controlled chaos and highly managed disorder.

Most of all, Alice Cooper was fun, in the same way that the mid-seventies were fun. In "School's Out," he sang, "Well we got no class / And we got no principles / And we got no innocence / We can't even think of a word that rhymes." That self-referential line—which really deflates the whole pseudo-horror scheme and reveals Cooper for the good-natured magician that he was, simultaneously—points back in time to the "second verse same as the first" line from the Herman's Hermits song

"Henry the VIII, I Am" and forward to the Ramones, who used the same line in "Judy Is a Punk." The problem was always how to translate the show onto vinyl; at his best, Alice Cooper rejected "concepts" on his albums and just made killer songs, which shouted so loud that they woke up the punks. The result was a very different sort of "punk rock" than that imagined by Grace Lichtenstein, who forever should be remembered and thanked for using words and phrases like "punk rock," "threw up," "legs spread wide," "fondles his privates," and "hacks a baby doll to pieces" in *The New York Times* in 1972, when, because nothing seemed possible, everything was possible.

> [Grace Lichtenstein, "Alice Cooper? David Bowie? Ugh! And Ugh Again!" *The New York Times*, September 24, 1972, pp. 7–8.]

## Cox, Alex

**British director, born in 1954.** His 1984 film *Repo Man* featured music by Iggy Pop, the Plugz, Circle Jerks, and others. A gloriously shaggy-dog film, *Repo Man* is characterized by the same DIY ethic that generated punk. It's funny and absurd and weirdly scary and surreal and wise and even sentimental, at times, and sometimes all at once. The movie is *punk* in a disarmingly radical way; beneath its humor is a sort of bubbling anarchy of ideas, none of them mixing together into a coherent whole. About punk, Cox has said:

> Well, this was a movement that encouraged the political. It encouraged anarchic tendencies because it had revolutionary expectations. Although punk's revolutionary tendencies may have been disappointed, its features fed through into a number of interesting films at the time. When we made *Repo Man*, Penelope Spheeris was making *Suburbia*, which is also quite an interesting film about the punk scene in a way.

And while Cox has remained a resolutely independent filmmaker, it is interesting that a film like *Repo Man* required old-fashioned, capitalist financing. Cox's Web site includes many of his original screenplays in pdf format, often along with studio notes, production cost information, marketing plans, etc. For *Repo Man*, Cox's budget information included a section entitled "Investors": "Film making is, of course, a risky venture even when the production is insured against lab damage and equipment loss. As such, it is best suited to venture capital, since there is always a possibility of project failure and loss of investment funds." And later we read about the "rapid growth of exploitable markets." For Cox, punk was something revolutionary and radical, associated with progressive rather than conservative ideologies. And yet, of course, it was also a commodity, something to be bought and sold in the marketplace. As Doug Henwood, publisher of *Left Business Observer*, noted in an interview in *Punk Planet*:

> In a practical sense, a lot of independent operations screw their employees and customers over as much as anybody else does. You could say that there's often something other than the logic of profit maximization at work in independent operations, but you can't be sure of that. There are lots of scum bags and frauds everywhere, including independent music labels and publishers.

Insisting on punk as a revolutionary movement reacting against the forces of big music labels and big media is itself a form of reactionary nostalgia. Stacy Thompson notes that within "a few months after the Sex Pistols signed with EMI, The Clash had signed with CBS, The Damned with Stiff, and The Stranglers with UA." And from the New York scene, Patti Smith signed with Arista, Television with Elektra, and the Ramones and Dead Boys with Sire, which was acquired by Warner Bros. in 1978.

Or consider this exchange from *Repo Man*, as the leader of a "punk gang" lies dying on the floor of a convenience store at the end of a failed robbery attempt. "Otto, the lights are going dim," he says. "I know a life of crime has led me to this sorry fate. In the end, I blame society. Society made me what I am." To which Otto replies: "That's bullshit. You're a white suburban punk, just like me."

[Alex Cox quoted by Xavier Mendik, "*Repo Man*: Reclaiming the Spirit of Punk with Alex Cox," in *New Punk Cinema*, ed. Nicholas Rombes, Edinburgh: Edinburgh University Press, 2005, p. 197; Doug Henwood quoted in Stacy Thompson, *Punk Productions: Unfinished Business*, Albany: State University of New York Press, p. 149; Stacy Thompson, *Punk Productions*, p. 19.]

## *C.P.O. Sharkey* / "Punk Rock Sharkey"

**An episode of the television show *C.P.O. Sharkey*,** starring Don Rickles, which aired in March 1978. Rickles visits an L.A. punk club, ultimately convincing a punkish girl to join the navy. The episode features the Dickies playing "You're So Hideous" as kids dance in a sort of corny, mediated, violent way followed by a gag in which one of the navy officers in attendance quips that he used to do that dance: stepping on cockroaches. It is only fitting that one of the first network television shows to incorporate punk into its plot featured Don Rickles, whose abrasive humor cut through the pieties of hypocrisy. "Don Rickles, a true punk himself, is the tube's prophet," John Holmstrom once wrote, recognizing the secret truth that punk is, above all, a stance, a way of carrying yourself in the world, a performance. Rickles was a performer who became famous for his alarmingly direct and assaultive responses to hecklers. The most radical thing he did was recognize and involve the audience, turn them into participants; there was always an element of anarchy and implied violence in his best routines. In this, he provided a context to his performance that recognized the artifice, even as audiences forgot this artifice, momentarily, as they lost themselves in his routine. At its finest, and only rarely, punk managed this same small miracle.

[John Holmstrom, "Punxploitation!," *Stop! Magazine* #5, Dec/Jan 1982/83, p. 12.]

## Cramps: Live at Napa State Mental Hospital

**Filmed by Target Video** at the Napa State Mental Hospital in June 1978, this is the sort of artifact that is so strange that you are tempted to think it's fake. It is probably the most disastrously confounding document of the punk era, something that, even more than thirty years later, has not lost its power to shock. What in God's name, you wonder when watching this, were the administrators of the Napa State Mental Hospital thinking when they let the Cramps in to play? Struggling to make sense of what's unfolding, to find some precedent, your mind races back to Johnny Cash's 1968 concert at Folsom State Prison. The black-and-white video—shot on a Sony Port-a-Pak with a single microphone—is so blurry and degraded that right from the start it looks like something beamed in from another plant, or the set of a movie gone wrong. The obvious question that crosses any sane person's mind after watching two minutes is, *Who is crazier, the Cramps or the mental patients?* And by the time the patients take the stage—and boy oh boy do they ever take the stage—the answer to the question is obvious.

Strangely enough, this is also one of the tenderest documents, as the late singer Lux Interior (Erick Purkhiser) plays the whole show straight without a trace of irony or mockery. When he stops midway through "Love Me," looks out into the audience and says, "Love me," and gets down on his knees, a few patients rush up to give him a tender hug, taking his plea seriously. It's a disorienting moment, because the song suddenly becomes something much different when taken literally. And for "Human Fly" and "Domino" he is joined by a female patient who takes the microphone and ad-libs her own lyrics. You keep expecting things to turn terrible, but they don't, even during the final song, "TV Set," as several patients start crawling awkwardly up onto the stage, like extras from George Romero's *Night of the Living Dead*.

In the end, what you remember is the interaction between the band and the patients, and wonder about but cannot answer half-formed questions in your mind about punk and madness and how glad you are that you know only a little bit about this strange concert so that it can remain, thankfully, as a full-blown mystery in your life when there are so few mysteries left.

# Criticism, Rock

**What is the purpose of writing about rock?** If the music is good, and if it means something, even for a moment, does there need to be writing? Doesn't the best music describe itself? Alone in a bedroom, or with someone else, what's the use of words interposed between music and bodies? (A bedroom with an unwatered plant that is dying and a life-changing book by C. S. Lewis that's yet to be opened: What's wrong with you? And don't you regret wasting your time on those Harry Potter books?) Is there even a place for words? Of course not. The fact that I've let a dozen "serious" scholarly projects slip through my fingers while writing this book shows . . . well, maybe it just reveals some defect in me that becomes more obvious the older I get. Many people—Dave Marsh included—have wondered why punk has become so critically valorized when other music from that era, such as disco, has not. There are many answers as to why punk's legacy seems outsized, ranging from the very serious (punk was "white" music in a racist society) to the very flippant (punk was simply better than disco, and you

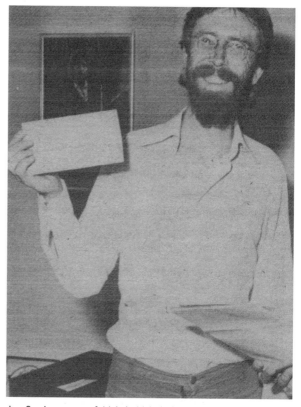

Jan Steele, winner of *Melody Maker's* Student Rock Essay Contest, August 1976

didn't have to dance to it while on drugs to enjoy it). But in truth punk has lasted because it was written about, and because it emerged at roughly the same time as self-conscious "rock crit" writing. At its best, the writing—by Lester Bangs, Greil Marcus, Richard Meltzer, Dave Marsh, Legs McNeil, Patti Smith, and others—was as unpredictable, absurd, funny, poignant, sarcastic, difficult, easy, egotistical, bitter, and self-consciously structured as punk itself. This shows up in big ways and in small. For instance, near the end of his 1973 *Creem* review of a Captain Beefheart album, Lester Bangs wrote, "The main thing to be said about this album is that, even at its most violent, it's *comfortable*. Its scope becomes endless by limiting itself (how's that for rock critic bullshit?)."

This open acknowledgment of "rock critic bullshit" is finally one of comradery: It's a secret communication between one loser and other. It's not quite the same thing as the Ramones counting out their "one-two-three-four" before a song, but it's close: both wink at the audience, but then deliver something that makes you forget that wink. In that same issue of *Creem*, several of the record reviews are "interrupted" by the editor, who interjects some italicized comment, correcting or mocking the author. This isn't exactly like breaking down the fourth wall in theater; it's more like the director leaning out onto the stage from the wings and correcting an actor in front of the audience.

The strange thing is, formal rock criticism—in all its contorted academic glory—briefly coexisted with more traditional rock journalism and with fan-clubish writing for several years in the mid-seventies. Consider, for instance, that *Melody Maker*—hardly a music theory forum—sponsored a Student Rock Essay Contest in 1976. The winning essay, by Jan Steele, a Ph.D. student in social anthropology at Queen's University, entitled "Tommy, Lennon, Mao and the Road to Revolution," noted that:

> We are near a great turning-point in history, the point in the West at which the products of capitalism, which could only be produced under capitalism . . . can be appropriated fully and finally by working people for the benefit of all people of the world . . . The rock musician in his song expresses a desire for freedom, but in the capitalist era freedom can only be attained through money. He pleads for more honesty in sexual relationships but participates actively in sexual exploitation. He is vehemently iconoclastic, yet wallows in his deification.

In his weekly *Melody Maker* column, Richard Williams asked why punk (in 1976) did not go one step further and disavow the critics who championed it:

> It's time for a change, and if that change comes in the shape of The Damned, the Pistols, and the Punk movement, then I'm all for it. Move over, redundant artys-fartsy nostalgia, and give dumb violence a chance!
>
> Don't misunderstand me: I don't want to have to listen to it. As Michael Oldfield pointed out in his review of the CBGB's live album last week, it's time these people made it clear that they aren't interested in the views of 30-year-old critics. They should disown and repudiate even the kindnesses. The mental contortions of the aged should be held up for ridicule by those they would praise.

To end with a question: Why didn't punk mean a rejection of the very critics who helped define it?

[Lester Bangs, "Low Yo-Yo Stuff: Getting Closer to the Captain," *Creem*, January 1973, p. 67; Jan Steele, "Tommy, Lennon, Mao and the Road to Revolution," *Melody Maker*, August 28, 1976, p. 25; Richard Williams, "Let's Have a Generation Gap Again," *Melody Maker*, August 28, 1976, p. 14.]

# d

# Dancing

**"[The songs of G.I., Youth Brigade, and Minor Threat were]** lost in sheets of white noise. However, that seemed to provide a context for the activist alienation of slam dancing, in which young men metamorphosize into bowling pins, while others act out the role of perpetually flowing bowling balls. It's a style which speaks to youthful angst and ambivalent violence." (Harrington, July 17)

"Violence is not new to rock 'n' roll, but it's never been so menacing. In the past, riots tended to come from overcrowding or things getting out of hand; now things start out of hand." (Harrington, July 19)

"Psychologists suggested yesterday that while the rock 'n' roll craze seemed to be related to 'rhythmic behavior patterns' as old as the Middle Ages, it required further study as a current phenomenon . . . Dr. Meerlo described the 'contagious epidemic of dance fury' that 'swept Germany and spread to all of Europe' toward the end of the fourteenth century. It was called . . . St. Vitus Dance (or Chorea Major), he continued, with its victims breaking into dancing and being unable to stop." (Brackner)

"The early music which emanated from the Restoration churches and their Dales and Downs Bible weeks was contrastingly raucous in tone. Many of their first creations were stampeding warfare songs such as 'It's God who makes my hands to war,' 'An army of ordinary people,' and 'The Lord is marching out in splendour.'" (Scotland)

"In the next three years [1804–1806] their [Richard McNemar and John Thompson, Presbyterians] services, particularly their intercongregational communions, became wilder and wilder, with not only jerking and swooning, but barking like dogs and formalized dancing. This style, almost as much as freewill doctrines, alienated those ministers and congregations from the main body of Presbyterians." (Conklin)

"The Pentecostal world of worship, shaped by the sounds, surrounds the worshipper. As part of the ritual field, these ritual sounds are one of the elements that helps to produce the matrix within which Pentecostals encounter their God and each other." (Albrecht)

We hit the floor, they all stand back
We start to vibrate and the floor starts to crack.
Well by the second verse they're all joining in
We don't do the hustle, hully gully or swim
We vibrate
Vibrate together, vibrate (Vibrators)

Whatever the explanation, enthusiasm mounted as the music approached the same points in each verse. The musicians were, in turn, stimulated to even more intense performance. A little girl jerked . . . A man "B," who had been active other nights leaped up with a shout, capered toward the rostrum and then returned to his seat. There were cheers. Someone raised his hands over his head and waved or vibrated them. A young man "C," shouted. His neck stretched itself back from his body and became stiff with the chin vibrating. Then his head vibrated while his body was relaxed. Then he danced. The trio was singing right on. Up jumped "A," jerking repeatedly. Then a girl near her jerked and other followed suit. (Wood)

[Daniel E. Albrecht, *Rites in the Spirit: A Ritual Approach to Pentecostal/Charismatic Spirituality*, Sheffield: Sheffield Academic Press, 1999, p. 144; Milton Brackner, "Experts Propose Study of 'Craze': Liken It to Medieval Lunacy, 'Contagious Dance Furies' and Bite of Tarantula," *The New York Times*, February 23, 1957, p. 12; Paul K. Conklin, *American Originals: Homemade Varieties of Christianity*, Chapel Hill: The Unversity of North Carolina Press, 1997, pp. 11–12; Richard Harrington, "The Sounds of the Slamdance," *The Washington Post*, July 17, 1981, p. B7; Richard Harrington, "Slamdancing in the City," *The Washington Post*, July 19, 1981, p. G1; Nigel Scotland, *Charismatics and the Next Millennium: Do They Have a Future?* London: Hodder and Stoughton, 1995, p. 56; Vibrators, "We Vibrate," November 1976; William W. Wood, *Culture and Personality Aspects of the Pentecostal Holiness Religion*, Paris: Mouton and Co., 1965, p. 12.]

# Dead Boys

**D. H. Lawrence once said** of Edgar Allan Poe that "he is absolutely concerned with the disintegration-process of his own psyche," and that "doomed he was. He died wanting more love, and love killed him. A ghastly disease, love. Poe telling us of his disease: trying even to make his disease fair and attractive. Even succeeded." Lawrence was schizophrenic about Poe; he wanted to dismiss him by loving him. He wanted to protect himself from Poe by making Poe's bloodlust safe and bourgeois, but in the end he didn't know how to do this. Instead, he wrote nine pages about Poe in *Studies in Classic American Literature*.

The same could be said of your efforts to laugh off the Dead Boys, who offer the first and most terrible glimpse of punk's annihilistic potential. Formed in Cleveland in 1975 out of the detritus of Rocket from the Tombs, Dead Boys consisted of Stiv Bators, Cheetah Chrome, Jeff Magnum, Johnny Blitz, and Jimmy Zero. Bators, Chrome, Magnum, Blitz, and Zero: The names are good enough to make a collective persona, and so was the music, especially on *Young, Loud and Snotty*, released in 1977. On "Ain't Nothing to Do," Bators sang, "There ain't nothin' to do / Gonna beat up the next hippie I see / Maybe I'll be beatin' up you / Look out, baby, here I comes."

The truth is, the Dead Boys were not that good. Of course, punk innoculates itself against this sort of judgment because it's not supposed to be "good." So let's put it this way: the Dead Boys were one of the first punk bands to drive off the cliff. Imagine them falling off a cliff, and making music as they are falling. Picturing it this way, questions of taste don't really enter into it. They are neither good nor bad: The fact that they succeeded in making music while they were falling makes them interesting. In 1977, Cathy Nemeth described them this way in *New York Rocker*:

> The effect of the music—rock fierce and pure—is devastating. But in their pursuit of ultra-violence, the Dead Boys are leaving themselves vulnerable to the stifling horror of mediocrity. There is just so much aggression that can be generated in reply to, say, boredom before it drives its own self into the ground.

So they were an interesting band, falling off a cliff. They frightened and angered some people, like Mary Harron, who covered the early punk scene and who would go on to direct some very fine movies, such as *I Shot Andy Warhol*. This is the last paragraph of Harron's 1977 article on the Dead Boys:

> There are times when ignorance and thoughtlessness and naivete are more danger- ous than deliberate cruelty. The Dead Boys are not responsible for everything that is going wrong with punk rock, but they and their fans are being swept away by a situation they don't understand and which will hurt them.

In songs like "Down in Flames" ("Dead eyes feeding your dead, dead brain / Dead boy, dead boy, always end the same") you can hear a prediction that will come true in the California hardcore scene, when the savagery of lyrics, sound, and album artwork combined to lay waste to the original impulse of nostalgia that gave rise to punk. "The group's only real forte is its blatancy," wrote *Los Angeles Times* critic Robert Hilburn. But the legacy of the Dead Boys is as prophets, not musi- cians. They tuned in to punk's destructive frequency early on. They were destroyers who destroyed themselves.

[Mary Harron, "The Dead Boys: Pretty Vicious," *Sounds*, August 27, 1977; Robert Hilburn, "Dead Boys Run in the Punk Pack," *Los Angeles Times*, November 5, 1977, p. B7; D. H. Law- rence, *Studies in Classic American Literature*, 1923; repr., New York: Viking, 1964, pp. 65, 81; Cathy Nemeth, "Dead Boys: CBGB's," *New York Rocker*, November–December 1977, p. 57.]

# "Death of Punk"

**The cover of the alternative newspaper** the *East Village Eye* from June 1980 features a drawing by John Holmstrom, founder of the seminal *Punk* fanzine, which first appeared in 1976. The headline? JOHN HOLMSTROM AND THE DEATH OF PUNK, THE ORIGINAL. The word "punk"—because of its distinctive lettering and its close association with Holmstrom—refers not only to *Punk* the fanzine but to punk as a movement and perhaps an idea. The beauty of this particular cover is its self-defeating honesty, its bittersweet acknowledgment that punk—at least in its initial formulation—was dead. The cover depicts Holmstrom and Legs McNeil sitting on a street curb, dressed in classic, simple black-and-white punkish clothes, sort of like bums, as the trendy, hip New Wavers (most dressed in pink) form an enormous line on the sidewalk behind them waiting to get into a fancy club (charging a fifty-dollar cover) whose sign in marquis lights reads SUPER-HIP NEW WAVE DISCO SUPPER CLUB. TONIGHT: BLONDIE, CORBETT MONACA, SUZANNE FELLINI, WAYNE NEWTON.

Holmstrom's line to Legs (who is trying to bum a cigarette off a horrified pre-valley-girl hipster who exclaims "Oh, Ick! My God!") is "Well, Legs, we blew it!"—a direct echo of Peter Fonda's line to Dennis Hopper in *Easy Rider* (1969), in many ways the quintessential sixties movie. Of all the words to put into Holmstrom's own cartoon mouth, these are the most self-damning and self-accusatory, seeing as how *Punk*, and punk in general, loathed and mocked the counterculture and the hippies. Inside, on page seventeen, Holmstrom has drawn a "*Punk* magazine scrapbook," with highlights from various back issues of *Punk*, including this quote (from issue #7) from R. Crumb:

> Who knows? Maybe hand-printed "punk" nihilism is the next **BIG** thing . . . slick, middle-aged businessmen with him up-to-date leather outfits will start approaching you with big bucks . . . then what? But maybe you'll be lucky and this won't happen and you'll be able to continue putting out a "tough li'l spunky" magazine for awhile until you get tired of not making money and have to look for work. . . . Eventually, everybody has to look for work, kid . . . you can't be a teen-ager forever . . . but it's fun while it lasts, huh?

## Demics

**A punk band from London, Ontario,** formed in 1977 by Keith Whittaker, Rob Brent, Iain Atkinson, and Nick Perry/Jim Weatherston. The name, slang for something like "loser," conjures a system of measurement, like metrics, in your nighttime mind. They are perhaps best known for "New York City," recorded in 1978. The song ("I'm getting pretty bored / and I want to get out") is nearly perfect, and it makes you love New York City even more than you do. Other songs are just mis-aligned enough to evoke mystery. "The 400 Blows" sounds like it was recorded in a garbage can; the lyrics are so garbled that Whittaker must have had stones in his mouth. "Factories" is like the Ramones in slow motion, with some of the bleakest lyrics: "Hoot, hoot, hoot go the factory horns / You hear it every morning from the time that you're born / Your time has come now to work within its walls."

# Destroy All Monsters

**Detroit/Ann Arbor antirock band** formed in 1974. Listening to them, you feel like your brain is being looted. Except it feels good. Here are two things that happened: The burning of once-magnificent Detroit. Ann Arbor awoke from its sixties dream—and it was a dream only—to the harsh reality of the real world in business suits. President Gerald Ford, for God's sake. The hippies had turned ugly, enforcing the worst sort of political correctness. Joined by Niagara—a woman to fall in love with—and Ron Asheton of the Stooges. Punk before there was punk. Impossible to tell now, as this is being written in 2006 (but in what year, loyal reader, are you reading these words? And what sadness haunts you?), whether the band hated itself or the world it sang about.

Ad for Destroy All Monsters from the Detroit-area fanzine *White Noise*, 1979

The 1978 single (released by IDBI Records, P.O. Box 7241, Ann Arbor, MI, 48107) contains the song "Bored," with lyrics that go "When I woke up this morning, I was really bored / When I woke up this morning, I was really bored / When I woke up in the afternoon, I was really bored / When I woke up in the afternoon, I was really bored" and "You're so boring when I think of you / You do nothing for my interview," and "You're not anywhere / You're not anywhere." But was it punk? That's an impoverished question. "I went to CBGBs once and it was just a brawling filthy bar," Carey Loren, who helped create Destroy All Monsters, has said. "Detroit had an even crazier version called Bookies Club . . . Punk rock was mostly uncreative drivel. It was all about fashion: safety pins and leather."

But hold that 45 in your hands. Take it out of the sleeve. Place it on the turntable. Gently drop the needle. Turn up the volume. "Bored" is the better song, mostly because near the end the lyrics shift from "You're not anywhere / You're not anywhere" to "I'll go anywhere / I'll do anything."

The other side, "You're Gonna Die," has a cruel surprise waiting for you at the very end. After the song is over, as the needle slides into the thick, ice-skatable black at the end of the single, Niagara's voice is repeated in an endless loop, echoing the last words of the song: "gonna die." At first, this sounds like a skip in the record, a flaw. But it's no flaw. It's a deliberate, nasty little trick, a death loop more eerie than anything concocted in *The Ring*. What this means is that you could die writing this very book, or die reading it, alone, and that damned record would still keep repeating Niagara's silky voice seeping into your no-longer-hearing ears.

Detroit has always anticipated its second musical renaissance following Motown. For a short while, punk was thought to be that renaissance. Then "electronic music." Then Eminem. Then the White Stripes. Then . . . The great secret is that the very anticipation of the never-coming renaissance is, in fact, the renaissance.

Detroit, among all major American cities, is alone in the fact that its anticipation for renewal is the strongest evidence of its renewal. *Ballroom Blitz*, a Detroit (well, Dearborn Heights) fanzine from the late 1970s, has a cover that proclaims DETROIT UPRISING and an accompanying article and photo spread that refers to the "aggressive avant-garde sound of DESTROY ALL MONSTERS."

Now you are holding another single in your hands, "What Do I Get? / Nobody Knows," from 1979, and you notice that IBDI Records is now located at P.O. Box 1038, Southfield, MI, 48075, and you wonder what that means. The switch from Ann Arbor to Southfield. Anything? Or nothing?

"What Do I Get" is not wonderful, except for the last blistering thirteen seconds of guitar fury. That, you love. "Nobody Knows" is much better. It's simpler. Niagara sings her lyrics likes she's reading them from a sheet she's just been handed. She doesn't care, but you do. And then there are the guitar solos, by Ron Asheton, and you are reminded how all categories of rock are obliterated in the face of vision and conviction. What does it matter what it's called?

Unlike the first single, this one has an actual photograph of the band on the back of the sleeve. Of course, Niagara is wearing a mini-skirt. There is the indisputable fact of her legs. Her eyes are closed. Her arms are crossed in front of her. She is thinking of someone, in a faraway place. You shut your eyes, too.

Although you want to rescue her, it is you who needs rescuing.

[Cary Loren, interview with Jeff Penczak, https://home.comcast.net/~leapday56/caryloren.htm; "Detroit Uprising," *Ballroom Blitz* no. 25, March 1978, p. 12.]

## *Dhalgren*

**A long novel (nearly eight hundred pages)** by Samuel R. Delaney, published in early 1975, two years after Thomas Pynchon's *Gravity's Rainbow*. William Gibson has described "the long slough of the pre-punk seventies, when *Dhalgren* was first published," and the book has the feel of impending disaster, but a disaster of what? "Do you think a city can control the way the people live inside it?" Kid asks at one point. The heated paranoia of the question, so close to Watergate and Vietnam and the bankruptcies and near-bankruptcies of cities like New York and Cleveland suggests its opposite: It is not control that will capture the imagination in the latter part of the seventies, but its opposite: anarchy. The escape from all systems of meaning and coercion:

> But I realized something. About art. And psychiatry. They're both self-perpetuating systems. Like religion. All *three* of them promise you a sense of inner worth and meaning, and spend a lot of time telling you about the suffering you have to go through to achieve it. As soon as you get a problem in any one of them, the solution it gives is always to go deeper into the same system . . . I gave up psychiatry too, pretty soon. I just didn't want to get all wound up in any systems at all.

As *Dhalgren* morphs into so many shapes that you can barely keep up, you become as hopelessly lost as the characters and realize that, like them, you have temporarily escaped from the system. Punk, as a highly compressed form of this escape, offered itself, briefly, as chaos. And in that chaos there was relief from the tyranny of meaning.

[Samuel R. Delaney, *Dhalgren*, 1975; repr., New York: Vintage, 1996, pp. 250, 251, 300; William Gibson, "The Recombinant City: A Foreword," *ibid.*, p. xii.]

## Dickies

**Formed in September 1977** in the San Fernando Valley area, the Dickies consisted of Leonard Graves Phillips on vocals; Stan Lee on guitar; Chuck Wagon (Bob Davis) on keyboards, sax, and guitar; Billy Club (Bill Remar) on bass; and Karlos Kabellero (Carlos Cabellero) on drums. In 1978 they appeared on the television show *C.P.O. Sharkey*, starring Don Rickles. They played "You're So Hideous." There is something very simple that the Dickies did. It was simple, but in its simplicity it said something profound about punk. The Dickies, in addition to writing their own songs, took other songs (often from the fifties and sixties) and played them very, very fast. For instance, they did this with "Sounds of Silence" and "Eve of Destruction." Both of these songs, originally, were serious, songs that even made

Right: The cover of the Dickies' 1978 LP, with *I'm OK–You're OK* in hand

Insert: Blow-up of the book in question

"statements" about personal alienation, world violence, etc. You could even say they were considered "important" songs. Now, other punk bands did this too, most famously the Ramones with their version of "California Sun," and the Dictators with their version of "I Got You Babe." (The Dictators's version puts an end to all irony and makes you fall in love again.) But neither of these songs were very "serious" to begin with; they were fun. They were good, fun pop songs. When you hear "California Sun" played at a faster pace, you think: *Yes, of course!* But the Dickies took serious songs—almost sacred to the ears of some people—and turned them upside down by eliminating entire verses and playing them so fast that they meant something entirely different. In doing so, they drained them of meaning and filled them with something else. But with what?

Here are the original dates of some of the songs from the sixties that they covered:

"Sounds of Silence," Paul Simon: 1964

"Eve of Destruction," P. F. Sloan: 1965

"Nights in White Satin," The Moody Blues: 1967

"The Tra-La-La-Song (Banana Splits Theme)," Nelson B. Winkless, Jr: 1968

Each new pop form creates its own reality out of the reality of the past. Whether it is the duty of pop (or art) to do this is another matter. The difference between 1967 and 1977 is that all sense of duty had been obliterated: Duty to nation in the form of social protest had become duty to self in the form of having fun. The Dickies tore through the painfully sensitive "Sounds of Silence" because there was no room for silence in punk: Those gaps had to be closed.

Were the Dickies' remakes ironic? A clue is an object held by one of the band members on a 1978 record cover. The object is a copy of the book *I'm OK—You're OK*, by Thomas A. Harris, originally published in 1967, reprinted year after year in millions of copies. "Are *you* OK?" asks the back of the book. "It's probably the most important question you'll ever have to answer. Because right now—whether you're aware of it or not—all the relationships with the most important people in your life are strongly influenced by a combination of how you feel about yourself (OK or not OK) and what you think of them (again, OK or not OK)." Punk framed the issue differently, with this question: Why should I want to feel OK?

Having avoided answering the question that begins the paragraph above, I'll ask it again: Were the Dickie's remakes ironic? And here is another evasion: According to *New York Rocker*, seeing "the band onstage is sort of like having the cast of a John Waters film invade for a jam-session." Which is to say, they were perceived as ironic by an audience for whom irony, satire, and camp were the new norm. According to the lead singer, Leonard Graves Phillips, the Dickies remade those songs out of a sense of solidarity, not camp: "When we were doing covers of 'Paranoid,' or even 'Nights in White Satin,' we actually believed in those tunes . . . We knew they were politically incorrect, we knew they were a little bit taboo at the time. It wasn't like, let's piss all over this band by doing a loud punk rock version of their song. And back then a lot of people didn't know how to wrap their ear around that."

[Leonard Graves Phillips, interview with Keith Brammer, www.thedickies.com; Pleasant, "The Dickies: L.A.," *New York Rocker*, vol. 1, no. 11, 1978, p. 67.]

# Dictators

**(By Ephraim P. Noble:)** The structural incongruities of this band are almost Faulkner-esque (were Faulkner to demote himself to a steady diet of White Castle hamburgers, bad reruns of *Happy Days*, *Mad* magazine, and the relentless barrage of nonsense that passes as TV news). Funny fellows, no doubt, as the front and back of their album *The Dictators Go Girl Crazy!* make clear. And so this is punk, eh?

Sounds more like Bad Company speeded up a few beats and with a few (failed) jokes thrown in.

"Who's that boy / with the sandwich in his hand?" begins the first song on side two of the album released in 1975 (it is the best album of that year, superior to *Horses* by at least a nose length). "He's no boy / and yet he ain't no man." Full of humor and flat-out living, a sort of high-speed replay of the best part of the early seventies, if there were any best parts, and by the time the fast drums start on the second song of side two, "California Sun," which of course reminds you of the more famous Ramones cover, you have given yourself over to "Well I'm out there having fun / in the warm California sun" even from the confines of northwest Ohio (where you first heard this, age eleven) and southeast Michigan (where you are now, when California still seems like a perverted dream) and your worst fear is that someday you will outgrow your love for this album, because by then you will be a different person, more refined, which is a fancy way of saying you will have rejected the things that made you who you are, and by the time you get to the fourth song on side two, "Weekend," the lyrics "Just give me a soda" and "I'm tired of this social change" make you wonder if you have misread the entire album: The end of this song makes you almost cry for its perfection, for the way it allows you to imagine yourself as perfect, briefly.

## Dils

**You knew nothing about this band** until much, much later. Her hair, swooped across her forehead. The way she practically melted into you in the theater in the dark during the obscure movie. The secret she would whisper into your ear years later, making you fall in love with her once again.

After the dust had settled, as they say, and you were a respectable property owner who scoffed at well-intentioned people like Michael Dukakis, just like the father in *Donnie Darko* who, watching the presidential debate on TV between George Bush, Sr., and Dukakis said something like, "You tell him, George." You hear that the Dils formed in 1977 someplace in California—San Diego? Ah, it's all the same, the places out there. At first, you were reluctant. At first, you hated the Dils without even hearing them. What is it with California bands and punk, anyway? It's too sunny, too close to Hollywood. California is Dreamland, and punk is not about dreaming, it is about waking up from dreams. You remember the scene from *Annie Hall* (also 1977) where Woody Allen reluctantly goes west and the absurdity of California with its new age trends and narcissism and fake people and ridiculous stars and suntans and health food and joggers and yoga and EST and UFOs and surfers. And that was before face-lifts and Botox.

But then you pick up a Dils record on vinyl because you are fortunate enough to live in a town that has record stores that stock such things as old Dils records on vinyl, and once again it is not the facts of the band but their music that converts you. You are reminded that two minutes of music can change the course of your life. It has been a long day full of some people who are terrible and some who are kind, and now it's late at night and you are well stocked with cheap Canadian beer, and your family is safe and asleep, and you have calmed your daughter's worries about memorizing her lines for her part as a Lost Boy in *Peter Pan*, and you made her laugh out loud for the first time in a long while, and in the cool of your basement you unsleeve the record and place it on the turntable and the first song is "I Hate the Rich," and the second is "You're Not Blank," both from 1977. The first ten seconds or so of "You're Not Blank" are like total war, and the first image you have is of the flames and fire and blood from *Apocalypse Now*. It has to be one of the most furiously alive songs ever, the kind that makes you wonder if you have any idea at all what you are talking about, if you have any idea at all about what you are at this moment (on the very day that Sadaam Hussein has been sentenced to death by hanging) typing on your PowerBook G4. The fact that it's only a song and that the Dils were only a band composed of an ever-changing lineup of flawed human beings like yourself does absolutely nothing to dispel the fact that the song has lodged in your brain as something forever great.

In a 1977 *New York Rocker* article about the Dils, Howie Klein began by noting that many U.K. punk and New Wave bands were, unlike U.S. bands, openly political:

American still have hope—dumb optimism coupled with a tradition of glossing over reality—and a distinctive ignorance of basic class consciousness. Although there are a few punk bands beginning to ape ultra radical anarchist sounds emerging from the U.K., as yet only one American band appears to have attempted any serious analysis of socio-political oppression. Ironically, this band—The Dils—comes from one of the most solidly middle class and homogenized parts of the country—San Diego.

Weeks later. Leaves have fallen. Sprinkler systems have been properly flushed out. November skies have darkened. You have read in several places that the recordings of the Dils live are a disappointment, that the vocals are muddled and syrupy. But there is "It's Not Worth It," recorded live in 1980, a song that confounds. "It's not worth it / You might as well spend your days in bed / It's not worth it / No matter what you do, you're better off dead." And yet the sound of "It's Not Worth It" is so beautiful, so soaring, the vocals barely hanging together and quivering almost like the Everly Brothers, the guitars and drums from 1:35 to 1:55 the perfect twenty seconds of the perfect song, annihilating any pretence of objectivity surrounding this entry, which, in its last sentence, was hijacked by Ephraim P. Noble, whose overly academic language once again threatens to ruin a perfectly good entry, which had until now avoided sentences that used words and phrases like *ideological constructs* and *interpellation* and which had avoided sentences that began and ended with the word And.

[Howie Klein, "Westcoastwaves," *New York Rocker*, November–December 1977, p. 47.]

## Diodes

**"The Diodes, a Toronto quartet,"** wrote Andy Mellen in the *Winnipeg Free Press* in 1977, "are the first Canadian punk rock band to sign a recording contract. It's still too early to gauge punk's popularity in Canada, although domestic releases by England's The Jam, The Clash, and The Vibrators are reportedly faring well." The Diodes were an important part of Toronto's emerging punk scene in the mid-seventies, as they opened the city's first punk venue in 1977, the Crash 'n' Burn. Although it lasted only a few months, it provided space for the scene to develop. The band, in its seventies version, consisted of Paul Robinson, John Catto, Ian Mackay, and John Hamilton. Although signing to a major seemed to be the ultimate break, it resulted in alienation from the emerging scene. "We were almost forced to fragment off because we had to go play," Mackay has said. "We had to go into the studio and record an album. We had to go nationwide. While we were at ground zero at the beginning, we in a sense disappeared from the scene. We had to."

Their song "Tired of Waking Up Tired" (1978) is untouchable. As a kid, you imagined the lyrics went "Talk like an explosion / walk like a heart attack." But who knows? It wasn't the lyrics that hooked you, but the totality of the song, its soaring melody, which reminded you of the Ramones channeled through the Everly Brothers. There is a nostalgia to the song that goes back to the fifties. In December 1969, far away from Toronto in Charleston, West Virginia, a small paper called *The Charleston Gazette*, published an article by Ray Brack that mentioned Lester Bangs, whose first record review for *Rolling Stone* had appeared eight months earlier, appeared: "Give credit to Lester Bangs of *Rolling Stone* for making the point precisely: 'The back-to-the-roots movement was cued by the Beatles' great, white-winged Graf Zeppelin of last winter' . . . The fad [fifties nostalgia] is rampant. Whether it will linger long enough to make an impact on youth dress, language, manners and mores is unpredictable at this point."

1. In 1974, the television series *Happy Days* debuted (Suzi Quatro would play Leather Tuscadero).

2. In 1976, the Ramones released their first album.

**3.** In 1977, the Diodes released their first singles.

It lingered.

[Ray Brack, "Out of the Sixties . . . Into the Fifties?," *The Charleston Gazette*, December 6, 1969, p. 12; Ian Mackay quoted in Liz Worth, "A Canadian Punk Revival," http://www.exclaim.ca/articles/research.aspx?csid1=111, June 2007; Andy Mellen, "Pop-Pourri," *Winnipeg Free Press*, October 26, 1977, p. 33.]

## Dogs / "John Rock n Roll Sinclair" / John Sinclair

**Featuring Loren Molinare on guitars and lead vocals,** Mary Kay on bass and vocals, and Ron Wood on drums, the Dogs were part of a vibrant Detroit-area music scene in the seventies that was too good to last. Detroit Jack has written that the "Dogs embodied the first of a new generation of rock and punk bands that melded the revolution fought by John Sinclair, the MC5 and the UP with the contemptuous spirit manifested in the 'Blank Generation.' 'Blank' perhaps because the utopian vision of the sixties was no longer believable in America's rust belt, and nowhere was the Decline of Western Civilization more apparent than in an economically devastated, racially divided Motor City."

The music the Dogs made sounds like it was coming from thirteen musicians, not three. If you hear them for the first time now, you will think there has been some terrible time-warp mistake, because when you listen they sound, at times, an awful lot like Nirvana. But Nirvana as channeled through Alice Cooper, AC/DC, and the Stooges. There is a fury to their sound that avoids the precious intellectualism of Pere Ubu and other Midwestern American bands. Basically, the assault the Dogs bring on leaves no room for escape; there is no ironic loophole of retreat. And this is precisely because there was (there is) no irony in Detroit.

Nowhere is this more apparent than in "John Rock n Roll Sinclair," which in its casualness ("'C'mon John" and later "J-J-J-J-J-J-J- Johnny") is both an honor and an insult to Sinclair, who by the seventies was the patron saint of the hippies (John Lennon even came all the way to Ann Arbor to sing at a "benefit" for him when he was jailed for possession). "We were a punk backlash to the counter-culture he [Sinclair] started in the Motor City," according to the lead singer Loren Molinare. But the song is a rejection of the sixties as imagined by the hippies in other ways. It's Chuck Berry–ish speed and pop—which in the hands of the Ramones would be transformed into punk—was really an embrace of the very antithesis of hippie music with its progressive complexity.

But who was John Sinclair? This is important to remember. Here are some words from the "White Panther Party Statement" from 1968: "Rock and roll music is the spearhead of our attack because it is so effective and so much fun. We have developed organic high-energy guerilla bands who are infiltrating the popular culture and destroying millions of minds in the process. With our music and our economic genius we plunder the unsuspecting straight world for money and the means to carry out our program, and revolutionize its children at the same time." Sinclair's link to punk—primarily through his involvment with the MC5, whose noise-drenched songs predicted the sonic growl and undertoe of punk—is important, for his revolution did indeed come to pass—just not in real life, but rather in music. "Rock and roll music," Sinclair wrote in "Rock and Roll Is a Weapon of Cultural Revolution" in 1968, "is a weapon of cultural revolution. There are not enough musicians around today who are hip to this fact. Too many of your every-day pop stars feel that music is simply a means by which they can make a lot of money or gain a lot of cheap popularity or whatever." When those words were published, Joey Ramone was seventeen, Richard Hell was nineteen, and Patti Smith was twenty-two. Sinclair believed in using popular culture—and rock and roll specifically—as a medium with which to revolutionize the nation's youth: "Westerners have absolutely no respect for content," he wrote;

> they're hooked on form image. "Image junk" is the way Burroughs put it, and once their forms are infiltrated you can get your own content in and they hardly notice the difference until it's too late, as long as they can relate to the form. Americans are the farthest out in this respect. That's how we can disguise ourselves as simple economic forces, like rock and roll bands, newspapers, etc., and continue to carry out our work with the blessing of the power structure, because they are so easily fooled by a graspable form. . . . We can work within these old forms, infusing them with our new content and using them to carry out our work.

So you can appreciate the dilemma here: A band like the Dogs owed its musical fervor to forerunners like Sinclair's MC5, and yet in many ways the music of the sixties and early seventies had attached itself to untenable, narcissistic ideologies that had to be rejected in punk. Punk's method of rejection was, more often than not, parody or mockery: There is good reason that *Mad* magazine was an inspiration to groups ranging from the Dictators to the Ramones. And yet on at least one level Sinclair's predictions came true: The entertainment culture industry so effectively absorbs street-level ideas as they blossom that there's hardly any need today for pop music—no matter how radical—to "infiltrate" anything.

In addition to looking backward, the music of the Dogs looked forward, especially toward what would come to be known as hardcore. This as more of a hunch than a fact; it is a statement based on gut feeling and instinct. But consider two Dogs songs recorded live at the Mabuhay in San Francisco in January 1977 as evidence. "Tuff Enuff" and "Are You a Boy or Are You a Girl" both move with the sort of blistering, choppy speed associated with West Coast bands like the Germs, X, and even

Black Flag. Both songs are powered by the force of thunder; the words "c'mon yeah" never sounded as good as they do in the chorus to "Are You a Boy or Are You a Girl," a moment equally matched when a chaotic guitar solo and drum break come after the line "Oh let me show you what you look like." At moments, the song sounds like it is so familiar with rock and roll conventions that it invented them. And another song, "Black Tea," sounds in its first ten seconds like either the beginning or the end of the apocalypse. Of course, this was inevitably the problem that punk confronted: how to deconstruct music with a glorious fury that made it sound instead like it was constructing something new. The punks discovered that tearing something down and building something new amounted, in the end, to the same thing.

[John Sinclair, "White Panther Party Statement," issued November 1, 1968, reprinted in *Guitar Army: Street Writings / Prison Writings*, New York: Douglas, 1972, p. 104; John Sinclair, "Rock and Roll Is a Weapon of Cultural Revolution," originally published December 1968, *ibid.*, pp. 113, 116.]

## "Dot Dash"

**A song by Wire.** So much has been written about this group and this song that you hesitated. But how can you hesitate about a song that has saved you more than once from the black depths you are prone to fall into? There are theories about Wire, because they are a theoretical band. The song begins with guitars, and then something that sounds like the fast ticking of a clock: It sounds like a bomb might go off, but then the guitars are so shimmering, so bright, that all the choppy, bleak theory of the lyrics disappears, and anyway you always took the lines "Don't crash / don't crash / don't crash / don't crash / don't crash / don't crash / don't crash" to be an affirmation, not a negation. When you first heard this song, you knew little about the band and worried that once you learned, you would see that you were wrong. In a creepily effective way, "Dot Dash" wipes out and erases the cold minimalism that is Wire's very identity.

Simon Frith has called "Dot Dash" a "punk ditty." He's right. Strange that Wire's finest song should be remembered as a throwaway.

## Down-and-out During the Punk Era, the Fun of Being

**What official political and economic histories** of the mid- to late seventies in the United States miss is the strange sense of gloomy, breezy, absurd fun that comes from living during a time when your nation has just lost a major war, when your president resigns in disgrace, when your major city—New York—is on the verge

*President Carter addresses Cabinet energy session as adviser James Schlesinger listens.*

UPI Telephoto

Jimmy Carter in 1977: presiding over disintegration

of bankruptcy, and when interest rates are soaring, along with unemployment and inflation. There's such a sense of lowered expectations and diminished optimism that you realize that, heck, the best strategy is to take comfort where comfort can be found. Today's economy is rigged so that even when times are tough you can buy enough toys—MP3 players, fancy and needless cell phones, plasma-screen televisions—that you never really feel in any danger of being cut off from what is new. (We are all firmly wired into the system now, but that's another story, another book. Someday, there's going to be a rebellion, isn't there, and it won't be the stuff of movies, and it won't be pretty.) But the seventies offered less protection, and the real danger of losing things (your job, your car, your heat, your house if you were old enough to own one) made everything more precious.

Jimmy Carter was the perfect punk-era president in two regards: He was an image of a do-it-yourselfer, an outsider, a peanut farmer who took on the big machinery of government and the experts and ran as a populist, and he articulated in painfully, doomily clear terms the malaise that became associated—fairly—with his presidency. In fact, Carter's now famous "Crisis of Confidence" speech, televised nationally on July 15, 1979, is really just an echo of the defeatist, self-deprecating attitude of so much punk music, and so much writing about punk, especially in the pages of places like *Creem* magazine. Here is some of Carter's speech:

The symptoms of this crisis of the American spirit are all around us. For the first time in the history of our country a majority of our people believe that the next five years will be worse than the past five years. Two-thirds of our people do not even vote. The productivity of American workers is actually dropping, and the willingness of Americans to save for the future has fallen below that of all other people in the Western world.

As you know, there is a growing disrespect for government and for churches and for schools, the news media, and other institutions. This is not a message of happiness or reassurance, but it is the truth and it is a warning.

These changes did not happen overnight. They've come upon us gradually over the last generation, years that were filled with shocks and tragedy.

We were sure that ours was a nation of the ballot, not the bullet, until the murders of John Kennedy and Martin Luther King Jr. We were taught that our armies were always invincible and our causes were always just, only to suffer the agony of Vietnam. We respected the presidency as a place of honor until the shock of Watergate.

Now, there is something about Carter's speech—a speech given three days after the Disco Demolition Night at Comiskey Park—that seems to revel in despair. Parts of the speech are steeped in a gleeful self-abdegnation, as when Carter rattles off a list of quotes from ordinary Americans ("men and women like you," he assures us), including "Mr. President, we are confronted with a moral and spiritual crisis," and "Our neck is stretched over the fence and OPEC has a knife."

Punk as a musical style and an expression of social dissatisfaction cannot be fully understood unless we revisit the everyday conditions that surrounded its

From the front page of the *Pittsburgh Post-Gazette*, 1977

movement into mainstream media. In early 1977, for instance, three states—Ohio, New York, and New Jersey—were under energy emergencies. In January, in newspapers across the United States, there were reports that the "fuel crisis in the Northeast threatened to add more than 250,000 new layoffs to the ranks of the estimated 400,000 already 'energy unemployed.'" In late January, readers would have read on the front page of *The Pittsburgh Press* that "President Carter called an emergency Cabinet meeting on the winter energy crisis and suggested both the government and private industry go to a 4-day, 10-hour-a-day work week to reduce the use of natural gas." Pennsylvania—which Carter visited during the crisis, warning of a "permanent energy shortage"—was hit especially hard. The *Observer-Reporter*, under the headline SHAPP ASKS MASS CLOSINGS BECAUSE OF ENERGY CRISIS, reported that the "natural gas crisis will force some Pennsylvanians into mass care centers unless nonessential businesses comply with Gov. Milton Shapp's request to shut down, a spokesman for the governor has predicted." When critics of punk—such as Martha Bayles—attack its nihilism and savagery ("destruction was the thrill, the messier the better," Bayles has written) what they miss is the economic desolation in the United Kingdom and the United States that made possible the grim humor and absurdity of punk.

When Carter said that "we've discovered that owning things and consuming things does not satisfy our longing for meaning" and that "piling up material goods cannot fill the emptiness of lives which have no confidence or purpose," he was speaking about a different sort of blank generation, one that tapped into the mythology of the hippie commune while rejecting its utopianism. Was what he said really that much different from what Jeff Raphael, the drummer for the San Francisco punk band the Nuns, said in 1977? "People didn't consider it any great accomplishment having a straight job and working . . . People were more interested in your ideas, what you had to say and how you carried yourself than by how much material wealth you had."

Jimmy Carter was a punk president, but this is only clear in retrospect. At the time, he was hated by ex-hippies and fresh punks alike. In *Sluggo!*—that greatest and most unpredictable of punk fanzines, published out of Austin, Texas—Poly Publius wrote:

> The point is this: you distrust politics and politicians so much by now that you don't want to be political even if you wanted to be that thing. You just see Billy Clements, Jimmy Carter, and the other members of the leisuresuit/cardigan sweater class and you think that is political and that is all that's political and you forget that anything else is political. Everything is political.

It was something that was there from the beginning of Carter's bid for the presidency, as demonstrated in these words from one of his television ads from the

1976 campaign season when he told the American people, "When I look around, this is what I see: eight million people, every one of them out of work; every trip to the supermarket a shock, cities collapsing, suburbs scared, hospitals closing, teachers fired, crime growing, police departments cut, fire departments cut . . ." Not "anarchy in the U.K.," but anarchy (*cities collapsing*) in the U.S. A kind of poetry of disaster, not from the underground margins of society but from the mouth of the man who would be president. Carter's mistake was not in articulating this economic and spiritual anarchy, this *blank*ness, but in repeating it over and over again. Quite simply, unlike the Sex Pistols or the Dead Boys, he didn't know when to quit.

Carter's language was basically that of lament, but a lament that finds a certain relief and even pleasure in the dead zone that was the seventies. In "Squatting in the Carrot Patch," his article in *Creem* on the bizarre wonder of local television in Detroit, Richard C. Watts begins like this: "As this is being written, early on a humid, over-heated and fetid Detroit August, while second-hand fans circulate and re-circulate the heavy unfriendly air thru my modest pseudo-slum dwelling, while my dog lies beached at my feet, exhausted from too much panting, and my cat slumps in the window pane watching with resignation as the grass of my untended lawn begins to caress the front door . . ." and then goes on, eventually, to write about Channel 62, which in 1979 shows classic, silent black-and-white avant-garde films like *Vampyre* and *Battleship Potemkin*, "though they're nearly unwatchable. The greys bleed into the whites, the edges of the film fade into black hole darkness, the sound is thin and crackling. It's maddening. It's Detroit's finest."

If that laid-back gloom strikes you as willfully perverse, remember that the theme song to *Welcome Back, Kotter* (which aired on ABC from 1975 to 1979) spawned a *Billboard* number one hit in 1976. The show's theme song, "Welcome Back" by John Sebastian, opened with these lines: "Welcome back, your dreams were your ticket out. / Welcome back to that same old place that you laughed about." Can you imagine a show like *Friends* or some other such nonsense including such self-defeatism? Kotter is the guy who didn't escape, who didn't make it, who didn't follow his dreams. Sure, there was a strong idealistic strain to the show—Kotter cared about the kids, after all—but still, as the song says, "We've got him on the spot."

*On the spot.* Not so much pinned down, but ignored by the impersonal forces that were driving up oil prices, interest rates, and inflation. As a young man or woman growing up in Cleveland in 1974, you—or your parents—might have come across this small article in the *Cleveland Press* that begins, "Swiss Credit Bank Chairman F. W. Schulthese says world inflation and unemployment 'may well destroy the democratic institutions of the West.'" This is perhaps why—just a few pages later—in a local article about an armed robbery in front of preschool children, there is a certain absurd humor in the second paragraph:

> Brandishing guns in the presence of 32 pre-schoolers, two men today robbed six women employees of their purses at the Community Day Care center in the basement of St. Philip Lutheran Church, 11315 Regalia Ave. . . . . The children took the incident philosophically and were laughing and playing when police arrived moments after the gunmen fled.

It is a humor born out of desperation, fended-off tragedy, especially when we learn a few lines later that "the gunmen threatened to kill the women unless they handed over their purses and then herded the women and the children into one of the rooms in the center."

Danger and disintegration and humor that come about only when there's nothing left to lose. Describing the Electric Eels, the Cleveland band that embodied a raw kind of punk that predicted the movement's entire trajectory, Mary Burzynski McMahon has written:

> Their [Brian McMahon and John Morton] house, like its occupants, was strange and disorienting. The floor plan was odd with weird long hallways and rooms whose functions remain a mystery. Built before electricity, the ground floor had no ceiling fixtures, relying on ambient light for illumination. All reference to time of day was obliterated by windows facing brick walls or so dirty and shaded that sunlight was indistinguishable from streetlight, . . . The Eels were impossibly impractical. Brian didn't mow, but sickled the front lawn. He kept his beer in the garbage can out back; warm beer being preferable to sharing.

In countless interviews from the mid-seventies, bands from the American Midwest would talk with a mixture of disgust, revulsion, and awe about their decayed, crumbling cities. This from an interview with Pere Ubu (DT = David Thomas, TH = Tom Herman, SK = Scott Krauss, TM = Tony Maimone) by Robot Hull:

> **TM:** Kids band together and break into a place; later, they're found twenty yards away, passed out in their cars with gallon cans of toluene and rags around their noses.
>
> **DT:** Did you hear about the two kids who killed their father because he, quote, wouldn't let them do what they wanted to do, unquote? So they paid some kid sixty bucks to have him killed.
>
> **SK:** The kid shot the father in the head and left the body in the house for nine days!
>
> **TH:** Then his kids took his credit cards and went on a shopping spree.
>
> **DT:** Because he wouldn't let them do what they wanted to do. It made *Newsweek*.
>
> **SK:** Then there's the kids who threw a girl off the top of a building, twice, because she didn't die the first time.

**TM:** We always end up telling Cleveland horror stories. In England one night, we came back from a gig all wired and started talking about Cleveland. We gave our sound crew nightmares.

**CREEM:** *Do you think we're headed towards the nightmare of annihilation?*

**DT:** Cleveland's totally out of control, way ahead of the rest of America.

**TH:** It's as if someone had written an absurd script like for the movie *Wackiest Ship in the Army.*

**SK:** We live downtown a block from the war zone. Our street hasn't had any lights for a year. It's the main hooker street. Gun fights on the street. Right next door is a plasma donor center.

The language of economic doom was everywhere in the seventies, because the reality of economic doom was everywhere. In a 1979 advertisement for a Buffalo, New York, used-record store—Play It Again, Sam—here are these words: "We at Play It Again, Sam have built our store with the recession in mind. If you need money for gas or any other necessity, you can sell us the albums you no longer listen to for cold hard cash."

There are strange lines in Ben Marcus's novel *Notable American Women* that have always reminded me of all this, though I'm not sure why:

I am probably Ben Marcus. I might be a person. There's a chance I lived on a farm meant to muffle the loud bodies of this world, a sweet Ohio locale called Home, where our nation's women angled toward a new behavior, a so-called Final Jane. We could have had special water there, a behavior television, a third frequency, after AM and FM, for women's messaging, for women to steal the air and stuff it with their own private code.

The best films from this era capture the fun and menace of boredom, of having "nothin' to do." Scorsese said about *Mean Streets* that the "studio critiques were that it had a very bare story line and it was filled with digressions. They didn't understand that the digressions are what the film is all about. That's the way life is down there, it's digression. It's never really dealing with the realities of life. Nothing ever really happens, but when things do happen they happen like they happen in the film."

*Nothing ever really happens.* This was the dream of punk, the dream of the seventies, a dream borne out of boredom. While it's easy to romanticize the bad times once the good times have arrived, it's also important to remember them for the savage blankness they offered. For punk was always, at least symbolically, for and about the losers, not the victors.

[Advertisement for Play It Again, Sam Records, *Rockers*, November 1979, p. 6; Martha Bayles, *Hole in Our Soul: The Loss of Beauty and Meaning in American Popular Music*, Chicago: University of Chicago Press, 1996, p. 307; Jimmy Carter, "The Crisis of Confidence

Speech," www.pbs.org/wgbh/amex/carter/fillmore/ps_crisis.html; Jimmy Carter, "Reality" television spot, 1976, www.missouri.edu/~commwlb/TVSpots%201976-2000.htm; "The Energy Crisis," *The Pittsburgh Press*, January 30, 1977, p. 1; Martin Scorsese quoted in Ellen Frank, "Movies: *Mean Streets*," *Ann Arbor Sun*, May 17–31, 1974, p. 25; Robot A. Hull, "The World According to Pere Ubu," *Creem*, November 1979, p. 63; Ben Marcus, *Notable American Women*, New York: Vintage, 2002, p. 45; Mary Burzynski McMahon, "At Home with the Eels," CD liner notes to *Those Were Different Times*, Scat Records, 1997, Poly Publius, "The Nihilist #10," *Sluggo!* #17, March 1979 (labeled "April 1999"); Jeff Raphael quoted in James Stark, *Punk '77: An Inside Look at the San Francisco Rock 'n' Roll Scene, 1977*. Stark Grafix 1992, p. 32; "Shapp Asks Mass Closings," *Observer-Reporter*, January 28, 1977, p. 1; Tom Skoch, "Women Robbed as Children Play," *Cleveland Press*, November 7, 1974; " 'Slumpflation' Is Called Threat," *Cleveland Press*, November 7, 1974; Richard C. Walls, "Squatting in the Carrot Patch," *Creem*, November 1979, p. 59.]

e

# East Village Eye

**A newspaper/magazine founded by Leonard Abrams** that first appeared in 1979 as the New York punk scene was morphing into New and No wave. As usual, the hippies were a catalyst. "The mid Seventies were kind of dismal," Abrams has said.

The hippie era was really fizzling, going right down the toilet. Sure, it was hot in the late Sixties but the East Village scene really burned out with drugs and all sorts of shit. The hippies went to California, they went upstate, they fled and all of a sudden in the mid Seventies things got real quiet which was actually pretty pleasant but also a little depressing.

A snapshot of the June 1980 issue:

Page 2: The Staff, which includes Richard Hell, and where we learn that the *East Village Eye* is published biweekly by Eye Productions, 120 St. Mark's Place. A review (by Gary Indiana) of the film *Invisible Adversaries* (directed by Valie Export); theoretical science fiction involving a psychic plague "instigated by Hyksos, extraterrestial beings who 'take over' the hapless beings of Vienna."

Page 3: A column, "Nice People: Farewell to Slugger Ann," by Steven Wolf, which features this line: "Ann [the seventy-four-year-old owner of the bar Slugger Ann's] might have gone about her business within the confines of her bar while three decades rolled by, while beatniks and hippies and later punks paraded past her window without affecting her life or business in the least."

Page 4: Lehman Weichselbaum's article "Price of Production: A Do-It-Yourself Guide to Putting on Events at Tompkins Square Park." The key sentence? "Fortunately, there's a loophole."

Page 5: An article on the old Filmore East.

Page 6: In "Rocking on Broadway: A Musical Editorial," Carle VP Groome praises the avant-garde musical *Ocean's Motion* by Twyla Tharp and laments that "there has been little serious consideration for the music of youth" in recent musicals and that "at most, producers of reviews will throw in a token stereotyped punk group in heavy eye make-up, leather and spiked hair, sneering and smashing fake instruments."

Page 7: A black-and-white, heartbreaking photograph by Klarpa Palotai of an airliner in the sky, the same perspective and size of the 9/11 planes. A sunny day, the camera capturing in a weirdly canted angle the shadow-rich side of an apartment building, and the plane seeming—but of course it's not—to be about to

Nostalgia for the fifties: Punk as a high-speed replay of *Happy Days*

crash into its side. And an article on the Loisaida neighborhood and St. Mark's place: "The street's potential for beggary and violence is as usual. When the cafes, clothing emporiums and the roller disco open, the street fills with strident hairdos of all colors, exposed boobs, legs and muscles, studs, leather and dayglow jumpsuits . . . it's the New Wave, whatever that is."

Page 8: The "New Yorker Avantgarde" feature, with lots of words in German.

Page 9: A review by Gary Indiana, of the Werner Schroeter film *The Death of Maria Malibran*.

Page 10: An interview with the band U.S. Ape. Mary Maniak, from the band, says this: "When I heard the Sex Pistols for the first time I couldn't believe it. It was like somebody had wired me up with a thousand volts."

Page 11: An article on the band the Raybeats by Richard Barone. What sort of music does the band hate to hear? "Punk/Funk crossover—put that at the top of the list."

Page 12: A full page of ads, including one for Rebop, selling 1950s clothing, at the corner of 10th Street and 7th Avenue South, upstairs. The photograph shows customers and clerks in the store. They are men, with pompadour haircuts. It is difficult to tell whether the photograph is from the fifties, or contemporary to 1980.

Page 13: Here is a line from Richard Fantina's review of the single "Pod Life / Into the Action" by Insect Surfers: "The band's name gives you a point of reference which the music reflects—we'll have fun, fun, fun as we surf the crest of the punk wave into the '80s, etc., etc."

Pages 14 and 15: A conversation between David Solomonoff (D) and Carola Von Hoffmanstahl (of Cult Des Ghoules) (C) on the morning after the *East Village Eye* benefit at the Mudd Club:

> **D:** A lot of the punk/new wave mystique and style has had to do with not being able to take responsibility for what you do either because you can say "I know this is bad" and claiming that it's stylistic (which is *not* the same thing as a really new style or esthetic) or maintaining a cold half ironic distance—again so that no one is sure what you mean and as a result can't accuse you of anything without taking risks you refused.
>
> **C:** That's interesting—it nullifies criticism.
>
> **D:** It forces the audience or critic to do what the artist refuses to do—or to be totally accepting.

Punk was continually offering theories of itself. And it was the most theatrical form of rock, despite its genuine disavowel of the Big Arena.

Pages 16 and 17: see *Death of Punk, the*

Page 18: A prose poem by Charlotte Pressler—the wife of Peter Laughner and chonincler extraordinaire of the pre-punk Cleveland music scene—entitled "The Oil Piece" that includes the lines "maybe she will / make this mistake it's waiting to be / made and three she would have some- / thing to talk about at work tomorrow."

Page 19: An obscurely written column called "Bridal Black Bouquet."

Page 20: Ads for music clubs, including one for Studio 10 that says, "Now open Thursday Nites for Avant Garde Experimental Rock."

Page 21: Music notes, including, "The Cure at Hurrah for three nites played intelligent, new-style dance music, reflective at times, pop-y at times, but sincere and enjoyable all the time," and "Debbie Harry signed a three year contract doing jean ads for Gloria Vanderbilt; so we're just waiting to turn on the tube to see Johnny Rotten gargling with Listermint."

Page 21: A half-page ad for O.P. Screen Filmmaking Workshop: "Practical 16mm—Single System Sound / 4 Three-Hour Sessions / $50."

Page 22: This, by Emily Listfield: "He came over late. She had put on a slinky negligee. She had chilled champagne. He was bored."

Page 23: A profile of the artist Chris Burden that includes these sentences: "In conjunction with the B-Car Burden has also conducted another exercise in primitive, Robinson Crusoe technology, the CBTV. CBTV is, of course, Chris Burden Television, actually a reconstruction of the world's first television, a *mechanical* television, invented by the Scottish inventor John L. Baird in 1915."

[David Insley, "Leonard Abrams: Documentary Filmmaker, Founder *East Village Eye*," July 11, 2005, http://gothamist.com.]


# Eater

**A U.K. punk band whose very young members**—("average age 16," wrote Caroline Coon)—made songs of infuriating, brutal noise. They consisted of Andy Blade, Dee Generate (who was fourteen when the band formed in 1976), Brian Chevette, and Ian Woodcock. Their early songs, especially "Outside View" and "Thinking of the USA," are like machines set on FAST; their lyrics make the Ramones sound like the Philosopher Kings. Here are the opening lines to "Get Raped": "I don't wanna see you no more / 'coz you're just a scabby whore / You know I really hate your guts / Go and join all the other sluts." But does this matter? Yes, because Eater prompted some great put-down sentences from reviewers, like Paul Silverton ("Eater, being a band that I wouldn't soil my typewriter ribbon writing about"), Jon Savage ("Eater are very lackluster, murdering Alice Cooper's "18" ["15"] unforgivably and unamusingly. Showing how much care has gone into their singles"), and Paul Morley, reviewing their LP, *The Album* ("The crude, dark side of inexperience is presented confidently, as if it's all been done before. There's the bitter insulting of pitifully viewed and tight authority; the dumb low side mastubatory fantasies; the utter selfishness; the impatience to grow up. Eater feel there's a place for all this in rock 'n' roll. Their appeal is nil."). They will "certainly develop into an important band," wrote Kris Needs in *New York Rocker*. But did they want to?

Like the Dickies, Eater played covers at breakneck speed. Their version of "Sweet Jane" is, honestly, the best music they ever recorded, because it throws the original all out of context, and because Eater's own melodies were never memorable enough to stick. Their apologists, today, defend the band in terms of their bringing back memories. But taken on its own terms, stripped of the gloss of nostalgia, their music is like the dead spaces of empty houses.

[Paul Morley, "Eater Classless Critic Fearless," *New Musical Express*, December 12, 1977; Kris Needs, "And the Best of the Rest . . . ," *New York Rocker* vol. 1, no. 7, May–June 1977, p. 22; Jon Savage, "Various: The Roxy London WC2 (Jan–Apr 77)," *Sounds*, June 25, 1977; Peter Silverton, "Generation X: Central London College of Art and Design," *Sounds*, December 18, 1976.]

# Ejectors

**I know almost nothing about this band,** except for what I have learned from listening to them, and except for what the back of the album sleeve tells me. Here is the first paragraph: "In early 1980, five high school sophomores from two rival high schools in Fort Worth, Texas, somehow got together to form a punk rock band. The Ejectors featured Ashley Parrish (guitar), Fred West (drums/vocals), Scott Tuomey (vocals), Richard Dotson (bass), and Scott Paulsel (guitar)." The album I hold in my hands in between writing these words was originally recorded in December 1981, without Paulsel.

The songs are good, and sometimes great. "Fade with the Summer" is great. It makes you wonder: What if Van Halen tilted toward power pop, or even punk? You can't be sure, but you think the chorus goes, "I'll always love you," and it's fast and almost heartbreaking. But faster still is "George Jetson." It's not a better song, just faster. Sometimes you love an album for just one song.

# Electric Eels

**The Cleveland band that between 1972 and 1975** made music so shattering and ridiculously alive that it made even the rawest post-1975 punk sound tame by comparison. Featuring Dave E. McManus (vocals, clarinet), John Morton (guitar, vocals), Brian McMahon (guitar, vocals), and Nick Knox (drums), the Eels' sound is almost always harsh and flat, partly because there is no bass guitar, and partly because that was Cleveland in the early and mid-seventies. "Art Terrorism" is a phrase sometimes used to describe their sound and their stage presence. Here is Brian McMahon: "As for the Eels being more than just a tuneful band—the ART TERRORISM thing—well, given our decretum that one's philosophy must be actionalized, it's no wonder apt behaviors found way into the lives of certain people around us and . . . it terrorized them." Such terrorization involved banging on a sheet of metal with a sledgehammer and running a gasoline-powered lawnmower on stage.

Recorded in April 1975, "Jaguar Ride" hints at the full, burning sound and fierce melody that characterized their best songs. Listening today to the Eels' most remarkable songs, like "Jaguar," "Agitated," "Wreck and Roll," "Stucco," and "Accident," it's clear that it was really, in retrospect, Johnny Rotten who sounded like Dave McManus, not the other way around. Electric Eels were so incoherent they fooled everybody: in 1979, Floyd Bennett reviewed in *Sluggo!* the "Agitated" / "Cyclotron" single, which was recorded in 1975 and released on Rough Trade in 1978. He wrote that "those madcap Brit bopsters have turned up those dial-a-matic RECORD PRODUCER knobs <u>all the way</u> so that <u>u can get</u> sonic fudgy sludge out of even the most expensive speakers."

"Jaguar" takes the core pre-punk sound of bands like the Stooges and the New York Dolls and heads off in a new direction, a direction that punk would soon make public. "Well I don't know if it's wrong or right / But I got no plans that I made today for tonight." The song recognizes—like few others—the power of juxtaposing raw, aggressive sound with a melody that hearkens back (almost, and slyly) to rock's early days. If there's an increasing desire today to go back to the music that just preceded punk's notorious emergence into the limelight in 1976 (variously called "pre-punk" or "proto-punk"), then it's not out of nostalgia so much as out of a sense that this music (what David Thomas of Pere Ubu calls "third-generation rock"), most of it never professionally recorded in studios with expensive equipment, was as much a return to early rock as it was a forward-looking breaking away from the bloated, serious supergroup sound of the seventies. Paul Marotta, who recorded "Jaguar Ride" at the Eels' practice space, used several mics, the idea being that "with so many live microphones the sound of the band—loud, distorted, and abrasive—would be captured, and I would still have some flexibility to make the vocals a little clearer."

"Wreck and Roll," recorded in May 1975, is the kind of song that makes you wonder if the Sex Pistols hadn't secretly materialized in Cleveland, recorded under the name Electric Eels, and then rematerialized in England to play their first show six months later. The song is loud and fast and full of fun phrasing, like the unexpected pause between the words "nervous / breakdown." But there's also plenty of menace and a sort of blank violence: "Wreck and roll / go fall in a hole / a hundred fifty thousand feet below." The song begins, carries on, and ends after two minutes and eight seconds. You keep expecting it to change, to break its monotony, but instead it keeps going and going, the words piling up on each other almost too fast. But this is nothing compared to "Stucco," which is basically two notes played over and over again like a demented nursery rhyme that is forever stuck. This is how the opening lyrics go: "Rowboat / cream glass / toadcrawl / window / jump rope / deadbeat / *Newsweek* / gumbo." Paul Marotta has said that "Stucco," recorded as a rehearsal tape in September 1975, was one of the last Eels songs. Reduced to two notes—the equivalent of watching a game of pong—it's not that hard to see why. Having traced rock and roll to its basest and most primitive form, the Eels had finally pushed themselves to the very margins. "There is 'something' about those recordings and I can't say I had a master plan as to how to get the sound," Marotta says. "All I can say is that I agree, there is some quality that allows them to still be very exciting and fresh." It would take decades before people finally came to realize that, rather than being on the margins, the Eels were at the very center of the radical, beautiful incoherence that was 1975.

["I can't say I had a master plan," e-mail from Paul Marotta to author, May 31, 2007; Floyd Bennett, "Your Singles Corner: Review of Die Electric Eels," *Sluggo!* March 1979; Paul Marotta, "Recording Notes," *The Electric Eels: The Eyeball of Hell*, Scat Records, 2001; Brian McMahon, "Yes, Emily," http://electriceels.com/jaguarride3.html.]

## *Entertainment!*

**The cover of Gang of Four's album *Entertainment!*** features three vertically aligned, color-saturated images of a cowboy shaking the hand of an "Indian." Snaking around the images is this text: "The Indian smiles, he thinks that the cowboy is his friend. The cowboy smiles, he is glad the Indian is fooled. Now he can exploit him." In a sort of reverse universe of the British Invasion—which was, after all, an extended acknowledgment of the American blues—Gang of Four had turned the mirrors back on "the U.S.A." and predicted a Thatcher/Reagan decade that would put an end to the "soft" seventies.

The fact that Gang of Four existed more powerfully as theory than as actual rock band is something that its ardent defenders would rightfully deny, even as they sense a dim truth behind it. Like a half-powered Wire, Gang of Four worked through a process of subtraction that threatened to erase the band completely. Their songs are always vanishing into themselves. "You could tell by listening to Gang of Four music that punk had happened," the guitarist Andy Gill has said, "but it definitely wasn't punk music." If punk deconstructed the pop song and then put it back together with a structure that was primitive, fast, and loud, then Gang of Four resisted putting it back together at all: "That first Television album was great," according to Gill, "and so was the first Talking Heads record. There's a shared interest in avoiding the rock-guitar cliché for sure. If you think of the first crop of punk stuff, it was all just tedious guitars cranked up through Marshalls. In the wake of the Damned and the Sex Pistols, it was heavy metal but faster and not as well played. Certainly Gang of Four, Television and Talking Heads weren't interested in going down that road at all."

Recorded, according to Gill, in May or June of 1979, *Entertainment!* casts a strange spell. While it's true that the album's greatness lies in its alienated sound and aphoristic lyrics, upon multiple listens the whole thing achieves a measure of warmth that's hard to explain. While much has been made of the overtly political, at times Marxist, lyrics, Gill has tended to downplay the political dimensions of the lyrics: "I think people saw us as political because if you look at the overall spectrum of music, they strive to be as apolitical as they possibly can be. If anything in your songs makes any kind of social or economic or political idea or can be interpreted in those kind of ways, then everybody starts screaming 'Rabid Marxist!' at you." A song like "Natural's Not in It" is a series of imperatives and fragments that hints at a larger story that the reader must create: "The problem of leisure / What to do for pleasure / Ideal love a new purchase / A market of the senses." So begins the song, and taken out of their musical contexts these lyrics sound like lines from a university student's cultural studies essay. But they don't sound that way in the song, mostly because by the time they arrive—about twenty-four seconds in—you have been captured by the music, which begins simply and starkly with a guitar, which is soon joined by drums, which is then joined by bass. The result is that you are either tapping your foot, nodding your head, or dancing to the music by the time you are confronted with "The problem of leisure."

By the time you get to "Natural is not in it / Your relations are of power," you realize that you are being told (or reminded) about mystification, about how ideology tends to mask the mechanisms that create social reality by making its workings seem natural, inevitable, and universal. There was once a cultural critic who espoused a Marxist form of literary theory before disavowing "theory" in general. His name was Terry Eagleton, and this is what he wrote: "It is in the significant silences of a text, in its gaps and absences, that the presence of ideology can be most positively felt." This is a theory that circulates throughout the blank spaces of *Entertainment!* There is a cruelty to the repeated line "Our bodies make us worry" in the song "Contract" because, well, why should rock songs remind us of things like that? And then, in "Damaged Goods," the lyrics "Sometimes I'm thinking that I love you / but I know it's only lust," and the truth of those words offers a demystification of a different sort, but you can't tell whose side Gang of Four is on, can you?

[Andy Gill interviewed by Jason Gross in *Perfect Sound Forever*, October 2000; Terry Eagleton, *Marxism and Literary Criticism*, Berkeley: University of California Press, 1976. pp. 34–35.]

## "Experts Propose Study of 'Craze'"

**In February 1957,** *The New York Times* ran several articles on the rock and roll phenomenon, including an article whose headline read: EXPERTS PROPOSE STUDY OF "CRAZE": LIKEN IT TO MEDIEVAL LUNACY, "CONTAGIOUS DANCE FURIES" AND BITE OF TARANTULA. This article said many things, including this, from Dr. Joost A. M. Meerlo, an associate professor in psychiatry at Columbia University:

"The Children's Crusades and the tale of the Pied Piper of Hamelin", Dr. Meerlo went on, "are reminders of these seductive, contagious dance furies . . . Rock 'n' roll is a sign of depersonalization of the individual, of ecstatic veneration of mental decline and passivity. If we cannot stem the tide with its waves of various craze, we are preparing our own downfall in the midst of pandemic funeral dances."

Early on, rock and roll was seen as "sign" of something; but what? Yes, it is tempting to mock the serious, stiff-shirt pronouncements by the likes of Dr. Meerlo (*Where have you gone, Dr. Meerlo?*), and yet punk itself was highly self-conscious and aware of itself as a "phenomenon." For Malcom McLaren and Kim Fowley were not the only ones who sought to manufacture bands in a scene; the phrase "blank generation" itself implied a deliberation, a conscious and public effort to create a generational identity by rejecting identity altogether. In the short span of twenty-five years—from 1952, when Alan Freed sponsored the first live rock and roll show, to 1977—rock rock and roll had become old enough that its history, preserved on vinyl, served as a ready-made archive available for plunder. The paradox of punk is that in its rejection lay a very nostalgic act of recovery. And beneath its fury— perhaps even guiding it—was an unspoken acknowledgment that punk could never recapture the energy and anarchy of the very first years of rock and roll.

[Milton Brackner, "Experts Propose Study of 'Craze': Liken It to Medieval Lunacy, 'Contagious Dance Furies' and Bite of Tarantula," *The New York Times*, February 23, 1957, p. 12.]

## Feelies

**A band that upon first listen** perhaps seemed out of step and time with the punk/ New Wave era from which they emerged in the late seventies. Their first album, *Crazy Rhythms*, was released on Stiff Records in 1980 and is so full of sound at odds with both punk's meanness and New Wave's preciousness that it almost seemed to disappear from history.

In 2008, Glenn Mercer noted that "Our sound is defined by what we left out and didn't play, as much as by what we did." In *New York Rocker*, Miriam Linna wrote that the Feelies "play like cool guys who know the real truth but who aren't gonna start screaming into microphones for nothing." The Feelies suggested, more radically than No Wave bands like the Contortions, that the scorched earth left behind by punk could once again be made fertile. Whereas No Wave's response was to up punk's ante until it reached maximum deformity, bands like the Feelies (and the Marbles and the Speedies) assumed that the fury of punk was already there in listeners' minds. They took a more radical approach than hardcore, and quieted down.

[Miriam Linna, "Meet the Feelies," *New York Rocke*r vol. 1, no. 10, November–December 1977, p. 54; Jon Pareles, "Reborn for the Fourth of July," *New York Times*, July 1, 2008.]

## Fifties, nostalgia for the

**It is strange but fitting that punk**, a movement that has come to be associated with anarchy and decadence, took its initial codes and signals from the fifties. One response to the collapse and failure of what the sixties had become during and after the Summer of Love was to ignore it and go back in time to the years of supposed innocence and simplicity. In a 1973 *Rolling Stone* article entitled "Fifties Trivia New Wave in England," Jerry Hopkins profiled Malcolm McLaren, who in his Ted revival phase was running Let It Rock, "a small store that is a veritable museum of Fifties effluvia." Why? "The reasons, of course, are obvious. Much of the Western world is currently jiving and rock-and-rolling its way through a Fifties revival and (in America at least) 'pop culture' is now considered a respectable subject for study in more than 50 universities."

Although Jac Holzman and Lenny Kaye's collection *Nuggets*, released in 1972, is often credited with forecasting the emergence of punk, the soundtrack to George Lucas's film *American Graffiti* (August 1973) was a more popularized anthology of songs from the fifties and early sixties, including "Do You Wanna Dance" by Bobby Freeman (1958), which was covered by the Ramones on their third album, *Rocket to Russia* (1978). The movie itself helped make the television show *Happy Days* possible, as an earlier version of the show was shelved until the unexpected success of *American Graffiti* demonstrated the popularity and potential marketability of fifties nostalgia. Garry Marshall, the show's creator, has spoken about the power of fifties nostalgia in the early seventies and of how aware he and others in the television industry were about it. Referring to *Happy Days*, he notes how producers came to him and "wanted to do this show of nostalgia . . . we all realized that if you got a nostalgic show on the air the reruns wouldn't look bad. Everybody was coming up with these reruns and they looked silly . . . because of outdated clothing."

In America, such nostalgia was generated at least in part by the disintegration of economic and political structures. In February 1974, several months before the Ramones debuted at CBGB, an article in *Time* magazine profiled a gasoline-rationing system that forced motorists with even-numbered license plates to buy gas on even-numbered days, and those with odd-numbered ones to purchase it on odd-numbered days. "These people are like animals foraging for food," one Amoco dealer said. "If you can't sell them gas, they'll threaten to beat you up, wreck your station, run over you with a car." The good old days of cheap gas, stable if bland political leaders, and well-defined Cold War enemies suddenly seemed not restrictive but endlessly possible. "Hey, ho, let's go" was really a cry of retreat into the past, at least until the Sex Pistols destroyed not only themselves but the whole idea of punk as fun and innocent.

Of course punk never was fun and innocent—but then neither were the fifties.

[See also entries on Marlon Brando, *Rebel Without a Cause*, and blank generation / beat generation]

["Gas Fever: Happiness Is a Full Tank," *Time*, February 18, 1974, www.time.com/time/ magazine/article/0,9171,942763,00.html; Jerry Hopkins, "Fifties Trivia New Rave in England," *Rolling Stone*, January 4, 1973, p. 14; Garry Marshall, Archive of American Television Interview, August 2000, www.youtube.com/watch?v=gDVJcbscOeM.]

## Foreigner, The

**A 1977 film by Amos Poe** that both documented the punk scene in and around CBGB and that stands as a testament to DIY filmmaking. Shot in black and white, the film's plot involves Max, a foreigner who arrives in the United States for some reason and who is immediately pursued by gangs of punks for some reason. It doesn't matter why. The film glories in the mundane nothingness of everyday life. In one segment, Max lays on his bed in his hotel room watching a television documentary on punk. It goes on and on. Not *boredom*, quite, but close. Nothing much happens. In another scene, Max encounters Debbie Harry in a beautifully trashed alleyway. She is radiant, practically begging to be kissed. She asks for a light and sings a song for the camera. Then Max stumbles into CBGB, where the Mumps are playing, and he gets into a fight and is almost killed in the bathroom. But before all that there is the best scene in the movie, where Max walks the seedy, crowded, neon-lit streets while being followed by a mysterious woman in a plastic raincoat. (In your mind, this is like a secret, discarded scene from *Taxi Driver*.) There is no dialogue, only music, and you wish it could go on forever, because it is the perfect scene in an imperfect movie. It is the perfect scene in any movie.

The film was inspired my many things. It was inspired by the films of the French New Wave, by Jean-Luc Godard and François Truffaut, for whom continuity, editing, and rationality were often abandoned in favor of randomness and the beautiful chaos of chance. A notice in *New York Rocker* in 1977 said this: "Eric Mitchell & Amos Poe just back from Paris after invitations from the film industry to promote their movies *Unmade Beds* & *The Foreigner*. The boys were the French's idea of New York New Wave creative artists. Anyway they wowed those frogs and left them with their mouths hanging."

Poe's films, along with those by Scott B and Beth B, Charlie Ahearn, James Nares, and others influenced directors like Jim Jarmusch, who went on to more mainstream careers. There was "a real hope of the possibility of making films," Jarmusch has said. "It wasn't like dreams of going to Hollywood or anything like that. It was just a really strong desire and a really strong sense that it was possible to make films, without much money and without really any expertise. And that was important. Amos Poe's film *The Foreigner* I felt was really kind of important for the spirit at that time."

[Janis Cafasso, "Pressed Lips," *New York Rocker*, November–December 1977, p. 58; Jim Jarmusch interviewed by Peter Belsito in *Jim Jarmusch: Interviews*, ed. Ludvig Hertzberg, Jackson: University Press of Mississippi, p. 29.]

# "Frankie Teardrop"

**A song by Suicide** from their 1977 album, as well as a story:

Years earlier, he had been a writer. And then a musician. He tried to forget this, but then someone would read him one of his poems or play him that song where he did terrible things and then died. But he doesn't remember doing terrible things. He doesn't remember the screaming. He doesn't remember dying.

The journey that landed Frankie inexplicably and in soul-threatening danger on the balcony of the decrepit motel in Kentucky began in Northern Michigan one week earlier—or one year, depending on when you started counting.

The story of the car crash that took the life of his wife and daughter on their way home from the mall on a bright and sunny Tuesday afternoon in February was already hardening into legend in his mind. Frankie remembered how Alan Pasternak, the principal, stood outside the hot gym waiting after the seventh-period assembly and put his big hand on his shoulder and looked at him with sad eyes that said, *they're dead,* and how the police officer told him the news with a sort of awkward familiarity, and how quickly and efficiently his wife and daughter were buried and spoken about by the passionless minister, the old house that they had moved into north of Detroit when they were married sold along with nearly everything they had owned. The funny purple couch, the antique filing cabinet they had bought together in Millersburg, Pennsylvania, the espresso coffeemaker that they had used only twice, the piano. Their daughter's computer, her new clothes for college, her trophies from track, her bulletin board. All these things were props, they belonged to someone else. He felt as if all the secret mechanisms that lay beneath the surface were exposed, revealing the absurd logic of events and consequences: death and burial, morning and night, waking and sleeping, talking and listening, standing and sitting. There was nothing magical in any of it, and it confirmed what Frankie had always secretly thought but was afraid to say. The random absurdity of it all, given some desperate form by rituals. He felt that maybe he was being punished for thinking this way, for harboring these thoughts.

He gave himself a couple of weeks and then went back to work. People had said it was the best thing to do. He assigned his English class *The Wonders of the Invisible World* by Cotton Mather and *Blood and Guts in High School* by Kathy Acker and was reprimanded at the end of the year, kindly but formally, by the superintendent in his absurdly cold air-conditioned office. Then Frankie slowly and deliberately cut off all connections to his limited and far-flung family; his wife's mother who at age forty-three abandoned her family to sell her art in an obscure Utah town, his older brother in San Francisco, his aunt with throat cancer who gave him all those rare books and the Roman coin. He sold the house and moved into a smaller one, and then, a while later, sold that and moved into a smaller one yet, a cabin really, that backed up against a five-hundred-acre woods outside of town. Sitting on the back stoop now, in the dark June night two days after summer vacation started and many, many months after the accident, nursing a beer, he could remember the dumbest of details about them—like how his daughter always skipped stairs or how his wife said "whew" and tossed her keys on the entryway table when she came home, no matter where she had been.

He remembered back to right before it all began, in New York in 1977. They said he worked in a factory, but this was not true. And he was never evicted. That was over thirty years ago, and he still heard the screams.

Their death had become solidly and permanently a fact, something beyond recall.

It was that it was.

On the first day of summer Frankie went to town for groceries, and as he was pulling out of the parking lot, he saw a girl waiting—for a taxi, she said later.

Her red backpack.

Her army fatigues.

Her beautiful face beneath her stringy hair.

She was standing in the sun, by the side of the road, watching him.

She seemed to have rings on every finger.

She got into his car because he leaned over and opened the door, unexpectedly.

It was not something he planned to do.

He drove away with her because she let him.

He took her to where he lived because she said yes.

He didn't kid himself about how ridiculous this was, and how dangerous, but he felt he had earned the right, and that nothing had been for anything, and that everything that had come before was merely the setup to an awful punchline that was to come no matter what he did or did not do.

She slumped down in the car seat on the way to his cabin, either because she was hiding or because it was some weird affectation, like the way teenage girls twirl their hair. He drove her past his old house, with a new SUV in the driveway, and past the familiar storefront landmarks and out to the edge of town to his new place on the edge of a woods that he had never been in.

"Can I stay here a few nights? Do you mind?" she asked, looking around at his sparse place like she was interested in renting it. Before he answered she tossed her backpack onto the couch and disappeared into the bathroom. It was either sheer confidence or an act.

The first night he slept in his bed and she on the couch.

The second night she slept in his bed and he on the couch.

On the day of the fire that drove him finally and evermore out of his old life, she wanted to talk, but not about anything that seemed to matter.

He didn't know if she was homeless, or a runaway, or what.

He guessed she was about nineteen.

Her face had a savage determination about it, but he couldn't tell if it was from lots of experience or something else.

Her eyes were bright green.

Perhaps people were desperately looking for her, or perhaps they were hoping she would never return. She was quiet about all that with Frankie.

He could see how she, with her long bare arms and fierce stare, could become the object of obsession or disdain.

She was eating an orange at the kitchen counter, digging her fingers into it, wearing a white tank top.

She had tattoo of an oversized drop of blood on her left shoulder. It was a place where you could put your lips.

"Have you ever been to Spain?" she said.

"No. Have you?"

"Yeah, it's nice. No one rushes around. The beaches are white."

"Beaches?" For a moment he forgot that Spain had beaches, but then he remembered that it did. Of course it did.

Then he said, "That doesn't sound so bad."

"Even the squid is good."

"Isn't squid like rubber?"

"Not there, it's not. You've got to get it fresh. With lemon juice." She passed him an orange wedge.

"What else is there?"

"Priests. You can have a drink with them at the cafe. They understand about sin."

"I'll bet they do," Frankie said.

"But I don't do confessions," she said.

"I understand, my child," he said, and put his hand on her shoulder in a gesture of mock forgiveness. She smiled and held his eyes. He just wanted to touch her tattoo. He sensed that she knew this.

"Do you want to know what I saw in one of the churches there? In Spain?"

"Sure."

"I've never told this to anybody. I shouldn't tell you . . . Maybe it's because you're a total stranger, you know?"

"I don't believe you, but go ahead."

"It is unbelievable, you're right. God. You'll think I'm lying. It's like something out of a horror movie."

"That's okay."

"Have you ever seen the movie *The Tenant*?"

"No."

"By Roman Polanski?"

"Nope."

"Well, I'll keep it short." She pushed the plate of orange rinds away. "In this old stone church in the country we went to one night, past midnight, when we were drunk. It was outside of Madrid. We had followed the dirt road through a forest. It was hard to tell if was even being used anymore. It was so dark. And then this church—or whatever—appeared, at the end of the road. The door kind of fell off its hinges when we went to open it. Should I really tell you this?"

"I don't see why not."

"I've wanted to tell somebody. Might as well be you. At first it was only a feeling, but we were drunk, so it's hard to say. It was pitch black inside. The floor was crooked, tilted. But everything was spinning anyway, so it was hard to tell. Why we were even there I don't know. It was one of those crazy things. I was the first one in, and it smelled rotten. Like a dead animal."

"This is like a campfire story, isn't it?"

"Sort of," she said. "But it doesn't have much of an ending."

"That's okay."

"Well, inside there was this *thing*. I don't know. It was dark, but you could still see it, standing there, like ten feet tall, by the altar."

"What kind of thing?"

"Like a person. But too big. Standing very still, but looking right at me. At first I thought it was a statue, something religious, like Mary, you know? But it was moving, swaying."

"Swaying?"

"It could have been. I think it was. My head was spinning."

"What did you do?"

"Nothing. I mean, I couldn't tell what it was. It was this . . . presence, you know? Like God's eye but not God. Or a statue of God. That's what I keep thinking now: a statue of God. I slowly backed up and ran out, and I could hear the voices of the others back at the Jeep. I heard it start and I thought they were going to leave without me. I ran to them in the dark."

"And then what."

"Nothing else happened. But the thing in the church, it saw me, it recognized me. What if I told you that it's searching for me?"

"That would be nice."

She looked at him fully, this girl. "What would?"

"To be hunted."

"What makes you say that?"

"I'm just kidding."

"Anyway," she said. "It's like it saw right through me and knows everything now. Even things that haven't happened yet."

"Sounds like mythology."

"Well, it's a story at least. That's what you wanted. But it really happened. It's a story that's true. You better watch out. You're the only one I've told it to." She laughed.

This seemed to Frankie like some sort of threat or promise, or maybe even a little bit like an invitation. For she touched his hand gently when she said it. Why she did this he couldn't fathom; what she wanted from him he did not know. He let her keep her hand on his for a few moments before withdrawing it and standing up. Whatever it was that she wanted he did not have to give, although her cryptic talk made sense to him in a strange way. As he listened to her, he thought that maybe she reminded him of his wife or daughter. But she didn't. She was just some girl, some person. She smiled, and there was something beneath her smile, something that he thought he understood.

Then everything changed again so quickly. Like the accident. Late into the night he awoke on the couch to the smell of burning popcorn. But it wasn't burning popcorn. In the dark he stood up and pulled on his pants and sweatshirt, his eyes watering, coughing, and for a moment he thought, inexplicably, that he needed to save his daughter. Then he remembered and called for the girl, as if he had always known her, but there were flames coming from the kitchen that stood between where he was and the bedroom. The heat was already nearly scorching him and the noise of the fire was building, filling his head like the hum of a box fan. The heat pushed him back, and he found his way in the dark to the front door, and then down the steps, across the street, and to his car, and didn't look back. And for a moment, in his alarmed grogginess, he believed that hell itself was coming for him in the flames. He got in his car and drove off, passing the screaming fire truck coming the other way.

What would they find back there?

Her body, charred in his bed?

Or perhaps not, perhaps she was bad and had started the fire herself, had waited until he was asleep on the couch, had tiptoed around and looked at his face one last time. In any case it was wrong to run, and now, in his car, his clothes reeking of smoke, it dawned on him that it wasn't randomness, that his bad fortune hadn't been a fluke of circumstance. No, his life was being actively destroyed, he was losing everything: wife, daughter, home; now even his freedom was in jeopardy.

He was, as they say, on the run.

o o o

It was strange to be driving without direction or purpose, but he was. Clutching the steering wheel, it was clearer than ever to him that it had been a mistake to stay in the same town after what had happened to his wife and daughter. There was nothing for him there. This made it easier to drive for hours into the night down through the northern Michigan openness toward Detroit, which loomed two hundred miles in the future like an abandoned set from a dystopian science-fiction film. Everytime he drove through Detroit it looked worse than the time before. It was an experiment in suicide. He expected all the time to be stopped by the police and arrested for abandoning the scene of a fire, or whatever they called it. At 1:00 a.m. he pulled off into a welcome center and slept on the leaned-back seat.

He started out again at about 4:00 a.m. About an hour later, he could see the dawn creeping up, illuminating the flat scrubby fields. It was June—why wasn't anything growing in them? It didn't matter.

The truth is, he could have traveled like this forever, through the unpoliced towns that dotted the Midwest, the freedom of its unkempt highways, its unexplored woods, its abandoned barns, its empty buildings from another era of physical labor. It was as if the real world had been abandoned to him alone.

There was no war.

There were no towers.

Frankie moved across the landscape unnoticed. Despite everything that had happened, he was godlike in his assuredness. His story was as complicated and tragic as anybody's—rottenness and bad luck times ten—yet not for all his trying could he believe that his pain was matched by anyone else's pain.

He didn't think he was fleeing, because he wasn't sure if he was being pursued. It was a question of semantics, a state of mind.

After all, had he started the fire?

He had not.

And that he, a forty-year-old widowed school teacher, had a nineteen-year-old girl sleeping in his bedroom—what about that? Who would believe that out of compassion and something else he had helped her by letting her stay there a few nights, by providing shelter for her, by feeding her? After all, she was no mean animal. It was too complicated, he knew, to explain away. He doubted if he would believe it himself.

Even in this time of great uncertainty, it was clear to him that his whole life had tended toward this catastrophic year, as if everything that had come before was a carefully plotted script designed to simply advance him to this point. Frankie found this oddly comforting, because if the whole universe conspired against you, what hope was there? And this lack of hope offered a tremendous release, a freedom even. The car crash, and now the fire, it all seemed so tragically and so fatalistically comforting at the same time, a kind of short-lived, self-deluded victory. He knew now how the terrorists must have felt.

In his car driving out of the ruined city, the rain pounded his windshield in the night.

Buildings and bridges disappeared behind him, fleeing into the distance of his rearview mirror.

Lightning filled the passageways of abandoned buildings and the underpasses of great highways.

On a sharp curve on I-75 he passed a nighttime road construction crew, illuminated in the lightning like some three-dimensional painting, their yellow hats and orange vests meant to protect them from swerving cars. They were carving out the underside of an overpass. He drove farther south, out of Detroit with its savage history written everywhere, the car radio playing a crackly version of a new White Stripes song that already sounded ages old.

He took Telegraph Road, laid out like the barrel of a gun, through the suburbs, past Dearborn and eventually into the dark countryside past Adrian and into the little town of Monroe, with its sad middle-of-the-night flashing-red stop lights, the rain coming down in heaves like something from an over-budgeted movie.

It was 6:00 a.m. Frankie slowed at an intersection as the shadow sped across the road, then stopped. A bony dog stood at the side of the road in the pale edges of his headlights and he stopped and opened the door and waved a half-eaten candy bar beneath the dome light. In the back seat the animal held the candy between its paws and chewed at it silently.

He drove on out of Monroe, south into the unfamiliar Michigan countryside, his window open to the sound of crickets in the fields. Farther south still, to the Ohio border. At the Red Roof Inn he paid in cash and carried the lame dog bundled in his coat up the dimly lit cracked cement stairs to room 218.

Everything looked fake, like props: The bed. The TV. The Walls. He kicked at the tiny table to make sure it wasn't painted cardboard. He lay the dog on the bed like a carcass, turned on the lights, and shut the door.

In the shower, he rubbed the little odorless white bar over his face and through his hair. In the foggy mirror he looked at his own blank face, even and smoothed out in the steam, except for his hair, shocking black like crow's feathers. And the scar above his left eye.

On the bed the dog whimpered and licked a bloody, mutilated paw. Its nails were long, like it had been unnaturally caged and recently set free. Frankie sat down beside the animal and with his knife trimmed them back, one by one, holding each paw firmly. Perhaps the dog understood, for it offered no resistance but lay on its side blinking at the ceiling. It lapped up the water Frankie brought it in the frail plastic-wrapped cup from the bathroom. It slept beside him in the bed, twitching and fretting all night. It comforted Frankie, somehow, to think that the dog had such troubled sleep, too.

He laid back on the bed and looked up at the freshly painted ceiling and fell asleep.

That night he dreamt of something coiled black in the trunk of his car, and of the girl's warning after she told him the story of the thing in the church, and of opening the trunk with the turn of a key, and of the something spiraling out of the trunk like a reverse tornado.

The next morning the dog let Frankie carry him out to the car and put him in the back seat. Frankie drove out to the main street, with its Dairy Queen and Pizza Hut and tire shop and every building that had been distractedly built, past Fetter's Iron Works and Meijer and Dough Boys and the pharmacies and banks and oil changers, past the brown brick bank with the time and temperature and the small farmhouse wedged between the insurance office and the church, past the lurking hospital, square like a bunker with its startling antennas on the roof and its thin, creaselike windows. He drove out to the edge of development where the new marriages and hopeless marriages fled, some age-old memory trace of butchery buried in the signs for the brand-new Indian-named subdivisions, Shawnee Trace and Tecumseh Point and Arrowhead Park.

Then the houses and businesses fell away and the road south opened up with no distractions. Frankie drove farther and farther still until it was dark, a blanket of numbness covering his mind.

o  o  o

Everything at the truck stop off I-75 was covered with a delicate sheen of grease.

He was somewhere near Ashland, Kentucky.

The food came in fried heaps, delivered by a somnambulist waitress with wild red hair and a torn dress.

Perhaps she wasn't the waitress after all, Frankie thought afterward.

The coffee set his ears ringing, and he had to strain to hear his own thoughts.

Two tables over, a young boy of about eleven or twelve with a pierced eyebrow poked at his food sullenly, a secret signal to his parents that he was soon leaving their world, that even this—this innocent stopover on the way to somewhere else— he could not tolerate. He was bored with his own boredom. His clothes were brown and baggy; he was loaded with the symbology of discontent. With his bare hands and thumbs Frankie could mold the boy's high-cheekboned feminine face into the face of his own child's, his daughter's, lost now, lost now, lost but visible in traces in the body of every child.

With shaking hands Frankie fished out his money and spilled it lazily in rattling coins at the cashier's counter. One coin spun and spun, beyond reason, until he stopped it with his hand. Out of his wallet slipped a small piece of paper with a phone number written on it. He turned it over in his hands, and knew without knowing that the girl must have put it in there. Perhaps her cell phone number. Why? He imagined her doing it in the dark, as he slept. He folded it in two and returned it to his wallet. In the car the dog was awake, watching Frankie approach through the foggy window. Frankie started the car and drove off, pulling onto the highway with all the banal order that such an act required, gripping the steering wheel in his hands with strangulation strength.

As the gray strip of highway gathered speed behind him he looked more than once in his rearview mirror, certain that someone was following him. Not the police. There was something bigger in store for him than that. Whatever it was, it was getting closer. Something to end it all. Everything that was happening was tending toward this final moment.

o  o  o

That night, in southern Kentucky, he pulled off the highway and took a sorry road to the James Motel just outside of Kensington. The dog slept beside him in the bed. In the pale blue light of the morning Frankie walked across the parking lot to the truck stop and ordered breakfast. A policeman came in and sat down in the booth across from him, his gun in his holster. He put his walkie-talkie down on the table and took off his sunglasses and looked over at Frankie. He smiled. The waitress came and Frankie ordered the number 2, and when it came he kept some toast aside for the dog.

Back in the room he fed the dog and checked its feet, which were healing quickly. He flicked on the TV but all that came up was the blue on-screen menu, which he couldn't get to work. He went to the window and drew the drapes closed and then turned on the lamp on the desk and the bedside table.

When he was in the bathroom, someone pounded on the door. The dog jumped down from the bed and stood barking at the door. Frankie came partially out of the bathroom and stood in the doorway, waiting. The dog quieted down, and then there was pounding again, louder, almost alarming, and the dog went back to barking, its body shaking. The dog threw its head from side to side as it barked. Frankie didn't move. After the pounding stopped, he went to the door and looked out the peephole, but it was fogged and he could see nothing.

Frankie sat down on the bed and the dog jumped up next to him. He rubbed the dog's head and wondered if it might have been the cop at the door. Or maybe the cleaning woman—but she would have let herself in.

Frankie had planned to leave, but somehow he didn't. He called the front desk and put another night on his card. He also told them the TV wasn't working, and they said he needed to press the yellow button on the remote, not the red one, and that it said that in the channel guide on top of the set.

He ordered room service that day and night, and again the next, and it slowly occurred to him that he would not be leaving any time soon. He had enough money to stay here for a long, long time. Before he knew it, five or six days had gone by, and he hadn't even opened the curtains or looked outside. He didn't answer the door when the knocking came again, nor did he answer the phone when it rang. If someone wanted to get him, they would have to come and get him, because for all he cared the world outside had disappeared, and as long as he had food and money to pay for this room he was content not to leave, ever. He ceased to look at himself in the mirror but sometimes caught sideways glances that revealed his growing beard, his scraggly hair, his wrinkled clothes.

At night he sometimes wondered about the boy in the diner, which made him think about his daughter and her long, graceful body in the coffin, and the way she covered her mouth when she laughed, and about how the dog was healing, and about the girl he had maybe left in the fire.

He remembered her number in his wallet.

He had regretted not touching her tattoo.

He wondered if she was okay.

Sitting on the edge of his bed, he dialed it.

It rang and rang.

He hung up and did it again.

This time she answered.

"Hello?" she said.

"I wanted to see if you were okay."

"What happened to you? Why did—"

Before she could finish, another voice interrupted them on the phone, and at that moment the dog, startled by something at the door, jumped off the bed, tangling its foot in the phone cord, pulling the whole thing down and disconnecting the call. Frankie put the phone to his ear, but it was dead.

The lamp on the bedstand suddenly seemed too bright, like two- or three-hundred-watt bright. He reached over and turned off the light. The dog was barking wildly at the door, showing more life than Frankie could imagine, the hair on its back standing up.

He knew that he would never call her again, and that he shouldn't have even tried, and that it was time to let the dog go. He leaned over and put the phone back on the table, got out of bed, and walked across the room to open the door. In his mind the name he had for it was Hellhound, but that was a terrible name. Frankie, in his Detroit Tigers T-shirt, opened the door and let the dog out. It was easy to let it go.

Frankie stood in the doorway and looked out into the black night, trying to see something, anything, even a light. Yet there was nothing but blackness. The air felt sweet in his lungs. His car must be out there somewhere in the parking lot that he could not see. In fact, it was so quiet, so still, that looking into the blank night Frankie could almost imagine that the world itself had disappeared, or had never existed.

*What happened to you?* she had said.

He wanted to answer her now, but it was too late.

As he stepped away from his room, what he had come to fear, and secretly hope for, was finally and actually there before him in its darkness, darker even than the gathered night.

## "Full Speed Ahead"

**A song released in 1981 on Dischord Records** by the D.C.-area hardcore band Youth Brigade, which formed after the Teen Idles and the Untouchables broke up. Its members were Nathan Strajcek, Tom Clinton, Bert Queiroz, and Danny Ingram. Here is a criticism of hardcore: Basically, it all sounds the same. Screamed lyrics, short songs, fast tempos. This can be denied by a thousand fans in a thousand different ways, and yet there is enough truth in the statement. But what if sameness is the point? Hardcore is an overwhelming triumph over the diversity of sound, and in that fact lies this contradiction: It is both anarchy and fascism, freedom and control. "Full Speed Ahead" begins with wailing, rolling feedback, a typhoon of noise for about twenty seconds. Then comes a slow, heavy, perfect section that looks back to Black Sabbath and forward to Nirvana. The song must inevitably speed up, but you wish that it wouldn't.

For around forty-five seconds, "Full Speed Ahead" is something that many hardcore songs are not: surprising.

## *Further Temptations*

**An album by the Drones,** released in 1977. Tends to be dismissed as sounding too much like the other U.K. punk music from that year. But this is only true insofar as rock criticism has elevated the more avant-garde aspects of punk and New Wave over the straight-ahead, workmanlike sounds of bands like the Drones. Shift the paradigm slightly and bands like the Drones will take a more prominent

place as fulfilling punk's promise of returning rock to its unpretentious, democratic roots.

In truth, *Further Temptations* is a classic-rock album disguised as a punk album.
It's got a big sound, a heavy beat. It's not at all angular. It's the opposite of Wire,
or Gang of Four, or Television. Songs like "City Drones" and "The Change" rely
on the sort of unironic macho sound that's not too far from the "heavy" sound
of guitar-driven sixties rock. "Persecution Complex" is a straight-ahead rock song
except for the fact that the phrasing of the chorus—"I got a persecution complex
yeah"—crams so many words into such a short span that it couldn't sound like a
typical rock song even if it wanted to. And slow down "Movement" just a hair and
you've got something that almost sounds like Deep Purple. It's no surprise to find
the Phil Spector wall-of-sound song "Be My Baby" on the album, rendered through
a snarl; for a few seconds, beginning at 2:20, in a flurry of drums and building guitars, the song almost completely turns its back on the whole punk scene to embrace
the sixties, the enemy. "Monarchy, monarchy, you're cashing in on everything," they
sing on "Corgi Crap," and you wonder: Why would the monarchy *need* to cash in
on anything?

# Generation X

**The title of a book by Jane Deverson and Charles Hamblett,** published in 1964. The
name of the band Generation X was taken from this book, a copy of which was
owned by Billy Idol's mother. "That evening [in 1976]," the story goes, "Tony
[James] found a Sixties paperback called *Generation X*, a romantic account of Mods
and Rockers, under Billy's bed, and thought it would make a great name for a
group." The book consists mostly of interviews of young people in England. What
they say is by turns philosophical, sad, funny, boring, and confessional, and offers
a snapshot of an England where "No Future" was on everybody's lips, before it was
reduced to a pinprick and then exploded by punk. "We find it a comparatively
bleak picture," the authors wrote of their interviews with young British males, "shot
through with only occasional flashes of originality or illumination, a far cry from
the cozy images projected by the advertisers and moralizers, packagers of false glam-
our and journalistic optimism." And then:

> We feel, however, that the situation has been brought about not so much by lack
> of essential drive or imagination on the part of the young, but as a result of the

drumming into them of false values, tawdry ideas, from their earliest beginnings as social animals. There is an occupational fear, on the part of our educators and formulators of public opinion, a fear of originality.

If the book is haunted by a single idea then that's it. Most of all, the voices of the young in the book are highly aware of their fate in a consumer culture where socially proscribed roles seem, well . . . inevitable. There is a sense that the various youth style movements of the fifties and sixties—the teddy boys, the mods, the rockers—were fairly modest expressions of social difference. Punk seemed to say fully and completely what they had only stuttered. "'Parents, now completely unsure of themselves,'" said Johnathan Seres, one of the young men interviewed in *Generation X*, "'try to conform to the newer modes because the youngsters seem so much at ease and at home in the new ambience. Maybe, they

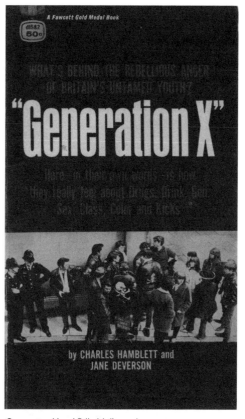

*Generation X* and Billy Idol's mother

think, if parents do likewise they will narrow the gap between the generations and achieve a form of mutual understanding. This explains the phenomenon of parents doing the twist, paying lipservice to Beatlemania, affecting to welcome the newest rave and latest wave.'"

Of Generation X's early performace at the Central London College of Art and Design in December 1976, Peter Silverton wrote in *Sounds* that "1976 has been a pretty good year for rock 'n' roll and, if Generation X stick around, 1977 could be even better." They did stick around for 1977, and released their debut album in 1978. One of the most generationally self-conscious albums to come out of the punk scene, *Generation X* always threatens to take off, and is always pulled back by its need to reject the past. "Trying to forget your generation," goes the opening lyric to "Your Generation" and, even more bitterly and truthfully, is this, from "Promises Promises": "The last lot made a few mistakes / They didn't die young, they got big waists." The gradual transformation of all culture into popular culture in the latter part of the twentieth century was both a blessing and a curse for punk;

by 1976 it was no longer possible to break with the legacy of the sixties gently. Instead, punk disavowed the counterculture and its music with extreme prejudice: its songs were faster, its stages were smaller, its politics (in America at least) were either invisible or reactionary.

> [Charles Hamblett and Jane Deverson, *Generation X*, Greenwich, Conn: Fawcett Gold Medal, 1964, pp. 109, 176; Peter Silverton, "Generation X: Central London College of Art and Design," *Sounds*, December 18, 1976.]

## Germ Free Adolescents

**The one-and-only album by X-Ray Spex,** from 1978, and one of the strongest and strangest rock albums ever—a "superior noise machine" Jon Savage once called the group—defeating attempts to compete with it in words. Poly Styrene (Marion Elliott), Jak Airport (Jack Stafford), Paul Dean, B. P. Hurding (Hearding), and Rudi Thomson (Lora Logic was in the band in its early stages). Inspired after seeing the Sex Pistols live in July 1976, Styrene set about forming her own band, and eight months later she had, and they were playing live. She wore braces. She was not skinny. In some ways, she was the opposite of Blondie's Debbie Harry, a sort of film negative of punk. A scrambling of the code. There apparently is, and has been, much to say about the fact that the band, in the notoriously male-dominated early punk scene, was fronted by a woman, and that the band was a precursor to the riot grrrl scene. Yes, this is worth acknowledging. But in fact it does a disservice to X-Ray Spex, as if they were not one of the great punk bands but merely one of the great female-fronted punk bands.

While *Germ Free Adolescents* is not a concept album, its obsessions—consumerism, plastic, the surfaces of everyday life, the relentless force of the present against the past—are everywhere. In "Warrior in Woolworths," Styrene sings, "Warrior in Woolworths / His roots are in today / Doesn't know no history / He threw the past away." About six months before the album's release, Styrene said this in an interview with Charles Shaar Murray:

> You have to be detached from everything in order to write. I have to observe things in order to write about them: I can't get too directly involved.
>
> That'd why I get a little frightened sometimes, because if I feel I'm getting too involved in hype and other things, all that sort of crap . . . interviews are all right, because they help work things out of your mind, but the other stuff is pretty self-indulgent.
>
> I don't want to become totally self-indulgent, because I write things that other people can relate to. If I totally get into myself I won't be able to do that. What I write will just become a reflection of me instead of a reflection of everything else.

Approximately one year later, Poly Styrene left the band.

[Charles Shaar Murray, "X-Ray Spex: Poly Styrene Is Still Strictly Roots," *New Musical Express*, May 13, 1978; Jon Savage, "X-Ray Spex: *Germ Free Adolescents*," *Melody Maker*, November 18, 1978.]

# Germs

**Listening to the Germs for the first time** was like being let in on a dark secret.

You wanted to turn away, and yet . . .

It was that "and yet" that separated you from many of your friends.

In David Lynch's film *Blue Velvet*—released a mere ten years after punk burst onto the national stage—there is this exchange between Jeffrey (the young man who has returned home from college to get sucked into a mystery) and Detective Williams, the father of Sandy, the girl whom Jeffery is falling in love with:

**Jeffrey:** I understand. I'm just real curious like you said.

**Detective Williams:** I was the same way when I was your age. I guess that's what got me into this business.

**Jeffrey:** It must be great.

**Detective Williams:** And it's horrible too. [pause] I'm sorry Jeffrey. That's the way it has to be. Anyway. I'm sure you do understand.

Of all the groups that arose in the immediate wake of the Ramones and the Sex Pistols, the Germs, out of Los Angeles, wrote music that most embodied and prophesized the spiraling dark side of punk. It is a side that some of us had been trying to avoid for much of our lives. Does that statement sound naive and maybe even moralizing? Since a human being, and not a committee, wrote this book, it is inevitable that statements like this will remind you that a specific person—specific like you are—wrote that first sentence of this entry, a sentence that in all likelihood does not mesh with your first experience of listening to the Germs. But let's assume you already know what you know about the Germs: You know why you enjoy listening to their music. Richard Meltzer has said that "when punk ended, which I'll call 1981, when I was living in L.A.—they had an incredible punk scene with the Germs, X, the Screamers, Nervous Gender . . . There were so many great bands there . . . Maybe 100, 200 people went to see all of them. By the usual rock club standards, there was 'no audience.' It couldn't be corrupted since there was no money to corrupt it."

It is commonplace to say, as M. C. Strong has said in his indispensable book *The Great Indie Discography*, this about the Germs: "Pioneers of hardcore punk, The

Germs made way for The Dead Kennedys, Black Flag, and a host of grunge devotees including Nirvana, Hole, etc." The divide between the "innocent" decadence of punk's first wave (Ramones, Television, Sex Pistols, etc.), which was so minimalist it could be called avant-garde, and the "guilty" decadence of punk's hardcore scene as embodied by bands like the Germs, is evident in this 1980 letter to the editor by Shane Williams in *New York Rocker*:

> I could forgive your magazine for not covering the L.A. scene; it is *NEW YORK Rocker* (even though you cover good English shit). Even your other L.A. columns have harped on the Xerox aspect of L.A., which is utter bullshit. But what really got me hot was this utter dolt, who supposedly hails from the Valley (his mailing address is right in my neighborhood) and has the sheer audacity to dismiss hardcore punk as "sullen, hardcore spikeheads, pogoing to two-chord thrash bands with disposition and artistic vision of maddened stoats."

The divide was already there: the arty, avant-garde New York scene, perceived as ironic going back at least to the Velvet Underground (wasn't Andy Warhol and the entire Pop Art movement the epitome of irony?) versus the emerging L.A. hardcore scene that, face it, traded in a more explicit rendering of punk's rough verdict against humanity. It was as if L.A. had taken what was a prank in New York and London and turned it into something very serious, almost deadly.

The Ramones were a group that your parents might actually like.

The Germs? Absolutely not.

Even the decadence of Cleveland's pre-punk scene was governed by a certain code that read, "Only So Far; No Further." Groups like the Germs took it further, and the result was annihilation. Jon Savage wrote about the Germs that for "English people dazzled by the Los Angeles sun, it is difficult to realize that this fantasy city can harbour oppression all the more cruel because it is masked by image and wealth." Perhaps it was the same darkness disguised in sunshine that lured people like David Lynch to the city. For in places like New York and Cleveland, there was almost a one-to-one correspondence between the city and the music: bleakness to bleakness. But what about sunny California? How could it be bleak with all those beaches, and that wine country, and Hollywood, and the legacy of the peace-love-and-understanding hippies?

But who cares about all that? The music is so good. The Germs' best and truest album, *GI*, with its ominous blue circle on a black background, begins with "What We Do Is Secret" and you can only make out some of the words, or what you think are the words. This is 1979, remember, before fast Internet searches to dispel mysteries and secrets. "Real," "worth it," "circuit," "astronaut," "across the border," and "order" are some of the words you think you hear. But it doesn't matter. The song is forty-one seconds long.

The next song, "Communist Eyes," has such perfect and fast drumming that for a while you believe that the true innovation of punk is not the lyrics or guitars but the drumming. You are from the Midwest of the United States of America; you do not know this band. So you turn the album over and look at the pictures of the band members—Pat, Lorna, Darby, and Don. You wonder who is the drummer. You suspect it is either Pat or Don. Probably Don. Drumming like that could never happen in Ohio.

The first side moves along pretty nicely, with no real surprises (a good thing) until the slower and heavier "Our Way." For some reason, this reminds you of Deep Purple or the Stooges, and you wonder what would happen if all the Germs' songs were slowed down by a few beats. Would it be blues?

"We Must Bleed" scares you, and you realize you are no longer in happy Ramones territory. What happened? The song plays and you imagine Kamikaze pilots crashing into a ship, the ship's guns a-chugging, a-chugging, blind force meeting blind force. The last minute of the song, with hoarse screams of "I want out now" reminds you, today, of Kurt Cobain, and a certain kind of rejection that you could never embrace, but sometimes wish you could. The song slows down like a dying clock. A countdown to nothing. It makes everything that came after make sense.

Side two. The last minute or so of "Let's Pretend" is pure punk. It's your favorite part of any song, but it makes you wonder: Since so much of the album sounds the same, would anybody notice? Repetition is the essence of punk, and also that which dooms it, ultimately, to a sort of perfection that keeps it a secret.

You have read that the album's last song, "Shut Down," is indulgent and too long. The back of the album says that it was "performed live." Does that mean live in the studio, or live in front of an audience? The answer is easy to find today. But in 1979 you knew not what. In a way, this song is a cruel joke. It's slow, almost bluesy. There is some strange piano. Near the end, the instruments seem at war with each other; this is when you realize the genius of Joan Jett's production.

And then—without warning—it's over.

Only years later will you realize that what had ended was much more than an album.

[Richard Meltzer interviewed by Jason Gross, *Perfect Sound Forever*, August 2000; Jon Savage, *England's Dreaming: Anarchy, Sex Pistols, Punk Rock, and Beyond*, New York: St. Martin's Press, 1992, pp. 437–38; M. C. Strong, *The Great Indie Discography* (2nd ed.), Edinburgh: Canongate, 2003, p. 74; Shane Williams, "Dear *NYR*," *New York Rocker*, March 1980, p. 4.]

## Gibson, William

**Born in South Carolina on March 17, 1948,** Gibson's writing has been inspired by the punk movement. About first hearing punk in 1977 in Canada, where he has lived since 1968, he has said, "I took Punk to be the detonation of some slow-fused projectile buried deep in society's flank a decade earlier, and I took it to be, somehow, a sign. And I began, then, to write." In an interview with Peter Murphy, he has also said this:

> 1977 seemed kind of like a roots movement . . . My take on it wasn't that it was brand new nihilism, it was like a return to something that had been the real beginning of the Sixties but had been collectively forgotten. I had forgotten it to some extent myself. And it actually wasn't so much the punk from England that did that for me; it was the stuff from New York that slightly predated what happened in London: Television and the first Patti Smith album. They were very consciously subversively retro in a really irony-free way, they seemed very, very sincere about it, and what I was seeing and hearing out of London was much more self-conscious material.

Gibson's stories, filled with the small details, the accident and mistakes, the dirt of everyday life, helped transform science fiction from sleek futurism to beautiful failure. His work is not ironic; at its heart, it is deeply sentimental. A nostalgia for a future looking back on our present. In "Fragments of a Hologram Rose" (his first published story, from 1977), there is the line, "The first three quarters of the cassette had been erased; you punch yourself fast-forward through a static haze of wiped tape, where taste and scent blur into a single channel. The audio input is white sound—the no-sound of the first dark sea . . ."

No sound. No Wave.

[William Gibson, "Since 1948," www.williamgibsonbooks.com; William Gibson interviewed by Peter Murphy, www.laurahird.com/newreview/williamgibson.html.]

## Glass, Philip

**Born in Baltimore, Maryland, in 1937.** The repeating phrases of Glass's work from the seventies (especially "Music with Changing Parts" and "Music in 12 Parts") evoke strange connections to bands like Suicide. There are correspondences, but they are difficult to trace. Alan Vega (who along with Martin Rev comprised the group Suicide) has said that the "Velvets came along and they were intimating something new with that continuum sound, that monotonous thing, it was also happening in classical music with La Monte Young, and Philip Glass." And in a profile in

*New Musical Express*, Paul Rambali wrote that "the sound of Suicide lies somewhere twixt kraut-rock and Lou Reed's *Coney Island Baby*. One could mention here Terry Riley and Philip Glass to lend avant-garde kudos."

Glass was in New York City during the punk era, driving a taxi from 1973 to 1978. "I liked it," he has said, "except for the imminent violence all around you . . . I was almost killed a few times." His music was sometimes received with the same shock and frustration that greeted underground and punk music from the time. One review of "Music in Fifths" ran under the headline MUSIC OF PHILIP GLASS CALLED SONIC TORTURE: " 'Music in Fifths' sent a number of listeners racing out, their hands covering their ears. Through the performance, the audience continued to dwindle steadily." Glass's notion of the additive process—the gradual addition of notes to musical phrases—finds mutated expression in songs like Suicide's "Ghost Rider," where everything repeats and builds to a steady roar that serves as a warning of some impending catastrophe—or else a distress signal from the other side of that catastrophe.

[Philip Glass interviewed in *Details Magazine*, www.yelp.com; Philip Glass review quoted from John O'Mahony, "When Less Means More," *The Guardian*, November 24, 2001, www.guardian.co.uk; Alan Vega quoted in Clinton Heylin, *From the Velvets to the Voidoids*, New York: Penguin, 1993, p. 68; Paul Rambali, "Suicide Is Not the Answer," *New Musical Express*, June 17, 1978.]

## "Going Underground"

**A song by the Jam, released in March 1980,** that reminds you why rock and roll overturned every other form of music (in the west, for a while at least). The lyrics, painfully, typically frustrated at times, are also sharp and unexpected: "You want more money—of course I don't mind / to buy nuclear textbooks for atomic crimes." It is a great and mysterious thing that a song like this, with such gloomsodden lyrics, can make you want to dance. Paul Weller loved to hate America, and many profiles and interviews with him during this time include the obligatory America-is-so-dumb-and-doesn't-even-get-art sentiments. Here, for instance, is how Simon Frith's article on the Jam from *Creem* ends: "The Jam have recorded as many good songs as Britain's biggest groups, and yet they are off to conquer America again, like learners. We all agree, before the conversation goes back to clothes, that there is still no sign of life across the Atlantic. The Ramones have been absorbed into their comic book and no one else mattered much to the Jam anyway. In America they would have been called the Jelly. We shake our heads and wonder."

The song's production is so clean and the lyrics articulated so clearly that there is absolutely no room for surprise, which makes it a magnificent species of pop-punk. "Going Underground" is a harbinger of the coming sternness and clarity of the eighties, which, unlike the murky and incoherent seventies, did not provide the sort of out-of-focus vision that gave rise to genres like disco and punk. The aesthetic militancy of hardcore would put an end to the contradictory impulses of punk: Songs like "Going Underground" are the last remnants before the new order.

[Simon Frith, "The Jam Is Packed Off to America," *Creem*, April 1980.]

## Graham, Bill

**Born in Berlin in 1931, died in California in 1991.** A rock promoter who in the sixties worked with bands including the Grateful Dead, Jefferson Airplane, the Rolling Stones, and Janis Joplin. In an October 1977 segment of Tom Snyder's *The Tomorrow Show*, he appeared, along with the *Los Angeles Times* music critic Robert Hilburn (an early supporter of punk), Joan Jett, Paul Weller (of the Jam), and Kim Fowley. During the segment, he came across as the resigned, slightly hostile skeptic, wearily and dutifully expressing doubts about the legitimacy of punk, and looking on dryly as Kim Fowley poked fun at the worst aspects of the counterculture and the sort of "arena rock" groups that emerged in the late sixties and early seventies. For a while, it seemed as if Graham and his aesthetics belonged in the dustbin of history. But then Snyder asked Weller if, someday, the "new" punk and New Wave bands would grow old, comfortable, and part of the mainstream. Weller suggested that yes, he hoped this would happen, and that the next generation should in fact overthrow punk. Joan Jett wasn't so sure, and there followed this exchange:

> **Graham (to Joan Jett):** I can count on less than one hand the artists that have become very successful and have not been caught in the swirl of what success does to you. You haven't been faced with that challenge, which I think is the biggest challenge of all. What will you do if you become a household word? You're going to live differently, you'll have a nice car, a nicer home. You'll have better clothes, and you *will* become the establishment because . . . I doubt very much if you will be able to catch yourself because the temptation is too big. Name someone who is very big, who lives a simple life.

> **Weller:** John Lennon, Pete Townshend, Bob Dylan, David Bowie.

> **Graham:** A *simple* life?

> **Weller:** I think so.

> **Graham:** Don't look at the hotel bill.

Graham's warnings turned out to be partially right. Punk and New Wave did become commodities, but with a difference: They didn't hide the fact.

Earlier in the segment, there was brief discussion of Nazi symbols as used by some punk groups. It is not clear whether those gathered on the stage with him knew that Graham—who was born Wolfgang Grajonca—was Jewish, and that his mother perished at Auschwitz.

## Gravity's Rainbow

**A Thomas Pynchon novel published in 1973,** the year that CBGB opened. Dark and paranoid and funny and long (over seven hundred pages) and rude and absurd and complex and Nazi-Germany obsessed and apocalyptic, the novel suggests fertile ground for the punk imagination. A line from a review of the book that year could easily be applied to punk, or to the Ramones specifically: "The risk that Pynchon's fiction runs is boredom, repetition without significant development, elaboration that is no more than compulsiveness." Boredom. Repetition. Compulsiveness. Although *Gravity's Rainbow* was selected in 1973 by the Pulitzer Prize jurors as the winner, it was rejected by the board as "unreadable" and "turgid." The jury refused to make another selection, and thus in 1973 no Pulitzer for a novel was awarded.

Richard M. Nixon (about whom Hunter S. Thompson in 1971 said "he represented what Robert Kennedy, in early 1968, called 'the dark side of the American character'") appears as "Richard M. Zhlubb, night manager of the Orpheus, who comes out against what he calls 'irresponsible use of the harmonica' . . . Zhlubb states that his queues, especially for midnight showings, have fallen into a state of near anarchy because of the musical instrument." It would take a lot to dispel the thick, gloomy paranoia of the seventies, and in some ways punk was a way to convert that disorder into something meaningful. Punk had no serious "message" to convey; its sound was its message. Like *Gravity's Rainbow*, the secret or key to its structure was in fact its structure.

"The silences here are retreats of sound, like the retreat of surf before a tidal wave: sound draining away, down slopes of acoustic passage, to gather, someplace else, to a great surge of noise." What if the noise retreated, was reduced, and then collected itself in places like Cleveland, where in 1974 Rocket from the Tombs were formed, writing songs like "Sonic Reducer," which Clinton Heylin has called one of American punk's most "potent anthems"? The "great surge of noise" in *Gravity's Rainbow* is terrifying in the way that ideas are sometimes more terrifying than their realization. Pynchon's novel is full of sentences that both predict and then condemn their peculiar historical moment, the great blankness of the years preceding punk: "We live lives that are waveforms constantly changing with time, now positive, now negative. Only at moments of great serenity is it possible to find the pure, the informationless state of signal zero."

In a review of the first album by Penetration, *Moving Targets*, Paul Morley wrote: "Ignore the packaging, especially the embarrassing luminous vinyl. This collection needs coloured vinyl like a Pynchon novel needs a nude on the cover."

[Hunter S. Thompson letter to Jim Silberman, June 1971, in Douglas Brinkley, ed., *Fear and Loathing in America: The Gonzo Letters, Volume II*, New York: Simon and Schuster, 2000, p. 421; Richard Locke, "One of the Longest, Most Difficult, Most Ambitious Novels in Years: *Gravity's Rainbow*, by Thomas Pynchon," *The New York Times*, March 11, 1973; Paul Morley, "Penetration: *Moving Targets*," *New Musical Express*, October 14, 1978; Thomas Pynchon, *Gravity's Rainbow*, New York: Penguin, 1973, pp. 769–70, 341, 410.]

## Great Jones Street

**In 1973 the writer Don LeLillo was thirty-seven years old,** and he published a novel entitled *Great Jones Street*. At its bare minimum, it is about a rock star, Bucky Wunderlick, who attempts to drop off the map, to stop touring, to stop making music, to disappear. The plot also involves "the product"—a mysterious and powerful drug that destroys the language center of the brain, reducing users to babblers—and the Mountain Tapes, Bucky's less polished, off-the-cuff, freewheeling, experimental, amateur music that his handlers want him to release as his entry back into the rock celebrity spotlight. While the novel is often described as a sort of black comedy version of Bob Dylan's reclusiveness and the mysteries surrounding his own *Basement Tapes*, in its dark heart the book is really about a moment in time—paranoid and tinged with violence—just before punk. There are the dog boys, a violent offshoot of the terrorist group the Happy Valley Farm Commune—whose random violence is detached from the political, socially correct violence of the sixties. They are an early-warning system for groups like the Dead Boys, the Viletones (led by Nazi Dog), and even the Sex Pistols. Here is an exchange between Bohack, who is trying to recover the product from Bucky, and Bucky:

"We've got a runaway contigent, Bucky. Their specialty is violence. Mindless violence. They talk about it all the time. When they're not talking about it, they're doing it. Mindless mindless violence . . ."

"I wonder how they define violence," I said.

"It defines itself. Mindless. In a way I can see what they're doing. They're scrupulous in avoiding any and all implications, political and otherwise. They have no real program or rationale beyond what I said. Mindless. I guess they're trying to empty everything out."

"Destroy," the Sex Pistols sceamed. "Mindless. I guess they're trying to empty everything out," Bohack said. "The Blank Generation," Richard Hell said. "Don't need no human race," the Dead Boys sang.

"Fame requires every kind of excess," the novel begins. "I mean true fame, a devouring neon, not the somber renown of waning statesmen or chinless kings. I mean long journeys across gray space. I mean danger, the edge of every void, the circumstance of one man imparting an erotic terror to the dreams of the republic." Fittingly, near the novel's end, Bucky himself is injected with the product, which promises to render him unable to make words—"Sounds, yes. Sounds galor. But no words"—like a punk in the most extreme sense, screaming inarticulately, noise with no content, not so much trapped in a cage of fame but extending that cage to everyone, just as promised by the DIY ethic, as if "meaning" itself was a dirty word, as if pondering over the "meaning" of the lyrics of the Beatles or Led Zeppelin or Pink Floyd was something for hippie kids, as if sound had to be reduced violently down to its most primitive state, beyond "meaning," approximated in punk by euphoria so strong it threatened total destruction.

[Don DeLillo, *Great Jones Street*, 1973; repr., New York: Penguin, 1994, pp. 1, 191, 255.]

## Gulcher

**In his review of Richard Meltzer's 1972 book *Gulcher*,** Andy (Adny) Shernoff of the Dictators wrote that it "takes ten minutes to write bad music but it takes ten years to write good music. So if you love music and have a desire to perform it, why the fuck should you waste all that time learning technique? Fuck the fundamentals and fuck all the formalities. Just play the music." Richard Meltzer is not as famous as Hunter S. Thompson or Lester Bangs or Charles Bukowski because he is not, in the end, a sentimentalist. There is a warmth to their writing, a we're-in-this-thing-together bond with their readers that Meltzer never establishes. *Gulcher* (the complete title is *Gulcher: Post-Rock Cultural Pluralism in America [1649–1980]*) is, aside from Herman Melville's *Pierre*, one of the strangest books ever published in the United States of America. It's like a demented, half-dreamed encyclopedia. From the entry "The Wonderful World of Booze":

> The drink is tequila, the effect is you're lying on your back constantly spinning in both directions if not all 7, at the same time all the time. It's when you try to switch direction that the spatial flashes hit, and you can't catch up with yourself even if you're the great Paavo Nurmi. You're always at least a step ahead of yourselves and it's a track meet from start to finish, very much like the vaunted lysergic. And it's a real cultural leveler, you don't have to be a hippie to love it.

That last part—"you don't have to be a hippie to love it"—is pure Meltzer. In a strange way, it makes sense that Meltzer was attracted to punk and New Wave publications such as *Creem*, *New Wave*, and others, despite his ambivalence about the punk scene. "Punk was something outside of rock," Meltzer has said. "It lasted about three years and then it circled back and rejoined the marketplace and became the same thing." It's because his writing, in terms of style and sensibility, was itself punk. He probably got the closest to any critic we've have ever had (with the possible exceptions of George W. S. Trow and Pauline Kael) to the nirvana of writing words that were as funny and mean and dangerous as the topics they described. Meltzer has said that in his writing, and in *Gulcher* especially, he was trying "to offer a pattern of disobedience." He also said that "I . . . sensed that the only sure way to avoid counterculture cliché (and with it the cloying sense that 'we'd' failed) was to go *beneath* its curve." He also said that he tried—and failed—to get Jacques Derrida to write an introduction to the 1990 reissue of *Gulcher*, which says a lot about what Meltzer was up to with his *Animal House*–like deconstruction of sentences and the ideas in them.

Meltzer wrote for many publications with interesting names. He wrote for *Zoo World*, for instance, a music magazine out of Ft. Lauderdale, Florida. His 1974 review of an album by the Creamcheeze Goodtime Band begins: "Sure woulda had a Good Time if the damn stereo hadn't busted down right in the middle of the first cut. Turntable just stopped turning, didn't even kinda settle down to a slow stop requiring several seconds or even a few: just stopped dead!" The review continues to talk about the broken turntable; there is virtually nothing about the album in question.

If you have never read Meltzer before, the best thing to do is to avoid the anthologies and collections of his writing, which chop them up and make them sound detached. Instead, track down a copy of *Gulcher*. In the meantime, here are some quotes from the book (really!), with page numbers:

- "Okay it's pud yanking time so get to it." (30)
- "He [Killer Kowalski] got a degree in metaphysics from some school in Ontario and he was a vegetarian." (40)
- "Like who the fuck cares about ballet except ballet fans?" (60)
- "Cause once you've eliminated one of the 2 essential ingredients in the formal structure of the female buttocks you can just forget the whole fuckin thing." (78)
- "Supermarkets are the best places for getting twist-off caps free. You just twist em off when nobody's looking." (87)
- "The best use of paper yet invented is spit balls and the second best is cardboard and the third best is postcards with pictures of famous places." (102)
- "The New York Rangers may have hornswaggled their name from the world famous Texas Rangers themselves but this has in no way aided their crusade in the prevention of serious groin harm to their super-stellar defenseman, the one and only Barney Aure." (106)

Here at last are the last sixty-seven words of this entry, from a letter to *Creem* by Lou Stathis: "Those turds who write for *Rolling Stone* every month really believe that worthless tripe they spew out. Most likely they regard themselves as perceptive sociocultural observers. But you guys is ok. Where else could I read eighty pages of lobotomized illiterates trying to imitate R. Meltzer every month?"

> [Richard Meltzer interviewed by Jason Gross in *Perfect Sound Forever*, August 2000; Richard Meltzer, "Afterward to the Reprint of *Gulcher*," in *A Whore Just Like the Rest*, Da Capo Press, 2000, p. 168; Richard Meltzer, *Gulcher: Post-Rock Cultural Pluralism in America (1649–1980)*, San Francisco: Straight Arrow Books, 1972, p. 55; Richard Meltzer, review of "The Creamcheeze Good Time Band" in *Zoo World: The Music Magazine*, August 29, 1974, p. 32; Lou Stathis, "A Weasel, A True Fan," *Creem*, October 1974, p. 98; Andy Shernoff, review of *Gulcher: Post-Rock Cultural Pluralism in America (1649–1980)*, by Richard Meltzer, *Creem*, January 1973, p. 64.]

## Gun Rubber

**The August 1977 issue of the fanzine from Sheffield,** United Kingdom. The Buzzcocks on the cover. Recommended by Job Savage in his survey of fanzines in *Sounds*. Like the best fanzines, there was an element of skepticism and even disdain about the punk scene. A cartoon by Robb Conn has a "hip TV bloke" interviewing a punk. "As a punk—a member of the blank generation—how do you react to being a product of the dole?" to which the punk answers, "Er, me mum buys me clothes."

*Gun Rubber* would go on to publish only one or two more issues, as the divide between punk's initial promise (as a music and an attitude that could somehow sustain its outsider status) and the growing reality (that punk was fast becoming a commodity like everything else) became too obvious to ignore. The closing editorial ended like this:

> So that's it, August 1977 and nothing's changed. Ask yourself, what's exactly so new about covering your old school blazer with safety pins and jumping up and down to the hit sounds made by today's superstars. Don't kid yourself, the Clash now cost 1,000 for a concert and are managed by a bloke who makes Malcom McClaren look honest. Very politically aware I'm sure. Oh yeah and while we're at it the Sex Pistols have recently turned down offers to play in Britain on the grounds that there wasn't enough money in it . . . It ain't no fun being a New Wave sheep. Get out and do something!

By the end of 1977, punk's first, naive phase was over. Depending on your perspective, it either evolved into its inevitable conclusion—hardcore—or devolved into the violence that was always implied and became an oppressive force.

> ["The End," *Gun Rubber*, August 1977; Jon Savage, "Fanzines: Pure Pop Art for Now People," *Sounds*, January 14, 1978.]

## "Gunning for Sex Pistols"

**A letter to the editor published** in the *Los Angeles Times* in 1977:

> I'm greatly disappointed at Robert Hilburn's enthusiastic review of the Sex Pistols'
> debut album. If this is what is best in punk rock, then I will never buy such trash.
> Thanks for the education, but no thanks. By the time I was listening to the second
> track I was becoming appalled by the lack of imagination, the sameness of the
> melodies (what melodies?), the musical aridity and the unrelenting noise through-
> out, which Hilburn, regretfully, prefers to call "intensity." Thank God and the
> Queen for sending us, instead, Paul McCartney and Wings and for their new and
> truly compelling and exhilarating "Girls' School."

> [Tony Rico, "Gunning for Sex Pistols," *Los Angeles Times*, December 4, 1977, p. X2.]

**h**

## Hannah, Barry

**An American author and a southerner.** (Skip this if you are looking for a straight-ahead
entry on punk.) In many ways, Hannah's 1970 novel *Geronimo Rex* is responsible
for the book you are reading now. Why? That's hard to say. Let the novel speak for
itself. Here are some key quotes:

> Before pulling the trigger in the auditorium, I seemed to be only verging toward
> life—say, like a man eating color photographs.

> What I especially liked about Geronimo then was that he had cheated, lied, stolen,
> mutinied, usurped, killed, burned, raped, pillaged, razed, trapped, ripped, mashed,
> bowshot, stomped, herded, exploded, cut, stoned, revenged, prevenged, avenged,
> and was his own man.

There is a madness to Hannah's writing that's mythically American to you, but
also alien, since you are a northerner. You read this book, *Geronimo Rex*, much
later, after you discovered punk, and although you realize that literally speaking it is
not *of* the punk era (and certainly not within the chronological parameters of this
book), there is something about it that is forever lodged in your brain as southern
gothic punk.

Of course, no such category exists.

And of course in your brain (the only place that matters) it does.

[Barry Honnah, *Geronimo Rex*. 1970; repr., New York: Grove Press, 1972, pp. 164, 231.]

## "Happy Birthday, Stephanie"

**An episode from the sitcom *Archie Bunker's Place*,** broadcast in November 1981, in which Archie's niece gets tickets to see Devo at Madison Square Garden. Archie and Barney go to the concert to stop her from attending (turns out she didn't go) and instead get arrested along with some other punks.

## Headlines, 1977

**In October 1977, an Associated Press article** by James Simon was picked up by hundreds of newspapers in the United States, many of them small-town newspapers, and helped spread, viruslike, the word about punk. The article is a perceptive, critical but open-minded account of punk and its significance, with references to John Holmstrom's *Punk* fanzine, the differences between British and American punk, the antipathy toward hippies, the role of minimalism, and a discussion of the do-it-yourself ethic.

What's of even greater interest is the role of headlines in preparing readers for the story. The headlines—reflective of each newspaper's own ideology—cast punk in many different lights. The articles often ran with pictures of either Patti Smith ("punk rock star") or the Dead Boys. Here is a sampling: different headlines from different papers for the same article by James Simon:

PUNK ROCK: OUTRAGEOUS AND GROWING (*Daily Journal,* October 14, 1977, Fergus Falls, Minnesota)

THE BIG QUESTION: IS PUNK ROCK HERE TO STAY? (*The Reporter,* October 14, 1977, Fond Du Lac, Wisconsin)

FANS OF PUNK ROCK GROUPS DRAWN TO OUTRAGEOUS COSTUMES, SIMPLE VIOLENCE (*Northwest Arkansas Times,* October 14, 1977, Fayetteville, Arkansas)

THE PUNK ROCK PHENOMENON ARRIVES IN AMERICA (*Nashua Telegraph,* October 15, 1977, Nashua, New Hampshire)

PUNK ROCK EXPLOSION HITS U.S. MUSIC SCENE (*Great Bend Tribune,* October 16, 1977, Great Bend, Kansas)

PUNK ROCK: WILDLY REBELLIOUS, BUT NOT NEW (*Brainerd Daily Dispatch,* October 18, 1977, Brainerd, Minnesota)

PUNK ROCK IS HERE—BUT WILL ROCK FANS LIKE IT? (*Chillicothe Constitution-Tribune,* October 19, 1977, Chillicothe, Missouri)

PUNK ROCK: WILL IT BECOME STANDARD FOR SEVENTIES? (*Aiken Standard,* October 19, 1977, Aiken, South Coliona)

PUNK ROCK CRAZE REACTION TO SIMPLICITY? (*The Courier News*, October 19, 1977, Blytheville, Arkansas)

PUNK ROCK IS THE NEW PHENOMENON OF THE MUSIC INDUSTRY (*Thursday's Muscaline Journal*, October 20, 1977, Muscaline, Iowa)

PUNK ROCK: NEW WAVE OF FANS COMING; THEY WANT THEIR OWN STYLE (*Gastonia Gazette*, October 20, 1977, Gastonia, North Carolina)

PUNK ROCK GROUPS SEND ROCK MUSIC TO DISGUSTINGLY LOW DEPTHS (*Idaho State Journal*, October 21, 1977, Pocatello, Idaho)

SCRUTINY: DEVELOPMENT OF PUNK ROCK STYLE (*Journal News*, October 22, 1977, Hamilton, Ohio)

PUNK ROCK CRAZE MAY REFLECT GENERATION GAP IN MUSIC INDUSTRY (*Huron Daily Plainsman*, October 28, 1977, Huron, South Dakota)

## Helen Keller

**The product of Norman Durkee, from Seattle,** the band Helen Keller never played a live show and recorded only one single in 1978. But what a single. The B-side, "Dump on the Chumps," is all right, but the A-side, "Surfin with Steve & E. D. Amin" is just about the most unforgettable song mentioned in this book. The voice is low and menacing, like someone shouting through gravel into the dark void. But then the soaring soprano, sung by Valerie Yockey, is extravagant and baroque and full of melody; it humbles you that no combination of words can do justice to the weird beauty of this song. "That chorus is a take off on the Beach Boys," he said, but instead of "shouldn't have lied, now" it's "shouldn't have died, now." There are facts about Helen Keller, the song "Surfin with Steve & E. D. Amin," and Norman Durkee that I should tell you:

1. Norman Durkee was born in Tacoma, Washington, in 1943, and sat next to Ted Bundy in class.
2. During childbirth, his mother was given the drug mixture morphine and scopolamine to produce the effect of "twilight sleep"; this combination of drugs—given commonly at the time—is no longer administered. Probably as a result of the drugs, Durkee was born with his umbilical cord wrapped around his neck and was nearly asphyxiated.
3. The song was written by Durkee and Douglas Beckowitz.
4. Distorted electric piano: Durkee
   Lead guitar: Beckowitz
   Bass: Dan Dean (also played the electric drill)

Drums: Fred Zeufeldt
Lead vocals: Durkee
Background soprano: Valerie Yockey
Engineered and mixed by Dr. A. (Richard Maltby) and Durkee

5. As for the distorted electric piano (above) which gives the song its deeply eerie and menacing vibe that seems to sustain forever, Durkee said, "The massive rhythm-guitar sound is actually a Fender Rhodes electric piano sent through a Peavy PA amp with all the settings set to maximum for distortion and sustain. The sound was so dense I could not play complete chords. I had to play open fourths and fifths."

6. As to why punk—and the weird sounds of third-generation rock—emerged at nearly the same time in different places, Durkee refers to the biologist Rupert Sheldrake and his theory of morphic fields, which suggests that phenomena (biological but also, potentially, artistic) become more possible the more frequently they occur. No matter where.

[E-mail from Norman Durkee to author, May 14, 2008; telephone conversation between Norman Durkee and author, May 13, 2008.]

# Herman's Hermits

**A major influence on the Ramones,** something that was widely acknowledged around the time of their first album's release in April 1976. "The infusion of the Kinks, Herman's Hermits, fake Mersey accents, DC5, MC5, and BCR into the Ramones' music is all the more crucial, vital to the survival of rock 'n' roll," wrote Gene Sculatti in 1976. Two years later, Roy Trakin noted that "ever so slowly evolving into the latter-day Herman's Hermits they always sought to become, the Ramones have achieved a larger-than-life, almost cartoon-character status in the rock world." But what did this mean, and how could the very roots of punk and even hardcore lie with a band like Herman's Hermits?

Herman's Hermits formed in Manchester in 1963. Originally, they were Keith Hopwood, Peter Noone, Karl Green, Alan Wrigley, and Steve Titterington. Derek Leckenby and Barry Whitwam joined later. "I'm into Something Good" went to number thirteen in the United States, and number one in the United Kingdom in 1964. "Mrs. Brown, You've Got a Lovely Daughter" and "I'm Henry VIII, I Am" also reached number one in the United States, in 1965. The band reunited and performed in 1973 to a full house at Madison Square Garden, as the New York underground/punk scene was forming. Despite the goofy, one-off band name, their best songs are so pure and balanced that it's easy to understand how the Ramones

Herman's Hermits as punk inspiration

and other mid-seventies bands were nostalgic for the energy, simplicity, and directness of songs like "I'm into Something Good," "Listen People," and "No Milk Today." In 1978, Derek Leckenby told the New Wave fanzine *Ballroom Blitz!* (out of Dearborn Heights, Michigan) that "groups like the Stranglers and the Sex Pistols possess a great deal of enthusiasm and rock and roll energy that has been sorely lacking from the BBC."

In fact, there is an underlying, melodic darkness to songs like "No Milk Today" that flies in the face of the band's highly controlled image as clean-cut lads. If the Rolling Stones and others were openly embracing the emerging darkness of the sixties, Herman's Hermits resisted, at least on the surface. The result is a sort of David Lynchian tension to this resistance, for darkness hinted at and fleetingly revealed is often more disturbing than darkness fully revealed. The achievement of the Ramones on their first three albums is all the more remarkable for how their music embodied the contradiction between pop sweetness and the utter degeneration of their time.

[Derek Leckenby interviewed by Mike McDowell in *Ballroom Blitz!* no. 25, March 1978, p. 23; Gene Sculatti, "The Ramones: *Ramones*," *Creem*, August 1976; Roy Trakin, "*Road to Ruin*: One Small Step for Man, One Giant Step for the Ramones," *New York Rocker*, September 1978.]

## High-Rise

**A 1975 novel by J. G. Ballard that,** as Jon Savage has noted, "was a big book" in England in the autumn of 1976 as bands like the Sex Pistols and the Clash were performing. The story is set in a drab, self-contained high-rise where all social order is disintegrating and reforming, chaotically and violently, along class lines, as the upper, middle, and lower floors war against one another. Published in the Unites States a few years later, the book, like punk, converts the raw materials of near economic collapse into art. Early in the novel, we are told that the "spectacular view always made Laing [a main character] aware of his ambivalent feelings for this concrete landscape. Part of its appeal lay all too clearly in the fact that this was an environment built, not for man, but for man's absence." *High-Rise* is an eerie novel (Isn't everything by Ballard eerie?) because, like punk, it's hard to tell in what measure its excess and violence are simply products of the seventies or critiques of it. Here is a key passage:

> Perhaps the recent incidents represented a last attempt by Wilder and the airline pilots to rebel against this unfolding logic? Sadly, they had little chance of success, precisely because their opponents were people who were content with their lives in the high-rise, who felt no particular objection to an impersonal steel and concrete landscape, no qualms about the invasion of their privacy by government agencies and data-processing organizations, and if anything welcomed these invisible intrusions, using them for their own purposes. These people were the first to master a new kind of late twentieth-century life. They thrived on the rapid turnover of acquaintances, the lack of involvement with others, and the total self-sufficiency of lives which, needing nothing, were never disappointed.

Richard Hell's blank generation. The Ramones' "now I wanna have somethin' to do." Pere Ubu's "Dub Housing." These are all signals of a collapse, disguised as pop art. The confusion and disorder go beyond content, for just as punk and underground and experimental music from the seventies did not fit squarely into pre-existing slots, Ballard's novel, in its American edition, is packaged in a similarly incoherent way. The cover features a *Publishers Weekly* blurb praising the novel as something that dwarfs *The Towering Inferno*, as if the book were a blockbuster adventure story, while the inside flap ("Tenants of Terror—These were some of the men

0-445-04181-1  $1.95

The disaster novel that dwarfs *The Towering Inferno* ..."Absorbing, chilling, frightening" —*Publishers Weekly*

by J. G. Ballard

Disintegration and disorder and opportunity

and women plunging to the depths of danger, destruction, and degradation in the hellish disintegration of—*High-Rise*") promotes it as if it were some campy exploitation novel.

But *High-Rise*, like the best of Ballard's fiction, is disturbing in a lasting way because, as theory disguised as entertainment, it offers a snapshot of what might happen when social disintegration opens up new spaces for thinking. Of course, in "real life" these open spaces are soon stabilized and culturally sanctioned: It's no coincidence that in the United States and the United Kingdom Reagan and Thatcher were elected as powerful forces of containment at around the same time. *High-Rise* offers no such solutions; there is no return to normalcy. Near the end of the book, "Laing thought about his good fortune as he sat on the balcony with his back to the railing. Above all, now, it no longer mattered how he behaved, what wayward impulses he gave way to, or which perverse pathways he chose to follow." For him—for us—the terrible truth is that disintegration often leads not to anarchy but to a form of destruction that is a precondition for starting over.

[J. G. Ballard, *High-Rise*, 1975; repr., New York: Popular Library, 1978, pp. 32, 48, 250; Jon Savage, *England's Dreaming: Anarchy, Sex Pistols, Punk Rock, and Beyond*, New York: St. Martin's Press, 1992, p. 232.]

## Hippies, Johnny Rotten's comments about

From The London Weekend Show, 1976:

**Q:** Who would you say is a good singer?

**Johnny Rotten:** I don't. I don't have any heroes. They're all useless . . . None. None are accessible.

**Q:** What's this thing you've got against hippies?

**JR:** They're complacent.

From a television interview, 1977:

**JR:** I know what I want.

**Q:** What do you want?

**JR:** Freedom, I think they call it. The hippies used to call it that. But I bet there's a better word for it.

## "Horror Business"

**A 1977 song by the Misfits,** a band that you want to forget. Why? Because their stand seems artificially remote. They are a stance. But this song, it sweeps you away before it even arrives: like the terrible calm you imagine occurs before a tornado. Obvious echoes of the Ramones singing about the "baysment." The last forty-five seconds are about as blistering as anything you have heard, and it reminds you that apocalypse is always in the mind. You realize now, listening to it again, that its New Jersey fury was in advance of California hardcore.

A strange story: You are a young professor, and one of your first memorable students is fiercely intense and intelligent, with a shaved head and a red metal, locked toolbox that he carries around. For some perverse reason, you dismiss his music (he liked the Misfits and recommended them to you in a spirit of camaraderie) maybe because you wanted to keep that wall up. Understandable. But now, years later, in part because of this book, you are forced to confront the Misfits and the tenderness of this melody, and the relentlessness of the song lays waste to all your petty reservations. Glenn Danzig, who wraps his voice around words in a thoroughly East-Coast-of-the-United-States-of-America way. Jerry Only. Bobby Steele. Joey Image. You prefer not to read about the shocking lives of any of these men: You love their music, not them.

## *Horses*

**The 1975 album, by Patti Smith,** that embodied punk even though today it sometimes sounds like something much different. Part of the confounding beauty (and mystery) of the album is that you can't tell if it is looking forward to the future or back at the past. It's hard to separate what that album first meant to us upon hearing it in the mid-seventies from how we have come to know it as "legendary rock album." At the time, there was the unadorned passion of Smith's voice, in total command. "I listen to *Horses* and I think of it as the culmination of all my most heartfelt adolescent desires," Smith has said. It is a testament to the album that, even today, people who trace their way back to the original punk scene get to this album and become lost.

Produced by John Cale, *Horses* sidesteps categories. Patti Smith had been famous in a small way in New York for at least a few years, which is why appraisals from further away are more revealing than up-close ones. In November 1974—roughly one year before the album was released—Richard Cromelin, reviewing her performance at the Whisky in the *Los Angeles Times*, summed up the contradictions that lay at the heart of her performance: "Patti Smith is at once very familiar—it's a classic tableau, the beatnik reading her poetry in a moody coffeehouse—and, though the sources of much of her style are readily apparent, strangely and strikingly new." Although he probably wasn't the first to use the term "punk" to describe her, he did note that she "chants from her own desolation row, confident and bewildered, assured and then not so sure, her own imagery linking with prime-time, punk-rock mythology."

*Horses*, appearing in the middle of the decade, roughly five months before the Ramones' first album would propel the underground/punk subculture into the public, was the last—and most beautiful—expression of the doomed romanticism of the sixties. Unlike Blondie, and later the Runaways, and even later the early Go-Gos, there was no irony in Patti Smith's band, not a trace of condescension. "I am a helium raven and this movie is mine / So he cried out as he stretched the sky / Pushing it all out like a latex cartoon, am I all alone in this generation?" she asks in "Birdland," the long track from side one. Smith was acutely aware that she was at the head of a new, brewing storm in rock. "I can understand why things have been calm for the last few years," she told Robert Hilburn of the *Los Angeles Times*. "We went through a lot of heavy stuff in the Sixties. It was like a whole season in hell together . . . everything just blew apart . . . We all had to pull ourselves together. To me, that's why our record's called *Horses*. We had to pull the reins on ourselves to recharge ourselves . . . It's time to let the horses loose again. We're ready to start moving again."

She moved in other ways, too. In her book *Babel* (1978), Smith wrote of Crazy Horse:

> he was shot in the knee and his knee opened and streamed and streamed the tears and wounds of his people. he wept and pissed and attempted to abuse his spoil and recapture the language of the lost.
>
> here he gripped his ear and the ear of his horse.
>
> he rode very fast and the wind whistled thru his wound. he manipulated the pain and reinvented the cliff and the waterfall.

[Richard Cromelin, "Patti Works Without a Net," *Los Angeles Times*, November 13, 1974, p. F21; Robert Hilburn, "Slipping the Reins on the Passion of Rock," *Los Angeles Times*, January 25, 1976, p. K72; Patti Smith, "The Salvation of Rock," *Babel*, New York: G.P. Putnam's Sons, 1978, p. 140; Smith quoted in *Velvets to Voidoids*, p. 191.]

# "How Could I"

## A song by the Mirrors, from Cleveland, Ohio. Recorded in June 1974. So influenced by the Velvet Underground that it's better than the Velvet Undergound. The precise moment when a little-known band on the edges of the rock canon supersedes the

VU happens at the 1:50 mark, when suddenly the tempo changes and a guitar hook kicks in that sets the song off in a whole new direction. Paul Marotta, who played keyboards and electronics on the song, has said that the Mirrors, when looking for new members to replace the ones who left, "wanted decent, funny, cool people to play with—no nut cases, assholes, artistes, and especially nobody that actually expected to make any money."

[Paul Marotta, liner notes to *Those Were Different Times* CD, p. 4.]

---

## "I Got You Babe"
(by Ephraim P. Noble)

**Covered by the Dictators,** on their debut 1975 album, *The Dictators Go Girl Crazy!* Who were these Dictators, and why was their music so good? Unlike Blondie, who also covered sixties songs, the Dictators did so without any traces of irony or camp. There are no gaps in this song that permit snarky laughter. It is as if the Dictators fall under the spell of the song while performing it, and believe it. They say this entry will show up in some so-called *Cultural Dictionary* something-or-other book on punk, and that I have a limited number of words—136 to be exact—for this entry, to be strictly enforced by one D. Barker, so I will say this: "I Got You Babe," as covered by the Dictators, is the most important punk song ever recorded because

## *Ice Age, The*

**A novel, published in 1977** by the British author Margaret Drabble, that captures in rolling waves of gloomy dirt and masochistic pessimism the social disintegration and fragmentation of British society at that time. Lester Bangs, in his 1978 article on Richard Hell, mentioned the book: "If the seventies are really going to be remembered as the decade when, like a character in Margaret Drabble's *The Ice Age*, people actually welcomed depression as a relief from anxiety, then the seething anxiety of Richard's music and his disturbing pessimism about the ultimate value of life itself are crucially important." From *The Ice Age*, Alison from her point of view on a train:

> The scenery outside the window altered, slowly, to the derelict Northern wastes
> and dump sites that nobody could now afford to landscape: was it true that the

0-445-04300-8 $2.25

Her newest bestseller!

# MARGARET DRABBLE

# THE ICE AGE

"A stunning novel from cover to cover...her best"
—Los Angeles Times

The cold logic of punk: human beings alienated from their inherited social landscapes

English had ransacked their riches for two centuries, had spent like lords, and were now bankrupt, living in the ruins of their own grandiose excesses?

And, after departing the train:

By the time she had struggled along for a few hundred yards, in the stink of exhaust fumes, shuffling through litter, walled in by high elephantine walls, deafened and sickened, she was feeling extremely cross with both Len and, alas, by association, Anthony. So this was what people complained about when they complained about the ruination of city centers. How right they were. It was monstrous, inhuman, ludicrous. It was just as well that the country had gone bankrupt, that property development had collapsed . . .

And a little later:

She looked around her, back at the plastic-fronted station: to her right, on another traffic island, an isolated church reared up, abandoned, a strange relic, a survivor from another age, another world. Piety had left it there, but what congregation could now ever gather in it? How could it be approached? It seemed a meaningless and ironic gesture, to have left it there, solitary, anachronistic, a pointing finger of ignored reproach.

Drabble created a world that was nasty and honest and opportunistic and visionary and cruel and masochistic. In other words, it approximated the beautiful absurdity of the real world. At its best, so did punk.

[Lester Bangs, "Richard Hell: Death Means Never Having to Say You're Incomplete," in *Psychotic Reactions and Carburetor Dung*, ed. Greil Marcus, 1978; repr., New York: Vintage Books, 1988, p. 262; Margaret Drabble, *The Ice Age*, New York: Popular Library, 1977, pp. 188, 190, 191.]

# "I waste hours keeping my soul out of the cauldron"

**In 1962, the poet Anne Sexton wrote to her friend** Tillie Olson that "I waste hours keeping my soul out of the cauldron but near enough the edge to hear any important messages." Peter Laughner—who was ten years old when this letter was written—likewise tried to live like this, and the terrifying beauty of their art emerged when they, in fact, made it to the very edge. For both, the fact of the cauldron became impossible to ignore or reject. Anne Sexton died, a suicide, in 1974; Peter Laughner, by acute pancreatitis, in 1977.

> [Anne Sexton, letter to Tillie Olson, Spring 1962, in *Anne Sexton: A Self-Portrait in Letters*, ed. Linda Gray Sexton and Lois Ames, Boston: Houghton Mifflin, 1979, p. 139.]

## *I'm OK—You're OK*

**The title of this 1969 bestselling book,** by Thomas A. Harris, has become a joke, a cliché, a stand-in for all the new age, self-help programs that have come and gone.

In some ways, the title was symbolic of the soft side of the sixties: Confronted with dark and complex social and personal problems, one response might be to *tune in, turn off, and drop out,* and another might be to declare simply, exhaustedly, *I'm OK—you're OK.* By the mid-seventies, punk had rejected the serious sixties—and the hippies especially—and on the cover of their 1978 seven-inch that included the songs "Paranoid," "Hideous," and "You Drive Me Ape (You Big Gorilla)," the Dickies posed with one of the band members holding the book *I'm OK—You're OK.* He looks at the camera with his mouth open with surprise, as if caught reading something embarrassing. The Dickies wrote the song "I'm Ok, You're Ok" with lines like "I'm in love with Sqeeky Fraum / I'd like to take her to the prom . . ."

But buried in the book, in the very back, is a critique of what was then

**ARE YOU OK?**

It's probably the most important question you'll ever have to answer. Because right now—whether you're aware of it or not—all the relationships with the most important people in your life are strongly influenced by a combination of how you feel about yourself (OK or not OK) and what you think of them (again, OK or not OK).

I'M OK—YOU'RE OK is the product of Doctor Harris's pioneering efforts in the field of Transactional Analysis—efforts that have already revolutionized therapy procedures throughout the world. After helping countless numbers of people help themselves establish mature, healthy relationships, he has translated startling theories into easily-understood language and adapted key ingredients of successful behavior change into practical advice. The result is a remarkable book that has already helped millions of hardcover readers lead more effective lives.

#1 FOR MORE THAN A YEAR ON
BESTSELLER LISTS ALL OVER AMERICA!
OVER ONE MILLION HARDCOVER COPIES SOLD!

The back cover of *I'm OK–You're OK*: a cliché waiting to be destroyed the emerging counterculture. It is profound and offers an analysis of the "greatest generation" that spawned the hippies and that had fallen almost completely out of fashion. Rejecting the notion that the student protestors were simply affluent kids who didn't know how good they had it, Harris suggests that their alienation from mainstream society was a lesson they learned well from their parents of the World War II generation:

> The age range of undergraduate college students is eighteen to twenty-two. Many of the student protestors were born from 1943 to 1946, and their most formative years were spent either partly during wartime or in the years immediately after the war. These years were characterized by unstable family constellations, movement from place to place, absent if not dead fathers, anxious, weary, troubled mothers, and general social patterns which magnified the unrest in the home. Many young fathers, returning from battle, entered colleges and universities under the G.I. Bill and reflected soberly on the state of a world which had demanded so much of them. Their Purple Hearts and wounded spirits supported their verbal expressions of the hatred of war and devastation. They did not capitulate easily to dead institutions and old clichés about how the world should be.

Harris suggested that there was an unease and a deep-seated alienation that the "greatest generation" passed on to their children. Far from the sentimental sugar-coated portrayal of the "greatest generation" peddled today, *I'm OK—You're OK* and other such books recognized the tremendous darkness and dis-ease that lay just beneath the surface of the "normal" fifties. The hippies saw this contradiction as hypocrisy and rebelled, making music and art that tried to "break on through to the other side." By the time punk emerged in the mid-seventies it was clear that many of the things that lie on the "other side"—Charles Manson, reckless hedonism, various social "movements" that despite good intentions became increasingly rigid and orthodox—were worth mocking.

[Thomas A. Harris, *I'm OK—You're OK*, New York: Harper and Row, 1969: p. 287.]


## implied velocity

**A phrase used by Leonard Graves Phillips,** the lead singer and songwriter of the California punk group the Dickies. Looking back on the punk movement, he said, in an interview with Keith Brammer:

> A song like [Black Sabbath's 1970] "Paranoid" when I was fourteen years old, was a punk rock song to me. It embodied everything, almost, that a Ramones song embodied ten years later. It had this implied velocity, and it was incredibly simple. It really did have kind of an edge to it that I wanted to try to reintroduce.

And:

[Current punk's] very politically correct, it's extremely parochial, and it all sounds the same. When I first heard the Ramones, or the Damned, or even the Sex Pistols, there was an implied velocity and an implied edge to what they were doing. Very quickly, a lot of what I consider second-generation punk bands went into virtual velocity. Play it fast! Play it faster! It became very formula.

The implied velocity of punk from the mid-seventies—as opposed to the literal velocity that developed later, especially in the D.C. and California hardcore scenes—is inseparable from its era. Punk became explicit in the early 1980s as a delayed reckoning: The terrible violence of the sixties could not be answered by that generation. It would take the relatively affluent, spoiled, narcissistic children of the seventies—unmoored from the utopianism of the previous decade—to make explicit what was only implied in early punk.

[Keith Brammer, "Implied Velocity and Puppet Shows: The Dickies in the Millenium," www.thedickies.com.]

# j

## Jarmusch, Jim

**American director, born in Akron, Ohio, in 1953.** His first full-length film, *Permanent Vacation* (which he began work on while at film school at New York University), was released in 1984. Jarmusch moved to the East Village in 1976 and was inspired by the emerging underground and punk scene: "It influenced me a lot initially," he has said, because in the late "Seventies, starting in like '76 or so, there was a really important spirit, especially in the music scene . . . you didn't have to be a virtuoso musician to form a rock band. Instead, the spirit of the music was more important than any kind of technical expertise on the instrument, which of course was—in

editor ALAN BETROCK

writers TRIXIE A. BALM   KEN BARNES   ALAN BETROCK   JANIS CAFASSO   JOSEPH FLEURY   DEBORAH FROST   JIM JARMUSCH GARY KENTON   HOWARD KLEIN   CATHY NEMETH   KRIS NEEDS STEVEN MEISEL   LISA JANE PERSKY   AMOS POE   SUKEY PETT BOB SENNETT   ANNA SUI   GENE SCULATTI   CRAIG ZELLER

Film director Jim Jarmusch listed as writer for *New York Rocker*, May–June 1977

New York—first Patti Smith and Television, and then Heartbreakers, the Ramones, Mink de Ville, Blondie, Talking Heads—all those bands."

Jarmusch wrote occasionally for publications like *New York Rocker* where, in 1977, he contributed a lengthy interview with Crocus Behemoth (David Thomas) of Pere Ubu about a city they both loved, Cleveland, which Thomas compared to the underground sea in the movie version of *Journey to the Center of the Earth* (1959):

> Well, remember when they came out and there's that underground sea, and it just went on forever, and the horizon is grey stone and these huge waves and it's just cold and grey? I can picture Cleveland sitting at the edge of that underground sea. And like, I think the city's been here for a thousand years. And it's real strange, the way people in Cleveland react to it . . . they sneak into the city in the morning, and they do their job and they make sure they're out of here before it gets dark . . . This city at night is always real frightening. Not because of any danger or anything like that, but because it represents something so astounding and incredible that people are real scared of it. I mean, just look out in the Flats and it's just, there's no facades, no facades of culture or anything. None of that. It's just Midwest, and it's this incredibly immense thing . . . We really think we have reproduced what it feels like in downtown Cleveland. We're servants: we don't create, we transmit.

Jarmusch's films are slow and are not peppered with punk- or New Wave era-music: The connection between his work and punk isn't immediately obvious. But, like the Ramones' first album, there is a singleness, a purity, a simplicity to his movies that shares with punk the impulse against adornment. His characters live within themselves so fully that their environments—cities, cars, apartments—take on such personality that they themselves become characters.

[Jim Jarmusch interviewed by Peter Belsito in *Jim Jarmusch: Interviews*, ed. Ludvig Hertzberg, 1985; repr., Jackson: University Press of Mississippi, 2001, p. 27; Jim Jarmusch, "Out of Darkness with Pere Ubu," *New York Rocker* vol. 1, no. 7, May–June 1977, p. 36.]

## Jim Basnight and the Moberlys

**"Live in the Sun," from 1978,** is like something from Shaun Cassidy channeled through the Ramones, and it reminds you that the crisis provoked by punk—how to reconcile the simple beauty of Beatles-type melody with the acrid void of No Wave and hardcore—was never really resolved. For this reason, "Live in the Sun" is one of the most dangerous songs of the punk era, impossible to decipher. It is so poppy, so chirpy: "the preacher who walked the beach"—a line that crisscrosses Kurt Vonnegut and Robert Bly. I said that this was a dangerous song, and this is why: Listen to it and you will want to dance; and dancing you will come to realize you are dancing on a grave. There is something braver in this song than in anything by the arty, pretentious distance of the rawer bands like the Pagans and Pere Ubu. There is a person you are dying to dance to this song with: You imagine this person's arms around your neck, this person's face close to yours but never touching, this person watching you with eyes that are telling you more than words ever could, this person who will likely never read this entry and never know how close everything came to being different than it has turned out to be.

"I Want You" is so perfect you worry that if you listen to it more than three times you will love it no more, and so you are warned: If you buy this record as a result of these words, please try to find Ephraim P. Noble, who first told me about this record, to thank him.

The first time you heard it, you knew that this song would have an entry in this book, but you're not sure why. In the dark of the Michigan night, you can admit it: The song represents a path not taken.

For you, the tragedy of Jim Basnight and the Moberlys is that they even existed at all, to remind you that bliss is possible.


## Jungle Rot

**On a Post-it note attached to this CD** I had scrawled the words—apparently after listening to it once—"learn to like this album." The fact that I do indeed like it now is either testament to my own powers of self-brainwashing or to the power of the music. I'll cast my lot with the latter.

George Brigman would probably cringe to find himself in a big fat book on punk. Baltimore in the early to mid-seventies was as burnt out and desolate as Cleveland, Detroit, or any other number of American cities. "The Dundalk area of Baltimore where George grew up," Rick Noll has written, "was either referred to as a blue collar neighborhood or a symbol of Baltimore's urban blight, depending on who was doing the talking. The Dundalk streets gave precious little hope of escape and the jobs that existed weren't really at the top of the food chain. Unemployment, crime, booze, and drugs, especially PCP, were rampant in the Seventies, but what's a poor boy to do, except play in a rock and roll band? Having no band, George started writing songs and sold his first song at the age of sixteen." Although Brigman did not hear or hear about the mid-seventies Cleveland bands until later, there is one connection: Pere Ubu's album *Dub Housing* (1978) got its name, as Simon Reynolds notes, from a view of Baltimore as the band drove through the city in their tour van. "In Baltimore they had these row houses, and somebody said, 'Oh, look, dub housing,'" according to Scott Krauss.

*Jungle Rot*—released in 1975—was basically a one-man show, with Brigman teaching himself guitar and later bass and recording tracks during the 1973–74 period. They were mixed at RMT Studios in Dundalk, with Brigman's friends Jeff Barrett laying down some drum tracks and Ron Collier providing vocals on one song and harp and conga on others. There was a certain freedom in the chaos and decay of the city. "It was like you can tear down the city but I'll still be standing," Brigman has said. The album was recorded on the cusp of punk. "Like most things around here the punk movement in Baltimore was a few years behind the rest of the country. I had to teach myself most of these things since everyone thought I was crazy to think I could do my music the way I wanted it done." The result is a strange, beautiful album, like some species that has, beyond all possibility, survived long after it was written off as extinct. The voice, a little like Iggy Pop's, is really there to surf on the guitars, which provide an ocean of fuzz. It's an example of what David Thomas has referred to as the "third generation" of rock musicians that were just beginning to find their way when punk exploded and laid waste to everything. But there, before the explosion, in the Baltimore of the film director John Waters (who has said that punk "put the danger back in music"), is the weird, self-made music of George Brigman, impossibly skinny in those old pictures, making music against all odds in the ruins of America.

["You can tear down the city," Brigman e-mail to author, June 14, 2006; John Waters quoted in Geoffrey Himes, "John Waters's Love Songs, Suitably Bizarre," *The New York Times*, February 11, 2007; Rick Noll, "Beware the Jungle Rot!," liner notes to *Jungle Rot* CD, Bona Fide Records; Simon Reynolds, *Rip It Up and Start Again: Postpunk 1978–1984*, New York: Penguin, 2005, p. 75.]

---

**k**

---

# "Keep Your Dreams"
(by Ephraim P. Noble)

**A song by Suicide.** It puts an end to all distinctions between genres. For what is this song? Canonically, Suicide has become known as a punk band, whatever that means, and it means nothing. Of course they are not punk. The word itself is practically meaningless. This contradiction is one of the great, last beautiful things left in our overadministered society of instant experts and database charlatans. God, how I hate them. "Exterminate the brutes," a wise man once said. There is a mystery at the heart of the band Suicide that this song, more than any other, encapsulates. For the record: I am no apologist. I know little about this band save through their recorded music, recommended to me by a Constantine Demoupoliputus, whom I doubt is even a real person. For facts and gossip, please go elsewhere. I am an interpreter, sir or madam, not a chronicler of ephemera and useless details.

This song must be listened to at high volume several times. If you are not an alcoholic, please drink several beers, or white Russians or black ones or even Diet and Morgan's or Bushmills, or something else of your choice. White Russians are nice because they are the drink of choice by the Dude in *The Big Lebowski*, and he is a good man, I and many others have come to believe. Perhaps the last good man. After all, he goes to witness his landord's avant-garde performace . . . but no matter. There is a symmetry to this song that keeps you off balance. Is this a strange thing to say? Perhaps.

The song reminds you of one of those cheap toy organs you might have received as a Christmas present. You cannot quite determine why this song is art and not some pathetic noodling by an anxious adolescent. To be honest, the song sometimes makes you cry. For those you have lost, of course. But even more, for even those who you know you will lose.

## Kentucky Fried Movie

**An irreverent, scrappy movie from 1977** directed by John Landis, who would go on to direct *Animal House*, *The Blues Brothers*, *An American Werewolf in London*, and others. While Landis's subsequent work was more professional and coherent, *Kentucky Fried Movie* is his most absurdly alive and anarchic. Composed entirely of short sketches, the movie is sort of a deformed mutant mixture of Monty Python, *Saturday Night Live*, *National Lampoon*, and tasteless homemade movies that kids might make in their garages and backyards.

While some critics dismissed the movie as adolescent tripe (which it was, but still) like Lawrence Van Gelder who, in *The New York Times* (of course!), wrote that "anyone interested in the condition of humor and wit in the United States stands likely to come away depressed" and that the movie seems "twice as long" as its eighty-six-minute running time, others detected the same DIY strain in *Kentucky Fried Movie* as was in punk rock. Under the headline PUNK ROCK OF FILM INDUSTRY, William E. Knoedelseder, Jr., wrote that the "comedy-sketch movie may be the punk rock of the motion picture industry . . . According to its creators, Jim Abrahams and Jerry and David Zucker, *Kentucky Fried* is a film by and for minds weaned on situation comedy, deodorant commercials, movie matinees, and nightly news. Theater for children of the video age."

The movie unfolds in short segments—over twenty in all, some as short as a few seconds—not unlike an album. In terms of race, sex, disability, and politics, the movie pokes fun at many of the sacred cows of the hippie era, a reminder that the rebellion of the counterculture had, by the mid-seventies, turned into a nightmare orthodoxy that was ripe for attacking. Here is the opening to one sketch, a fake commercial for a new board game, showing a white-bread family sitting around playing:

> New from Parker Brothers, a game for the entire family: "Scott Free." Your team has just assassinated the president. Can you get away scott free? Shake the dice and see. Great! You've found a patsy! Go again. Bonus card! You get Jack Ruby to kill your patsy. That's good because dead men don't talk. Oh no! Abraham Zapruder has filmed the assassination. Tough break, but now you go again. And a stroke of luck: twenty-two material witnesses die of natural causes.

The Dead Kennedys were formed a year latter, in the summer of 1978. There is no connection.

> [William K. Knoedelseder, Jr., "Punk Rock of Film Industry," *Los Angeles Times*, July 28, 1977, p. G16; Lawrence Van Gelder, "Kentucky Fried a Yolky Film," *The New York Times*, August 11, 1977.]

## "kids will go to New York, and you know what that means"

**A sentence in a 1955 *New York Times* article** about the emerging rock and roll phenomenon, entitled "Bridgeport Ban Stops the Music: 'Rock 'n Roll' Teen Dances." The headline refers to the banning by the police superintendant John A. Lyddy (not John Lydon) of such dance parties in Bridgeport, Connecticut. The article profiles William E. Kelsey, Jr., a businessman and organizer of rock and roll parties, as well as the director of the Bridgeport Teen Club. "Clear through from here to Stamford the problem exists," he noted. "The kids will go to New York, and you know what that means. I've always tried to let them all in, good and bad. The police tell me the bad ones must be kept out, so we are going to issue identification cards hereafter to let the good ones in."

> ["Bridgeport Ban Stops the Music: Halts 'Rock 'n Roll' Teen Dances," *The New York Times*, March 26, 1955, p. 17.]

# "L.A. Punk"

**A 1981 article by Mick Farren** of the sort that is rare today—rare because it took a skeptical, lengthy, critical look at a musical trend in a way that was not snarky or dismissive, but serious. Appearing in *New Musical Express*, Farren's essay suggests that the hardcore L.A. punk of bands like Black Flag, Circle Jerks, and Fear is a fulfillment of the harsh minimalism of Ronald Reagan; a violent purging of the excesses of the soft seventies. "Something nasty is lurking on the fringes of Reaganland. The children of this polluted capitalist utopia are being dragged by a grim, black anger into the nihilist world of Darby Crash. They are being infected with an inarticulate rage against everything that has been sold to them as good and desirable since the time they could crawl." A far cry from today's hero worship.

Farren's critique was serious because what he saw and heard around him was serious. Jettisoning the humor and absurd self-deprecation of the seventies punk scenes, hardcore had more in common with the austere, swaggering machismo of the Reagan era than it could ever admit. The brutal police tactics against so many of the L.A. punks were, in fact, central to their identity and myth. They needed the cops, whose violent response to the violence of the concerts reaffirmed the importance of violence to the whole scene. Rather than the enemy, the cops were unwitting promoters of the scene, conveying on it an importance that gave it mythic status.

But what about the kids? As Farren noted:

These are the children of the best that capitalism can offer. They come from the solid upper middle class suburbs of L.A., Mirada, Anaheim, Newport Beach, Huntington Beach and Fullerton. With their pools and their manicured lawns, their three car garages and Mexican gardens, these places are the strongholds of the American dream. It's the world of *The Graduate* and Mrs. Robinson. It's these people who have invested their votes and, in some cases, even their money to make sure that Reagan and his right wing new deal will protect and preserve this lotusland from the pressures of change. Somewhere along the way, though, something went wrong with the next generation. They want nothing more than to throw it all away, to trash and burn it.

But did this generation ever really become a "generation" in the same way that the Who's "my generation" did? Was the punk movement a part of a widespread cultural movement, or a more limited subcultural one? The raging discontent expressed in California hardcore is important not just because of the enduring, complex body of music and style it produced, but because its "youth revolution" never really coalesced into meaning. Why? Because it occurred at the dawn of the digital age, when the speed at which dangerous and radical ideas are absorbed into the cultural mainstream is so rapid that they have no time to ferment into something of real social consequence. In this regard, the hippies—ironically—were the last subcultural group to really threaten, in a meaningful way, the status quo. They had time to grow, quietly and over many years, testing out their ideas and their aesthetics in poetry and in music. Punk, in contrast, emerged in a time of greater speed: Its ideas were quickly dispersed, commodified, and ultimately recycled back into the mainstream in less threatening forms.

[Mick Farren, "L.A. Punk," *New Musical Express*, April 11, 1981.]

## La Guardia, Fiorello Henry

**The mayor of New York City** from 1934 through 1945. In *The New York Times* in 1936 there appeared this cryptic headline: "PUNK" THE MAYOR'S WORD; MAN WHO USED IT FREED. The brief article is even stranger:

> Mayor La Guardia has a "copyright" on the word "punk," Magistrate Rudich declared in Pennsylvania Avenue Court, Brooklyn, yesterday in dismissing a charge of disorderly conduct against Cecil Cohen, 35 years old, of 257A Tompkins Avenue. Cohen was arrested on the complaint of Mrs. Margaret Boiselle of 655 Lafayette Avenue, who said he called her a "punk" during an argument.
>
> Explaining he was dismissing the charge because he could not learn the correct definition of the word "punk" as used by the defendant, Magistrate Rudich added: "Our Mayor has a copyright on that word and uses it on many occasions. But I have not been able to learn other than the dictionary definition of the word, which describes 'punk' as the stem of a plant that burns slowly."

Forty years later—and about ten miles away from the courtroom where this decision about the meaning of the term punk was reached—a different kind of punk would be gaining national notoriety at a place called CBGB.

["'Punk' the Mayor's Word; Man Who Used It Freed," *The New York Times*, July 26, 1936, p. 6.]

## *Ladies and Gentlemen the Fabulous Stains*

**A terrifically punk film,** so overloaded with contradictions that it's like watching someone trying to walk with two broken legs and a missing foot. Filmed in 1980 and released in 1981, the film stars Laura Dern (in some scenes it looks like she's

MELODY MAKER, September 25, 1976—Page 3

# Caroline Coon reviews the new singles

## Runaways sexplode in glory

"THE ONLY thing girls are good for is going out shopping for glue," wrote the redoubtable Mark P in the first issue (the third is imminent) of his photocopied punk-rock fanzine, Sniffin' Glue.

He was reviewing The Runaways' debut album. But after this up-front chauvinist wise-crack he overcame (just about) his prejudice against women Rock 'n' Rollers. "Great stuff" was his final verdict.

Mark, 19 from Deptford, is one of the growing band of youths who, no longer apathetically grumbling about the State of Rock, is actively changing the scene.

A confident opinionator (Can and 'The Mothers of Invention are his all-time favourites), I wondered what he'd make of this week's singles — especially since he rates the Bay City Rollers new album "Dedication" (Bell) at the top of his list of this year's greats. Agreed.

The Runaways: "Cherry Bomb" (Mercury). "The lyrics are the kind I like from girls," he began. "They sound as if they will explode all over you and I can see girls I know singing them.

"I like the idea of girl bands but the Run-

Caroline Coon: punk chronicler and consultant to *Ladies and Gentlemen the Fabulous Stains*

warming up for *Blue Velvet*), Diane Lane, and Ray Winstone, as well as the ex–Sex Pistols Paul Cook and Steve Jones and the Clash bassist Paul Simonon. The early punk chronicler Caroline Coon—whose columns in *Melody Maker* and whose 1977 book, *The New Wave Punk Rock Explosion*, were among the first to explore punk critically—served as a special consultant for the film, helping to shape the look of the band. The film's writer, Nancy Dowd, has said that the New York punk scene inspired her: "I was so riveted when I saw the Ramones. You have to remember that during the seventies everything in terms of music was *junk*."

The movie's plot—concerning an all-female, pre–riot grrrl band that experiences the love and hate of audiences on their rise to fame—is less interesting than its individual scenes, which work as awkwardly blocked set pieces that teeter on collapse. After a concert, Corinne Burns (Diane Lane) and the Looters' manager, Dave Robell (David Clennon), have this Beckett-like exchange:

**Robell:** All those little girls back there, they're gonna be out here, in the stores, tomorrow morning, looking for your records.

**Corinne:** What records?

**Robell:** There are no records, are there? Right? There should be. In a week, five days, your next gig, I'm gonna show you the meaning of promotion. I'm gonna make people aware of you.

*Stains* juggles at least four related musical styles: punk (although it's already a form of nostalgia as performed by the Looters), glam metal (the movie means this to be a parody: the band is the Metal Corpses, whose lead singer is the Tubess' Fee Waybill); reggae (half formed in the movie, but there nonetheless), and New Wave/post-punk (as embodied in the Stains). It should be obvious that the movie "promotes" the Stains' genre as the most authentic, genuine of these styles, but it's not. For one thing, to its credit, the movie's tone is so uneven as to disrupt any clear identification with any one character or band. At one point, Robell tells Corinne, "What you were was a concept and you've blown the concept," which might just as easily be a commentary on the movie itself, especially when considering the ending.

The ending. At some point, it became clear that Paramount—which had hosted a disastrous pre-screening of the movie in Denver, Colorado—was not pleased with the film. Adler and others struggled with editing for a year. A new ending was shot, so upbeat and Go-Gos–like, so much a disavowel of the film's bleak message, that it almost appears to be ironic. MTV-like, the video shows the lip-synching girls in a kaliedescope of absurd out-of-context situations (pushing each other into a swimming pool, dressed in World War II uniforms dancing, driving a Jeep around, on the cover of *Rolling Stone*, etc.) singing "The Professional" (by Cook and Jones), whose lyrics go, "Join the professionals / be a professional / you're gonna be one anyway." Taken from one angle, the film's ending is a copout (A *swindle?*), an example of a commodity becoming the very thing it stands against. But from another angle, the "happy" ending is a gleeful, spit-in-your-face acknowledgment that it's what you wanted "anyway." Taken in this light, what's surprising is not that the band (and the movie) finally give in to pure pop sensibilities, but that it took them so long to come around.

[Nancy Dowd, "Behind the Movie," http://fabulousstains.com/behindmovie.html.]

# Leon, Craig

**A record producer whose work on early albums** by the Ramones, Blondie, Suicide, and others helped shape and define the sound of recorded punk in the mid-seventies. "In the Seventies I had a sense of pop music being quite ephemeral but still reflecting the spirit of the time and place it came from," Leon has said. "Kind of like the broadside sheets of older times. In fact this 'folk' communicative process was the primary criterion for any album to be recorded in my thinking at that time." It's easy now to overlook just how close, historically, the early punk movement was to the 1960s. The Ramones were performing their first shows less than a decade after Dylan went electric, and five years after Altamont. "When you'd go [into the studio], you'd have people that were still unaccustomed to live, loud music. They were still trying to dampen things down, even in 1973 and 1974," says Leon.

Leon's use of the word "folk" to describe his sense of music and recording during the punk era is disarming and radically truthful. Simon Frith describes folk like this: "'Folk' culture is thus created directly and spontaneously out of communal experience . . . There is no distance between folk artist and audience, no separation between folk production and consumption." Leon's greatest work from the punk era was with the Ramones and Suicide. In different ways, he achieved a separation of sound on both albums that allowed the music to reveal the conditions of its production. And so the songs are never just about the songs, but also about how they were made.

[Simon Frith, *Sound Effects: Youth, Leisure, and the Politics of Rock 'n' Roll*, New York: Pantheon, 1981, p. 48; Craig Leon, "In the Seventies," e-mail to author, May 27, 2004; Howard Massey interviewed by Craig Leon, www.craigleon.com.]

## Lofgren, Nils

**Born in Chicago, Illinois, in 1951.** Lofgren played piano, with understated beauty, on Neil Young's *After the Gold Rush*. As an illustration of just how flexible the term "punk" was before the first album by the Ramones (released in April 1976), consider this sentence from the 1975 *Creem* review of Lofgren's album *Nils Lofgren*: "And the vocals are as perfect rock 'n' roll punk as ever." Lest you damn the writer for that line, consider this one, from a little bit later in the review: "Most notably, he is not willing to write more tired hump tunes."

And that, as they say, is that.

[Mark Jenkins, review of Nils Lofgren, *Nils Lofgren*, *Creem*, June 1975, p. 66.]

## Lowell, Robert

**An American poet, born in 1917** and died in a taxi cab in New York City in 1977. He is known as a "confessionalist" poet, although this term seems pejorative today. It wasn't that Lowell confessed in his poems, but rather that his poems invited you into a world where his words became your confession.

In April 1976, the month that the Ramones' first album was released, Lowell wrote in a letter to Elizabeth Bishop that "New York is weird now, or so it seemed coming from the calm of Kent or even London. America and England are mirages and happy islands to each other, both an escape from prices." Lowell never mentions punk, yet the conditions that produced it are everywhere in his letters. In 1974, Anne Sexton—who along with Sylvia Plath took Lowell's graduate writing workshop in 1958 at Boston University—wrote in a letter to Erica Jong that "I never get down to New York (if I can help it)."

In 1959, Lowell published *Life Studies*, one of the major books of his career. In that collection there is a poem, "Memories of West Street and Lepke," that has these lines: "These are the tranquilized *Fifties* / and I am forty," which in its awareness of its time and place is as damning as Joan Didion's essay "Slouching Towards Bethlehem" (1967) and Lester Bangs's "The White Noise Supremacists" (1979). Lowell identified the fifties as *tranquilized*; punks identified the seventies as *nothing*. Both were painfully aware of the hand they had been dealt, and converted that knowledge into furious beauty.

There is a noise beneath the order of Lowell's poems and letters that, like punk, served as a warning. In another letter, also from April 1976, Lowell wrote that after "our exciting whirl through New York, we [Caroline Blackwood and Lowell] both feel it is too fast and fallen for us."

[Robert Lowell, *The Letters of Robert Lowell*, ed. Saskia Hamilton, New York: Farrar, Straus and Giroux, 2005: pp. 648, 649; Anne Sexton, letter to Erica Jong, June 1974, in *Anne Sexton: A Self-Portrait in Letters*, ed. Linda Gray Sexton and Lois Ames, Boston: Houghton Mifflin, 1979, p. 414.]

## m

## *Mad* magazine, punk and

**First there is the connection** between *Mad* magazine and *Punk* magazine, founded by John Holmstrom and Legs McNeil.

This entry is not about that but about *Mad*'s parody of a punk concert, which appeared in their June 1978 issue, "*Mad*'s 'Punk Rock Group' of the Year" (written by Larry Siegel and drawn by Harry North). There are some great exchanges between the hosts of the concert, Anita Tyrant (based on conservative crusader Anita Bryant) and Bernie Rakeoff:

> **Bernie:** Anita, meet a really swell bunch of guys! "JOHNNY TURD AND THE COMMODES"!!
>
> **Anita:** I'm going to throw up!
>
> **Bernie:** So are they!! But they're saving that for the big concert!

And:

> **Punk Band (performing):** Oh, man, the world is garbage / and life is full of crap / The United Nations has got the clap! / Down with charity / and

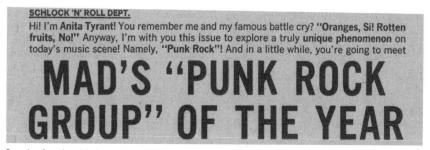

SCHLOCK 'N' ROLL DEPT.

Hi! I'm **Anita Tyrant**! You remember me and my famous battle cry? **"Oranges, Si! Rotten fruits, No!"** Anyway, I'm with you this issue to explore a truly **unique phenomenon** on today's music scene! Namely, **"Punk Rock"**! And in a little while, you're going to meet

# MAD'S "PUNK ROCK GROUP" OF THE YEAR

Parody of punk in *Mad* magazine, 1978

down with laws! / Down with everything / and up, up yours! / Up, up yours, bay—bee / up, up yours / Down with everything— / and up yours! / Yeeaaaaaahhh!

**Anita:** Good Heavens! What do they call THAT?!?

**Bernie:** "The Bluebird of Happiness"

When I was sick, my father or mother would buy me a copy of *Mad* at the local drugstore and bring it home to me to read in bed. It was in the fourth grade, I think, that I caught mono and—miraculously!—missed four entire weeks. I remember the winter sunlight moving across my shag floor, day after day. A cousin of mine, a few years older than me, gave me a whole pile of his *Mad*s, dating back to the mid-sixties. I'll never forget the "Crockwork Orange" cover, with Alfred E. Newman decked out like one of the violent youth thugs in Kubrick's terrible movie.

There was a spirit to *Mad* as anarchic as anything by the Sex Pistols or the Dead Boys. No authority was safe, not even the writers of *Mad* themselves. *Mad* seemed to me the only place that acknowledged so fully that the world was absurd, and that one response to that absurdity was laughter. For a kid whose heart melted every time a girl looked at him, and who almost literally perished the first time a girl kissed him, the fact that in *Mad*'s pages the playing field was leveled was a small miracle. So, when I first heard punk (the Ramones) and I first saw those skinny and yet strangely macho guys on the cover of their 1976 debut album, I immediately recognized that punk was already something that I was familiar with, even though I had never heard it before.

# Marbles

**Coming on a like a cross between** the Monkees at their euphoric best, Television, Peter Laughner had he been sunnier, and the Dictators, the Marbles made perfect sense for a world that never materialized. Formed in 1974, the band consisted of David and Howard Bowler, Eric Li, and Jim Clifford. According to David Bowler they were "auditioned" by Television's Richard Lloyd, who saw them play at Columbia University. They played many times at CBGB, headlining with bands like Ramones, Blondie, and Talking Heads. More than any New York City mid-seventies punk-era band, the Marbles illustrate the path not taken by punk, which depended upon a radical narrowing and refinement of its primal sound for its coherence as musical movement. "We were actually closest to Blondie in our pop sensibilities," Bowler says. "And the Ramones. I think that's why Alan Betrock managed both Blondie and us. He was a big 60's pop music fan." The messy truth is, there was no coherent sound at the beginning, and that's why you've likely never heard any songs by Marbles.

About halfway through the remarkable song "Red Lights"—their first single—everything slows down: "I would sell my mother / for a chance to play guitar in his band / we're still playing all the old songs / in the garage / but it's just a mirage." A new musical vista opens up in these fifteen seconds and then closes just as fast, and you are left to wonder if what you just heard was an accident or a sound that was just too good to survive. Because, and you know this in the secret recesses of your heart, nothing good can last. Recalling the early CBGB scene, Bowler says that "there was no ego yet. As soon as the suits arrived, it changed and went downhill from there. The scene became no longer ours. Careers were being formed and destroyed." "Red Lights" is the sort of song that could convert evil people into good, wife beaters into wife lovers, cynics into optimists, slave owners into abolitionists, sweatshop owners into labor rights activists, demons into angels, obsessive writers of massive books into normal people who exercise and laugh easily.

"Free World" begins with a just-before-the-execution snare drum, and then Spanish guitars, and then quiet, and then snippets of lyrics like "I know inside I'm something more than I'm supposed to be / I feel outside there's something more than is told to me."

"She's Cool" is more in keeping with the sound of the punk / New Wave scene and hints at an alternative future for the Marbles. Plus, it has lyrics that for a boy at a certain age are more prophetically true than any words from Holy Books: "She's just about having sex / can't you see the reason why my mind is vexed?"

"Fire and Smoke" is cinematic: You can imagine a long take lasting the whole song, the camera moving down a seventies Lower East Side street, following lovers trying to forget.

In a 1977 issue of *New York Rocker*, Alan Betrock wrote this of the Marbles: "One of the last living NY bands, Marbles' strength lies in their musicianship and handful of originals, but they unfortunately lack a lead singer or frontman to carry it off. If a change in direction is not forthcoming soon, this band may shortly exist only as a pleasant memory."

[Alan Betrock, "The Top 40," *New York Rocker*, February–March 1977, p. 44; David Bowler, "The scene became no longer ours," e-mail to author, June 9, 2007.]

## "Maybe the present decade . . ."

**In 1975, in an early overview** of the emerging New York underground music scene in *New Musical Express*, Charles Shaar Murray wrote, "Maybe the present decade is less of a specific area in its own right than simply a viewpoint from which to reassess the 'Fifties and 'Sixties." It's strange that punk—which has been defined so often as being an outright rejection of the sixties—was, early on, often imagined as a remix of sixties musical styles through seventies tastes.

[Charles Shaar Murray, "The Sound of '75?," *New Musical Express*, November 8, 1975, p. 6.]

## "The Menace and Charm of Punk-Rock"

**An article by the music critic Robert Hilburn that** appeared in 1976 in the *Los Angeles Times*. In it Hilburn wrote that the Ramones were "the final extension of the punk-rock movement; a band whose flashy, pugnacious stance pushes rock 'n' roll conventions to the point of anarchy." Later, he wondered about the durability of punk: "Its biggest problem, however, may prove to be its attempt to use a single rock emotion (the rebellion, defiance and punk-rock sensitivity to a song like the Stones' 'Satisfaction') and build a whole career around it." The Ramones were indeed the final extension of punk's first phase; California hardcore would pick up the signal and transform it into something darker and more literally violent.

[Robert Hilburn, "The Menace and Charm of Punk-Rock," *Los Angeles Times*, August 1, 1976, p. K72.]

## Milk 'n' Cookies

**Could a band with a name like this ever have made it?** Formed in 1973, Justin Strauss, Ian Horth, Sal Maida, and Mike Ruiz created music that slipped between categories. It wasn't quite glam, punk, pure pop, or heavy metal (before it became heavy metal) and yet it was all of those things. "We're middle class sure," Maida told Max Bell in *New Musical Review*. "Our music, lyrics, and whole image is innocence, but with a knowing behind it." Opening up at CBGB for bands like the Ramones, Milk 'n' Cookies clearly chose against emerging trends. And yet, the relative obscurity of the band makes discovering them for the first time akin to finding a fossil: There, in all its preserved glory, is a path not taken in the underground New York music scene. Writing prior to the release of their one and only LP, Linda Danna described them this way: "A band called Milk and Cookies were born as a healthy antidote to the then prevalent 'decadence' of New York's glitter scene. Their self-appointed task was to be young and adorable—something the kids could fall in love with."

Does it matter that their two best songs were unreleased? The soaring "Typically Teenage" was a demo track recorded in 1976. "Are you one of those kids on a Saturday night?" the song asks, and you can't tell if the song invokes matinees and malt shops out of nostalgia or mockery. Either way, there is a confidence on this song that's absent on many of their others. "Tinkertoy Tomorrow," recorded in 1975 and intended as a second single but never released, is almost as good. "Push your plastic button / everything's for certain." As with the best Milk 'n' Cookies songs, it's impossible to tell if that line is sung from within the teenage world or against it, in recrimination.

[Max Bell, "Milk 'n' Cookies: Sweetness & Light with Milk & Cookies," *New Musical Review*, March 8, 1975; Linda Danna, "N.Y. Notes: Milk 'n' Cookies," *Trouser Press*, February–March 1976, p. 22.]

# Minimalism

In an interview from 2005, John Holmstrom, who cofounded *Punk* magazine and whose impact on the look and feel of punk was important, said that "one cultural influence [on punk] that's been forgotten is Seventies minimalism. There was a concerted effort by bands like Suicide, Ramones and Talking Heads to follow the aesthetic that 'less is more' and to strip music down to its core . . . After all, most of the bands at CBGBs' had gone to art school or were aware of the art scene of the time."

The Ramones were the consummate minimalist American band; Wire the consummate minimalist U.K. band. In the United States, at least, the Ramones' sound—fast and simple and unadorned—was in direct opposition to the cultural and political excesses of the time, the free and easy swinging seventies, marked by the full retreat of post-Watergate conservatism. Minimalism is usually associated with "art"—painting, sculpture, photography, music, and writing (Raymond Carver despised the tag). What unifies these forms is their disavowel of "depth." In minimalism, the object and the idea are one and the same. Minimalist artists, according to Kenneth Baker, strive to "make us 'see the whole idea without any confusion,' by seeing the object as the idea, that is, making meaning identical with the object's physical presence." Of course, discovering punk for the first time, as a child, you never thought about whether it was minimalist or not. All you knew was that you loved it, and you wanted more. Why did you love it? Why did you want more? Because it said so much with so little. Now, many years later, you are writing this book about something you loved uncritically as a kid, and you are torn. There is a part of you that is still just a kid, putting the Ramones on the turntable for the first time while your girlfriend is in the other room; in fact, it is her bedroom, it is her album. That moment of first hearing. Well, it is a revelation, a secret code revealed.

In Don DeLillo's strangest novel, *Great Jones Street* (1973), a member of the radical guerilla group the Happy Valley Farm Commune says this to the rock star Bucky Wunderlick, who has deliberately withdrawn and dropped off the public radar: "You've always been one step ahead of the times and this is the biggest step of all. Demythologizing yourself. Keeping covered. Putting up walls. Stripping off fantasy and legend. Reducing yourself to minimums." In retrospect, it seems natural that punk's minimalism was a reaction to late-sixties and early-seventies excess, but it was really part of a larger movement—in art, film, and the avant-garde in general—to reject excess not just in terms of style but in terms of meaning. Legends operate in a funny way: The more you know about them, the less you see them as legends. The mystique evaporates. By the mid-seventies, with the expansion of television into ever more homes, and with more channels offered via cable, and with the emergence of home-taping systems and the "time-shifting" viewing habits they made possible, it became increasingly difficult for legends to exist for long in pop culture. If, for instance, in the 1930s and 1940s Hollywood tightly controlled the public image of its stars (who were "owned" by specific studios), by the sixties and seventies, after the collapse of the studio system, stars became free agents. Available to the public on their own terms, they sacrificed the mystique and aura that surrounded them when they were periodically withdrawn from the public sphere and made purposefully scarce by the studios.

So what to do in an era such as the seventies, when the expansion of media into everyday, private life (television, Betamax and VHS, the Walkman, etc.) threatens to reduce any star—movie, television, or music—into a parody of stardom? People like Bob Dylan had one solution: periodically withdraw yourself from public life, thereby increasing the value of your legend status. "Your power is growing, Bucky," a character in *Great Jones Street* says. "The more time you spend in isolation, the more demands are made on the various media to communicate some relevant words and pictures . . . The less you say, the more you are." This is one sort of minimalism. But it is not the minimalism of punk, which stripped away the veneer of stardom even further. Rather than abundance, punk celebrated reduction. Much has been said and written over the years about the amateurism of punk, but it wasn't a case of musicians deliberately trying to sing or play their instruments poorly, but rather, because so many of them were amateurs, they did not have to unlearn anything. In this respect, minimalism in punk was a condition of necessity, not choice. This separates punk minimalism from the minimalism more often associated with the art world or the art-music world where many of the minimalist composers, painters, sculptors, and architects were formally trained in "classical" traditions and were talented practitioners. For instance, Philip Glass studied at the Peabody Conservatory of Music and at Julliard; for him and many others, minimalism had very little to do with amateurism. As Robert Fink has noted, "Glass in particular began as the ultimate musical insider, a gray-flannel composer whose well-mannered style and Julliard connections got him fellowships, publications, and the BMI Young Composer of the Year Award in 1960."

Punk, with very few exceptions, did not need to first learn "the tradition" before breaking it. Its primary strategy—to convert limits into possibilities—was less a self-conscious choice than a gesture of fact.

[Kenneth Baker, *Minimalism: Art of Circumstance*, New York: Abbeville Press, 1988, p. 39; Don DeLillo, *Great Jones Street*, 1973; repr., New York: Viking, 1994, pp. 194, 128; Robert Fink, *Repeating Ourselves: American Minimal Music as Cultural Practice*, Berkeley: University of California Press, 2005, p. 69.]

## "Mistakism"

**A term used by the director Harmony Korine** to describe a method of filmmaking that allows for errors and mistakes. It is a descendant of the French New Wave, but also of punk-era cinema. Here is an exchange between the editors of the fanzine *Damage* and the filmmaker Nick Zodiak:

> **Damage:** There's a real fear of making mistakes. That was broken through in music a while back when people could start learning how to play in front of an audience . . .
>
> **Zodiak:** They're so scared of making mistakes and they're so scared of being too ambitious. This is the case in all forms of expression—we're inundated by professionalism . . . It's a means to prevent people from expressing themselves.

["They Eat," *Damage* vol. 1. no. 5, 1980, p. 35.]

## Mo-dettess

**The Mo-dettes made the most beautiful music** from the shards of punk, which probably accounts for why they are so little known. Formed near the beginning of 1979 in London as the Bomberettes, they consisted of Ramona Carlier, Kate Korus, June Miles-Kingston, and Jane Crockford. "White Mice," from 1979, spirals into melody so completely sincerely that you almost ignore the tone of the lyrics: "Smile so sweetly, so completely / Girls in every way / A smile like yours should be on show." Their cover of "Paint It Black" is groovy, thumping, with just the proper tinge of reggae to suggest a double meaning for the term "black." "Dark Park Creeping"

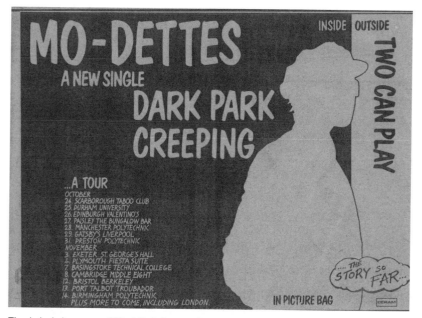

The dark, dark menace of "Dark Park Creeping"

(which was, according to Kate Korus, "a late night song. After you've been down to the pub you've got nothing to do and nobody to talk to, you go and have a fight.") has such a dark, dark, menacing, strong undercurrent. But their best is the overlooked "Foolish Girl," whose first line, "She was once a feminist," sets the tone of the rest of the shaky, dreamy vibe of the song, which knocks back and forth between seduction and rejection.

They were the subject of a less-than-enthusiastic profile in *New Musical Express* in 1980 during their U.S. tour: "The Mo-dettes's music seemed safe, took few risks," wrote Richard Grabel. "The new pop has developed its own mainstream, and the Mo-dettes are firmly in it." In retrospect, their music is closer to the soft comfort of late Go-Go's rather than the brash recklessness of the Slits. And this was their greatness, really, to understand that punk had already self-extinguished, leaving in its wake something called hardcore, which bore about as much relation to punk as disco did to jazz. Which is to say: The Mo-dettes dared to be melodic and sweet at the beginning of a harsh new decade.

On October 28, 1980, the Mo-dettes played at Manchester Polytechnic. That same evening, in the United States, President Jimmy Carter debated Ronald Reagan in Cleveland, Ohio, just a week before the general election. Carter further doomed himself at several points throughout the debate, as in his response to this question: "And would it be an act of leadership to tell the American people they are going to have to sacrifice to adopt a leaner lifestyle for some time to come?" Carter: "Yes. We have demanded that the American people sacrifice, and they have done very well." Contrast this to Reagan's response, in which he said, in part:

> Since then [1980], he [Carter] has blamed the Federal Reserve System, he had blamed the lack of productivity of the American people, he has then accused the people of living too well and that we must share in scarcity, we must sacrifice and get used to doing with less. We don't have inflation because the people are living too well. We have inflation because the Government is living too well.

["The Carter-Reagan Presidential Debate," October 28, 1980, www.debates.org/pages/trans80b_p.html; Richard Grabel, "The Mo-dettes Don't Quite Crack the States," *New Musical Express*, October 18, 1980, p. 25; Kate Korus interviewed by Kris Needs, "The Mo-Dettes," *ZigZag*, December 1979.]

## "Most absurd year in the history of rock 'n' roll, the"

**Here is the full opening sentence** from an article by Greg Shaw in the December 1975 issue of *Phonograph Record*: "I predict that 1976 will be the most absurd year in the history of rock & roll." Shaw's article—"1976: Rock 'n' Roll in the Year of the Hetero-Centennial"—is part satire and part serious prediction. As with the best rock criticism from the era, it manages to go beyond the confines of its genre. "While all this is going on," Shaw writes, "there will be a new underground cult

Greg Shaw's sly prediction of punk

gaining popularity across the land. Ironically (if irony still means anything in the world of pop, which I strongly doubt), this new underground phenomenon will be a fanatical revival of the most popular, commercial music of the last decade, the teenage rock of 1964–66 that the very first generation of 'underground' aficionados was rebelling against."

[Greg Shaw, "1976: Rock 'n' Roll in the Year of the Hetero-Centennial," *Phonograph Record*, December 1975, p. 30.]

# MTV (and "Dancing with Myself")

**MTV launched in August 1981,** just five years after punk broke. And yet, those early MTV years seem far, far away from punk. The smiling VJs, the looming sense that what you are seeing is promotion as careful, scripted, and empty as some five-year plan drafted long after five-year plans have gone out of fashion. Greil Marcus's just pronouncement in 1987 still rings true today: "For every new art form there's someone to come along and pronounce it dead, but rarely has an art form been born dead—as is the case with rock video, and its major outlet, MTV."

MTV may have been dead by 1987, but in the early years it was, as Simon Reynolds notes, "a curious animal, almost inadvertently radical," with videos by the likes of Devo, Boomtown Rats, the Pretenders, Blondie, Talking Heads, and others. Strangely, punk cast a far darker shadow than any of these groups from an unlikely and critically neglected presence: Billy Idol.

Billy Idol stares down innocence in *New Musical Express,* October 1980

Young viewers who were just coming of musical age in the early 1980s might be forgiven for not knowing that Idol had been the singer in Generation X, one of the early English punk bands, formed in 1976, and that "Dancing with Myself" was one of their songs (as Gen X), released in 1980. Idol later covered the song and made it, and himself, famous. Tobe Hooper directed the video.

Hooper's 1974 film *The Texas Chainsaw Massacre*—itself a low-budget, DIY production as subversive as any so-called punk movie, and a lot less self-serious—had inspired "Chain Saw" from the Ramones' debut album in 1976. Was Hooper chosen to direct "Dancing with Myself"—a sort of pop/heavy metal/club version of punk—because *Massacre* had inspired a song on a seminal punk album? Probably not, but in the secret logic of how these things work, it makes sense. Hooper's video was really honest and really sick, if you thought about it. A rock star (an idol) who looks like the idea of what a punk should look like (the blond spiked hair, as pale as death or Sid Vicious at the final Sex Pistols concert at the Winterland in 1978, the snarl, the leather) sends off electrical charges or something that knock back his mad-craved fans before they get too close. But, fan-zombies that they are, they keep coming, like a herd of animals.

[Greil Marcus, "Born Dead," *In the Fascist Bathroom: Punk in Pop Music, 1977–1982*, 1987; repr., Cambridge: Harvard University Press, 1993, p. 345; Simon Reynolds, *Rip It Up and Start Again: Postpunk 1978–1984*, New York: Penguin, p. 338; Dick Tracy, "More T.V. Rock," *New Musical Express*, February 21, 1976, p. 9.]

## "Music is primal, mindless, without climaxes"

**A line in a very early review of the Ramones at CBGB.** Actually, it was a review of Savage Voodoo Nuns, which veered into a review of the Ramones. "The band is a quartet of young kids who play at being hard-ass leather rockers . . . None of their songs lasts longer than a couple of minutes . . . The songs have titles like 'I Don't Want to Go Down to the Basement' and 'I Don't Want to Walk Around with You' and 'Beauty Is a Punk.' They epitomize early sixties simple-minded rock-and-roll, but are played with a 1974 vengeance and violence."

[R.B., "Savage Voodoo Nuns, 10–31–74," *Soho Weekly News*, November 11, 1974.]

**n**

## "Neat, Neat, Neat"

**The second single, from 1977,** by the durable U.K. punk band the Damned, which was among the first U.K. punk bands to sign to a label and was the very first U.K. punk band to play at CBGB, in April 1977. As the first track on their debut album, *Damned, Damned, Damned*, the song offers a glimpse into the playful, pure-pleasure side of punk that always existed alongside the more politically "serious" and avant-garde dimensions of punk. Two April 1977 articles in the *Los Angeles Times* helped solidify the band's reputation and provided an early taste of hardcore. On April 20, Richard Cromelin wrote that the "Damned work in the frustration/aggression tradition of the Stooges, combined with a minimal/musical approach that reflects the

Ramones' influence." And in a longer profile on April 23, he noted that "[David] Vanian, wearing Alice Cooper-Meets-Dracula make-up and tattered black clothing, raced around the stage in the frantic, out-of-control manner of a mechanical ghoul whose batteries had been overcharged. The music was simple, straightforward. The emphasis was on energy."

What distinguished the Damned—and "Neat, Neat, Neat" especially—was the sheer speed: The song is simply and purely fast, as if it was recorded as quickly possible, right before the power was cut. In fact, for about twenty seconds near the middle of the song—from 1:22 to 1:44—the guitar work is so fast it sounds as if the song itself is going to fall apart. When, in an interview in *New York Rocker*, the guitarist Brian James said that the group had recorded the entire album in "about twenty-four hours," you're tempted to believe him on the merits of "Neat, Neat, Neat" alone, which sounds as if it was made in one take, in real time, in two minutes and forty seconds, the length of the song itself. In this regard, a song like "Neat, Neat, Neat" is the cinema-verité of punk rock: The very fact that it barely holds together reminds you of the conditions of its own production.

Some of the song's lyrics—"no crime if there ain't no law / no more cops to mess you around"—suggest a political meaning, but of what sort? The rest of the words are even murkier: "A distant man can't sympathise / He can't uphold his distant laws." But at other spots the lyrics sound as if they were made up to simply move the song along to its next moment as quickly as possible. And of course the title and chorus—the spat out, staccato, rapid-fire "Neat, Neat, Neat"—sandwiched between lines like "She can't afford a cannon" and "She can't afford a gun at all"—evokes the rat-tat-tat of gunfire.

The fastness of punk has always reminded you of the quick editing of certain movies. "Neat, Neat, Neat" is the *Taxi Driver* of punk, dipping and plunging into sudden mood changes. In that movie, Travis Bickle (Robert DeNiro) sends a sweet card to his parents and is later covered in blood as the camera moves slowly above him like God looking down. You realize what terrified you about punk was the same thing that terrified you about *Taxi Driver*: The moments when the engine cut off and the entire thing went into free fall.

[Richard Cromelin, "The Ambassadors of Punk Rock," *Los Angeles Times*, April 23, 1977, p. B10; Richard Cromelin, "A New Wave of English Rockers," *Los Angeles Times*, April 20, 1977, p. E7; Brian James quoted in Sukey Pett, "The Damned . . . Not the Beautiful," *New York Rocker* vol. 1, no. 7, May–June 1977, p. 24.]

## Nervous Breakdown

**The first EP by Black Flag,** featuring Keith Morris on vocals, Greg Ginn on guitar, Chuck Dukowski on bass, and Brian Migdol on drums. The sound is punk boiled down to a level of frightening purity. There is no fat on these songs, no excess. Although in the imagination Black Flag lingers as a brutal transformation of early punk, which often veered between menace and camp, there is nothing campy about this, or any, Black Flag song. The fact of hardcore Southern California is there, or is just about to be there: the relentless sound, the speed, the sonic sense of inevitability.

"It could well be their best recording," Michael Azerrad has written. "It was definitely the one by which everything else would be measured." What strikes you

BLACK FLAG (Los Angeles)

Keith Morris, vocals
Greg Ginn, guitar
Chuck, bass
Robo, drums

Black Flag began in Hermosa Beach, an LA
tidewater with a strand and cruising street
where activity centers for the surfers and
the cruisers. Shunned by Hollywood promoters and bands, they played the occasional
party and self-promoted gig, anywhere, for
anyone, until the "Nervous Breakdown" EP
was finally released in early 1979. Since
then Black Flag has been playing clubs around
town.

Black Flag

on listening to it again is how the Ramones' and the Sex Pistols' influence are still there on the surfaces of songs. There is a snarl but not a scream. That would come later. "I was a hippie / I was a burnout" sings Morris on "Wasted." In fact, the connection between classical punk from the 1975–77 era and the emerging hardcore of Black Flag lies with the rejection of hippie softness. But whereas the Ramones suggested an open affinity for certain styles of sixties pop music, Black Flag rejected this completely and pushed punk further into the realm of abstract noise. "I see a lot of the music coming out now is similar to the early 'Sixties. It's just, 'let's forget about things, let's have fun, let's hop around and have a good time.' That's not why I play music, and that's not why I listen to music," Ginn said in a 1980 interview. Of course, for many fans, having a good time is what rock and roll is about. At its most extreme—and this is almost fully realized on *Nervous Breakdown*—the music of Black Flag was a stern and serious tyranny of noise.

Strangely, for a band often associated with anarchy, Black Flag conjured an almost militant orthodoxy enforced, dutifully and sometimes pitilessly, by its fans.

[Michael Azerrad, *Our Band Could Be Your Life: Scenes from the American Indie Underground 1981–1991*, New York: Little, Brown and Company, 2001, p. 19; Greg Ginn, "Black Flag," *Skitzoid*, March 1980, http://homepages.nyu.edu-cch223/usa/info/.]

# Nervus Rex

**Formed in 1977, Nervus Rex** made music and were doomed. They were doomed because the music they made seemed, on the surface, to be of its time. But deeper, deeper, their songs were far too . . . nervous. Jittery, they jumped out of categories. Founded by Lauren Agnelli (who also wrote under the name Trixie A. Balm) and Shaun Brighton, they were later joined by Miriam Linna and sometimes Dianne Athey and Jonathan Gildersleeve. They released a single, "Don't Look," in 1978, and one self-titled album, produced by Mike Chapman, on the Dreamland label in 1980. The album's cover and back are a riot of overstaturated color, bright reds and purples and oranges, like a band pretending to be a band, a complete reversal of punk's black-and-white aesthetic. The second song on side one, "Go Go Girl," creeps so close to dark pop perfection that it's easy to see why the band self-destructed, as bands like the B-52s mined this territory with more ruthless efficiency. You will listen to that song one hundred times and never tire of its soaring beauty, or the perfect last twenty seconds.

In 1977, the band was profiled in *New York Rocker*: "They call them elitists and solipsists, but they want to be great popularizers. They like punk, and they hate punk. Lauren came up with the final self-defining contradiction: she defined the band's attitude as 'melancholy jubilance.' And since paradox is the ultimate Seventies art form, this band just might make it work." But they didn't, in part because there was no dynamic presence à la Blondie (who, it must be admitted, they sounded a lot like) but also because some bands are just destined to make one very good album and a handful of jittery songs that leap off the turntable like electric shocks.

[Tom Carson, "Nervous Rex," *New York Rocker*, February–March 1977, p. 12.]

# "New Dark Ages"

**A song by the San Francisco area punk/art-punk band** the Mutants, who formed in 1977 and whose lineup included Brendan Early, Fritz Fox, John Gullak, Sue White, Paul Fleming, Sally Webster, and Dave Carothers. They were powerful, funny, absurd, and had an alarming stage presence, singing and destroying things (like television sets) at the same time. In the *New York Rocker*, Happy Geek (aka Howie Klein, whose 415 Records, founded in 1978, was among San Francisco's first punk and New Wave–oriented labels) wrote that "the S.F. Mutants aren't like anything else in the world—well, maybe a little like the B52's." And several months later, in a profile of the band, Klein (this time writing as Connie Chung) said that from "the outset, the Mutants' creative tension had revolved around a dynamic clash between chaos and spontaneity on the one side, and musical proficiency and professionalism on the other." In the *Oakland Tribune* in December 1977 there appeared this announcement under the heading PUNK BANDS TO PERFORM: "Not content with destroying the old values of music, punk bands continue to expand that genre's once-limited horizon. The Mutants, a self-proclaimed quartet of artists turned punks, will stage a 24-hour multi-media experience beginning Friday, Dec. 17, at 8 p.m., at Target, 743 47th St., Oakland."

"New Dark Ages" is like an accusation disguised as a pop song. "Business people with long hair / hiding plastic things everywhere / recording shows while they're not there / since they got it they don't care." And that's just the first part. One of the great, chaotic, contradictory things about punk—especially West Coast and U.K. punk—was that it could be as socially engaged as the folk music of Dylan's era. The line "recording shows while they're not there" is as theoretical as Marshall McLuhan, but in the beautiful fury of the song you forget about theory and want to dance. "We've always been on the verge of falling apart," Fleming said in 1982. They stayed together long enough to see the new dark ages turn even darker.

[Connie Chung (Howie Klein), "Moo Moo Mutants," *New York Rocker*, September 1979, p.28; Paul Fleming quoted in Suzanne Sefanac, "Courting Chaos with the Mutants," *Bay Area Music*, December 15, 1982, p. 24; Happy Geek (Howie Klein), "San Francisco," *New York Rocker*, February–March 1979, p. 32; Charles Shere, "Punk Bands to Perform," *Oakland Tribune*, December 13, 1977, p. 38EE.]

## "New Music, The"

**"The New Music" is a story by Donald Barthelme (1931-89)** in the collection *Great Days*, first published in 1979. It is not about punk, or New Wave, or No Wave, and yet it is. "If one does nothing but listen to the new music, everything else drifts, goes away, frays," someone says. And later: "The new music burns things together, like a welder. The new music says, life becomes more and more exciting as there is less and less time." Many of Barthelme's short stories (Are they really stories?) first appeared in *The New Yorker*, and if you read the safe, ironic, overly patterned stories published in its pages today, you will wonder at how someone like Barthelme could ever have been welcomed there. "Fragments are the only form I trust," he once wrote, and his stories are the musical equivalent of the strange and absurd and sometimes terrifying music of Pere Ubu, or the Electric Eels, or Destroy All Monsters, or, later, James Chance and the Contortions, or Mars, or Theoretical Girls. "The new, down-to-earth, think-I'm-gonna-kill-myself music, which unwraps the sky," is another line.

Donald Barthelme was not a minimalist, just as punk was not minimalist, because there is something too large in his stories. But reading them, you *feel* that they are minimalist. They are spare, lacking in exposition, sometimes hanging by just a few details of place or setting. They seem to be made of facts, but they are not. They trap you somehow.

Barthelme's brother, Frederick, was the drummer for the avant-garde, Houston-based rock band the Red Crayola (later the Red Krayola) from 1966 to 1968. The band is claimed, by some, to be a forerunner of No Wave.

[Donald Barthelme, "The New Music," in *Great Days*, New York: Pocket Books, 1980, pp. 21, 37.]

## New Wave, the (1)

**Throughout the emerging scene** around New York City, terms like "underground," "punk," and "New Wave" were used to describe the music and the sense of fun and style. While these terms are arbitrary and their meanings in constant flux, under-

Donald Barthelme's short story collection *Great Days*

standing how they were used in the early years helps to shed light on the vitality and diversity of the emerging scene in the mid-seventies. As Bernard Gendron has noted, "Initially, in England, 'new wave' was simply put forth as a comple-mentary label for those bands and movements *also* designated as 'punk'. The expressions 'punk' and 'new wave' were nearly convergent in their mid-seventies applications and equally volatile in their definitional shifts." The term had been used earlier, perhaps not surprisingly, by Dave Marsh, who had helped popular-ize the phrase "punk rock" in 1971. In a 1973 article in *Melody Maker* entitled "New York New Wave," Marsh sensed the very beginnings of an emerging scene: "Great white rock has not often come from New York City and its surrounding boroughs, even though—or perhaps because—the American music business is centred here . . . Things have changed. There are now not two or three excellent local rock acts in the area, but a dozen . . . Even though it is the glam-rock groups who have attracted most of the attention on the New York scene so far, not all of the bands wear lipstick." Marsh goes on to praise Blue Oyster Cult and New York Dolls as harbingers of this new wave.

New Wave R.I.P., *Trouser Press*, October 1977

According to some, by the time the Ramones were in the studio recording their first album in early 1976, the term "New Wave" was still more prevalent than "punk." Craig Leon notes that if "my memory serves me well, we never used this term [punk] at all. Seymour Stein nicked the term 'New Wave' from the Fifties French film guys to describe the music but no one used 'punk' other than the title of John Holmstrom and Legs McNeil's magazine of lower NY at that time." In a cover story for *Trouser Press* ("New Wave, R.I.P.") in 1977, Ira Robbins wrote that the New Wave, as a legitimate, meaningful movement, ended as soon as it was co-opted into the mainstream: "Let's talk about co-option. Every movement has to be co-opted to be destroyed; I think Lenny Kaye said that. In the past few months the new wave has been the subject of almost every possible form of exploitation: films, 'best of' albums, foreign tours, press junkets—the works. There's nothing left to be taken . . . Along with the induction of new wave bands into the rock hierarchy comes the inevitable onset of dry rot; no band can stay fresh forever."

For some in the emerging hardcore scene, the term "New Wave" suggested the softening, the de-fanging, of punk's initial combustive fury. "At the time [the late seventies]," notes Michael Azerrad, "the major labels were in the midst of co-opting punk rock by dressing it in skinny ties and modish haircuts, virtually willing a trend called 'new wave' into existence. Many fans bought in, as did plenty of bands, pushing punk back to the margins." But of course these elements had been there since the very beginning, as bands like Talking Heads, Blondie, and many others never embraced punk's anger and furious sound. At its most radical, the New Wave did—as Leon and others have suggested—owe its meaning to the film movement know as the French New Wave (*La Nouvelle Vague*), whose directors included François Truffaut, Jean-Luc Godard, Claude Chabrol, and others. Their movies—ranging from *The 400 Blows* (1959) to *Breathless* (1960) to *Week End* (1967)—appear to teeter on disaster with their jump cuts, open endings, unmotivated camera movement, sudden violence, and in-the-street guerilla-style shooting. The influence of the French New Wave—both direct and indirect—on the punk and New Wave movement is perilously difficult to trace. Other than Richard Hell and several others, few of the original punk pioneers talked—or were ever asked—about the influence of this film movement. But even a group as supposedly "stoopid" as the Ramones were at least aware of the heady art and avant-garde film culture in and around the New York City area. Tommy Ramone recalls "hanging around the Museum of Modern Art . . . I would take three-hour lunch-breaks and watch all the movies there and I got into avant-garde films."

Godard's films, in particular, were an enormous influence on punk. Their detached coolness and the way they converted alienation into freedom rather than introspective gloom was echoed in punk's detachment. David Thomson has said that "the very thing his [Godard's] films lack is emotion. They deal with moments of cinema and with his jungle of reference, but never with feelings." It may seem strange to speak of the aloofness of punk, especially compared to the alienating arena-rock mentality that it reacted against, but in truth punk thrived on "dead" or "blank" emotions. It was, after all, a rejection of the introspective, get-in-touch-with-yourself residue of the sixties. Whereas the previous generation of rock stars at least pretended they cared about the audience, the punks gloried in openly defying this code. Their performances, like the movies of the French New Wave, were chopped up and speedy, undercutting the sort of emotional momentum that builds up in long movie scenes or long rock songs like "A Day in the Life" or "Stairway to Heaven." In one of the best New Wave films, *My Life to Live* (*Vivre Sa Vie*), Anna Karina plays a woman who becomes a prostitute. In an early scene, she is sitting at a café (of course!) when the silence is interrupted by machine-gun fire from outside. The camera pans from her face to the front door, where a bloodied man stumbles in. But the panning shot is staccato, interrupted with violent jump cuts in keeping with the rat-tat-tat of machine-gun fire. It's a simple, powerful technique: Even forty-plus years later, it takes your breath away. In that moment, Godard's technique perfectly mirrors the content of the film: as the plot is about machine-gun fire, so is the editing. The "New Wave" in music collapsed the difference between content and style even further and at its most extreme—as with the Sex Pistols—obliterated that difference altogether.

[Michael Azerrad, *Our Band Could Be Your Life: Scenes from the American Indie Underground, 1981–1991*, New York: Little, Brown and Company, p. 123; Bernard Gendron, *Between Montmatre and the Mudd Club: Popular Music and the Avant-Garde*, Chicago: University of Chicago Press, 2002, p. 269; Tommy Ramone quoted in Clinton Heylin, *From the Velvets to the Voidoids: A Pre-Punk History for a Post-Punk World*, New York: Penguin, 1993, p. 169; Craig Leon e-mail to the author, May 27, 2004; Ira Robbins, "New Wave, R.I.P.," *Trouser Press*, no. 22, October 1977, p. 22; David Thomson, *The New Biographical Dictionary of Film*, New York: Knopf, 2002, p. 342.]

# New Wave, the (2)

**In the preface to his book** *The New Wave: Truffaut, Godard, Chabrol, Rohmer, Rivette*, the film scholar James Monaco wrote:

What is "The New Wave"? Like most such critical labels it resists easy definition. Coined by Françoise in the pages of *L'Express* in 1958, it originally referred to a new, youthful spirit then making itself felt in French film. It quickly gained currency and became a versatile catchphrase applied not only to film, but to any cultural phenomenon that was seen to be new or rebellious or hip.

That was in December 1975. The same month, in Richard Hell's notebook, there is this entry:

*WRITERS: Hamsun, Chandler, Huysmans, Godard, Baudelaire, Poe, Cossery, Burroughs, Vellejo, Breton, Lautreamont, Borges, Kabir.*

[Richard Hell, entry from December 24, 1975, in *Artifact: Notebooks from Hell, 1974–80*, New York: Hanuman, 1992, p. 43; James Monaco, *The New Wave: Truffaut, Godard, Chabrol, Rohmer, Rivette*, 1975; repr., New York: Oxford University Press, 1976, p. vii.]

# New Wave, the (3)

**Sire Records, in particular, took advantage** of the ambiguity between the terms "punk" and "New Wave" and used it as part of a promotional campaign to sell records by the likes of the Ramones, Talking Heads, Dead Boys, Tuff Darts, Richard Hell and the Voidoids, the Saints, and Patti Smith. NAMES WILL NEVER HURT US ran the banner over one ad in a 1977 issue of the *New York Rocker*: "First it was 'punk,' then 'new wave.' As each term for the new rock 'n' roll falls by the wayside, people are getting

Sire's use of "punk" and "New Wave" in *New York Rocker*, 1978

the idea there's a wide range of rocking going on within the new sound." Whether or not Seymour Stein, who cofounded Sire in 1966 with Richard Gottehrer, was the first to use the phrase "New Wave" in relation to the New York "underground"

Dead Boys, Saints, Talking Heads, and Richard Hell and the Voidoids all New Wave in December 1977 advertisement

music of the time, Sire Records promoted and popularized the phrase—especially after 1977, when Warner Brothers became their distributor. As Greg Shaw, the founder of BOMP Records, recalls: "I was invited to give an orientation talk to Warner's creative people. I went over the ways this 'new wave' differed from the album rock they were more familiar with and discussed the politics. They went on to market 'punk' under the name 'new wave' and quietly forced Sire to drop the rest of its punk roster."

[Greg Shaw quoted in Mark Spitz and Brendan Mullen, *We Got the Neutron Bomb: The Untold Story of L.A. Punk*, New York: Three Rivers Press, 2001, p. 262.]

## New Wave Theatre

**A Los Angeles television show** begun in 1981—eventually picked up nationwide by the USA Network—hosted by Peter Ivers. Ivers was a Harvard University graduate whose career is difficult to describe because it was full of beautiful contradictions. Instead of a neat bio, here are a few facts/legends/quotes:

- He majored in classical languages.
- He played the harmonica.
- He was friends with Peter Rafelson, whose father, Bob Rafelson, directed several American films, including *Five Easy Pieces* (1970).
- He was friends with Steve Martin. Here is something that Steve Martin has said about the era preceding punk:

  Around this time I smelled a rat. The rat was the Age of Aquarius. Though the era's hairstyles, clothes, and lingo still dominated youth culture, by 1972 the movement was tired and breaking down. Drugs had killed people, and so had Charles Manson. The war in Vietnam was near its official end, but its devastating losses had embittered and divided America. The political scene was exhausting, and many people, including me, were alienated from government. Murders and beatings at campus protests weren't going to be resolved by sticking a daisy into the pointy end of a rifle. Flower Power was waning, but no one wanted to believe it yet, because we had all invested so much of ourselves in its message. Change was imminent.

*New Wave Theatre* was where the most dangerous California bands performed live, but in Ivers's alternate universe they didn't seem as dangerous. This was partly because of the philosophical, ruminating way Ivers talked about things, dressed in his brightly colored clothes and sunglasses. He looked tanned. Was he a faux-new-age guru? Was he even a fan of the bands? Was he serious when he said things like "Songs are rituals" and "One of the last roads to freedom left is through the world of art and entertainment" (this spoken in front of an enormous map of our solar system, with quiet organ music in the background and crickets chirping)? What to make of the Angry Samoans, or Fear, or Geza X, or 45 Grave, or Kaos, or Circle Jerks, as they hurtled through songs as if summoning catastrophe? In the context of the studio, with the weird camera angles and the raw, unproduced sound, even the most violent slam dancing (with Keith Morris hurling the words of "Wild in the Streets" at the audience, who responded by hurling themselves at each other) took on an aura of absurdity. *New Wave Theatre*—like some of the experiments being produced by Joe Rees at Target Video—was a parallel-universe version of MTV, where the music was fresher and rawer and where the narrative was not within the songs themselves but within the strange collage of Ivers's monologues, the bands performing, and Ivers's interviews (often onstage) with the bands. Around 1978, he wrote about his desire to "produce high quality, mass-marketable video and audio works from low-budget underground sources." Perhaps it was inevitable that music and video would merge in the shape of MTV, which debuted in 1981.

The truth is you had heard Peter Ivers's music long before you heard of Peter Ivers. He wrote "In Heaven (Lady in the Radiator Song)" for David Lynch's film *Eraserhead* (1977), in which Henry (Jack Nance) is so the opposite of punk that even his stand-on-edge hair and skinny tie could not put your imagination back together again after seeing the film. For years, pathetically and impractically, the *Eraserhead* soundtrack was the most radical music you owned: The entirety of side two is the radiator song. You listened to it in the dark and swore you saw her face. Some of your friends thought *Eraserhead* was the weirdest, sickest, most boring movie that they had ever seen, and you wondered about yourself—really wondered—about why it seemed so normal to you, so realistic, so honest. The river behind your childhood home was beautiful and terrifying at night, there in the dark, moving swiftly and quietly. How could so much motion, so much force, be so quiet?

In 1978, in the pages of *Search & Destroy*, David Lynch was asked whether he had "heard much of punk rock":

I was reading those magazines, for instance. And I haven't heard much punk music—you know Pete Ivers? He was playing me the RAMONES and some other bands. I really believe they're on to something, like going back to the roots of real rock 'n' roll, and I love that. Rock 'n' roll has gotten so watered down in so many different mixtures that it's nothing, it doesn't do anything for you, and when you hear the REAL stuff, it just drives you crazy. The politics, I don't go for, I'm not into that one bit. I'm into doing something and doing the best job you can at it, trying to get as deep into it as possible, down at the roots.

[David Lynch quoted by Kent Beyda in *Search & Destroy* No. 9, 1978, www.davidlynch.net; Peter Ivers quoted at http://ghosttownfilms.net; Steve Martin, *Born Standing Up: A Comic's Life*, New York: Scribner, 2007, p. 144.]

## "New Way" [1979]

**A seven-inch put out by the group the Wall**—which at the time consisted of Ian Lowery, Andy Griffits, John Hammond, and Bruce Archibald—on Small Wonder Records. Side A ("This Side") is a testament to the swirling, complex sounds of punk that are overshadowed by its fast and simple side. With echoes of Richard Hell and the Voidoids, the Sex Pistols, Television, Patti Smith, Gang of Four, and many others, "New Way" is a series of biting aphorisms. "Work, work, work sets you free / If this is freedom, give me chains I can see" the song begins, and by the time you hear "I don't want to work in tomorrow's dream," you can't help but agree. Side B ("That Side") has two songs, including the small masterpiece "Uniforms," which proceeds at breakneck pace to lay waste to the tinny, timid sounds of the emerging post-punk bands. Plus, the song is simply anthemlike. "Buy a new one when the old one's worn / Everybody's gotta have a uniform," the band screams, and when you realize that they are referring to themselves as well—as members of a rock band in the business of making records that people will buy and of performing on stages where people will watch—you find the fierce critique of conformity in "Uniforms" to be even more darkly funny.

## Nirvana (1986–94)

**If Nirvana was so good, why did they become so popular?** (This is one of those entries that does not fit within the so-called scope of this book. But the inclusion of Nirvana is imperative.) If this is a question that haunts all great radical art that achieves mainstream success, then it's a question worth asking about Nirvana, whose music elevated remorse to the status of art. The destruction at the heart of Nirvana's music—and I mean destruction—was real: Things could only end in catastrophe. Nirvana mocked their own success from the beginning; at some point this effrontery to achievement was no longer viable. When Nirvana passed from successes to icons—when they became "representative" of a certain generational strain—there was no further room for evolution. Or, to be more precise: At some point there was a choice to not evolve.

In fact, the band tried. Their November 1993 performance on *MTV Unplugged* was the closest they would come to acknowledging that their music was, at heart, steeped too deeply in pop to satisfy the savage blankness that their hardcore fans wanted.

At its heart, rock and roll has always offered a double vision of the world, one that must satisfy the demands fans who dedicate themselves to a "scene" as well as a broader audience of fellow travelers for whom the purity of the music must not interfere with its accessibility. It would be a cliché to say that Nirvana became a victim of their own success. But, as it happens, this is one cliché that turns out to be true. In a culture that demands success and then punishes you for it, Nirvana punished themselves before others had a chance to.

Nirvana's demos and early, rough performances are heartbreaking, because there is so little difference between them and their polished, studio-produced counterparts. The "gap" that would suggest artifice or calculation just isn't there. It's telling that an early cover by the band—Led Zeppelin's "Immigrant Song"—is the antithesis of punk. Recorded on videotape in 1988 at Krist Novoselic's mother's house in Aberdeen, Washington, the rehearsal shows that, at their heart, Nirvana were a heavy metal band steeped in big guitar. In the video, there are just some guys standing around drinking beer and playing with the light switches, listening to loud music. It's hard to tell where regular ends and art begins. You look at their faces and you wonder, can they tell that the band that is rehearsing in front of them is breaking into new territory? Nirvana is just a local band, playing in a house with bookshelves and doors and pretty nice carpeting. Kurt Cobain faces the paneled wall, and you are reminded of the jittery last moments of *The Blair Witch Project*, in the basement.

Grunge was as much an attempt to skip the needle off the record as was punk's attempt to return it to the record. In her book of poems *In the Surgical Theatre*, Dana Levin asks, "Are you becoming enslaved / to a bad idea? / That it all / just happened"? The terror here—as in all disconnected art—is that you can only answer these questions if you choose to hear the questions themselves. And if you choose to answer the questions, then the answer, of course, is "yes."

In truth, Nirvana was the last logical outcome of punk and represented a serious version of the "blank" in blank generation. Incoherence, if you take it seriously, can end only in chaos. The gun in Kurt Cobain's hand at the very end.

The demo for "Smells Like Teen Spirit," recorded in 1991, is like a warbly signal from another planet: The flatness of its lo-fi sound reminds you only of three-dimensional potential: The Creature from the Black Lagoon suddenly switching from black and white to terrible color. The tight, Butch Vig mix isolates the sounds, as most professional mixes do, and renders the song both more commercial and more powerful. That's a hard contradiction to swallow: the careful, methodical professionalism that goes into a song that bursts forth with so much power. "I think we probably spent the better part of a day doing the guitar overdubs," Vig has said of the recording of "Teen Spirit."

Like the Sex Pistols, it could only end in disintegration.

[Dana Levin, "Chill Core" from *In the Surgical Theatre*, Philadelphia: The American Poetry Review, 1999, p. 38; Butch Vig, from liner notes to Nirvana box set.]

# Nixon, Richard

**There are many things to say about Richard M. Nixon.** Many things have already been said. Nixon's relationship to punk is obscure. Unlike Jimmy Carter and Ronald Reagan and James Callahan and Margaret Thatcher, he did not preside over its flowering. But he came to symbolize the era's radical incoherence, an incoherence that gave rise to punk. Nixon was a law-and-order Republican who was not a conservative as conservatism came to be defined in the Reagan and post-Reagan era. He supported, often and openly, environmentalism, affirmative action, and government's involvement in helping rescue urban areas in decline. "The great question of the seventies is," he proclaimed in his January 1970 State of the Union address, "shall we surrender to our surroundings, or shall we make our peace with nature and begin to make reparations for the damage we have done to our air, to our land, and to our water? . . . This requires comprehensive new regulations."

In a strange way, the early punks shared Nixon's disdain of the hippies and the counterculture. In the hundreds of hours of available transcripts from his presidency it becomes clear that part of Nixon's disdain for the hippies emerged from his bewilderment about why young people raised in affluence would turn on the very establishments that provided them with relative comfort and luxury. Here is a portion of a 1971 conversation between Nixon, John Ehrlichman, George Schultz (Nixon's director of the Office of Management and Budget), and Ronald Zielger (Nixon's Press Secretary) concerning a planned Federal Employees for Peace demonstration:

> **Ehrlichman:** We're denying a permit to Federal Employees for Peace across the street tomorrow—
>
> **Ziegler:** [Unintelligible].
>
> **Ehrlichman:** —for a rally [unintelligible].
>
> **Ziegler:** Oh, good. [Unintelligible].
>
> **Ehrlichman:** Four hundred people.
>
> **Ziegler:** [Unintelligible].
>
> **President:** Any reason that we don't use fire hoses on these people—
>
> **Unknown:** Nothing better.
>
> **President:** —rather than that darned, uh, tear gas?
>
> **Ehrlichman:** No, uh, slippery streets slow traffic—
>
> **President:** Yeah.
>
> **Ehrlichman:** —and, uh, that's one of the, one of the major considerations on Monday, but, I, I, that was my initial reaction was, we ought to soak 'em down. Chief says, "Please don't make the streets wet." He says that slows the traffic by fifty percent.

**President:** Oh.

**Ehrlichman:** He says the name of the game is to keep the traffic moving, so, uh—

**Ziegler:** Of course, fire hoses turned on the crowds; that makes a worse picture than tear gas.

**President:** Does it?

**Ehrlichman:** Yeah, there isn't much of a picture with tear gas—.

**Ziegler:** [Clears throat] Just people running and a little smoke. You get, you know, those big fire hoses goin' on a crowd—

**President:** I see.

**Ziegler:** —of people like that, you could probably—.

**President:** It's awfully effective.

**Ehrlichman:** Yes, sir, it's very—

**President:** And maybe—

**Ehrlichman:** —effective, and the Europeans use 'em, you know, frequently.

**President:** The Germans.

**Ehrlichman:** Yeah.

**President:** They, when we were in Berlin, they took those fire hoses out, and they cleaned those streets fast.

**Ehrlichman:** Those trucks, they have trucks with water guns.

**President:** [Unintelligible].

**Ehrlichman:** —and—.

**Ziegler:** Those things really pour out the power too.

**Ehrlichman:** Yeah, they can knock a guy quite a ways. The, uh, uh, we were hoping there would be no rain Monday for the same reason.

**President:** Yeah—

**Ehrlichman:** [Unintelligible].

**President:** —there wasn't any.

**Ehrlichman:** There was none, and it was, it was a good thing. The damn hippies opened fire hydrants a number of places, and, uh, that caused a slow-down. They just, they just ran from one to the other and they [unintelligible].

[Part of a conversation among President Nixon, John D. Ehrlichman, George P. Shultz, and Ronald L. Ziegler in the Oval Office between 3:17 pm and 3:19 pm on May 4, 1971, http://www.nixonlibrary.gov/forresearchers/find/tapes/finding_aids/tapesubjectlogs/trn490-24.pdf. Richard Nixon, "Annual Message to Congress on the State of the Union," January 22, 1970. The American Presidency Project, www.presidency.ucsb.edu.]

# No Policy

**The one and only EP by the D.C.-area band** State of Alert (S.O.A.), fronted by Henry Garfield (who later became Henry Rollins), with Mike Hampton, Simon Jacobsen, and Wendel Blow (and later, briefly, with Ivor Hanson). "Along with a few other D.C. bands," Michael Azerrad has written, "S.O.A. was inventing East Coast hardcore." The speed of the band and the brevity of the song—the record clocks in at under nine minutes—approaches the abstract.

Seven things about *No Policy*:

1. "In its simplist definition," according to Edward Strickland, "minimalism is a style distinguished by severity of means, clarity of form, and simplicity of structure and texture."

2. Although the song "Lost in Space" lasts forty-three seconds, it only takes Garfield sixteen seconds to sing the entirety of the lyrics, which include the lines "Snort that coke / What a joke / Who's gonna wind up dead—You."

3. The guitar solo, such as it is, on "Draw Blank" lasts around six seconds. The song itself lasts thirty-six seconds.

4. On "Gate Crashers," Garfield sings, "Your loving fans are growing few / With tunes so old they're sick of you / Your hair's too long and so's your set." Pictures of Garfield around that time look positively military.

5. Near the beginning of "Riot" there is laughing, and someone says, "Are you crazy, Wendel?" To which he replies, "What?" It is a moment of humanism on a machine-like album.

6. "Public Defender," at one minute, twelve seconds, is the longest song. It also has the heaviest sound, bubbling in your ears.

7. "Gonna Hafta Fight" is the last song, rock and roll boiled down to its essence, for good or for ill. In truth, there was no reason for hardcore to evolve beyond this: It had already reached its limit.

[Michael Azerrad, *Our Band Could Be Your Life: Scenes from the American Indie Underground 1981–1991*, New York: Little, Brown and Company, 2001, p. 27; Edward Strickland, *Minimalism: Origins*, Bloomington: Indiana University Press, 1993, p. 4.]

# No Wave

**No Wave represented a disavowal—even a betrayal—of punk** insofar as it rejected the populist, melodic streak that animated punk's first wave. It is true, as Bernard Gendron has written, that "no wave music was quite naturally perceived by its media devotees as also teetering aesthetically between these two worlds, that is, as incorporating avant-garde components and rock components equally into its musical practices, and thus itself musically neither strictly avant-garde nor rock, really a new muta-tion." Maybe I'd better let Ephraim P. Noble take over here, because in truth it's hard to write about No Wave without sounding a little bit like a dissertation. (D. Barker has threatened to subtract one dollar from my advance for each sentence that smacks of something that sounds like a "dissertation," so I'm being careful not to let Ephraim P. Noble write too many of them.) But I'm afraid if I let him get started on this topic he won't ever stop, so I'll just say this: No Wave is music for people who hate music. Rarely does it offer the sort of compromise that results in surprise: Once you hear a song by the Contortions, and then another, you have figured out the combina-tion, and the door of the safe swings wide open, revealing . . . nothing. The safe is empty. When Michael Azerrad writes that "when Brian Eno recorded four no wave bands . . . for 1978's *No New York* compilation, he unwittingly fomented the scene's demise, as jealousies were sparked by the fact that some bands were picked to record and others weren't," what he misses is a judgment about the music itself, which was so self-consciously dry and angular. All art involves, on some level, a disavowal of tradition. The problem faced by No Wave was that the tradition it was rejecting in the late seventies—punk—had not yet really hardened into tradition. There was still room for evolution, as bands as disparate as the Clash and Black Flag showed. By the time punk had fully morphed into its fully commercialized "pop" phase (Green Day, Blink 182, etc.), No Wave had come and gone.

The real question raised by No Wave was this: Was it a symptom of the times, or an indictment? The hollowness, even cruelty, at the heart of this music cannot be ignored, even by its most fanatic apologists. We enter the realm, in the music of No Wave, where banality swerves off unexpectedly into the realm of art. Do the defenders of No Wave really enjoy the music? Or is this a bourgeois question that's predictably beside the point? Here's a theory: No Wave upped the ante, and kept upping it, out of sheer curiosity about how far punk could be boiled down until it disappeared. No Wave swerved so far into the realm of self-conscious art that in order to like it you had to hate music, because No Wave is, at its heart, music for people who hate music. Listening to it, you feel it hollows out a part of you.

[Michael Azerrad, *Our Band Could Be Your Life: Scenes from the American Indie Underground 1981–1991*, New York: Little, Brown and Company, 2001, p. 231; Bernard Gendron, *Between Montmartre and the Mudd Club: Popular Music and the Avant-Garde*, Chicago: University of Chicago Press, 2002, p. 279.]

## Nobody's Heroes

**The second LP by Belfast's Stiff Little Fingers,** released in 1980. It is, you discovered later, not their most well-regarded album, which is *Inflammable Material*, from the previous year. *Nobody's Heroes* features Jake Burns, Henry Cluney, Ali McMordie, and Jim Reilly. The back of the album shows a "letter" from Chrysalis to Gordon Ogilvie (who managed the group and cowrote many of their songs) that reads,

> Dear Mr. Ogilvie,
>
> Many thanks for sending your tape which I have been given careful consideration. Whilst we feel there is some potential within the material, we feel at this present time we are not the company to be able to assist you in furthering your recording career.
>
> In the meantime, may we wish you the very best of luck in the future.

It reminds you of Charles Bukowski, of the hilarious, endless letters of reprimand from various anonymous supervisors in *Post Office* (you wonder why movie versions of Bukowski's books are never half as *funny* as the books themselves). The music is clean and bright. You know Stiff Little Fingers were a "political" band, but as with all art, the truth is more complicated. What are the politics of clean production? There are spaces between the instruments in which you maneuver. In "At the Edge" (which has got to be one of the greatest underappreciated punk songs, but you must wait until :38 to understand why), they sing, "Here's your room and here's your records," and the song lifts into a melody as glorious as one of the cloudy dream sequences in Terry Gilliam's *Brazil*. And then there are the great rhymes that come so fast, as if shot out of the barrel of a gun: "I've got no time to talk about it / All your stupid hopes and dreams / Get your feet back on the ground son / It's exams that count not football teams."

On songs like this and on "Tin Soldiers," Stiff Little Fingers offer up fast melodies and then subvert them just as quickly. They are always building a wall of sound and simultaneously taking it down. There is—dare it be said—a Thatcherite economy to the songs that cools them off just as they are heating up. In "Tin Soldiers" this comes near the 2:30 mark, when the boys count out, Ramones-like, "one, two, three, four" but then proceed to pull back and offer up an almost art-rock guitar solo.

Or take "Gotta Getaway," a song for falling in love. A darkened room, the flicker of LED lights, the sound of distant footsteps, unanswered cell-phone calls because your hands are all over each other, the shape of furniture against your bodies, the bass line beginning at :24 that makes you wonder, and then glorious guitar waves at :44, and then those opening lyrics, "You know there ain't no street like home / to make you feel so alone."

## Non Compos Mentis

**Non Compos Mentis was a band from Dallas, Texas,** consisting of the brothers Caldwell and David Hill. They recorded just a handful of songs, none of them much known. So to discover these songs is a thrill, and the fact of their obscurity is sad but also gives you hope because human beings create such marvelous things. "Ultimate Orgasm" (1980) is a fierce and melodic song about, you know, suicide. "You don't need a girl, you don't need a boy / you don't need any miracle toy," the lyrics go, and there is the sleeve cover showing the woman with the gun to her head. The ending sounds like haunted metal. But better still is the B-side, "Twist the Blade," which explodes the usual categories (punk, post-punk, pop punk, etc.) and rattles around in your brain like a marble. This song too ends weirdly, like a machine revving up to explode. There are a few other scattered songs too, like "Quick to Compliment" and "Six Feet Under," but that first single from 1980 is so sharp that you feel the music zooming out of one decade and into another.

## "Normals"

**This, from a 1977 article** about punk fashion:

> Desiree Hunt of Hollywood came to the Whisky in a white silk shirt, black satin gloves ("I'm an expensive punk"), keychain earrings, heart-shaped glasses, jeans, black boots and a swastika pin attached to her neck scarf . . . "The swastika doesn't represent a thing about the past," she insists. "It's just something to shock the normals."
>
> [Marylou Luther, "Shock Chic: The Punk Persuasion," *Los Angeles Times*, July 31, 1977, p. E1.]

## Nostalgia

**Out of the disorder of the seventies** came a barely disguised longing for the past. Was it a real or an imagined past? It doesn't matter. In movies of the "new Hollywood" this nostalgia was most obvious: *American Graffiti, The Godfather, Chinatown, The Long Goodbye*—a look backward, the past as an escape from the escapades, disasters, and high dramas of Vietnam, Watergate, the Saturday Night Massacre, U.K. unemployment, heat waves, racial violence, stagflation, the energy crisis, bussing violence, the Patty Hearst kidnapping, wage and price controls, the Pentagon Papers, *Roe v. Wade*, the New York City blackout, the Jonestown mass suicide, Three Mile Island, and the Iranian Hostage Crisis. Was it any wonder that the sources of punk were

Nostalgia in the punk era: *New Musical Express*, 1975

so deeply historical (Marlon Brando in the fifties, early British Invasion music, Phil Spector girl groups, fascism) as to be nostalgic?

"Remember Those Fabulous Sixties?" the *New Musical Express* asked on its cover in November 1975, in the same issue as Charles Shaar Murray's extensive profile of the emerging New York underground/punk music scene, a full five months before the release of the Ramones' first album. Fascination with certain sixties bands—the Searchers, Freddie and the Dreamers, the Merseybeats, and others—had everything to do with the fact that they failed, in terms of the music "business" and longevity. By 1975, the meaning of the Beatles, or the Stones, or Pink Floyd, Queen, or Bob Dylan had become perfectly clear: They were established so fully that even their forays into diversity and experimentation (i.e., concept albums or thematic albums, synthesizer-free albums, etc.) seemed predetermined and inevitable. But other "failed" sixties bands—like those collected on *Nuggets*—had not survived long enough to acquire the burden of predictability. Punk transformed that nostalgia into action of two basic sorts. Bands like the Sex Pistols—modelled on the often-short-lived *Nuggets*-type groups—disintegrated before their meaning became static. Bands like the Ramones endured, but, remarkably, without "evolving" in the same way that survivors from the sixties (the Beatles, the Stones) did.

Punk's fuel was nostalgia, borne of the absurd and terrible circumstances of the seventies. By the mid-eighties, when the incoherence and contradictions of the sixties and seventies had been resolved under the banner of conservatism, punk had already gone through its hardcore phase and had itself become an object of nostalgia.

# "Not exactly what you would consider melodic"

**In January 1977, roughly seven months after** the release of the Runaways' first album, and two months after the Sex Pistols' "Anarchy in the UK" was released as a single, the following letter to the editor appeared in the *Los Angeles Times*:

> I'm concerned over Robert Hilburn and Richard Cromelin's article involving Kim Fowley and his all-girl/bad-boy music group, the Runaways. Why do worthless bands with nothing to say and musical arrangements not exactly what you would consider melodic attract publicity while good musicians are starving for deserved recognition? I'm not saying that the article wasn't well written but I'd rather that you spend your time concentrating on people who have something to offer the music world. You better get someone down [in] the typesetting room. The man keeps substituting the letter p for the j in junk rock. —J. P. Spain, Sepuiveda

In fact, there is more than an element of truth in the letter: The Runaways, charming as they were (*Oh boy, here it comes. I knew he hated The Runaways. —Ed.*), really did not have much to say and were lacking in melodic hooks. But that, of course, was precisely the point. The cool detachment of the Runaways was in direct opposition to the earnest feminism of the late sixties and early seventies, when gender became—it had too, of course—no fun. The Runaways put the fun back. And they were not, exactly, melodic.

[J. P. Spain, "Punk Rock as Junk Rock," *Los Angeles Times*, January 16, 1977, p. T2.]

# "Notes on the New American Cinema"

**Before there was the DIY, underground,** amateur movement that came to be called punk in music, there was something similar in cinema, the ideas of which were articulated in a journal called *Film Culture*, founded in 1955 by the Lithuanian-born filmmaker and writer Jonas Mekas. Among his many essays that championed the spirit of independent filmmaking, "Notes on the New American Cinema," from 1962, is the most forceful and accidentally predictive of a similar wave that would sweep music approximately ten years later. Two quotes:

*Dan Drasin. Burton Brothers.*

In *Sunday* (1951), Dan Drasin's uninhibited camera, zooming in and out and around the action, caught the clash between the folk-singers and the police in New York with an immediacy and aliveness seldom seen in the documentary film or television. Drasin was greatly assisted by his ignorance of certain professional techniques which would have hampered his freedom. He came to cinema completely free of professional inhibitions. He moved with his zoom freely, against all textbook rules, not afraid of shaky movements or garbled sounds. The shooting circumstances didn't even permit much time for perfectionism. He lost the slickness but he gained the truth, both in sound and image.

*Ron Rice. Vernon Zimmerman. The Poetry of the Absurd.*

The *Flower Thief* (1960), by Ron Rice, and *Lemon Hearts* (1961), by Vernon Zimmerman, are two of the latest and most successful examples of post–*Pull My Daisy* cinema. Both are made with the utmost creative freedom, with the utmost disrespect for the "professional" camera, plot, character conventions . . . Their imagination, coming from deeply "deranged" and liberated senses, is boundless. Nothing is forced in these films. They rediscover the poetry and wisdom of the irrational, of nonsense, of the absurd—the poetry that comes from regions that are beyond all intelligence . . .

Mekas and others championed an "uncontrolled" cinema, characterized by shaky, handheld camera movement, improvisation, and what Harmony Korine would, decades later, call "mistakism." "Drasin was greatly assisted by his ignorance of certain professional techniques," Mekas wrote. In 1974, the Ramones elevated ignorance to the level of performance.

[Jonas Mekas, "Notes on the New American Cinema," in *Film Culture Reader*, ed. P. Adams Sitney, 1962; repr., New York: Cooper Square Press, 2000, pp. 94, 101.]

# Nuns

**Among the first punk bands from the West Coast,** San Francisco's the Nuns illustrate the imprecision of terms like "punk." At their early best, they consisted of Jennifer Miro, Jeff Olener, Richie Detrick, Alejandro Escovedo, Michael Varney, and Pat Ryan. They released a few singles prior to their self-titled 1980 LP (recorded after Escovedo left the band). The Nuns, along with Crime, signaled the birth of something new in San Francisco, the symbolic heart of the hippie counterculture—but of what? Jeff Olener describes the early scene:

What I saw happening was just the tail end of people hanging on to an old era. The only progressive thing that was happening was probably the Tubes, if you call them progressive. There was basically no real scene. There was no club scene. It was the same old bands coming in and playing. Around this time, I went back to New York City to visit and I went to CBGB's and I saw Patti Smith, the Ramones, and a couple of other bands, all playing stuff that I was into. There was no scene like that in San Francisco yet. So the Nuns were formed in 1976 and then we got Jennifer.

Ad for the third single by the Nuns, 1980

Precisely because San Francisco was so deeply saturated in the sixties, many of the early punk bands that emerged there exhibited a powerfully strange breed of mixed-up styles and genres. An early article about the band by Michael Snyder that appeared about six months after their first show at the Mabuhay asks, "Sex and violence? Fanfare for an era of crumbling morals? Wholesome family entertainment?" The answer to these questions was yes and no. If groups like Blondie, Talking Heads, and the Ramones showed just how diverse the early New York underground/punk scene could be in terms of musical styles and stage presence, then bands like the Nuns suggested that in San Francisco the codes were even more scrambled. In *New York Rocker*, Howie Klein wrote that the Nuns "are at once, for example, sublime and grotesque; imagine a melding of the Talking Heads and the Dead Boys (if you dare)."

In songs like "Media Control," "Suicide Child," "Lazy," and "World War III," the Nuns come across as funny, dangerous, mean, tender, and fully aware of a range of musical styles cartwheeling from cabaret-like lounge singing, to garage rock, to droning psychedelia. Their music from the late seventies is incoherent in the best sense of the word. Nearly thirty years later, it still makes no sense.

[Howie Klein, "The Nuns: Whisky a Go Go, L.A.," *New York Rocker*, 1978; Jeff Olener quoted in James Stark, *Punk '77*, Stark Grafix, 1992, p. 6; Michael Snyder, "The Nuns Confess," *New Wave*, August 1977, p. 6.]

O

## *Oblique Strategies*

**A set of cards created by Brian Eno** and the artist Peter Schmidt in 1975 (followed by subsequent editions) for the purpose of, as Glenn O'Brien suggested, "solving problems in artistic processes." According to Eno:

> The idea of *Oblique Strategies* was just to dislocate my vision for a while. By means of performing a task that might seem absurd in relation to the picture, one can suddenly come at from a tangent and possibly reassess it. So I had about five or six little principles that I carried in my head at that time [during art school]. Then when Roxy started and we made our first album, although I liked the album a lot, as soon as we had finished it and I was in a position of sitting at home and listening to it as a record, I began thinking "If only I'd done this, or that." I could suddenly see lots of places where a slightly more detached vision or a different angle of approach would have made a lot of difference. So the next time we recorded, I compiled a set of about twenty-five little cards which I'd just stick around the studio and keep reminding myself of all the time.

For every card that veers into the territory of the power-of-positive-thinking ("Ask your body") there are three or four that go against your natural instincts. Taken together, they offer a form of randomness that verges on controlled anarchy. If a method of "punk" is ever written, it will have to take into account the *Oblique Strategies*, which come as close as possible to a creative manifesto. Writing in *New York Rocker*, Howard Wuelfing (who would himself become a force in the D.C. hardcore scene as a writer, musician, and producer) noted that "in fact there is no coherency to the cards' observations, no system of thought one can absorb and apply."

Weirdly, some of the cards could easily be the working rules of an emerging punk band in the mid-seventies. Here are a few:

- Disconnect from desire
- Do something boring
- Emphasize repetitions
- Emphasize the flaws
- Honor thy error as a hidden intention
- Look closely at the most embarrassing details and amplify them
- Make a blank valuable by putting it in an exquisite frame
- Repetition is a form of change

- Use fewer notes
- Use "unqualified" people

[Glenn O'Brien, "Eno at the Edge of Rock," *Interview*, June 1978; Howard Wuelfing, "Don't Be Afraid of Cliches," *New York Rocker*, August 1979, p. 23.]

## "Old New / New New"
**From *New York Rocker*,** early 1978:

| Old New | New New |
|---|---|
| • sneakers, S & M spike heels | • loafters, boat shoes |
| • chains, safety pins | • plain pumps or flats |
| • brown and black lipstick | • costume jewelry |
| • thin eyebrows | • pocket watches |
| • acid green socks | • red or white lipstick |
| • striped T-shirts | • heavy eyebrows |
| • black leather | • white socks & underwear |
| • leopard skin | • white T-shirts |
| • sharkskin suits | • oversized old sportsjackets |
| • studied ivy league look | • polka dots, houndstooth black or white suits |
| • 1950's + 1960's | • 1978 |

Punk, as music and fashion, had been aware of itself as style since the beginning, evolving out of (and eventually rejecting) glam and glitter rock. By 1978, the early ambiguity of bands like the Ramones had evolved into a more regularized code whose most important premise was to shock. But of course, audiences now expected to be shocked. Everything was permitted, and nothing was shocking anymore.

[Cindy Sui, "La Mode Change," *New York Rocker*, vol. 1, no. 11, February–March 1978, p. 35.]

## "Ongoing force of *me*, the"
**During a 1987 video interview** for Finnish television, Johnny Rotten (John Lydon) said this in response to the interviewer's statement that there had not been anything as revolutionary as the Sex Pistols:

There *has* been something as revolutionary as the Sex Pistols. The ongoing force of *me*. And this you must never forget. I'm as relevant now as I was then. In fact more so. You need me. I don't need you.

In the film *Michael Clayton*, Arthur (Tom Wilkinson) says, "Is that the correct answer to the multiple choice of *me*?"

## Only Ones

**Powered by Peter Perrett's detached voice,** the Only Ones made serious, fun, and dark music during the punk era. Their members had been around, in other bands, in the years preceding punk. Perrett had been in a group called England's Glory (the great song "Peter and the Pets" is from that era), and bassist Alan Mair, from Glasgow, had been in the Beatstalkers. Mike Kellie was in Spooky Tooth, while John Perry played in the Rats. Their influences included Bob Dylan, Pink Floyd, Jonathan Richman, and the Kinks. They formed as the Only Ones, in August 1976. "The music we're doing is something I've been writing for six years," Perrett told Ian Birch in 1977, "and I'm not going to go out and get my f—— hair cut. We're just individuals and if it coincides in any way with what's going on, then that's OK." In that same interview, Mair said, "To the hippies we were punk, and to the punks we were hippies."

The band never fit neatly into the musical slots that were destroyed and then quickly re-created under other names in 1976–77. Their first single—"Lovers of Today" b/w "Peter and the Pets" from 1977—was released on their own Vengeance label and suggested that, in the harsh light of punk, the sort of casual narcissism that was the secret code of the sixties was no longer secret. "We ain't got feelings / We ain't got no love / We ain't got nothing to say / We're lovers of today," sang Perrett. Of course, in their continual rejection of feelings, the punks created an awful lot of them among their fans. "Peter and the Pets" is such a sad, strange song that at moments you believe it is something that Peter Laughner might have done. "Special View" lurches forward like a drunk sailor determined to fall off the dock into the dark sea water only to have the girl from earlier catch him at the last moment, pull him to her breast, and kiss him until he's breathless. It's a perverse imitation of reggae, far more radical than anything concocted by the Clash. "It's the Truth," with backing vocals by Koulla Kakoulli, is all old-time cabaret infected by the rottenness of the modern world. In other words, it is romance, so doomed that the song—which should go on for four or five minutes—ends too soon, at 2:07, like a divorce. The secret beauty of this song, as well as "No Peace for the Wicked," is that you become convinced that Perrett is singing directly to you, and this is because the production has the illusion of being so simple and clean. The clean, slow tempo of these songs is almost a blasphemy in the punk era. Even more perversely slow is "In Betweens," from the 1979 album *Even Serpents Shine*. But it's more than slow; it's the measured focus of Perrett's voice, and the steady, well-spaced drone of the band

> If you try to follow me home tonight
> you will find everything that you've heard is right
> you'll never return to the home you knew
> leave it all behind, it's up to you.

These are the opening lines to "Someone Who Cares," and they are a warning and an invitation. The band itself was a mild threat. The sounds they made on your turntable broke categories and in the darkness of your basement alliances shifted suddenly and without reason. "I don't ever wanna sleep again / now that I've found love" go the words to "The Big Sleep," from their final album in 1980. But you don't believe it, because it's impossible to sustain an idea like that. And besides, by their final album you were older.

Such words, you had to reject them. And that was, for a while, the saddest thing of all.

[Ian Birch, "The Only Ones: One-off," *Melody Maker*, September 3, 1977.]

## "Ottawa Today"

**A fierce song by Canada's the Red Squares,** released in 1978. The song flutters, with clean guitars that remind you a little bit of Television. It goes fast, like a wind-up toy that you keep expecting to run down but that never does. Near the middle, the song becomes a speech: Ottawa today "is a delightful monument to the uninspired bleakness of a bureaucratic mind. Drabness, frustration, and boredom are its jewels." The conversion of social distress into a song of beauty and power.

## *Out of Vogue*

**An EP released in 1978 by the Middle Class,** a band from Orange County, California. As Brendan Mullen, the founder of the Masque in Hollywood, has noted, "Many hold the Middle Class up as probably the first American hardcore band, which basically meant playing faster downbeat tempos than the first wave of 'Hollywood' proto-hardcore bands like the Germs and the Bags." They consisted of Jeff Atta (the Atta brothers grew up in Santa Ana) on vocals, Mike Atta on guitar, Bruce Atta on drums, and Mike Patton on bass. The four songs—"Out of Vogue," "You Belong," "Situations," and "Insurgence"—are short and fast, as if the only lesson from the

Ramones was speed. In "Out of Vogue," Atta sings "We don't need no T.V." and there is humor in the fact that the one-two-three-four chant popularized by the Ramones comes near the middle of the song, not at the beginning. "Situations" is a bit slower, and the great thundering bass makes you realize that, slowed down a bit, hardcore has more in common with heavy metal than with punk.

In truth, the label "hardcore" has never sat too easily with the band. "Sorry kids," Mike Atta has said, "Middle Class was about as hardcore as Dr. Pepper (which, by the way, fueled our speed). We were very fast, tense, tight, sonic, loud, young, excited, nervous, naïve, and only slightly pissed . . . actually more annoyed than pissed. Our *Out of Vogue* era gigs did manage to whip up a frenzy, but nothing so aggressive or violent as hardcore would later be known for." The four songs convey the intensity of four people learning to do something together for the first time. Like the best punk, the violence is implied by the aggressiveness of the music rather than by anything overt.

[Mike Atta, "An Interview with Mike Atta from the Middle Class," *Agony Shorthand*, http:agonyshorthand.blogspot.com/2006/07; Brendan Mullen quoted in Matt Coker, "Suddenly in Vogue," *Orange County Weekly*, December 5, 2002.]

## Outsider, The

**A book by the philosopher Colin Wilson,** published in 1956, which was in some ways a ghostly premonition of the punk stance:

For the bourgeois, the world is fundamentally an orderly place, with a disturbing element of the irrational, the terrifying, which his preoccupation with the present usually permits him to ignore. For the Outsider, the world is not rational, not orderly. When he asserts his sense of anarchy in the face of the bourgeois' complacent acceptance, it is not simply the need to cock a snook at respectability that provokes him; it is a distressing sense *that truth must be told at all costs*, otherwise there can be no hope for an ultimate restoration of order . . . The Outsider is a man who has awakened to chaos.

The dominant idea in Wilson's book—creation arising from destruction—is mirrored in groups like Patti Smith ("positive") and the Dead Boys or the Sex Pistols ("negative"). Of course it's much, much, much more complicated than that . . . but not really. Wilson's name emerges in lots of writing from punk's first era: Sandy Robertson, in *Sniffin' Glue*: "recommended reading: Anything by Colin Wilson, especially 'The Outsider' and 'Introduction to the New Existentialism.' " Robertson, in *Sounds*, reviewing Patti Smith's *Easter*: "A song for Colin Wilson fans: 'Outside of society / Is where I wanna be.'"

John Morthland, in *Creem*, reviewing the Dr. Feelgood LP *Malpractice*: "The cover photo gives a good enough introduction to the music inside: They stand there looking outside even *The Outsider*, like the villains in a Colin Wilson nightmare."

There are, in certain songs by the Dead Boys, or Rocket from the Tombs, or the Sex Pistols, or Black Flag moments when, in truth, it seems that the center is not holding, and Wilson's line about awakening to chaos takes on the force of truth, not theory.

[John Morthland, "Dr. Feelgood: Malpractice," *Creem*, July 1976; Sandy Robertson, "O! Nothing Earthly . . . —Poe," *Sniffin' Glue*, July 1977, reprinted in Mary Perry, *Sniffin' Glue: The Essential Punk Accessory*, London: Sanctuary, 2000; Colin Wilson, *The Outsider*, 1956; repr. New York: Dell, 1967, p. 15.]

**p**

# Pagans

**The Pagans, from Cleveland, Ohio,** consisted of Mike Hudson, Brian Hudson, Mike "Tommy Gunn" Metoff, and Tim Allee. For a while they played music that seemed to predict something. But what was it predicting? A clue lies in their name. According to Mike Hudson, whose essay "The Pagans" is indispensable:

One day, I was reading the collected works of the Cleveland poet Hart Crane. At the end of the book was a listing, showing where each of the poems had been published, and as I scanned the first page I saw again and again the name of the magazine that had given Crane his first exposure. The other words on the page seemed to fall away, and what I saw was this:

*The Pagan*
*The Pagan*
*The Pagan*
*The Pagan*
Hmmm, I thought. The Pagans.

Who was Hart Crane? Does it matter that he wrote, for a time, for *The Plain Dealer* (Cleveland), or that he jumped to his death into the Gulf of Mexico from a steamship in 1932, and that his body was never recovered? He was a fierce poet, under the spell of T. S. Eliot but simultaneously breaking that spell. "We make our meek adjustments" is the first line of his poem "Chaplinesque." And the beginning of the final stanza: "The game enforces smirks; but we have seen / The moon in lonely alleys make / A grail of laughter of an empty ash can."

Well, there is that, and there are the songs of the Pagans. The noise that the Pagans made was different from the noise that Hart Crane made. The first thing to know about their most famous song, "What's This Shit Called Love," recorded in March 1978, is that the guitars sound wavy and low and crackling. The second thing to be aware of is the sly humor and theory of the opening lyrics, which are easy to miss because your brain wants to correct the lyrics: "Saw it in books / I read it on TV / It don't mean nothin' to me."

"Little Black Egg," recorded in 1978 by the Pagans, is a remake of the Nightcrawlers song, one of the forgotten gems of the Midwest punk scene; it makes you want to live rather than kill yourself. You picture yourself in the basement with the girl: Everything is right, and in what seems to be a gift from God, you happen to put this song on just as she is willing—for the first and last time—to dance with you. It is dark. She steps in close to you and puts her arms around your neck. You pray to God the song won't end. All meaning except for her has evacuated itself from your mind.

First the guitars. And then some drums. And then the snarling voice. But oh, what a melody. And the lyrics: "I want my little black egg." It makes you wonder, and then you wonder no more. She is almost in your arms. She has missed yet another shot in Ping-Pong, and she throws down the paddle. This is your opportunity: You go back to the stereo, place the needle at the beginning of "Little Black Egg," and walk over to her. You take her by the hand. Her hand is sweaty and she is still oh-so-mad about losing that Ping-Pong game. She dances with you at first, sort of noncommitally. Her mind is elsewhere, on missed shots. But then when the song breaks into its wordless guitar parts, she lets you. She lets you, and you are sure it is the music. This much is clear to you: Were it not for the music, there is no way she would let you. You are thankful for the Pagans, even though you know very little about them. The song has the sort of drive that makes any turning back impossible. This works in your favor, especially at the 1:41 mark, when the lyrics drop out and the only thing to concentrate on is each other's bodies. The song has the sort of drive that pushes you both forward into new territory.

Another Pagans song, "Street Where Nobody Lives," was recorded in the spring of 1978. Mike Hudson recalls that the song was "written in my car stuck in traffic on the way home from work one night." It begins à la the Stooges and never lets up. The song is a reminder of all that post-punk would forsake in its terrible rush to mediocrity. There is a push and confidence in the music of the Pagans that was not evaporated by the harsh light of success. In fact, failure was the key to bands like the Pagans. "Ever tried. Ever failed. No matter. Try Again. Fail again.

Fail Better," Samuel Beckett said. Even at its best, punk wasn't a success, but a better sort of failure.

[Mike Hudson, "The Pagans," www.geocities.com/pagan_pages/index.html.]

## "Paint It Black" (1)

**A Rolling Stones song covered by several punk-era bands,** suggesting a secret connection that's difficult to decipher. The Avengers, Television, Patti Smith, Blondie, the Feelies, and many others covered it. The terrorizing thing about the lyrics is the absolute rejection, the absolute negation. It's like Joseph Conrad's *Heart of Darkness* boiled down to hot tar. Because the Stones' song has such melodic force, the nihilism of the lyrics is easy to overlook.

> I see a red door and I want it painted black
> No colors anymore I want them to turn black
> I see the girls walk by dressed in their summer clothes
> I have to turn my head until my darkness goes.

Those words are as shockingly negative as anything by the Stooges; one day histories of rock will acknowledge the radically disaffirmative force of the Stones, whose legacy has been tarnished by longevity. In Steven Soderbergh's film *The Limey*, Peter Fonda—playing some breezy, likeable, immoral record executive—describes the sixties to his girlfriend as a sort of dream. But then he stops and corrects himself: what he means by "the sixties" was something very specific, not the entire decade: "It was sixty-six . . . early sixty-seven. That was all," he says.

"Paint It Black" was released in May 1966, the same month that tens of thousands of anti–Vietnam War protesters picketed the White House. In a poem from that era, "At a March Against the Vietnam War," Robert Bly wrote:

> We have carried around this cup of darkness.
> We hesitate to anoint ourselves.
> Now we pour it over our heads.

In 1966, black was loaded with meaning: It could refer to race, it could refer to moral depravity, it could mean depression; It could refer to the desire to be blind to the horrors of the world. Ten years later, when punk bands covered "Paint It Black," the rejection the song embodied must have seemed quaint. Yet it is a testament to the brutality of the Stones' song that even the campiest punk remake could not dispel the absolute zero that resides at its core.

[Robert Bly, "At a March Against the Vietnam War," in *Selected Poems*, 1967; repr., New York: Harper Perennial, 1986, p. 67.]

## "Paint It Black" (2)

**The cover version of the Rolling Stones' song** by the Avengers, which threatens to cast the entire terrible and romanticized sixties in a new light. There is a hint of boredom—but only a hint. Of course, the Avengers' version is faster: Punk was faster, Penelope Houston's voice was faster, as if the sixties could not be escaped from fast enough, or as if by playing the music of the sixties faster, the entire decade could be replayed as a high-speed car chase. That was the whole point. We must return to 1966, the year of "Paint It Black"'s original recording and release, and 1967, when the song flowered in the summer of love. The Stones were not the Beatles, but they were still competing. Soon, Altamont would separate them forever, and the full monstrous transformation during that time from altruism to unrepentant narcissism would come into focus. In December 1967, President Lyndon Johnson gave a joint interview for the television networks. The Summer of Love had come and gone. The warm mud was now cold. The war in Vietnam was escalating. For the next several years, there would be burning cities in the United States, campus violence, further assassinations, the real threat of anarchy. There was this exchange between Dan Rather and Lyndon Johnson:

> **Rather:** Mr. President, if I may, let's turn to the subject of youth. I think everyone expects youth to rebel and be restless. But there seems to be an unusually large number of American youth at this particular point in history who feel alienated to the traditional American ideas of God, patriotism, and family. Do you sense this alienation. What can be done about it?
>
> **Johnson:** Yes, I sense it. I think we have that condition. And we are trying to meet it as best we know how. I have seen it several times in my lifetime.
>
> I remember the days of the zoot-suiters in World War II. I remember the doubters who thought all of our youth were going to the dogs because of the sit-down movements in some of the plants in our country at certain periods of our country. I remember the doubt expressed about our ability in World War II to take a bunch of beardless boys and resist Hitler's legions.
>
> There have been some disappointments. But I have visited the campuses of this country. My Cabinet has gone and met with the young people of this country. We deal with young folks every day in the Peace Corps, in the poverty program, in the VISTA program, and in the job camps.
>
> And I think it is a very small percentage that have given up, who have lost faith, who have deep questions about the future of the country and of themselves.

Despite periodic efforts to recast punk as a political stance, punk in fact utterly detached itself from politics. In the hands of punk's most aesthetically radical groups—the Ramones, the Sex Pistols, the Slits, and Wire—the music, almost magically, created a tyranny of sound that left no room for the old ways of thinking. Bands like the Clash were in fact part of the inevitable reactionary backlash against punk, reintroducing the old sixties notions that music needed to be politically engaged.

The Avengers' version of "Paint It Black," coming at the end of it all, was a reminder of the early radical fun of punk, when the old orthodoxies had not yet been replaced by the new orthodoxies.

[Lyndon Johnson, "A Conversation with the President," December 19, 1967, The American Presidency Project, www.presidency.ucsb.edu.]

## Para-Punk Cinema

**Although the term "para-punk underground"**—originally used in 1979 by J. Hoberman to describe New York's emerging punk-era cinema—has fallen out of favor, its close relative "para-punk cinema" is worth resurrecting because of its strange ambiguity and because it is a term of its time. Other descriptors—especially "no-wave cinema" and "the cinema of transgression"—have come to replace "para-punk," but these terms link the movement (if it can be called that) too closely to specific styles and personalities, when in fact the films were highly diverse. Hoberman's article appeared in *The Village Voice* in May 1979; portions of it would also appear in the book *Midnight Movies* (1983), written with Jonathan Rosenbaum. In *The Village Voice* piece, Hoberman wrote:

> Drifting across the Bowery, fallout from the 1977 punk "explosion" continues to spawn art-world mutations. For the first time in the decade since the structuralists zoomed in on the stuff and ontology of film, a radically divergent group sensibility has blossomed on New York's independent film scene. Closely linked to local art-punk, no-wave bands, these filmmakers parallel the music's energy, iconography, and aggressive anyone-can-do-it aesthetic, while using the performers themselves as a kind of ready-made pool of dramatic talent.

Hoberman focused on directors such as Beth B and Scott B, Vivienne Dick, Charlie Ahearn, Eric Mitchell, James Nares, and Amos Poe, noting the cross-fertilization between many No Wave bands and the new breed of filmmakers. What did they have in common? Most of them made films using Super-8, and many of their films were initially shown in places like Max's Kansas City, bypassing the usual distribution channels. Nick Zedd (who sometimes went by Nick Zodiak at the time) would also become a force on the scene, eventually publishing the "Cinema of Transgression" manifesto in 1985 in the *Underground Film Bulletin* (Amy Taubin had used the term in 1979 in a *SoHo Weekly News* article "The Other Cinema"). Their films gloried in the shattering of taboos, but to what end? For one thing, they disavowed all affinities to traditions and movements. "Two opposing forces are now in existence," Nick Zodiak said in an interview in *Damage* after the release of *They Eat Scum*. "I just wanted to offend everyone, including people who like disco and including punks. Because nowadays there's a new breed of asshole called the punk that replaces the old breed of asshole, the hippie. And soon a new breed of asshole will replace the punk."

Some of the films achieve genuine and hallucinatory menace, such as Scott B and Beth B's *Black Box* (1979), about a man kidnapped, tormented (by Lydia Lunch), and stuffed into "the refrigerator" (a sheet-metal-lined cube wired for heat and cold) where he was assaulted by light and noise. The ending recalls the fury of the final flashing-light-nuclear-explosion minutes of *Kiss Me Deadly* (1955), except that that film's moments of transgression were all the more shocking because the film as a whole worked within the constraints of the production code and the mores of the fifties. Charlie Ahearn's *The Deadly Art of Survival* (1979), with its images of the vast crumbling concrete wasteland of New York City, is more bleakly dystopian than any million-dollar Hollywood movie set. And James Nares's *Rome '98* (1978) plunges so deeply and even earnestly into camp that it's hard not to take it seriously.

And yet, watching the films today—when everything is permitted (or at least discoverable)—it is difficult to feel anything but shame at what has been gained. The theorist Andreas Huyssen has written of the avant-garde movements of the seventies that "*the avant-garde*—embodiment of anti-tradition—has itself become tradition . . . its inventions and its imagination have become integral even to Western culture's most official manifestations." Which is to say: What happens when transgression itself becomes "traditional"? Yes, it could be argued, "mainstream" cinema is just as conservative as ever, as each new wave of blockbusters barely tinker with "the formula." But it is this very conservatism that makes moments of transgression all the more shocking all the more radical. The extended dialogue-free sequence in Alfred Hitchcock's *Vertigo* (1958) is startling because it comes within the context of a relatively commercial film—not in spite of it. Para-punk cinema and No Wave music dispensed with the very structures of their mediums, and in doing so eliminated the elemental contrast that makes transgression meaningful. Of course, art and pleasure are (sometimes) two very different things, and it would take a true philistine

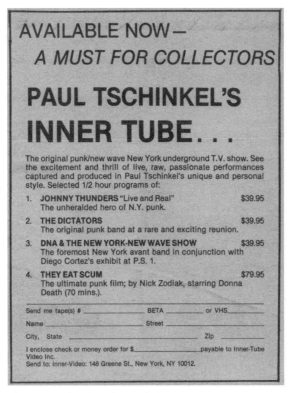

Punk movies for sale in the era of videotape

to object to the unsanctified violence in a Nick Zedd or Richard Kern movie today, when mass culture itself trades so openly and shamelessly in humiliation and degradation.

The secret truth about para-punk cinema is that we all have in our hearts and minds our very own No Waves that sometimes wash over us suddenly and without warning and that sometimes creep up slowly. Soon, we find ourselves in our own dark thickets. Watching even the most extreme and extremely transgressive para-punk films, the most shocking thing is how mild they are compared to the savagery of the imagination.

[J. Hoberman, "No Wavelength: The Para-Punk Underground," *The Village Voice*, May 21, 1979, p. 42; Andreas Huyssen, "The Search for Tradition: Avant-Garde and Postmodernism in the Seventies," *New German Critique*, Winter 1998, p.23; Nick Zodiak interviewed by Mia Culpa, "They Eat Scum," *Damage* no. 5, 1980, p. 34.]

# Patti

**She called herself Patti Smith,** but who could know for sure?

In those days I was living in a tiny room above an Italian restaurant off the corner of an alley. Everything that could be wrong with the room was wrong, and I could even see down into the kitchen from a broken cold-air return duct beneath a metal grate on my floor.

The owners, a husband and wife, had lost a son in Vietnam, and they hired me to wash dishes because they said I reminded them of him. I washed dishes most nights, and then a few afternoons I worked at the video counter of a U-Haul place. That was back before the big chain video-rental places when they were rented out of places like U-Haul and neighborhood grocery stores. Then one day the father came to me and pressed a key into the palm of my hand.

"Upstairs," he said, "is yours." They were full of gestures like this. They were unreasonable in their love for me.

They never charged me rent, and I lived there for many years, a fugitive from the world. Each Thursday a boney-elbowed man named Paul did the dishes instead of me, and I sat at small table in the shadows near the back of the restaurant, drinking red wine and having all the homemade bread I could eat.

That's when she came up to me at my little table in the corner, her eyes as black as her hair. She was wearing jeans and a black leather jacket, a little silver bracelet on her wrist. Her fingers were so long they reminded me of spider legs, but in a good and happy way. I didn't recognize her at first—the only picture of her I really remembered was from the cover of *Horses*—but as she came closer I could tell it was her.

"Hey," she said, "aren't you the guy from the video store?"

"Yeah," I said. "Patti, right?"

She sat down across from me and took off her jacket. She must have noticed I was looking at it.

"Like it?" she said. "It's my 'don't fuck with me' jacket."

"Oh, I'll have to remember that."

Beneath her jacket she wore a loose black tank-top. Now, this will sound funny, but I knew then that she was someone with secrets, and that those secrets were darker than your run-of-the-mill secrets. I just knew. I had been right before. For instance, when I was fifteen I dated a girl whose father had recently remarried. The new wife seemed all sunshine and roses, but I knew something darker lurked beneath the exterior of fine china, carefully folded napkins, and flawless rose gardens. I even told my girlfriend this, warned her that her step mom wasn't all she was cracked up to be. But she didn't believe me. Neither did her father when I went to him with my suspicions.

"I'm warning you," I told him. "She's not a good woman. Watch your back."

He was outraged at my audacity and banned me from setting foot on his property again and forbade me from seeing his daughter. A month later I got a call from my girlfriend informing me that, while her dad was at work the day before, a moving company came in and emptied the contents of the house into a huge moving truck. Everything: coat hangers, TV, VCR, furniture. Even the carpet scraps in the basement. All gone. When my girlfriend's father got home he thought he had been robbed and called the police. In his embarrassment he even rescinded the ban on me, but I only saw his daughter once or twice more. The old spark just wasn't there.

And there were lots of other cases, too, where it turned out my unscientific gut-level reactions ended up being right on target. So I felt pretty confident that Patti had some secrets, which was okay by me. Anyway, our conversation didn't go as I expected, and I think I let it follow the strange course it took because I was, as I said, unable to create a vision of my own future in my head. In other words, I was defenseless.

"Let me cut right to it, Nick," she said, putting a cigarette between her lips and lighting it with an old canary-yellow bic. Who used those anymore? "Before I was performing, I used to have a shell around me. I felt alien. It was like my shell was there and I was two feet behind it." She paused, inhaled, exhaled. A line of smoke from the tip of her cigarette drifted up in a wobbly line. "I'm not here to deceive you," she said, settling back into her chair, which I thought was an odd way to begin, something out of a sinister movie like *The Manchurian Candidate* or some example out of a textbook on psychology, an example that illustrates Freud's theory that people rarely initially say what they mean to begin a conversation, and that in fact they very often say precisely the *opposite* of what they mean, such as when someone says, "I don't believe we've met before" when in fact the person might *at that very moment* be thinking, "I believe I have met this person somewhere before."

"Okay," I said. What else could I say? She smiled. She took a deep drag on her cigarette.

"Good. Shall we go ahead?"

"With . . . ?"

"Oh, just a few questions."

"Why not."

"How old are you?"

What did I have to lose? I answered her. "Twenty-five."

"What were you doing one year ago?"

"Uh, let's see. Well I was in grad school. Working on my dissertation. Teaching some freshman composition classes. Then I got kicked out."

"Really?" Patti asked.

"No, not really. But I was asked to leave. They were polite about it."

"And now?"

"Well, now I'm just, you know. Hanging around. I'm writing a little bit but, ah, mostly just, you know, kind of drifting." She didn't seem too interested in that.

"Are you claustrophobic?" she asked, tapping her ashes into my empty wine glass.

"No," I said.

"Afraid of the dark?"

"Mildly."

"Yes or no for questions that can be answered yes or no, please," she told me, looking at me in the eyes.

"No," I said.

"Do you smoke?"

"Sometimes."

"Are you afraid of tight places?"

"Tight like . . ."

"Like let's say you were wedged between two rocks, and you knew you were in no danger of being crushed, but you also knew that you'd have to work hard to get free. Would *that* frighten you?"

"I suppose a little."

"Would it *terrify* you?"

I considered this, and imagined myself wedged between two rocks that would not crush me.

"No," I said.

"Does the idea of being blind frighten you?" she asked, shutting her eyes. Was this her idea of a joke?

"Sure," I said. "It'd be awful."

Patti opened her eyes again. "Can you swim?"

"I can."

"Do you work better on a team or alone?"

"I've never worked on a team."

"Have you ever seen a dead body?"

"I prefer not to answer," I said, finishing off my beer.

"I need a yes or no answer," she said.

"I prefer not to."

"I'll give you that one. What's your earliest memory?"

"Um, my earliest memory is of . . . Let's see . . . Getting stuck under my dad's riding mower. But the blade wasn't engaged."

"Do you remember it well?"

"Yes."

"How much of it do you remember?"

"Pretty much the whole thing. Kate—Katie—Katherine—my sister—believe it or not—snapped a Polaroid of it."

Patti smiled. She played with her earlobe. She waited. What did she wait for?

"Is your memory," she said finally, twisting out her cigarette, "from the actual event or from the photograph?"

"What's the difference? Photographs capture images of real things."

"Not really. One could conceivably remember a photograph but forget the event it captured."

"I still don't see the difference," I said.

"Well, let's take a hypothetical situation and say we're talking about a picture of a birthday party for a cousin when you were just five or six. You happened to be sick and weren't there. But your sister is in the picture, sitting at the table wearing a party hat. And the picture implies that you were there; you ought to be there. Hypothetically you are just outside the frame of the picture, in the space that the camera doesn't capture. But let's say you aren't there, and the picture ends up in a photo album, where you see it every once in a while. Pretty soon you forget that you were sick on that occasion and missed the party. Pretty soon you think, 'Well, too bad I'm not in that picture because I was in another room or at the other end of the table or going to the bathroom.' So now I ask you and you say you remember your sister at your cousin's birthday party, but what you really remember is a picture of your sister at your cousin's birthday party."

"Well, I can tell you—trust me I can tell you—which memories are from experience and which are from photos. Trust me I can make that distinction."

"I trust you."

On the far side of the room, the Joey Miserable band worked their way through an old Pink Floyd song—something from *Dark Side of the Moon*: "Breathe, breathe in the air / Don't be afraid to care / Leave, don't leave me . . ." Not exactly a song you'd expect to hear from the Worms, who scorned covers. And if they did a cover it would likely be something from the Sex Pistols or Bikini Kill or Nick Cave and the Bad Seeds. But they played the Pink Floyd song beautifully, somberly, stately, and it reminded me of the synchronicity of *Dark Side of the Moon* to the film *The Wizard of Oz*, how playing the album as the soundtrack to the movie really matches what's going on in the film in an uncanny way, and how Dorothy becomes some other, ahead-of-her-time figure when watched that way, looking mournfully to the sky as the fighter jets scream out of one of those sound effect Pink Floyd song interludes, and how the ringing of the bells (the "tolling of the island bell") predicts the Wicked Witch's arrival.

"Okay, that's it," Patti said suddenly, putting her black jacket back on and standing up. "You did very well. Hey, can we get out of here and get some air?"

"Sure, let's go."

We moved out of the bar slowly, accompanied by the blaring Pink Floyd, past the tables of the happy, the lonely, and the inscrutable. As the music droned we seemed happily trapped in time—at least that's how I remember it—like one of those throwaway scenes in a film that you later recollect as, in fact, the film's key scene, the scene that functions as the engine that drives the plot.

Outside it was night. The sidewalk was still giving off heat from the day. We were on the edge of campus, the place where it dwindled from bar district into cheap apartments with weedy lawns and barbecue grills on porches and eventually into corn and wheat fields. We walked out and out, and I was very happy to be there with Patti beside me in the dark.

"So, it's my turn now. What do you do now?" I asked her.

"Now?"

"Now that you don't make music any more."

"I always make music. I just don't record it anymore. I don't perform."

"Why?"

She paused and smiled. "I prefer not to."

"Of course," I said. "I understand."

"I knew you would. That's why I came to you. That's why I found you. Now I make maps. I'm a cartographer."

"Really? What do you make maps of?"

"The human heart," she said, turning to me, laughing. "Just kidding. Well let's see, all sorts of things. People hire me to map places, I map them."

"What kinds of places?"

"All kinds. Forests. Abandoned mines. People want to figure out how to get around in a place. Before they go there they send me first to figure it out for them."

"What kind of people?"

"You know. Corporations that want to buy some uncharted foreign land. Wealthy guys who want to explore some exotic place. Developers who need to know the locations of mine shafts or underground water or whatever before they build."

"Sounds dangerous."

"Hmm," she said. "Not really."

We walked on through the night, out away from campus, into the darkness. For some reason I thought about two Pink Floyd albums: *Set the Controls for the Heart of the Sun* and *Dark Side of the Moon*. Hot and cold. Ying and yang. Near and far. I thought about Patti there next to me, her black leather jacket, her lean body beneath that jacket. Near and far.

We didn't say anything for a long time as we made our way farther and farther out along a country road that cut between vast, dark wheat fields on either side. The heavy night air was sweet. Sometimes it was so dark and quiet I wasn't sure if she was there at all, but then I could hear her breathing. The quiet purr of videotapes rewinding in my mind.

"Can I ask you just one more question?" she said, taking out a cigarette. She stopped to light it, her face appearing in the small, unsteady glow of the flame. Her hands were trembling. Why were they trembling?

"Of course," I said, cupping my hand around her lighter, steadying her.

"What do you fear most?" She tucked a lock of hair behind he ear with a graceful touch of her fingertips.

"What kind of fear?"

"The real, terrible thing. Not just physical, but existential. You know, the one true fear that freezes your heart in the middle of the night."

I knew the answer right away—I knew it before Patti even finished the question—and I didn't even turn it over once in my mind. As we walked down the road in the night, the crickets screaming in the wheat, our shoulders touched a few times, and I wondered if this person named Patti liked it when our shoulders touched. I had only known her—how long?—a few hours, really. No longer than that. And what did I know about her? Nothing, except that she made maps and smoked and that I had let her ask me all sorts of absurd questions. So why did I tell her—this stranger named Patti—why did I tell her about Katherine, about my sister? Because there was no one to stop me; I had nothing to lose.

"That I'll never see my sister Katherine again. That's my greatest fear."

"What happened to her?" she said.

I told her—the first time I had ever talked about it to anybody, except one other time when I was drunk—about that night in 1980: how my sister and I had spent an evening at a carnival on the rides that turn you upside down, how we came back home dizzy through the plowed fields, how our parents put us to bed for the night, how I heard her in her room telling herself a story, how my room spun that night, how I dreamt of an enormous black machine that filled my head and then my room, a machine like a maze, with no beginning and no end, and of how in the dream Katherine climbed through the dark gears and wires, and how I tried to follow her, exhausted, on and on, deeper and deeper into the labyrinth, and how I lost her there, and how the machine came to life like some beast, and how I escaped without her. The next day, on the island, I told her about my dream, and then later I went to get her forgotten watch and when I returned home she was gone.

"So where'd she go?" Patti asked.

"I don't know. No one knows. She just vanished. Or ran away. Or was taken away. Disappeared."

"It doesn't make any sense. People don't just disappear."

"That doesn't matter anymore. What matters is that she's not here. She's somewhere else, or she's no where."

"She can't just be 'no where.'"

"That's where I think of her."

"Well, that's one way of looking at it, I suppose. Were there suspects?"

"There were a few people. But it all went cold."

"How did—what did your parents do?"

I didn't say anything. We walked on quietly for a while. The stars shimmered in the sky like little bits of shattered glass.

"Truth or dare," I said. "Now you tell me your fear. What terrifies you?"

Patti was quiet, and I could see her face barely in the moonlight, as colorless and smooth as a soft lake stone.

She stopped and tossed her cigarette aside. She looked up at the sky.

"Her," she said, quietly.

I looked up, too, at the black-ink sky filled with glass stars. Millions of miles away. What was our world of problems to them?

"Her?"

"She tried to hurt me once, and she'll try again. She's searching for me even at this very moment. Even as we speak right now. She's searching for me because that's all she knows how to do. And she won't stop until she finds me."

"Who?"

"Someone I knew once. A terrible . . . someone."

"Tell me."

"I can't, not now."

In the dark I wanted to reach over and touch Patti's face, her skin. I took a few long, deep breaths, letting the pure night air fill my lungs.

"Let me show you something," she said, stepping closer. "Shut your eyes."

"It's already dark."

"Trust me. Just shut them. Now, I'm going to put your hand on my heart. Don't get any funny ideas, I just want you to feel my heart. Here."

She took my hand and slipped it inside her jacket and pressed it to her chest. Her body was warm beneath my hand, her chest moving up and down, but other than that, nothing. No heartbeat.

"I don't feel anything," I said, my eyes still shut.

"Are you sure?"

"Yeah."

"Spread your fingers apart."

I spread my fingers, and the tip of my pinky touched the curving flesh of her breast. I could hear us breathing. It was intoxicating. But still no heartbeat.

"But yet it's in there," she said, whispering. "I know it is. My heart's inside there, beating fast, beneath your hand. I can feel it. I know it's there. I know it is. Do you understand?"

It was quite a moment, I can tell you, and it filled my head with such . . . such expectation. Is that the right word? I don't know what else to call it. Expectation.

We walked back toward the campus without saying much, my hand tingling. In fact, I don't believe we said a word to each other all the way back.

Finally she said, "Do you want to find your sister?"

Her question caught me off guard, and I didn't respond for a time.

"What if she's not to be found?" I said at last.

"Listen, silly: Do you want to find your sister?"

Who was this person, taking such interest in my past?

"Yes," I said. "If she's to be found."

"What, you think it's fated?"

"I believe in that. In fate. And you, do you want to escape her, the person who's searching for you?"

"Yes," she said. "If she's to be escaped."

By now we were back on the edge of campus, the buildings dark and quiet.

"Well then we're in a real quandary, aren't we? I want to find someone. You want to lose someone. Quite a pair."

"Obviously we need to meet again. To discuss our dilemma."

"Obviously," I said. Then, before I could say anything else, Patti reached up to me, put her hand lightly on my cheek, and gently kissed me. A soft, sweet kiss, her lips on mine. Then, just as quickly, she turned and walked away into the night.

"Good-bye," she said, her voice distant in the dark. "I'll visit you at the Outpost."

I don't remember walking back to my tiny room. Perhaps I went directly there; perhaps I wandered the dark streets. I don't recall. But I do remember lying on my mattress that night, staring up at the black ceiling, thinking of Patti, and of my hand upon her body beneath her jacket. I shut my eyes, then opened them. The same black ceiling. I thought, *If I try hard enough, I can see the sky. If I try hard enough, I can see the stars.*

And then I did.

# Penetration

**Pauline Murray, the lead singer of Penetration,** has said that Patti Smith was an inspiration, and in songs like "Life's a Gamble," "Lovers of Outrage," and "Reunion"—all from their 1978 album, *Moving Targets*—you can hear, in the soft spaces between the words, Patti Smith. The band Penetration (formed in May 1976, recorded their first demo in June) included, by 1978, Murray on vocals, as well as Gary Chaplin, Robert Blamire, Gary Smallman, Neale Floyd, and Fred Purser. "People's expectations of you get you down," Murray told Phil Sutcliffe in 1977, and listening to that first album your expectations evaporate at the first noise, because the sound defies category. Penetration succeeded in minimizing gender just when you expected it to be important; for this reason, the groups is less acclaimed than X-Ray Spex or the Slits or even Patti Smith, who self-consciously invited and then rejected such ideas. (The Slits always wanted you to remember that they were women, even as they wanted you to forget; this tension, of course, drew the interest of the critics. Penetration was less inclined to play this way.) But was the music good? In fact, it was too good. "Distance from London," Jon Savage has noted, "gave these metropolitan groups [Penetration and others] room to grow as they were shielded from the worst aspects of the signing frenzy in the capital."

Listening to *Moving Targets* now, it's easier to hear what a radical album it is, conforming to neither punk's blank nihilism or to post-punk's nervy, echo-chamber hollowness. Instead, it offers up an alarming dose of big, kick-ass rock, complete with guitar solos.

[Jon Savage, *England's Dreaming Anarchy, Sex Pistols, Punk Rock, and Beyond*, New York: St. Martin's Press, 1992, p. 300; Phil Sutcliffe, "Penetration: Anarchy in County Durham," *Sounds*, June 18, 1977.]

# Penetrators

**A garage/punk band from Syracuse, New York,** whose music—like that of George Brigman—shared with punk a nostalgia for early-sixties rock and roll. But unlike groups like the Ramones, whose music was stripped down to the force of a single idea, the Penetrators were less wedded to the idea of purity and speed. The band was originally—in 1976—Eliot (Spike) Kagan and Jack Lipton. It would, by 1979, also include Curtis Seals, and then Christian D'Orbit, Paul Bawol, and Henry Brent. Recorded in 1976 and released in 1979, "Baby Dontcha Tell Me" was entirely Kagan—on vocals, guitar, drums, everything. Haunted by the sounds of the Rolling Stones (as were all their songs), this one achieves a sort of doomed fury, shifting moodily between surf rock and noise rock, Eliot's voice coming on like someone singing from the back of an abandoned subway car during a thunderstorm.

# Pere Ubu

**The Cleveland band Pere Ubu's affinity** with punk is thorny. Here is what David Thomas, the lead singer and force behind Pere Ubu, says about punk:

> Personally I was uninterested and considered punk to be tiresome and backward-looking. Punk was and is a Madison-Avenue corporate scheme to try to keep rock dumb. It was the worst thing that happened to music in the Seventies. It destroyed an emerging generation of Third-Gen rock musicians. The best bands of the period are all ones that were already working when punk was organized, were already shaped and had formed an identity independently. After that pre-punk wave there was a desert for years. Unless you think rock music should be dumb. Your call.

Originally formed in 1975, Pere Ubu's first incarnation included Peter Laughner (at that time the guitarist and sometimes singer in Rocket from the Tombs), who only recorded two songs with the band: "30 Seconds over Tokyo" and "Heart of Darkness." Laughner, who died in 1977, was enamored of the developing underground New York scene, while Thomas and many others associated with Ubu wanted nothing to do with New York. According to Tim Wright, Ubu "never wanted to play New York. They just wanted to be a Cleveland band."

Despite Thomas's disavowel of punk, Ubu's philosophy was resolutely DIY and, at times, minimalist. Like the practitioners of the Dogme 95 film movement, whose "Vow of Chastity" was written by the Danish directors Lars von Trier and

Ad for Pere Ubu at the Crypt, from Cleveland *Scene* magazine, December 1976

Thomas Vinterberg, bands in the early-to-mid-seventies Cleveland music scene recognized that limits and self-imposed constraints—rather than unlimited freedom—could unleash tremendous creative force. Diminishing the sheer number of creative choices in any artistic endeavor can free the artist to work expressively and fully within boundaries. Here, for example, is the basic Ubu methodology, as expressed by Thomas in the article "Story of Pere Ubu":

- "Don't ever audition."
- "Don't look for someone."
- "Don't seek success."
- "Choose the first person you hear about."
- "Take the first idea you get."
- "Put unique people together. Unique people will play uniquely whether or not they know how to play."
- "Delay Centrifugal Destruct Factors for as long as possible then push the button."

The path not taken into punk is illustrated on two versions of "30 Seconds over Tokyo," written by Laughner, Thomas, and Gene O'Connor (Cheetah Chrome) in 1974. The Rocket from the Tombs version was recorded in February 1975 at the band's rehearsal loft, described by Craig Bell as a twenty-by-fifty-foot space through a Sun six-channel mixer onto a 2-track tape machine. Named after the 1942 raid on Tokyo by James Doolittle, the song, according to Thomas, was "a good choice for our cinematic approach. Brief synopsis. U.S. needed to strike propaganda blow against Japan right after Pearl Harbor and to suggest to Japanese leaders that they were not safe from retribution. Stripped down a flight of B-25s of everything but a few bombs and launched them off a carrier which they'd never be able to return to (fuel) or land on (size)."

The Rocket from the Tombs version, despite the fact that it was recorded crudely (or perhaps because it was), is superior in almost every way. Clocking in at 6:41, there is a relentless fierceness to this version that is positively frightening and that captures the symbolic madness of the Doolittle raid. Where the Pere Ubu version is studied and distant, the Tombs version builds, at the 2:19 mark, into a thunder of guitars that wipes away all irony and pretense. It's as if Cleveland had been reduced to nothing but the Flats. A screeching, electro-shock guitar that begins at 4:25 and lasts approximately thirty seconds is a sonic earthquake that hearkens back to the crazy ending of Robert Aldrich's 1955 cold-war paranoia movie *Kiss Me Deadly* and the terrible, romantic scene at the end where the two characters stumble at night through the roaring surf, fleeing the nuclear explosion but caught in its strobe-light flashing and hounded by its shrieking, piercing sound.

By comparison, the Ubu version of "30 Seconds" is a catalog of missed opportunities and false starts. This isn't to say that it isn't a great song, in its own coldy alienated way. But it's much more of a thinker's song, a song that's too self-conscious to rock out. Instead of a gun waiting to be fired, it's a gun lying on the table, waiting to be picked up. Charlotte Pressler—who was married to Laughner—has said of Ubu and the scene at the time that "we would sit around and elaborate the aesthetic. We'd just sit there and go, 'What's cool?'" The difference between Rocket from the Tombs and Pere Ubu is that Rocket from the Tombs forgot that question for one brief moment.

Pere Ubu rarely did.

John Berryman's collection of poems *The Dream Songs*, published in 1965 and 1969, are wonderful and terrible and like a hallucinogenic prophecy of the bleak and funny center of the seventies. *How*, you wonder, *did he know?* "Dream Song # 364" sits before me now, the *Twin Peaks* soundtrack holding it open, the Michigan frogs singing some mystery to each other in the deep forested wetlands behind our home. The poem begins like this:

*There* is one book that Henry hasn't read:
*Ubu Roi*: He feeling ignorant whenever his mind brings it up.
Everytime anybody says
—Mr Bones, you has read everything—he singles out instead
*Ubu Roi*, to prove he is an idiot
and should be, as one, blest.

"Final Solution"—originally released in March 1976, one month before the Ramones' first album—is the kind of song that makes all the above words about Ubu being too coolly intellectual seem irrelevant or wrongheaded. The song uncurls like a rattlesnake in terrible slow motion. "Buy me a ticket to a sonic reduction / Guitars gotta sound like a nuclear destruction." There is a moment of silence after these words, as if the world had suddenly gone out, and then the lyrics continue: "Seems I'm a victim of natural selection." The song's title was "inspired by a Sherlock Holmes story, 'The Final Problem.' Concern that one final solution might be associated with another caused the band to delay its re-release for several years." Could the band really have been unaware of the "other" associations to the phrase "final solution"?

"Heaven" is, in its sweet, reggae-tinged softness, among the most confounding Ubu songs. Of course, there is the strange synth-growl sound that stalks the song, like some soft monster breathing very slowly, and even after a lifetime of listening you cannot decode this song. Originally released in 1977, this is the first Ubu song that seems connected to something outside, a more familiar form of music, although that familiarity is defamiliarized at every turn. The first line, "Here she comes," puts you in the mind of a love song, but of course there is no love song here.

[Craig Bell, from liner notes to the RFTT CD p. 4; John Berryman, "Dream Song # 364," *The Dream Songs*, 1969; repr., New York: Farrar, Straus and Giroux, 2007, p. 386; Pressler quoted in Clinton Heylin, *From the Velvets to the Voidoids: A Pre-Punk History for a Post-Punk World*, New York: Penguin, 1993, p. 221; Tim Wright quoted in *ibid.*, p. 222; "Story of Pere Ubu" available at http://users.rcn.com/obo/ubu/ubu_story.html; David Thomas interviewed by Craig Johnson, "I Never Volunteer Information," available at http://spikemagazine.com/0305davidthomas_pereubu.php; Peter Thomas, e-mail to author, May 7, 2006]

## Pettibon, Raymond

**An American artist, born Raymond Ginn in 1957,** whose early work was used on record sleeves and flyers for Black Flag and other punk bands, especially those associated with SST Records, founded by his older brother, Greg. His reputation and body of work has grown so that his punk-era illustrations are just part of what he is known for today. He earned an economics degree from UCLA and was, for a time, a high school math teacher. His drawings ooze with thick black lines that suggest pathetic violence and humor; it's not surprising that he has been influenced by noir. Of his work during the punk era he has said, "My work was just drawings, and basically drawings just as I would do now. They weren't done with any aspirations of becoming a part of that [punk] scene. They were just collections of drawings, some of which I xeroxed and sold. But you couldn't even say they were sold in the punk scene . . . It was never my goal to capitalize on punk."

In the same interview, Pettibon mentions Henry James as among his favorite writers, Henry James of the notoriously slowly unfolding ambiguity. In his 1902 novel *The Wings of the Dove*, Kate says this to Densher about Milly, who is dying: "She doesn't see the future. It has opened out before her in these last weeks as a dark confused thing." At its best, Pettibon's work is as unsettling as Milly's future; there is a violence waiting just off the page, but we are not certain when or how it will strike.

[Henry James, *The Wings of the Dove*, 1902; repr., New York: W. W. Norton, 1978, p. 213; Raymond Pettibon interviewed by John O'Connor, *The Believer*, Dec/Jan 2004–2005, p. 63.]

## "Police State"

**Released in 1979, the single "'Police State"** (b/w "Set Program") was the product of Jim Jacobi of Lincoln, Nebraska, who played all the instruments except drums, which were played by Herb Hill. He called the project Crap Detectors. It is a low, fuzzy, crunchy song, with a guitar solo that is savage and careens like a car with no breaks speeding down a mountainside. That solo is like listening to the MC5 through cabin walls. There are simulated gun shots and sirens at the end. "Corporations want you to take it / Justice for the rich / That's the little hitch," he sings, and you wonder about all the space around Lincoln, Nebraska.

"Set Program" is a synthesizer-heavy mechanistic drone, with Jacobi's voice coming across like the computer HAL from *2001: A Space Odyssey* speaking from hell. At moments, the song reminds you of Devo, if Devo had been locked in a dark castle for years and learned to play dark-castle songs. No, this is not, strictly speaking, punk music, and yet it shares with seventies punk the radical unfamiliarity that came with the do-it-yourself ethic. And this is the strange and sometimes wonderful thing about music like Jacobi's: Just because it was made in basements and other familiar places by people sort of like you and me does not make it any more populist than the overblown music of groups like the Eagles or Yes. For at its best, music like "Set Program" manages a level of alienation that arena-rock bands spent careers trying to achieve.

## Punk, alternate meanings of

**The term "punk" is a notoriously slippery term.** Right away, let us dispense with the obvious meanings it has come to be associated with today: a do-it-yourself ethic, spontaneous amateurism, primitivism, fast songs, resistance to mass commodification. Instead, let us turn to its less obvious, historically eclipsed meanings. A sampling:

- *A Dictionary of Slang and Unconventional English*: "punk, adj. Worthless; decidedly inferior; displeasing; 'rotten'"
- *A Dictionary of the Underworld*: "punk, n. A no-good, a waster, a person of no importance"
- *Dictionary of Smoky Mountain English*: "punk *noun* Partially decayed wood, often used as kindling"
- *Dictionary of Caribbean English Usage*: "punk . . . A stupid person"
- *Black Talk: Words and Phrases from the Hood to the Amen Corner*: "Punk i) A cowardly, passive person; a nonfighter"
- *The New Zealand Oxford Dictionary*: "punk n. nonsense"

In 1976 especially, when the term "punk" was increasingly attached to groups like the Ramones and the Sex Pistols in the press and in fanzines, there was the possibility of arguments like this, expressed in a letter by reader Anthony Cerqueira, in *Melody Maker*:

I would like to congratulate Steve Lake for confronting that so-called rock artist Patti Smith and criticising her and her Learn-As-You-Play Music School dropouts. Those poison arrows of Lake's were long deserving of that little girl living out her rock and roll fantasies.

We'll ignore the fact that Patti Pretentious is pushing thirty. Smith is representative of the so-called New York punk rock scene.

What is going on now in the New York area is the amnesty programme for all past teens who ignored punk rock in their youth.

This writer is and I am excused from the services at CBGB's. I have paid my dues to the great god of Rock and Roll . . . I couldn't hear for two days after sitting in the second row of a Deep Purple/Fleetwood Mac concert. This is what comes into my mind when I hear the term "punk rock": not the Ramones or Patti Smith. The groups named above are what I feel is the true definition of punk rock. Groups such as Thin Lizzy are carrying on the tradition.

Early on, the "return to basics" that characterized what came to be known as punk was playing out in several different ways. From one angle, bands like the Ramones and the Sex Pistols could be seen as stripping down rock and roll to its basics, returning it in spirit (if not lyrically) to its populist, garage rock dimensions. But from another angle, these bands were too self-conscious, too arty, too invested in image. That's why a band like Eddie and the Hot Rods—which had been around in one form or another since 1973—could disavow, or at least warily embrace, what was rapidly becoming known as the punk movement. "We've never put a false front on," the Hot Rods' Barrie Masters told Chris Welch of *Melody Maker*. "We've started getting labeled Punk now, but fair enough, if they want to call us that. All those who want to be Punk bands aren't. Half of them. Especially like the main culprits, they're just art-school boys who are into image, which is all wrong."

A good example of how everything was still gloriously mixed up in 1977—before the record companies had fully begun to break the scene into sellable units—is evident in an advertisement for Drome Records ("your NEW WAVE record store") from Cleveland Heights, which in July ran a half-page ad that began with the phrase "and the SUMMER OF METAL continues with . . . The Dictators and AC/DC and KISS." Under the banner of "New Wave," "metal" seemed a perfectly viable category.

[Richard Allsopp, ed., *Dictionary of Caribbean English Usage*, New York: Oxford University Press, 1996, p. 456; Anthony Cerqueira, "Lizzy, Not Patti, Is Future of Rock," *Melody Maker*, September 25, 1976, p. 19; Tony Deverson and Graeme Kennedy, *The New Zealand Oxford Dictionary*, New York: Oxford University Press, 2005, p. 911; Michael B. Montgomery and Joseph S. Hall, *Dictionary of Smoky Mountain English*, Knoxville: The University of Tennessee Press, 2004, p. 469; Geneva Smitherrman, *Black Talk: Words and Phrases from the Hood to the Amen Corner*, New York: Houghton Mifflin, 1994, p. 186; Chris Welch, "Hot Roddin," *Melody Maker*, September 25, 1976, p. 47.]

## Punk, as "honored"

**One of the goals of this book** is to go back to that moment in time when the term "punk" was unstable, ambigious, loaded with so many suggestions. Once the Sex Pistols made punk notorious after their incident with Bill Grundy on British television, the term hardened into a rigid, more specific set of meanings. And then it became the name of a specific sort of music. And then it became an industry. But in May 1976, Larry Rohter could write in *The Washington Post* about punk like this:

> The punk is one of the oldest and most honored figures in rock 'n' roll. He dates from the mid 'Fifties, when Elvis Presley and James Dean first popularized the image of the sullen but vulnerable leather-jacket tough guy, and had been a part of the rock scene ever since. He nurtured the Beatles through their early "teddy boy" phase; lately he's reappeared as the hot-blooded hero of many of Bruce Springsteen's songs.

> In truth, the tramps of early Springsteen songs are only a few heartbeats away from the alienated, fun-seeking kids in Ramones songs. But although Springsteen's songs were full of hostile romanticism, they were never ironic. Punk itself was never fully ironic either, but bands like the Ramones, the Sex Pistols, Talking Heads, Blondie, Wire, the Cramps, and Television made it impossible to attach yourself fully to the characters in their songs; this was their art. Rohter was right to associate James Dean with punk (Nicholas Ray, who had directed *Rebel Without a Cause*, was a hero to Richard Hell), for his gloomy detachment was simply a method of keeping violence at bay. Punk's first wave in the mid-seventies was an experiment in loosening the reigns but still carefully containing this hostility. Punk's second wave—hardcore—was a rejection of containment altogether.

> [Larry Rohter, "The Time-Honored Punk Syndrome," *The Washington Post*, May 9, 1976, p. 167.]

## Punk, influence on something other than music or fashion

**A not-so-secret truth:** Punk rock was a sort of music that lasted a fairly short time, probably not even until 1982. It was just too tied to its historical period to live beyond that period and its unique circumstances. In truth, the DIY spirit has long characterized music, from the early blues to early rock and roll to rap and hip-hop to street musicians throughout the ages playing any type of music. The myth surrounding punk—that it was characterized primarily by the fact that anyone could just pick up an instrument and play—was created early in the movement, first through fanzines, where musicians, reacting against the hyper-professionalism of the late sixties and early seventies, distinguished themselves by taking on amateurism as a badge of honor. But almost all pop music begins this way, regardless of genre. Punk distinguished itself by maintaining this cult of amateurism, which was quickly picked up by the mainstream press as an angle into the phenomenon of punk itself.

In popularizing the DIY philosophy, punk did not revolutionize the future of music so much as it did the future of film. The rhetoric surrounding the rise of digital cameras and the Dogme 95 movement is deeply intertwined with the do-it-yourself language of the punk movement, as well as its claims of authenticity. The director Amos Poe, a contemporary of Jim Jarmusch, notes, in the DVD director's commentary for his film *The Foreigner* (1977), connections between his style of punk filmmaking and the Dogme 95 movement: "This soundtrack, by the way, has no mix . . . When we hear music, there's no other sound, and when you hear dialogue there's no other music . . . It's just cut. Straight cut. This pre-dates the Danish school . . . of Lars von Trier . . . Dogme . . . this is the Dogme thing, twenty years before." In both punk and Dogme, claims about creating something more "authentic" or "real" are based upon very complicated forms of technology. According to Simon Frith, "[Punk's] ideology may have been anti-technology, but the late Seventies rush of home-made records and independent labels was dependent, in fact, on the lower cost of good quality recording equipment." The Danish directors Lars von Trier has said that "[T]he reason why I laid down the Dogme rules or put a camera on my shoulder was to get away from all this perfectionism and concentrate on something else." Indeed, technologies of production can never be separated from production itself.

Von Trier has offered among the most utopian defences of digital cameras; like the punks before him, he argues for simplicity: "I think technology right now is great, because it makes filming so easy, you know. Early on, when I was young, everyone would say, No, you can't make films, it's too difficult to make films. Which was always a lie, it's always been a lie that it's difficult to make films. But now, nobody believes it anymore, because of the technology." The speed of punk—short, fast songs—has had tremendous influence on the look of film and on visual culture in general. As Maria Demopoulos suggests, filmmakers and audiences have been deeply affected by the fast editing that characterizes television commercials, promos, and, in its heyday, MTV, which were all in turn influenced by punk's speed:

> If viewers can now process cuts as brief as two frames, the equivalent of one-twelfth of a second, it's because MTV and its surrounding advertising-marketing complex have finely tuned our optic nerves, both promoting and portraying a more accelerated pace of daily life and, consequently, a new rhetoric of emotional and psychological fragmentation and disorder. More than a decade of translating music

into visuals has yielded a new, self-taught, self-generated way to connect moving images. This highly mannered editorial aesthetic embodies the very essence of advertising: compression . . . Where classical film editing melds transitions into seamless, gliding passages, New School editing slams images together in head-on collision. Rooted in rebellion, this aggressive, anarchic, fuck-the-line approach, landing you at your next edit faster, evokes the youth culture that spawned it.

Like the films of the Dogme 95 movement, which also exploited self-imposed limitation, films like *The Blair Witch Project* embraced simplicity in ways that generated their own degree of complexity. Joshua Leonard, one of the *Blair Witch Project* actors, has said that "Sony could have $50 million and a sound stage and A-list actors and never make the same film. The constraints on this film became the essence of this film, became the power of this film." This constraint—a sort of anti-aesthetics that produces its own aesthetic—is similar to punk's rejection of complexity and elaborate, expert production. The digital camera evokes punk's dream of do-it-yourself autonomy with its point-and-shoot technology that promises to elevate the untrained amateur to filmmaker.

The ripples generated by punk moved quickly through music. But they also moved, more slowly and mysteriously and in harder-to-trace ways, through other cultural forms, especially film.

[Maria Demopoulos, "Blink of an Eye: Filmmaking in the Age of Bullet Time," *Film Comment*, Fall 2000, p. 38; Simon Frith, "Art vs. Technology: The Strange Case of Popular Music," in *Popular Music: Critical Concepts in Media and Cultural Studies. Vol. 2: The Rock Era*, 1986; repr., London: Routledge, 2004, p. 117; Joshua Leonard quoted in "Something Wicked," at Salon.com, www. salon.com/ent/; Amos Poe, "Commentary Track," *The Foreigner*, Eclectic DVD Distribution, 2001; Lars von Trier, *Lars von Trier: Interviews*, Jackson: University Press of Mississippi, 2003, pp. 149, 155.]

# "Punk is inconceivable without the bleak failure of the sixties"

**Elsewhere in this book you are now holding in your hands,** or resting on your lap, or hurling out the upstairs window of your pathetic "apartment" or comfortable home in the blank suburbia you swore never, ever to permit to devour you, and yet here you are, nonetheless, being devoured and denying it . . . elsewhere in this book there are words about "punk as theory," etc. It is not an act of nostalgia when I say that writing about pop music during the punk era was more historically nuanced, self-critical, and skeptical than it has ever been. Since part of the fun of punk was making fun of the hippies, many of the musicians and writers from the punk era openly considered what was different about their own era. This led to critiques—sometimes devastating, sometimes funny, sometimes both—about previous generations. Here is Marian K., writing in 1980 about the sixties in *Damage*:

> The fact remains that punk is inconceivable without the bleak failure of the Sixties' thrust. Drugs, political ideas, the arts, and especially the "personal" innovations like group living, nonhierarchical organization, and sexual liberation—all these went bankrupt in the course of a few short years. It wasn't soley that they were lousy ideas or that the free social energy which fueled them just ceased to be available; any social thrust followed too long and too blindly engenders its own healthy negation—nostalgia.

And again here, writing about the seventies:

> Society has never before suffered from such utter drift, unable to command for itself an appropriate style, looting the cultural past at a speed that threatens to overtake the rate of history itself, paralyzed by a morbidly self-conscious confusion that raises doubts, like Zeno's Paradox, about how you ever get from one point to the next . . .

Four years later, the literary critic Fredric Jameson wrote of "slowly becoming aware of a new and original historical situation in which we are condemned to seek History by way of our own pop images and simulacra of that history, which itself remains forever out of reach." Although the word "kitsch" is barely used any more—maybe it never was used very much—punk was such a fine example of it that it practically obliterated its meanings. It was Clement Greenberg who drew the sharpest distinctions between the avant-garde (which imitates art) and kitsch (which is consumer driven, i.e., for those who vaguely desire "culture"). Greenberg's essay "Avant-Garde and Kitsch," is elitist and full of so many assumptions about "genuine" art and culture that it rings strangely out-of-tune in our present-day circumstances when we tend not to think of "high" or "low" culture (comic books are now "graphic novels" that win prestigious literary prizes). But back in 1939 it was exciting to trace out such distinctions, and Greenberg did it with harsh clarity. "The precondition for kitsch," he wrote, "a condition without which kitsch would be impossible, is the availability close at hand of a fully matured cultural tradition, whose discoveries, acquisitions, and perfected self-consciousness kitsch can take advantage of for its own ends. It borrows from it devices, tricks, stratagems, rules of thumb, themes, converts them into a system, and discards the rest." Punk was a system whose working parts conspired to reject what the sixties had become.

[Clement Greenberg, "Avant-Garde and Kitsch," in *Clement Greenberg: The Collected Essays and Criticism, Vol. I.*, ed. John O'Brian, 1939; repr., Chicago: University of Chicago Press, 1986, p. 12; Fredric Jameson, *Postmodernism, or, The Cultural Logic of Late Capitalism*, 1984; repr., Durham: Duke University Press, 1991, p. 25; Marian K., "Retro-Spectacle," *Damage* no. 4, Jan. 1980, pp. 10–11.]

# "Punk Rock: the Arrogant Underbelly of Sixties Pop"

**This was the title of Greg Shaw's** *Rolling Stone* review of *Nuggets: Original Artyfacts from the First Psychedelic Era*, compiled by Lenny Kaye and released in 1972. Kaye himself had used the word "punk" in his liner notes, and Shaw explored its meanings with a more critical eye. "Punk-rock at its best is the closest thing we came in the Sixties to the original rockabilly spirit of rock & roll," Shaw wrote, and, "Punk-rock didn't produce many big hits, because it was too primitively undisciplined for most PDs and a lot of kids." And, most significantly: "But punk-rock—defined rather strictly by fuzztone, Fender or Standell amps, Vox organs, the limits of a year's worth of guitar lessons, and that certain tone of aggro in the vocals—had gone the way [by 1967] of the dinosaur." Sixties punk, the way Kaye and Shaw and others described it, was relatively obscure, unshapely, and experimental, "nuggets" to be discovered and savored later, its hostile beauty largely ignored by the mainstream of the time. It is perfectly strange and wonderful that the term punk—which ever since 1976 or so has designated a new, aggressive, fast style of music that broke with the past—was used in the early seventies to refer to music of the sixties. "Following the rock & roll revival, the surf music revival, and the reggae revival," wrote Mike Saunders in *Shakin' Street Gazette*, "the punk music revival is now in full swing." Punk rock, he wrote, originated as a term "in the early 1970's when rock writers en masse began writing about all the albums they threw away in 1967 (only to scour the bargain bins for in 1971), and which reached its height in 1972 when the *Nuggets* collection stormed the nation's charts." And this is a beautiful and unsolvable fact:

Punk rock in *Rolling Stone*, 1973

The phrase "punk rock" did not exist prior to 1975 in the way that we understand the term today.

And it did.

[Metal Mike Saunders, *Shakin' Street Gazette*, November 7, 1974; Greg Shaw, "Punk Rock: The Arrogant Underbelly of Sixties Pop," *Rolling Stone*, January 4, 1973, p. 68.]

## "Punk rock is a put on"

**A quote from a Canadian Broadcasting Corporation** documentary about punk rock, aired in 1977, which profiled the Poles, Teenage Head, and the Viletones, as well as some fans. The reporter, Hana Gartner, was incredulous and openly skeptical. At the end of her report, she said:

> Punk rock is a put on. What makes it offensive is not the volume of the music or the obscenity of the lyrics. It is the seventeen-year-olds who actually believe what the punks are saying: that life is boring, meaningless, that self-inflicted wounds and living for today is good for you. The musicians—they're in it for money, fame, kicks, and chicks.

Gartner's rebuke, based on her immediate, visceral reaction to the punk scene, has been echoed in the decades following. Martha Bayles has written that today "the punk legacy persists wherever noise, shock, and ugliness are cultivated for their own sakes, and wherever the fires of adolescent anger and aggression are stoked in ways that are almost totally destructive."

Bayles's rant—while tempting to mock—is not too far off from the sort of critiques offered by Lester Bangs ("The White Noise Supremacists") or Joan Didion ("Slouching Towards Bethlehem"), except for the fact that they were more daring writers. The ugliness of punk rock, though, is so obvious it hardly needs pointing out. The point *is* nihilism. The point *is* ugliness. The point *is* destruction. Isn't that, in fact, the point of any rock and roll that means anything? In 1974, at the Rock Critics' Symposium at Buffalo State College (which featured Patti Smith, Lenny Kaye, Richard Meltzer, Nick Tosches, and others) Bangs said, "My feeling about rock 'n' roll is that it's a bunch of garbage! It's everything your parents ever said it was, it's in one ear and out the other, it's trash." I am not the only person to note that punk's meanness, in its initial, mid-seventies wave, was a reaction against what had become the bland niceness of the counterculture that was itself fast hardening into a numbing orthodoxy that would be embraced by both the Left and the Right: Altamont; the Manson murders; grim, bloody, cruel foretastes in real life of what would take the stage as performance in punk.

"Destroy!" Johnny Rotten would scream on stage, but of course it had already happened.

Punk was only an echo.

[Martha Bayles, *Hole in Our Soul: The Loss of Beauty and Meaning in American Popular Music*, Chicago: University of Chicago Press, p. 13; "Canadian Punk Rock," reported by Hana Gartner, Canadian Broadcasting Corporation. Aired September 27, 1977, http:// archives.cbc.ca; Lester Bangs quoted in Jim DeRogatis, *Let It Blurt*, New York: Broadway Books, 2000, p. 97.]

## "Punk Rock Rises Again!!" (*Creem* headline)

**This headline—leading off the August 1976** record-review section of *Creem*—makes a lie of the notion that punk was a radically new musical style in the mid-seventies. But if not new (or at least not perceived as new), then what was it? Let's stick to the facts of this issue. The first three record reviews are of the Ramones' first album, *Ramones* (by Gene Sculatti), the *Runaways* (by Robot A. Hull), and the *Modern Lovers* (by Peter Laughner).

The review of *Ramones*—appearing just three months after the album's April 1976 release—never uses the word "punk." Instead, it contains this sentence: "Even if it turns out *not* to be the clarion squawk of a raw new age, the Ramones' *Ramones* is so strikingly different, so prevailingly out of touch with prevailing modes as to constitute a bold swipe at the status quo."

Although the *Modern Lovers* review does not reference the term "punk," it does reference *Ramones*: "Only one guitar solo . . . which makes one more than on the Ramones album, which is however more consciously dumb: vis-à-vis the Ramones don't sing about Pablo Picasso or Cezanne or things being 'bleak in the morning sun.' "

[Robot A. Hull, review of *The Runaways*, *Creem*, August 1976, p. 66; Peter Laughner, review of *The Modern Lovers*, *Creem*, August 1976, pp. 66–67; Gene Sculatti, review of *Ramones*, *Creem*, August 1976, p. 66.]

## "Punk Root"

**An advertisement in the Washington, D.C.,** fanzine *Descenes*: "Rare Rock: 100's of obscure mid and late Sixties punk root lp's and 45's being liquidated by hard-up private collector who got fired. Yardbirds, Pretty Things, Kinks, Davy Dee, Nazz, Chocolate Watch Band, you name it."

["Rare Rock" advertisement, *Descenes* vol. 1, no. 3, July 1979, p. 2.]

q

## "Question of Degree, A"

**A song by Wire,** released as a single in 1979. It comes on with the ferocity of a violent military coup, then backs down, then stages a coup against itself. The lyrics are just as menacing: "I didn't simply fall out / I was thrown at great speed / from a passing car / I didn't touch the ground / till I landed at your door." Some songs are cinematic in the sense that they spool out stories in your head. Somehow, the song recognized that the last year of the seventies was more than just the last year of the seventies: It was the transition into a whole new era of conservatism that would last, and last, and last. It's hard to say precisely how the song knows this, but it does. For one thing, the song is very strong. It is not weak. Whatever its intentions, it exudes none of the temerity of U.K. and U.S. leaders in the years immediately preceding Thatcher and Reagan.

I challenge you, if you have never heard this song, to shut your eyes and listen until the opening lyrics kick in.

There's your movie.

Now go make it.

r

## *Radio On*

**The masterful 1979 post-punk film** by the director Chris Petit, who had worked at *Time Out* as the editor of the film section prior to making *Radio On*. The film's plot—a man (Robert, played by David Beames) investigates the mysterious death of his brother—is really just an excuse to infuse the dreamy, gloomy black-and-white-photographed English landscape with a forlorn beauty. Petit's great gesture here is to actually let the songs—by David Bowie, Kraftwerk, Wreckless Eric, Devo, and others—play themselves out. There is no MTV (remember that?) style editing here, no fast cuts. Instead, the film is composed almost entirely of languid, mobile long takes, sometimes from moving cars, that trace Robert's disconnection from human beings even as the film renders these human beings more deeply and fully than scores of films that focus on so-called character development.

Wim Wenders served as associate producer. This is important to note because if you have ever seen Wenders's *Wings of Desire*, then you have seen a sort of re-make of this film, with Nick Cave filling in for all the post-punk music in *Radio On*. The other significant connection is to Amos Poe's 1978 film *The Foreigner*, which also relied on the barest of plots as a vehicle for a punk soundtrack.

There are three perfect scenes in *Radio On*:

1. The opening sequence, with credits appearing on the screen as if being typed, as Bowie's "Heroes" plays. Basically one long take: We glide up some stairs, into a hallway. We pass an open door, where there is a man in the bathtub, not moving. We don't see his face. The camera floats through the apartment, hovering at a handwritten note on a bulletin board above a desk that reads, "We are the children of Fritz Lang and Werner von Braun. We are the link between the '20s and the '80s. All change in society passes through a sympathetic collaboration with tape recorders, synthesizers, and telephones. Our reality is electronic reality."

2. About thirty minutes into the film, Robert stops at a pub and puts the song "Whole Wide World," by Reckless Eric, on the jukebox. Nearly the entire song plays during one long take, as the camera slowly pulls back as Robert looks out the window at the rainy street and then walks over to the bar to finish his pint as gloomy-looking youth sit alone or play billiards. The song is full and swelling, and Robert is beaten down and passive. The shadows are as dark as black ink stains. He is most certainly a child of Lang in a scene that would not have been out of place in *M*.

3. The last minutes of the film. Robert abandons his car on the edge of an enormous gravel pit, but not before inserting a cassette tape of Kraftwerk's "Ohm Sweet Ohm." Leaving both car doors open, the music follows him as he makes his way toward a train depot. The early-morning sun breaks through the clouds and for a few glorious moments, everything turns pastoral: the sort of England we Americans sometimes dreamed of as children. Everything is going to be okay.

## "Radio Wunderbar"

**An EP and a song by the Carpettes,** from Newcastle, released near the end of 1977. "We know what you like and you like what you hear 'cause we know you / It's all manufactured just to fit your ears and we know you," the lyrics go, and this was punk's inevitable contradiction. Because for every rallying cry against conformity, against packaging, against the absurd limits of manufactured taste, there was the creeping sense that punk itself was headed swiftly in these same directions. But for twenty seconds—from 1:32 to 1:52—"Radio Wunderbar" forgets all that and is pure beauty. It is a guitar solo as played by a six-year-old. Simple and repetitive: the very essence of punk. There is nothing dazzling, nothing virtuoso about it, and in its wide-open-space directness, it gives you freedom. It is best listened to in the dark of a summer night, with the humming and ticking of insect noises, and within the full mystery that those twenty seconds can mean more to you than any reasonable person could possibly understand.

## Raincoats, the

**Stranger, in a more quiet way,** than the Slits, the Raincoats made music that trailed off like a long math equation you never quite finished. Formed in 1977 in London, by 1978 the Raincoats had become Ana da Silva, Gina Birch, Palmolive (from the Slits), and Vicky Aspinall. They were the classic "important" band that was not much heard, especially in the United States, until interest by Kurt Cobain and Kim Gordon resulted in the re-release of three of their albums in the 1990s. In *Damage*, M. C. Parker called their first LP a "curious vision of punk and urban folk." "Women in rock" means something different today than it did in 1980. Here are three quotes. This first one is from the Raincoats, as recounted by Greil Marcus:

> The basic theme in rock 'n' roll is what goes on between men and women . . . Rock 'n' roll is based on black music. And it's based *in* the exclusion of women and the ghettoization of blacks. Which is why we want to put a bit of distance between what we do and the rock 'n' roll tradition.

And this one is from Angela Carter, whose 1979 collection of stories, *The Bloody Chamber*, revised and updated the classic fairy tales (Little Red Riding Hood, Beauty and Beast, etc.) in ways that short-circuit the gendered power relations that governed them:

> I'm basically trying to find out what certain configurations of imagery in our society, in our culture, really stand for, what they mean, undercutting the kind of semi-religious coating that makes people not particularly want to interfere with them.

This last one is lyrics, actually, from the song "Fairytale in the Supermarket," from *The Raincoats*, their first album (1979):

> I don't know the books that you read
> But you don't say that
> love never externalizes
> You're re-reading a book
> to feel reassured
> By the life of your favorite hero

There is a nearly perfect song on their first album, *The Raincoats*, called "No Side to Fall In" that builds on overlapping vocals and the sort of melody that drips in your head. Like all great art, it transcends whatever "message" people get out of the Raincoats about gender or politics. It is a song to take you someplace else. It is both punk and not-punk, in the way that the Talking Heads, or the Weirdos, or Gang of Four were both punk and not-punk. And yet this is what Gina Birch had to say in 1996: "I think, basically, though, neither of us [she and da Silva] would have dreamt in a million years that we would be doing anything like this if it hadn't been for punk. So I think the major kind of focus and kind of landscape in which we operated was really to do with punk."

[Gina Birch interviewed by Richie Unterberger, December 12, 1996, www.richieunterberger. com/birch.html; Angela Carter interviewed by Cindy Katsavos in *The Review of Contemporary Fiction*, Fall 1994, vol. 14.3, www.centerforbookculture.org/interviews; Greil Marcus, *In the Fascist Bathroom: Punk in Pop Music, 1977–1982*, 1980; repr., Cambridge: Harvard University Press, 1993, p. 113; M. C. Parker, "Raincoats LP," *Damage* no. 5, 1980, p. 32.]

# Ramone, Joey (and Joey Miserable and the Worms)

**This is a story** of what happened many years later, after the Ramones became so famous that the idea of the Ramones became more important than the band itself. You could see this happening even as far back as the late seventies, and by the mid-eighties—after hardcore—it was clear that, although they had changed the face of music, they themselves would never change. By that time, history seemed to have passed them right on by. They had become a legend. They had become trapped. This was around 1985. The weather had turned cold, and I had lost my job. I hated graduate school. The radiator clanked like a defective timebomb in my apartment, and I kept the drapes shut. A friend—my last one—had told me that Joey Ramone was sick of the Ramones and was performing under an assumed name—Joey Miserable—right here in our town, with a makeshift band.

Joey was such a part of my imagination that sometimes, listening to the records, I wondered if he was even real. The first thing he told us was that he was a hunted man, though he never acted scared until the very end. I came to know—everyone did—that he was in the new band to save himself from something, some "terrible terrible," as he once said. Worse than guns, even; than hot bullets tearing through flesh. But he talked so often in apocalyptic language that after a while it didn't mean anything. Bullets were too abstract to scare us. We were all on our way to being fired or kicked out of school. The campus was falling apart under the weight of bad ideas.

The Outpost Bar and Lounge for Loungers was an old brick schoolhouse (so they said) converted to a tavern not far from my apartment at the edge of campus.

It was some fevered Hieronymous Bosch hallucination of hell: the blood-red décor; the enormous ink-black shadows from life-sized carved-wood sculptures of naked men and women in fight scenes; the long, warped mirror behind the bar that cast back a wavy, distorted reflection of the place. I'd sit at a small table in the corner and make my way through a few pitchers of cheap beer as Joey Miserable and the Worms tore through their first set like lightning, and then slowed down for their second set—their "midnight" set—into some kind of trancelike waltz of distorted feedback and crackling guitar. Joey writhed on the stage like a worm stuck with a pin.

That's when I became, for a brief time, the lyricist for the bad.

"I'm a hunted man," he said to me, shaking from fear or delirium. "Wanna write the words to my songs?" From a distance his face looked clawed at, but up close you could see right through him, like one of those deep-sea fish from miles down. We called him Joey Miserable, but he could have been Joey Transparent. His skin was so tight on him it threatened to split apart at any second.

It was one of those desperate decisions that turn out to be good. Somebody told him I was a writer who had published some poems. He never even asked me my name. It was easy for me to say yes. I'd sit at the table in the corner as the band played, penning lyrics about drowned lovers, bloody revenge, head-on car wrecks, hopelessness, ghosts, destruction, mutilation, total war, power. I'd always try to write the songs from the point of view of the "bad" person, to give voice to his or her perspective, to create a space in the song where the worst parts of human nature could roam free. For instance, "Blood Brothers" told the tale—in the sparest of terms—of Brother A, whose affair with Brother B's beautiful wife is not at all the secret that he thinks it is. In fact, Brother B lives with the knowledge of the affair. At a banquet for his cheating wife's birthday, Brother B drugs them both and scoops out their eyes with spoons before hanging himself. Another song, "Three Bullets for Four People," tells the story of an ingenious hit man who is sent to murder a family of four. When he discovers he only has three bullets for the job, he, shall we say, makes good use of bullet number three, concocting an elaborate, cruel method to kill two people with one bullet.

And then there was Cindy.

I really only knew her long enough for her to claim attempted poison.

She had a little scar over her left eyebrow that somehow made me love her.

She turned up one night at the Outpost, standing alone up at the bar, writing some secret thing on a napkin. Her hands moved like slow spiders. She might be the person to love me. Even from a distance, I could see that. I was about to get up and walk up to her when she caught my eye, smiled, and came over. She was wearing jeans and a black leather jacket. A little silver bracelet twisted like a secret code on her wrist.

"Hey," she said, "aren't you the guy from the video store?"

She came into the store once in a while.

She sat down across from me and took off her jacket. I must have been staring at it.

"Like it?" she said. "It's my don't-fuck-with-me jacket."

"That's funny. Someone said that exact same thing to me not long ago."

She began to ask me a very strange and dark-turning question, but I stopped her right away, before she could finish. I even put my hand on her arm to stop her.

"No, you're right," she said. "I was wrong to ask."

Then I said, "It's not that I don't trust you . . ."

"You don't need to say that," she said.

On the far side of the room, the Worms were on the cramped stage working their way through the desert part of one of my songs. You could practically see the blood coursing through Joey's body. He was that transparent, as if his skin was nothing more than damp wax paper. His veins were like a million thread-blue rivers on a map.

"She's the one who's gonna pop me," Joey told me the next night, before he went on stage. "Shit. Why'd it have to be your girlfriend?"

"Jesus, Joey. Come on. She's not my anything."

He said, "Do me a favor. Afterward, don't write about it. Don't put it in a song. And make the songs slower. They're too fast again."

"Sure."

"I hope she does it with a gun," he said. "A bullet is small. Half the time you can't even see the hole it makes."

Joey's band played my songs like it was the end of the world that night, miserable dirges that all ended in various forms of bloodshed. He took the stage like a Revelations man, like some creature that had been sent here to imitate a human, drenched in sweat, wielding the microphone like it was a weapon, hurling abuse at the crowd. The band thundered through song after song, like an earthquake, like uniform noise. "It's fucking something, these songs," Joey Miserable would tell me afterward, wiping his drenched body down with a towel. "I want more. Can you give me more?"

I didn't see Cindy for many weeks after this. The campus was looking more and more like a neglected movie set. August came and went. While I continued writing songs for Joey Miserable, I could feel the end waiting for me like an open furnace. Everything was falling apart. A gun went off during one of his shows, tearing the finger off some kid's hand. They found the bullet lodged in a wooden beam above the ceiling. Joey was sure it was meant for him, that Cindy had sent someone to do it. In awaiting his death he became desperate, prone to hysterical fits that began with shouting and ended with bloodshed. His skin became even more transparent, showing through to the very blood speeding through his veins. If he were naked you could see the architecture of his circulatory system, the crazy activity around his heart, the nothingness around his limbs.

Something changed in Joey, and in us. It was whispered that he was Joey Ramone, and the crowds gradually got larger. A reporter for the college paper tried to ask him some questions. He retreated from the edge of the stage. By fall we were barely hanging on. The spirit of the times was changing in ways that made the type of songs I was writing for the band seem irresponsible, even dangerous. The shootings at the high school out west. The crashing-down towers in the east. My songs—which had always been received by the audience as darkly funny, ironic tales of obsession—now seemed serious and threatening in all the wrong ways, as if they were actually a part of the context from which the new violence had arisen. My songs weren't funny anymore: It was fine to glamorize violence in the abstract, but not when the images in my songs matched too closely images from the real world.

And Joey felt more hunted than ever, convinced that someone near him would be the one to kill him. He suspected and hated Cindy, who knew a hundred ways to kiss. She showed me all the time. One night, after a particularly brutal show, Joey confronted me at our table, his eyes sped up like a rabid dog's, blaming me for his impending ruination, going on and on about how my songs were all surface and shock and had no depth to them, and then suddenly reversing himself, berating me because my songs were too complex and difficult.

He showed me an unfired bullet that he said he found in his shoe one morning, shaking it in my face like proof.

I shrugged it off, but I knew it was true: We were tied into this thing together somehow, all of us. Cindy, too. How did we let that happen? And then, within a week, we became untouchable. Cindy's father was killed in a car wreck on the way home after visiting us. My old English professor jumped off the roof of a parking garage, splattering himself onto storefront windows. The electricity in my apartment went out for nearly a week. All my plants withered and died. A boy Cindy knew fell through the ice in Canada and drowned. Everything we touched, we shattered. It confounded Joey most of all. He was certain he was next. One moment he was all sound and fury, stomping around and gesticulating wildly, like a reborn Mussolini; the next he was all whimpers and tears, as soft as a marshmallow, collapsed with his bald head on his arms at my table. When Cindy reached into her purse he jumped back like he had already been shot.

That's when the guy with the gun in his pocket came walking over, a blackened figure dragged out of the Old Testament. Then the gun was in his enormous hand, so real it looked fake. The bullet was screaming to get out. The man's finger was the most important thing in the world. In the mirror above the bar I watched it unfold like a movie trailer: the plotted-out sequence of steps, the Jack Ruby extension of the man's arm, the swift, sly, slick move of Joey's hand over Cindy's beer, the man's sudden veering away and through the crowd and out the door.

Who knows what Joey slipped in our beers? He practically begged us to drink. Perhaps the man in black with the gun was just a diversion, an excuse. Cindy took a sip, and was sick for a week, the inside of her stomach burning like acid. She curled up on my couch like an anthrax victim. But it could have been anything.

For weeks after Joey disappeared, all I heard was gunshots. All the time. All around me. Everywhere. The sky above campus was full of flying bullets. And everyone I saw—every person on the street—looked at me like they had just murdered somebody. Do you know that look? And these people . . . there wasn't anything I could do to stop this. It wasn't one of those things you could just call off.

Cindy recovered, convinced that Joey had poisoned her to save himself.

"It wasn't Joey who was hunted," she said when she was better. She was sipping tea in the sun on the patio, her knees pulled up beneath her chin. "It was us."

Like I was seeing bullets, she was seeing him. Everywhere.

It made everything between us impossible.


# Ramones (1974– )

**Boy:** C'mon, say you like 'em.

**Girl:** I'm sorry. They're terrible. They're not even funny.

**Boy:** Funny?

**Girl:** You said they were funny, remember?

**Boy:** I said ironic. Not funny.

**Girl:** Whatever. They're not either.

**Boy:** Why are you so mean?

**Girl:** I'm not mean.

**Boy:** Do you want to talk about the Ramones or not?

**Girl:** No, I don't want to talk about the Ramones. What is there to say? You already tried to make me read those books about them.

**Boy:** What about that little one I lent you, the one on their first album?

**Girl:** What about it? I think I lost it under my pillow.

**Boy:** Did you read it?

**Girl:** Yes, I read it. And then I lost it. I think it got mixed up in the laundry. It went through the wash with bleach. All the words disappeared off the pages.

**Boy:** So you didn't lose it.

**Girl:** Well, I practically did. C'mon, what's the use of a book with no words? It might as well be lost.

**Boy:** You know something, you're just not fun anymore.

**Girl:** What a thing to say! Look at you! Mr. Rock Critic. Honestly, who cares?

*(Silence)*

**Girl:** Okay, what do you want? Some sort of confession?

**Boy:** Tell me you love the Ramones.

**Girl:** Most of them are dead! What do you mean!

**Boy:** Please, just tell me.

**Girl:** Okay. I love the Ramones.

**Boy:** Say, their first album in 1976 is the functional product of a direction-less culture.

**Girl:** Their first album in 1976 is the functional . . . product of a direction-less culture.

Unlike the serious prog-rock and concept albums of the era that distanced themselves from the mundane triviality of popular culture, *Ramones* is laced with references to movies, news events, history, and the ordinary happenings of everyday life. As Donna Gaines has noted, "The Ramones' songwriting reflects their obsession with popular culture and Americana. Johnny and Dee Dee were war-movie fiends, and the whole band loved television, surf culture, comic books, and cartoons." The filmic world evoked in *Ramones* is one of B-movies, cult movies, and horror films. *The Texas Chainsaw Massacre* was released in 1974, the year many of the album's songs were written. The film scholar Robin Wood has written that, "central to the film—and centered on its monstrous family—is the sense of grotesque comedy, which in no way diminishes but rather intensifies its nightmare horror . . . The film's sense of fundamental horror is closely allied to a sense of the fundamentally absurd." This sense of comic horror infuses the album's fifth track, "Chainsaw," a sort of homage to the film. This was also the era of the vigilante film, most forcefully expressed in *Straw Dogs* (1971) and *Death Wish* (1974), in which Charles Bronson plays a tolerant New York City architect who turns to vigilantism after his wife is murdered. Mixed in with the album's humor is a deeper menace and sense of pervasive violence running through songs like "Beat on the Brat" and "Loudmouth" ("I'm gonna beat you up") that is reminiscent of films like *Death Wish* and that in fact constitutes a wholesale rejection of the feel-good, peace-love-and-understanding ethos that informed the rhetoric of the counterculture. For if in 1969 audiences were expected to see the violence of *Easy Rider* as tragedy visited upon well-meaning (if not innocent) drifters, by 1974 films like *Death Wish* had audiences pretty much rooting for those committing the violence.

Like the emerging punk scene itself, films in the mid-seventies contained a heady mix of high and low, art and trash, domestic and foreign. Ads from an August 1975 issue of *The Village Voice* (during a time when the Ramones were playing at CBGB) offer a glimpse of the variety of films playing in New York City. At the Bleeker Street Cinema, you could see Bergman's *The Seventh Seal* and *Wild Strawberries*, Hitchcock's *The 39 Steps*, and Satyajit Ray's *Two Daughters*. *The Eiger Sanction* was playing (for only $1.00) at St. Mark's Cinema, while a theater on Broadway at 49th showed *The Texas Chainsaw Massacre*. The Elgin, meanwhile, offered Mick Jagger in *Performance*, Jonathan Demme's *Caged Heat*, as well as *Don't Look Now*, *El Topo*, and *The Harder They Come*. Or you could catch Russ Meyer's *SuperVixens*, rated X—in the mid-seventies, X-rated movies were advertised alongside "family" movies in both underground and mainstream newspapers in New York City, including *The New York Times*. The blurb for *SuperVixens* might just as well have come out of the punk imagination: "an all out assault on today's sexual mores, and more, a frontal attack against women's lib . . . blasting through the male 'machismo' syndrome, kicking the hell out of convention, hang-ups, convictions, obsessions! The whole bag . . . cops, robbers, sexually aggressive females, rednecks, sick men-of-war, unfaithful wives, impotence, athletic prowess, the 32-second satisfaction, cuckolding, breast fixation vs. hat jobs, egotism and other fun 'n games, racing cars, self-abuse . . . and even death and reincarnation!" And of course the PG-rated *Jaws* ("8th Record Week!") was playing just about everywhere, with its own image of a huge shark about to munch a practically nude female swimmer.

The most punk moment in any movie from that era has nothing at all to do with punk rock or punk style. About midway through Martin Scorsese's *Taxi Driver*—which opened in 1976 just months before *Ramones* was released and which was shot in the summer of 1975—Travis Bickle (Robert DeNiro) sits in his New York apartment watching *American Bandstand* on his crappy TV. Scorsese cuts between kids slow dancing to Jackson Brown's "Late for the Sky" and Travis watching in a kind of resigned numbness ("sitting here with nuthin' to do") as if the "normal" world being depicted on TV were utterly and forever out of reach for him. He has a gun in his hand, which he occasionally aims at the screen. Later, in a startling shot, we see a transformed Travis standing outside at the edge of a crowd listening to a hackneyed speech by a politician. Travis has changed: He is sporting a Mohawk (punk?) haircut that signals his radical rejection of the "normal" world depicted on *American Bandstand*. While the film escalates into increasing and frenzied violence at this point, I think it is the few quiet moments where we see Travis watching the TV with a sort of deep and menacing sadness that capture best the spirit of loneliness that punk emerges from and addresses.

In *Midnight Movies*, J. Hoberman wrote that, seen "strictly as a youth movement, punk was a kind of perverse, high-speed replay of the counterculture—complete with its own music, press, entrepreneurs, fellow travelers (including more than a few ex-hippies), and, ultimately, movies." Punk films from this era include John Waters's *Pink Flamingos* (1973) and *Female Trouble* (1975), Derek Jarman's *Jubilee* (1977), and Amos Poe's *Blank Generation* (1976) and *The Foreigner* (1977). However, while these and other films are no doubt central to the articulation of a punk sensibility, it is another film—David Lynch's *Eraserhead* (1977)—that, like *Taxi Driver*, captures the sense of Outsiderness that informs punk. In *Eraserhead*, Henry (Jack Nance) is the ultimate outsider, existing in a world so degraded that it's simply beautiful. He is practically inarticulate, defining himself though his actions, not his words. And that electroshock hair is as alarming as anything worn by Richard Hell or Sid Vicious. Above all, *Eraserhead* offers the illusion of a complete and separate world; like punk, its influences can (and have been) traced and demystified in dry studies of influence, and yet there is something about *Eraserhead*, and about punk, that manages to escape the most determined efforts to explain away its mystery.

From the very beginning, do-it-yourself "punk" cinema was an important part of the emerging punk music scene. Filmmakers like Amos Poe—who was also a writer for *New York Rocker*—helped define the punk aesthetic in film and often wrote for or were featured in the music newspapers and fanzines that emerged in New York City in the mid-seventies. In a 1976 profile on Poe in *New York Rocker*, Matthew Fleury, in his discussion of Poe's films *Night Lunch* (1975) and *Blank Generation* (1976), called Poe's work "presence filmmaking" and noted that Poe considered the Zapruder film of the Kennedy assassination "the greatest single footage ever shot" because it captured—unintentionally—history.

The Ramones were not rebelling against popular music, but rather against how popular music had come to be defined and experienced. If today we tend to think in terms of selling out versus not selling out, we need to be careful not to project these concerns backward to the seventies. For there was less worry about "selling out" to the mainstream than there was desire to replace mainstream music with something better, something more alive, something unexpected. The Ramones in particular desired a hit; after all, they believed in and were passionate about their music and wanted to share it with others beyond the cramped space of CBGB. As Seymour Stein, the cofounder of Sire Records who signed the Ramones to Sire in 1976, has said, "their melodies were very catchy and stayed with me, dancing around in my head, and it was absolutely clear that for better or worse, underneath it all was a pop-band mentality." Others, such as Craig Leon, who produced *Ramones*, share this view: "Quite honestly, we thought we were creating a hit pop record. The Bay City Rollers, Herman's Hermits, and the Beatles were our competition in our minds. But do bear in mind we were laughing all the way through it."

Casting the Ramones and other bands as anti-corporate and anti-mainstream means that you have to ignore the tremendous amount of care and energy that they put into promoting themselves. The Ramones in particular were very much aware of the press and publicity they were generating, and they were active participants in shaping their image and generating further press interest, as this 1977 interview with Roy Trakin from *New York Rocker* suggests:

> *What was the turning point?*
> **Dee Dee:** That festival [the 1975 summer rock festival at CBGB].
> **Tommy:** The turning point was . . . when Lisa Robinson came down . . . actually we got some nice writeups from some people and we sent them out to the people in the trades, with a little picture of us.
> **Johnny:** I think we had a list of 100 people and we hit everybody.
> *Did you lick the envelopes yourselves?*
> **Tommy:** Yeah, addressed them and everything.

This form of do-it-yourself publicity, while much different in scale than the massive promotional engines that sustained supergroups like Led Zeppelin and the Eagles, was nonetheless driven by a desire to reach a broad audience. Rather than look at their success as something to be ashamed of, or as some sort of selling out, the Ramones remained keenly aware that, as one of the earliest punk bands to sign to a label, they were in many ways responsible for the potential success and viability of the emerging punk scene. "We were the first CBGB-punk-type group to get signed," Tommy told Trakin, "and that was important because I think we opened up the doors." While punk in the 1980s and '90s has very much cast itself in opposition to mainstream, corporate interests, and while recent writing on punk (often by academics) casts punk as a sort of Marxist music-for-the-people-and-by-the-people, it's instructive to remember that, in punk's early days, many punk bands desired and actively courted mainstream success.

The first three albums by the Ramones do make you wonder, though, how seriously should I be taking this? The punk generation grew up not only with TV, but with cable, and with all the repetition ("repeats"), irony, and camp that the medium engendered. As Robert Ray has noted, the "new self-consciousness also flourished on television, where 'Rowand and Martin's Laugh-In' (1968–73), 'The Carol Burnett Show' (1967–78), and NBC's 'Saturday Night Live' (1975– ) all featured irreverent media parodies, particularly of movies and TV news. Other regular series could not be taken straight: 'All in the Family' (1971–79), 'The Rockford Files' (1974–79), 'Happy Days' (1974–84), 'Mary Hartman, Mary Hartman' (1976), and 'Soap' (1977–81) all traded on obviously ironic uses of standard television formulas." The beautifully complicating thing here is not that *Ramones* offered itself as an ironic rock album, but that it might be received that way by an audience raised in a TV culture that always questioned the codes of sincerity. Or, looked at another way, punk irony was gradually evolving into the new norm, replacing the macho sincerity and you-better-take-this-concept-album-seriously of progressive rock, which would help explain punk's delayed acceptance into the mainstream and its late-blossoming stature: It came at the very beginning of a decades-long process of incorporating irony into the mainstream, of which a show like *Late Night with David Letterman* would become key. In 1976, *Ramones* sounded both very wrong and very right. Today it just sounds very right, not because the music on the album has changed but because the conditions into which that music enters has. Listeners coming to *Ramones* for the first time today are conditioned to accept it because they have heard it before—perhaps without knowing it—in the very music that the Ramones helped to create. In this sense, the Ramones' career is about creating the conditions under which their music would be retrospectively accepted. As Jon Savage has suggested in his study of British punk: "In the mid-Sixties, pop had been modernistic: reveling in an everlasting present, without reflection or theory. In the late Sixties, pop became 'progressive,' an idea implying some forward, unitary motion. Early seventies stars like David Bowie and Roxy Music broke up this linear motion with a plethora of references taken from high art, literature and Hollywood kitsch. As the new generation, the Sex Pistols were a finely tuned mixture of the authentic and the constructed."

Besides, isn't all performance—whether writing, acting, singing, dancing, or whatever—self-conscious by its very nature? Perhaps, but punk was predicated on a deliberate assault on the elaborate, overproduced, self-serious music of the era, and it is this reactionary nature that imbued punk with a complicated ironic stance. In short, unlike the music of its day, which sought to extend a tradition (i.e., Led Zeppelin or Eric Clapton's "extending" the blues), punk sought to reject tradition. For even though it's true the music of the Ramones points back to an earlier time, as Craig Leon and others have noted, this earlier music is referenced not so much for its sound or style but rather for its energy. While it's pretty easy to hear the blues in Zeppelin's "Dazed and Confused," it's not so easy to hear Herman's Hermits in "Loudmouth." It's harder to think of another rock album that, upon its initial appearance, sounded so little like anything that had come before it.

Is it surprising that a movement like punk—with its rejection of the musical indulgence and decadence of progressive rock—would embrace the iconography of fascism, which also rejected "decadence"? Mary Harron comes closest to best explaining the use of fascist imagery in punk and by the Ramones in particular. "Joey Ramone was a nice guy, he was no savage right-winger," she has said. "The Ramones were problematic. It was hard to work out what their politics were. It had this difficult edge, but the most important thing was needling the older generation." If liberal humanist rock critics and scholars today are wary of dwelling on the conservative, sometimes reactionary political dimensions of punk (Johnny Ramone was a longtime conservative) while at the same time devoting page after page to delineating the socially engaged political subtleties of Bob Dylan or Bruce Springsteen or Ani DeFranco, then it's at the risk of minimizing one of the many complexities of punk.

[Seymour Stein quoted in Jim Bessman, *The Ramones: An American Band*, New York: St. Martin's Press, 1993, p. 42; Donna Gaines, liner notes, *Ramones* (reissue), Warner Archives/ Rhino, 2001, p. 9; J. Hoberman and Jonathan Rosenbaum, *Midnight Movies*, New York: Harper and Row, 1983, p. 275; Craig Leon, e-mail to author, May 26, 2004; Robert B. Ray, *A Certain Tendency in the Hollywood Cinema, 1930–1980*, New York: Oxford University Press, 1985, p. 260; Jon Savage, *England's Dreaming: Anarchy, Sex Pistols, Punk Rock, and Beyond*, New York: St. Martin's Press, 1992, pp. 162–63; Mary Harron quoted in *ibid.*, p. 138; Roy Trakin, "Ramones," *New York Rocker*, November/December 1977; Robin Wood, *Hollywood from Vietnam to Reagan*, New York: Columbia University Press, 1985, p. 93.]

# Ramones, the first album in ten tracks

1. In early 1975, Lisa Robinson, who edited *Hit Parader* and *Rock Scene* magazines, saw the Ramones at CBGB and began championing them in her magazines. As Joey Ramone recalls, "Lisa came down to see us, she was blown away by us. She said that we changed her life. She started writing about us in *Rock Scene*, and then Lenny Kaye would write about us and we started getting more press like *The Village Voice*, word was getting out, and people started coming down." Robinson also convinced Danny Fields—who had managed the Stooges and was influential in the New York music scene—to see the band; he would eventually end up managing them, beginning in November 1975. According to Fields, the "Ramones had everything I ever liked. The songs were short. You knew what was happening within five seconds. You didn't have to analyze and/ or determine what it was you were hearing or seeing. It was all there."

2. The Ramones received further exposure—this time on a more national scale— after the CBGB 1975 summer festival of unsigned bands. On September 19, the band made a demo of "Judy Is a Punk" and "I Wanna Be Your Boyfriend," both produced by Marty Thau. Craig Leon, who had arrived in New York in 1973 to work for Sire Records and who was on the prowl for new talent, had seen them perform shortly after the summer festival and was enthusiastic, eventually bringing the Thau demos to the attention his boss, Seymour Stein. According to Tommy Ramone, "Craig Leon is the one who got us signed.

Singlehanded. He brought down the vice president and all these people—he's the only hip one at the company. He risked his career to get us on the label." Stein's wife, Linda Stein, also played a crucial role in convincing her husband to sign the band. The Ramones auditioned for Stein in the late fall of 1975; they signed with Sire in January 1976.

3. In her classic 1969 essay "Trash, Art, and the Movies," Pauline Kael wrote of "trash" films that when "you clean them up, when you make movies respectable, you kill them. The wellspring of their *art*, their greatness, is in not being respectable." While it could be said that punk fought long and hard against respectability, there is no denying that the early to mid-seventies New York scene from which it emerged was a heady mix of artists, filmmakers, writers, and performers. It's almost inconceivable today to imagine a contemporary music scene as peopled with artists, writers, and filmmakers as the early punk movement was, with people like Andy Warhol, William S. Burroughs, Patti Smith, Mary Harron, Arturo Vega, Amos Poe, Gerard Malanga, and others all being part of the scene. As Dick Hebdige has noted, "the New York punk bands had pieced together from a variety of acknowledged 'artistic' sources—from the literary *avant-garde* and the underground cinema—a self-consciously profane and terminal aesthetic."

   This isn't to suggest a calculated effort—at least not by the Ramones—to draw on artistic sources but rather that part of what made the band great was its emergence from a vibrant New York movement where distinctions between pop culture and art were blurred.

4. Prior to his involvement in the band, Tommy Ramone had even made avant-garde films: "I was [getting] into film-making. I guess I was jumping around. I went to work for this film company. I was hanging around the Museum of Modern Art 'cause the company was right next to the Museum. I would take three-hour lunch breaks and watch all the movies there and I got into avant-garde films. I started making some stuff like that." The Pop Art movement of the fifties and sixties—of which Andy Warhol was the American Giant—had already smashed distinctions between "high" and "low" culture; by the seventies it wasn't that what punk was doing by mixing styles was new, but rather that they reinjected a sense of fun and danger into the process.

5. *Ramones* was recorded in seventeen days in February 1976 for roughly $6,400. According to Craig Leon, most of the work with the band was completed in seven days: "It took just three days to get the music down, four for the vocals." In the era of bloated, supergroup excess, $6,400 was a paltry amount of money. "Some albums were costing a half-million dollars to make," Joey noted in *Please Kill Me*, "and taking two or three years to record, like Fleetwood Mac . . ." At

first, the process sounds like the ultimate do-it-yourself, amateur, reckless ethic that is associated with punk. In truth, however, the Ramones approached the recording process with a high degree of preparedness and professionalism and a fiercely self-contained, unified sound. But this had not always been the case. In July 1974 Tommy became the Ramones' drummer, and the band's sound underwent a change: "To them it was just a hobby," he told *Punk* in 1976; "to me it was an avant-garde thing. Then we started getting really good and I said, 'This isn't avant-garde, this is commercial!' And that's when I started playing drums. When I saw the $signs$ . . . I changed the whole sound of the group into the way it is now—you know—hard rock."

6. Near the end of 1974, the band recorded fifteen demos in one day. These were, according to Jim Bessman, "just basic tracks and vocals and mixes of most of the songs that made up their first album." In September 1975 they cut two more demos ("Judy Is a Punk" and "I Wanna Be Your Boyfriend") with Marty Thau who had previously managed the New York Dolls). The sound on the Thau demos is somewhat richer and warmer than that on the other demos, and it hints at a more pop-oriented, melodic sensibility that shows how, with a slightly different approach, the Ramones sound could be less assaultive.

7. Although the band wanted to suggest the intensity of their live performances, the album was in no way intended to be "live." As Craig Leon notes, "capturing the energy of the live shows was quite important. But if you jump to the conclusion that the sound of the recording was just the sound of the band live you would be mistaken even though that was what I was trying to convey. The album is quite layered and structured and took full advantage of the studio technology of its time without being obvious." This tension—how to transfer the spirit of live performance without simply replicating it—was something that haunted, and in some ways worked against, punk. For if progressive, virtuoso rock encouraged deep, repeat listenings and a cultivated appreciation for complexity, punk assaulted the listener in a way that almost begged for a live audience. One of the reasons punk did not move gently into the mainstream or receive more radio play was precisely because it was always about more than the music on the album: It was a stance, an attitude that was difficult to transfer to vinyl.

8. "I actually toyed with the idea," says Leon, "of the recording being one long band with no breaks" in a way that would capture the no-break-between-songs live performances. There are hints of this at the end of the album's second side, where "I Don't Wanna Walk Around with You" is followed by "Today Your Love, Tomorrow the World" with no break in between. There were other experiments that didn't happen, either, according to Leon: "There was a quadraphonic

version that I played around with doing. I did a lot of quad-encoded work in those days and almost did the Ramones album that way." By the time they went into the studio record, the Ramones had developed an archive of songs and had honed their sound before audiences at over seventy shows. "We had the songs for the first three albums when we did the first one," Johnny has said. "We already had 30 to 35 songs, and we recorded them in the chronological order that we wrote them. I didn't want the second album to be a letdown by picking through the best songs for the first one and using the lesser songs for the second album."

9. It was difficult for a good band to make the transition from live act to meaningful recorded presence. Indeed, the pages of the mid-seventies underground music press in New York City are full of ads and enthusiastic write-ups for enormously popular punk bands at the club level who subsequently failed to transfer that spirit to vinyl. In "The State of Pop Music in New York: A Symposium," from *The Village Voice*, the musician and record producer Tony Silvester noted that the "reason a lot of great acts don't happen on records is because they don't feel that tension that they feel live—9 out of 10 times on a record they try to duplicate the club scene and it doesn't happen." What's missing, Silvester claimed, was "simplicity from the standpoint of production."

Here is Craig Leon addressing the album's production:

The album was recorded purely. Nothing covered up. The same way that you would record a classical or jazz work. We use the same mic placement techniques on the London Symphony Orhestra or the Orpheus Chamber Orchestra today that we used on the Ramones in 1976. These techniques are the same as what you would have gotten on classical or jazz recordings or for that matter good pop recordings in 1956. The sound of the music in the room. Minimal effects other than those created naturally. But it was not "cinema verite" all live and raw.

We did a lot of overdubbing and double-tracked vocals, going for a bizarre emulation of the recording values of "A Hard Day's Night." The stereo image was inspired by that as well. Due to the limitations of 4-track recording in the Sixties the image on the old Beatles records in stereo used to have the entire backing track on the left and vocals and tambourine overdubs or whatever on the right. This is not so evident on the U.S. releases but very clear on the UK versions. This fit the three-piece sound of the Ramones perfectly. There was a conventional mix of the recording but it wasn't as effective. Also, a mono mix. Some of those tracks surfaced on singles. The mono version is quite powerful.

We also did the recording quickly. Mainly because of budget restrictions . . . but also because that was all the time we needed. I think that getting a performance down on a recorded medium quickly helps duplicate the sense of being in the room when it was being made.

10. The important thing was to resist complicating the simplicity of approach that characterized the Ramones' sound. As Tommy (who coproduced the album) has noted, "What we had was an idea that it's not the virtuosity that counts, it's the ideas themselves that are important . . . Virtuosity is not only not necessary, but it might get in the way." But for all the talk of amateurism, the early punk bands—and the Ramones especially—were hard working and serious about the music, honing their skills through relentless gigging. The fast, easy sound was the product of hard work; even a brief glance at their tour dates leading up to the first album reveals the sort of relentless touring—mostly gigs at CBGB and the Performance Studio—that would characterize their career. Unlike the Sex Pistols, who in interviews were likely to laugh off questions about musical influences, technique, etc., the Ramones talked seriously about the ideas and techniques that lay beneath their music. "In retrospect," Tommy noted, "it's a great lo-fi album, almost avant-garde. It captured our music at that time."

[Jim Bessman, *Ramones: An American Band*, New York: St. Martin's Press, 1993, p. 38; Dick Hebdige, *Subculture, The Meaning of Style*, 1979; repr., London: Routledge, 1987, p. 27; Pauline Kael, "Trash, Art and the Movies," in *Going Steady: Film Writings 1968–1969*, 1969; repr., New York: Marion Boyars, 2000, p. 98; Craig Leon, e-mails to author, September 13, 2004, and May 26, 2004; Legs McNeil and Gillian McCain, *Please Kill Me: The Uncensored Oral History of Punk*, New York: Penguin, 1997, p. 229; Danny Fields quoted in Monte Melnick and Frank Meyer, *On the Road with the Ramones*, London: Sanctuary, 2003, p. 60; Tommy Ramone quoted in *ibid.*, pp. 55, 195; Tommy Ramone quoted in *Punk* no. 3, 1976; Larry Rohter, "A Loving Re-Creation of Sixties Rock 'n' Roll," *The Washington Post*, June 2, 1976, p. B8; Tony Silvester, "The State of Pop Music in New York: A Symposium," *The Village Voice*, September 8, 1975.]

# Ramones, first lines of songs on first three albums

**From *Ramones*** (April 1976):

- "Hey ho, let's go"
- "Beat on the brat"
- "Jackie is a punk"
- "Hey, little girl"
- "Oh, oh, oh, wohoho"
- "Now I wanna sniff some glue"

- "Hey, Daddy-o"
- "You're a loudmouth baby"
- "PT-Boat on the way to Havana"
- "Next time, I'll listen to my heart"
- "If you think you can, well come on man"
- "Hey baby don't you take a chance"
- "I don't wanna walk around with you"
- "I'm a shock trooper in a stupor yes I am"

From *Leave Home* (January 1977):

- "Gonna take a chance on her one bullet in the cylinder"
- "I was feeling sick I was losing my mind"
- "I remember you"
- "I met her at the Burger King we fell in love by the soda machine"
- "Wondering what I'm doing tonight"
- "Ooo-weee, do it one more time for me"
- "Gabba gabba we accept you"
- "Now I wanna be a good boy"
- "Winter is here and it's going on two years swallow my pride"
- "I know your name I know your game"
- "Well I'm going out west where I belong"
- "They do their best, they do what they can"
- "I saw her walking down the street he jumped down"
- "Mama where's your little daughter"

From *Rocket to Russia* (November 1977)

- "There's no stoppin' the cretins from hoppin'"
- "Chewin' at a rhythm on by bubble gum"
- "Oh oh oh, oh oh oh"
- "Lovely lovely locket love"
- "I don't care"
- "Well the kids are all hopped up and ready to go"
- "We're a happy family"
- "Lobotomy, lobotomy, lobotomy, lobotomy"
- "Do you wanna dance and hold my hand?"

- "Yeah, I wanna be well"
- "You better know what you want"
- "Hey Johnny, hey Dee Dee, Little Tom and Joey"
- "Well everybody's heard about the bird"
- "Hey hey hey"

## Ramones, as "trivial" / "great"

**Two early views of the Ramones**—both published in July 1976, just months after the release of their first album—suggest a bipolar response that would characterize reactions to the Ramones throughout their entire career. In his review in *Circus*, Paul Nelson praised their "deceptively simple LP of 14 short songs," noting that it cost "$6,400 and was made in less than a week." "Thankfully," he wrote, "*Ramones* is not an album for sleepwalkers. There are real people on it, and they are enthusiastic. They care."

Allan Jones, meanwhile, reviewing the group's performance at the Roundhouse in London, wrote that "it's impossible to find the Ramones, and those nouveaux-punk stylists one has had the opportunity to see, anything more than trivial . . . They and their contemporaries are merely conforming to the mood of the times, rather than creatively disrupting established opinions and attitudes." Nearly twenty years later—long after the threat of the Ramones had passed—the critic Martha Bayles would make a similar argument, decrying the "cult of incompetence" of punk: "Only a fool with a tin ear, or a conformist terrified of not being on the 'cutting edge,' would credit the Ramones with recapturing the old energy."

While it's tempting to dismiss such characterizations of the band (after all, the Ramones themselves rarely made such grandiose claims about being "cutting edge"), there is a truth to the charges that rings in your ears. To what extent were the Ramones the pioneers of a new sound and a new spirit of DIY music-making, and to what extent were they simply expressions of their era, the seventies, the musical equivalent of minimalism in art? This is obviously an unfair question, as all cultural productions—from music to computers—are products of their time. The problem comes, I suspect, from claiming that the Ramones were somehow ahead of their time, that they were prophets of a new sound. There is a truth to Jones's dismissive remark that the Ramones "are merely conforming to the mood of their times." Of course. And yet in the hands of the Ramones the mood of the times was transformed and distilled to such purity that both characterizations—"trivial" and "great"—are fair.

[Martha Bayles, *Hole in Our Soul: The Loss of Beauty and Meaning in American Popular Music*, Chicago: University of Chicago Press, 1994, pp. 303–304; Allan Jones, "Ramones," *Melody Maker*, July 10, 1976, p. 18; Paul Nelson, "Why the Ramones Are Great (I Think)," *Circus*, July 6, 1976, p. 18.]

## "Read About Seymour"

**The debut single, from 1977,** by Swell Maps, who were from Birmingham, England. Although they formed in the years preceeding punk, it was punk that cast them in a new light. Like Wire, Swell Maps reduced songs to sheer energy; you can practically hear the popping and hissing of electricity in "Seymour." But there is an essential difference between the post-punk minimalism of Wire and Swell Maps: Whereas Wire are cold and efficient and obscure, Swell Maps are more playful, hearkening back to a sort of Merry Pranksters with guitars and drums. And yes, the last sixteen seconds descend into crashing noise, anarchy, the falling apart of things—the only proper way to end the song.

## Reagan, Ronald

**The fifties ended.** The sixties ended. And the seventies ended. In fact, when Ronald Reagan was elected, there was no doubt that the seventies had ended. In his nomination acceptance speech at the Republican National Convention in Detroit in July 1980, Reagan said, "I will not stand by and watch this great country destroy itself under mediocre leadership that drifts from one crisis to the next, eroding our national will and purpose." It's no wonder that hardcore bands thrived, and then died, under the reign of Reagan, the Stern Father. After all, the secret premise of even so radical a punk film as Penelope Spheeris's *Suburbia* (1984) was that broken families and absent fathers had flung children out into the streets, where they formed substitute families with like-minded punks.

The deserted cities—so alluring and full of inspired menace for the likes of David Thomas and Jim Jarmusch and countless other musicians and artists during the seventies—were in Reagan's view something altogether different. And yet, in an October 1980 debate with Jimmy Carter, Reagan used the same code words as punk: despair, desolation, no future:

> I stood in the South Bronx on the exact spot that President Carter stood on in 1977. You have to see it to believe it. It looks like a bombed-out city—great, gaunt skeletons of buildings. Windows smashed out, painted on one of them "Unkept promises"; on another "Despair." And this was the spot at which President Carter

had promised that he was going to bring in a vast program to rebuild this department . . . There are whole blocks of land that are left bare, just bulldozed down flat. And nothing has been done, and they are now charging to take tourists there to see this terrible desolation. I talked to a man just briefly there who asked me one simple question: "Do I have reason to hope that I can someday take care of my family again? Nothing has been done."

It's commonplace in rock-crit writing—so much so that it hardly needs saying—to describe the Reagan era as shallow, materialistic, selfish, bullying, television-fake, militaristic, Puritan, and socially reactionary. "Throughout the country," Michael Azerrad has written, "anyone with the slightest bit of suss was disgruntled by the pervasive know-nothingism Ronald Reagan fobbed off as 'Morning in America.'" Or Greil Marcus, writing in 1981, that the "secret message behind the election of Ronald Reagan on November 4th was that some people belong in this country, and some people don't; that some people are worthy, and some are worthless."

And yet hardcore punk was infused with the spirit of musical triumphalism. It too was a return to basics, a clearing away of the clutter, the resurrection of the simple and direct. Back in 1975, James Wolcott, in his *Village Voice* article "A Conservative Impulse in the New Rock Underground," noted that "what's changed is the nature of the impulse to create rock. No longer is the impulse revolutionary— i.e., the transformation of oneself and society—but conservative: to carry on the rock tradition." During the early to mid-1980s, Reagan provided a ready target for anybody who felt alienated from "society." And nostalgia cannot be measured solely in economic or social-policy terms. What matters and what is worth saying is that Reagan had things in common with the punk imagination: a return to basics; a rejection of the excesses of the counterculture and the hippies; a mastery of performance; a do-it-yourself work ethic. In fact, suburban cool, as a reaction to the flamboyance of hippie decadence and glam rock, was very much a part of the New York underground music scene in the years leading up to Reagan's ascension. In 1975, John Rockwell wrote that the Talking Heads looked "almost preppy cool. The two men tend toward the kind of T-shirt that has little alligators on them; Miss Weymouth generally sports stylish jumpsuits." The restrained, minimalist cool of Talking Heads and the Ramones was a version of the Velvet Underground stripped free of excess and commandeered down to the pinprick simplicity that would be the hallmark of Ronald Reagan's speeches.

"It was almost as if there were a power vacuum at the center of American power and identity," Stephen Paul Miller has said of the late seventies. In filling that vacuum, Reagan quickly assumed the status of mythic figure either out of some utopian or dystopian fantasy. In 1977, Richard Robinson noted that it "is very possible that punk political and social attitudes, although they seem extreme at the moment, may be as perceptive about the 'Seventies as the hippie peace-love-end-the-war-politicians-are-crooks attitudes were perceptive about the 'Sixties. Unfortunately, as Johnny Rotten of the Sex Pistols has noted, there cannot be change without violence. Rotten and many other punk leaders feel something has to be done about society other than making promises." Reagan's "return to order" shared so much with punk—which by and large cast him as the Enemy Father—that it will likely be decades before it becomes acceptable to draw this comparison.

[Michael Azerrad, *Our Band Could Be Your Life: Scenes from the American Indie Underground, 1981–1991*, New York: Little, Brown and Company, 2001, p. 9; Greil Marcus, "Life and Life Only," *Rolling Stone*, January 22, 1981, reprinted in *In the Fascist Bathroom: Punk in Pop Music, 1977–1982*, Cambridge: Harvard University Press, 1993, p. 169; Stephen Paul Miller, *The Seventies Now: Culture as Surveillance*, Durham: Duke University Press, 1999, p. 62; Ronald Reagan, "Nomination Acceptance Speech: July 17, 1980," available at www.4president.org/speeches/reagan1980conventionhtm; Reagan, "The Carter-Reagan Presidential Debates," October 28, 1980, available at www.debates.org/pages/trans80b_p. html; Richard Robinson, "Punk Rock at the Edge of Commercial Breakthrough," *Inside: A Supplement to the Valley News* (Van Nuys, California), November 20, 1977, p. 20; John Rockwell, "Talking Heads: Cool in Glare of Hot Rock," *The New York Times*, March 24, 1976, p. 25; James Walcott, "A Conservative Impulse in the New Rock Underground," *The Village Voice*, August 18, 1975, p. 6.]

## *Real Life*

**Released in 1978.** The first LP by Magazine, the band that featured Howard Devoto, formerly of the Buzzcocks. Although the group is usually characterized as post-punk, Magazine sounded as if they had avoided punk altogether. What to make of this album, that sounded like Suicide and Television mixed with a not-yet-existent New Order? Simon Reynolds has written that Magazine was "another postpunk band that had failed to deliver on high expectations." And it was in precisely this failure that Magazine navigated new sounds that left punk behind without disavowing it.

The strongest, most haunting songs on the album sound like broadcasts from someone so demented he must be speaking the truth. There is nothing forgiving about them, and you wonder if they are even songs in the way that you have come to understand that word. In "Motorcade," the narrator sings:

Here comes the motorcade

Moving so slow and hard

Like a snake in a closet

Holding sway in the boulevard

Here is your man

All faces turn unanimously

The small fry who sizzle

In his veins

In all security

In the back of his car

Into the null and void he shoots

The man of the centre of the motorcade

[Simon Reynolds, *Rip It Up and Start Again: Postpunk 1978–1984*, New York: Penguin, 2005, p. 301.]

## *Rebel Without a Cause*

**Elsewhere in the book, James Dean** has been invoked—as has Marlon Brando—as a prototype for the gloomy, alienated, middle-class teenager of mid-seventies punk. In 1978, the Jesuit scholar Neil P. Hurley wrote this: "In *Rebel Without a Cause*, [Dean] crystallized the smouldering discontent of U.S. youth in the Age of Anxiety, the age of the 'organization man,' of sexual awakening (the Kinsey reports) . . . The U.S. family and U.S. youth have never been the same since the Eisenhower period." Strange that one of the more radical groups of the late seventies were the Jesuit liberation theologists, whose idealism and bravery saw through the shallow apologetics of irony.

The film took its name from Robert M. Lindner's book *Rebel Without a Cause: The Hypnoanalysis of a Criminal Psychopath*, published in 1944, two years before Benjamin Spock's *The Common Sense Book of Baby and Child Care*. Although the movie has practically nothing in common with the book except for the title, the book offers a vision of disaffected and alienated youth that is strangely prophetic not only of the Beats, but of other subcultures such as the punks. What characterizes the "rebel" in Lindner's book is his (it is almost always a "he") detachment from any larger social meaning: "a rebel without a cause, an agitator without a slogan, a revolutionary without a program," Lindner writes. He attributes the rise of the rebel figure, in large part, to the closing of the frontier, which had until the end of the nineteenth century provided a culturally sanctioned outlet for, among other things, violence. "So when the geography," he writes, "of a nation or a community or even a civilization becomes fixed, behavior of an unsocial variety which has been flung there by centrifugal action, now works itself out in a harmful manner in the culture itself. Especially is this true where they psychological horizon is similarly limited by economic under privilege, lack of educational opportunities, the immediacy of poignant social contrasts and repetitious occupational activity; in a word, by social disinheritance."

In the film, James Dean's character, Jim Stark, is a CinemaScope punk before his time, in a red (not black) jacket.

[Neil P. Hurley, *The Reel Revolution: A Film Primer on Liberation*, Maryknoll, New York: Orbis Books, 1978, p. 150; Robert M. Linder, *Rebel Without a Cause: The Hypnoanalysis of a Criminal Psychopath*, 1944; repr., New York: Other Press, 2003, pp. 2, 13.]

## "Receiving End"

**A song by London Zoo,** released in 1979 on the Zoom label. They were Robert Sandall on vocals and guitar, with Nick Eldridge, Ed Shaw, and David Sinclair. Earlier, they had been Blunt Instrument, with Bill Benfield instead of Eldridge. The band broke up in the spring of 1980. But these are mere facts in the face of the "Receiving End," which blunts the senses with its beauty. The opening forty seconds make a complete mockery of other songs and almost ruined you for the writing of this book. Those forty seconds almost make you believe in the old universal human truths again: If the entire world listened, no one would want to kill each other anymore. There is a separation to the sounds that reminds you of "Redondo Beach" and other clean songs. The spaces become so big about three-quarters of the way into the song that you could almost fall through them.

## Rent Act

**U.K. legislation designed to control excessive rents** charged by landlords. The 1977 Rent Act, according to Kevin Boone, was paradoxical, as "it led to a more-or-less complete absence of affordable rented accommodation throughout large parts of the U.K. Potential landlords would prefer to leave their properties empty than risk someone taking occupation at a low rent forever." In 1976, Joe Strummer told Caroline Coon that "all the laws are against you. Whoever's got the money's got the power. The Rent Act's a complete mockery. It's a big joke. I just have to f- off into the night for somewhere to sleep."

[Kevin Boone, "The K-Zone: Protected Tenancy," available at www.kevinboone.com; Caroline Coon, "The Clash: Down and Out and Proud," *Melody Maker*, November 13, 1976.]

# Rimbaud, Arthur

1. Margo Jefferson: "Patti Smith is being hailed as the Rimbaud of rock. The 28-year-old performer and songwriter in fact considers herself Rimbaud's disciple, and her first album is something the debauched poet would understand."

2. Patti Smith: "The French poet, Rimbaud, predicted that the next great crop of writers would be women. He was the first guy who ever mad a big women's liberation statement, saying that when women release themselves from the long servitude of men they're really gonna gush."

[Margo Jefferson, "Touch of the Poet," *Newsweek*, December 29, 1975, p. 51; Nick Tosches, "Patti Smith: A Baby Wolf with Neon Bones," *Penthouse*, April 1976.]

## *The Road Warrior*

**A film (*Mad Max 2: The Road Warrior* is the full title)** directed by George Miller, released in 1981, whose costumes and tightly choreographed chaos suggest the punk imagination. There are the Mohawks, yes, and the leather, and the violence. There is Humongous. But beyond that, there is the sad glory of a postapocalyptic world. "In the future," the ominous voice in the movie's trailer tells us, "cities will become deserts. Roads will become battlefields." Bands like Pere Ubu and Destroy All Monsters from cities like Cleveland and Detroit had already conjured these images; Miller's genius in *The Road Warrior* was to go outside the cities into the open spaces with their natural desolation and beauty: *This is what cities might become*, the movie whispered in secret, *if we are lucky*. The movie's precursors include *The Searchers* (John Ford, 1956), *North by Northwest* (Alfred Hitchcock, 1959), *Duel* (Steven Spielberg, 1971), and *Picnic at Hanging Rock* (Peter Weir,

Apocalyptic-punk fashion in *Road Warrior*, from the cover of John Holmstrom's *Stop! Magazine*, 1982–83

1975), where open spaces suggest a sort of blank terror, and where the human form itself is the alien element. In an issue of *Stop! Magazine*, John Holmstrom said this:

> *Road Warrior* is the first film to capture the real essence of punk . . . An underlying theme in this movie is the war between the hippies and the punks. The punks, led by Humongous and starring Wes, want the gasoline that the hippie tribe is hoarding. They kill and rape any hippies they meet up with, they torture them and burn them and get what they want. The hippies live in an armored compound that protects their school busses and gasoline, and wear long hair and robes. Mad Max saves a hippie to pick up some free gas, then joins the tribe after the punks kill his dog.

In truth it is just a movie, made by the right people at the right time. All meaning is imposed later, by writers like me.

[John Holmstrom, "Punxploitation!," *Stop! Magazine* #5, Dec/Jan, 1982/83, p. 14.]

## Rocket from the Tombs, four sentences about

**Periodically, listening to Rocket from the Tombs,** who made music in and around Cleveland, Ohio, in 1974 and 1975, you feel like a knife fight has broken out in your speakers. If you happen to be listening to them while sitting in your basement, in the dark, or in a small shady barn on a farm in France, or in a train speeding across the high plains, you are forgiven if you flinch. And if you wonder, about two minutes into "30 Seconds over Tokyo"—which is hands-down the very best song by any group mentioned in passing or written about in depth in this entire book—if you wonder how in the world it is possible that such catastrophic music can mean so much to you, then you are not alone in wondering. David Thomas, Peter Laughner, Craig Bell, and Gene O'Connor ("Cheetah Chrome") recorded more than ten songs on tape, including "30 Seconds over Tokyo" and "Ain't It Fun," songs that pointed toward a future that punk would never reach because it became aware of itself too soon, which is the fault, really, of no one, except that you wish that punk had not clarified everything so quickly.

## Rocket from the Tombs, two songs by

1. "Ain't it Fun": If there's any pop song that merits an entry with no words, this is it. However:

   > Recorded live—one of twelve tracks—to tape on February 18, 1975, at the Rocket for the Tombs Rehearsal Loft with music by O'Connor ("Cheetah Chrome") and lyrics by Laughner.

According to band member Craig Bell, "We recorded it in our rehearsal loft on West 4th St. It was a large space, maybe 20 x 50, which suited our purposes considering the volume we played at."

The most heartbreaking moment of the song happens at the 3:11 mark, when Laughner, in a genuine plea that wipes out any lurking traces of irony, laments, "Oh God."

And then there is this:

Ain't it fun when you jus jus jus jus jus just can't find your tongue
You stuck it way too deep inside of something that really stung

The song is confounding in other ways. For one thing, it suggests that punk (and, later, grunge) was, at its heart, an extension of the blues, fueled by a postmodern nihilism and speed that transformed its simple chords and repetitive lyrics into a teenage howl. Listening to "Ain't It Fun," it's no surprise that the night before he died—at age twenty-one—Laughner would record, in his parents' home, an acoustic tape that contained numbers by Robert Johnson.

Was punk's lament the result of a sort of pampered white alienation, as opposed to the dirt-poor alienation—a potent result of racism—that characterized the great Black blues tradition? I suspect this is a question that punk fans would rather not ask, or else would dismiss as irrelevant. And yet, one can't help but wonder: Is something like "Ain't It Fun" borne out of a luxury that raises alienation to the status of art? Against the "Yeah, so what?" that you might be thinking right now let me say this: It does matter. The slow guitar solos on the song sample an American past that is impossible to ignore.

2. "Amphetemine": The sad thing about this song, sung by Peter Laughner, is that you hear your own possible demise in the five minutes and twenty-seven seconds that it takes to unfold. It is one of the best rock songs ever written, and it is recorded live in Cleveland on July 24, 1975, at the Piccadilly Inn, and there are people talking and laughing in the background. It's hard to tell what this song is trying to become: There are such moments of tenderness: "I was standing at the ledge of the bridge / staring down into the water's edge / it rolled back and then it rolled away / don't know why that I feel this way / you got to come on down / you got to come on down / you got to come on down." But that's not how the song begins. It begins over the din of background conversation: "Take the guitar player for a ride / he's never once been satisfied / thinks he owes some kind of debt / it'll take him years to get over it." The drums come on like machine-gun, clearing the way for the push of guitars, and then a breather with delicate bass work, and then more vocals, and then a fiery and short guitar solo, and then a calm, and then "I was standing at the ledge of a bridge." Why is it that, coming out of Peter Laughner's mouth, you are sure he is talking about you?

You wrote this entry on two separate occasions—separated only by about fifteen months—yet they seem decades apart. The first paragraph: Your children are still children. They love you as Dad. The forest behind your Michigan house is dying. The second paragraph, on a bitterly cold night in March 2008, your children in their rooms, older now, Barack Obama looking like he will be the Democratic nominee. Do they still love you as Dad? Yes and no. It's good, of course, that they no longer love you as they used to love you. Right? They should love others more than you. You hope this for your children—that they will detach. This is the right and proper thing for them to do. But this song makes you miss them. You never met Peter Laughner. For all you know, he was a jerk. You don't like to romanticize celebrity, even minor celebrity. That's why you hate rock concerts. You worship at no man's feet. No woman's. You want to be the one cheered, not the one cheering. And yet Laughner's voice on this song and those beautiful last fifty seconds transport you away from such bittersweet thoughts.

## Rockwell, John

**Although not as well known as Lester Bangs,** James Walcott, Richard Meltzer, Robert Hilburn, and other critics who wrote about punk as it was emerging, John Rockwell contributed pieces to *The New York Times* in the mid-seventies that provided widespread national exposure to the scene. His writing also conferred a strange sort of legitimacy to some of the emerging bands—not that they wanted or needed such a thing. In the column "The Pop Life," as well as in many feature articles, Rockwell delineated the tremendously fuzzy and not-yet-defined contours of New York's underground music. In March 1975—a full eight months before Charles Shaar Murray's "Report on the Genus Punk" in the November 1975 issue of *New Musical Express*—Rockwell mentioned CBGB in the context of the "seedy little club[s]" that Patti Smith was playing at the time. "Patti Smith," he wrote, "must see herself as some sort of alien muse who has come down and captured the essence of the stylized punk defiance that is at the heart of rock music."

The following month, he described Lou Reed's image of "unstable, android-punk indifference." Rockwell was the first to mention the Ramones in the *Times* in May 1975, nearly a full year before the release of their debut album, and several months before James Walcott's piece "Ramones: Chord Killers" in the July 21 issue of *The Village Voice*. "The Ramones, a young rock quartet from Queens, have been playing here and there recently (at CBGB's earlier this week), and it's a lot of fun. This is yet another group in what has become a fixed New York pattern: black leather jackets, a parodistic macho-camp swagger, and furious, blasting rock 'n' roll.

But what the Ramones offer is nonstop energy (based on double-time guitar strumming), a few clever hooks, and sudden, stop-and-start endings to their songs. For all their underground image, this is a band with obvious commercial potential."

In some ways, of course, it doesn't matter who the "first" New York journalists to cover the punk scene were. What's strange is the beautiful collision between punk's defiance and anarchy, and the staunch traditionalism of "the gray lady." Rockwell's prose was not as electric or impressionistic as that of Bangs and others, and it is precisely this disjunction between the anarchy of what he describes and the stylistic conservatism of *The New York Times* that transforms his articles into instances of jittery formalism. Art history is littered with stories of writers and artists and filmmakers who have produced their best and most shocking work not in total freedom, but rather within constraints, sometimes self-imposed. The discussion of punk within the constraints of *The New York Times* (as opposed to, say, *Creem*) produced a sort of supercharged tension. In Rockwell's columns, Lou Reed was Mr. Reed, Martina Weymouth was Miss Weymouth, Tom Verlaine was Mr. Verlaine. When this proper approach collided with the implied anarchy of punk, the result was a form of static that, like punk, was a small act of liberation.

[John Rockwell, "Patti Smith Plans Album with Eyes on Stardom," *The New York Times*, March 25, 1975; John Rockwell, "Lou Reed Concert at the Felt Forum Both Good and Bad," *The New York Times*, April 28, 1975; John Rockwell, "Speculation About Rock Spectacles," *The New York Times*, May 16, 1975, p. 24.]

**S**

# Saints

**The first album by Australia's the Saints** is almost too good to be punk. Released in 1977, *(I'm) Stranded* is, at its core, a fifties-style album disguised as punk. Formed in Brisbane in 1974, the Saints' early lineup included Chris Bailey, Ed Kuepper, Kym Bradshaw, and Ivor Hay. Early footage of the band from Australian television shows why they never really fit in with the emerging punk scene in the United States and the United Kingdom, as the band tears through "(I'm) Stranded" with barely any physical movement at all, as Bailey—laconic, bored looking, with cigarette in hand—comes off as a thinner version of David Thomas from Pere Ubu. But there is a radicalness in the anti-performance of it all, as if to underscore the fact that the music is fierce enough: Why create a spectacle on stage when the music is spectacle enough?

By the time the Saints arrived in the United Kingdom in June 1977, where they opened for the Ramones and Talking Heads at the Roundhouse, the punk scene was already hardening into its own strict categories of sound and style. In the summer of 1977, they were interviewed in *Gun Rubber*, a Sheffield fanzine:

**Me:** What do you think of the tour so far? And of the New Wave scene?

**Ed:** The reception so far has been 50/50, some really great audiences and some not so good like tonight. I think the New Wave thing has lost a lot, it's got too involved in fashion, which is superfluous.

**Me:** You're not fashion conscious at all?

**Ed:** No, we don't care about all that, we play this music because it's what we've always played and we don't care who likes us, just because we've been named as a "punk" band doesn't mean that we're going to start dressing the part.

They had received early positive reviews of their first single. In *Sniffin' Glue*, Mark P. wrote that "this single is a brilliant effort. The Saints recorded and released it themselves. They're what rock 'n' roll's all about. They move—fast, loud, very like the Ramones, but they're no take-off." According to Ed Kuepper, the single was made in June 1976, when it was recorded and mixed in about five hours. As with the Ramones, the Saints did not see themselves as breaking with the past musically so much as recuperating its lost energy. "It wasn't recognized at the time," Kuepper has said, "but I think in a strange sort of way, my main influences was stuff I thought, was the absolute epitome of rock and roll . . . mostly done in the Fifties with the likes of Bo Diddley, Eddie Cochran, Chuck Berry and people like that. That sort of music, I thought, had never been really surpassed."

In truth, the Saints—especially on their first, and best, album—assault the fifties as much as love it. "Like a snake calling on the phone / I've got no time to be alone" begins "(I'm) Stranded," and the song never lets up. You feel as if machines, not humans, are playing the instruments, and all your theories about the "meaning" of punk disappear. "Nights in Venice" is even stranger; it reminds you in its end-of-time destruction of "30 Seconds over Tokyo" and how the best punk songs are not necessarily the shortest ones. The song builds to annihilation, and what is clear now, in retrospect, is that the rock industry had no place for a song like that whose doom-struck sound could not be recuperated by the marketplace. The Saints' first album was a theory of something darker and fiercer than punk, in its adolescent violence, could ever imagine.

[Ed Kuepper interviewed in *Gun Rubber*, August 1977, p. 11; Ed Kuepper interviewed by Joe Matera, *Australian Guitar*, 2004; Mark P., "Stranded with the Saints," October 1976, in Mary Perry, *Sniffin' Glue: The Essential Punk Accessory*. London: Sanctuary, 2000.]

# Screamers

### A punk band (Synth-punk? Punk-ELO? Techno-punk?) out of Los Angeles, consisting of
Tomata du Plenty, Tommy Gear, K. K. Barrett, and Paul Roessler. Active from 1977
(there was an earlier incarnation called the Tupperwares) until the early 1980s. A
band without guitars. A band that never released a record. Their interviews were an
expression of theory. They answered questions in deceptively simple aphorisms.

From a 1977 interview with *Slash*:

> **Tomata:** I would just say we make sounds.
>
> *Slash*: What will happen to Johnny Rotten?
>
> **Tomata:** When he makes some money he'll probably get his teeth fixed!
>
> *Slash*: Are you a "musical" band?
>
> **Gear:** I personally don't like music per se.

From a 1979 interview with *New York Rocker*:

> **NYR:** Or go video-disc.
>
> **TG:** I don't know. It would be real exciting to release video before audio
> recordings. That may be the standard in the future.

From a 1979 article by Jon Savage:

> **Tomata:** I think advertising is more exciting than the product most of the
> time.

In stage presence, they are likely to remind you of Devo or Talking Heads. In
sound, they are likely to remind you of nothing, except maybe Pere Ubu. In truth,
they seem to have sprung from some strange, undiscovered garden. Pioneers of video
before music and video were linked together for mass audiences, it is only recently,
in the YouTube era, that their work has the potential to reach unsuspecting viewers.
As documented by Target Video in the late seventies, in both live and studio performances, the Screamers performed not so much *for* the camera as *at* it. "Early September [1978] saw them up north in San Francisco, Oakland to be precise, spending
a week at Target Video doing promotional videos," Jon Savage wrote in 1979.

The most remarkable of these are two videos filmed at Target Video Studios
in 1978, "122 Hours of Fear," which recalls, distantly, Rocket from the Tombs'
"30 Seconds over Tokyo," is a soundtrack to the B-horror movie that your life could
be if you strayed too far. "Wow! What a show! One-hundred-and-twenty-two hours
of fear!" Tomata screams. Most of the video is one long take with no cuts or
edits; there is none of the fast cutting that would come to characterize MTV and
its distracted audience. More frightening yet is "Eva Braun," a video stretching

over nine minutes. The band is surrounded by television sets showing themselves. Tomata stands perfectly still, like a mannequin, for the first few minutes. About six minutes into the song the band calmly walks off the set, the music droning on without them. The stage is now empty. At around the 8:00 mark, the band returns, the song resumes, and then it ends.

There is an idea behind this all, but what is it? Is it pop music? Performance art? What are its intentions? The most exhilarating and menacing thing about the Screamers is that they remained undefined, unclassifiable. The very existence of a band as strange as the Screamers poses a question that, thankfully, has yet to be answered.

[Steve Ellman, "Screamers: Past Their Primal?" *New York Rocker*, August 1979, p. 34; "Interview with the Screamers," *Slash* #2, June 1977; Jon Savage, "The Screamers," *Melody Maker*, January 6, 1979.]

## SCUM Manifesto

**Valerie Solanas's screed—insane,** but with just enough truth to make you wonder— was published in 1968 and was part of Malcom McLaren's and Vivienne Westwood's remodeled shop, Too Fast to Live, Too Young to Die. As McClaren noted in 2004, "I ripped out the dance floor and used the wood to make parallel bars. I covered the walls with sponge and sprayed slogans from pamphlets I'd picked up in NYC—the SCUM (Valerie Solanas's Society for Cutting Up Men) Manifesto, adding the words, 'Does passion end in fashion, or does fashion end in passion?'"

Punk's disaffection with the hippies—sometimes violently expressed, sometimes humorously, most often both—was nothing compared to Solanas's. In a section of the *Manifesto* entitled "Isolation, Suburbs, and Prevention of Community," Solanas writes:

Our society is not a community, but merely a collection of isolated family units. Desperately insecure, fearing his woman will leave him if she is exposed to other men or to anything remotely resembling life, the male seeks to isolate her from other men and from what little civilization there is, so he moves her out to the suburbs, a collection of self-absorbed couples and their kids . . . The "hippy" babbles on about individuality, but has no more conception of it than any other man. He desires to get back to Nature, back to the wilderness, back to the home of furry animals that he's one of, away from the city, where there is at least a trace, a bare beginning of civilization, to live at the species level, his time taken up with simple, non-intellectual activities—farming, fucking, bead-stringing . . . The "hippy" is enticed to the commune mainly by the prospect for free pussy—the main commodity to be shared . . .

Punk, too, was about negation and rejection. As Johnny Rotten told Carolyn Coon in 1976:

> I haven't seen a hippie in two weeks. That's something! They were so complacent. They let it all—the drug culture—flop around them. They were all dosed out of their heads the whole time . . . Yeah man, peace and love. Don't let anything affect you. Let it walk all over you but don't stop it . . . We say b—! If it offends you, stop it. You've got to or you just become apathetic and complacent yourself . . . You end up with a mortgage watching TV with 2.4 kids out in suburbia—and that's just disgusting. All those hippies are becoming like that.

[Johnny Rotten quoted in Caroline Coon, "Sex Pistols: Rotten to the Core," *Melody Maker*, November 27, 1976; Malcom McClaren, "Dirty Pretty Things," *The Guardian*, May 28, 2004, http://arts.guardiann.co.uk.]

# Second Extermination Nite

**The Second Extermination Nite** at the Viking Saloon in Cleveland, on January 19, 1975, was, as Paul Marotta notes, "the fourth gig of the [Electric] Eels' five-gig career." The songs they played come across like all the trees in a forest falling at precisely the same time. The sound is from every direction. There is scattered applause. "Mustard" builds to fury in just over a minute. "When you're using / lots of hotdogs / in the peat moss / you can feel it," go the lyrics, by John Morton. An ad for the show in Cleveland's *Scene* is small; the names of the bands are not even listed. Approximately 450 miles to the east, at CBGB on that same night, Television and Blondie performed. It was near the midpoint of the decade. There was no telling how things might turn out. Approximately three months later, the Ramones would release their first album. The sounds began to coalesce around some unified whole. Strangely, although punk is often memorialized in terms of disorder and anarchy, it was order that defined it. The Extermination Nites at the Viking was the furthest expansion of that disorder. Soon patterns developed. Personalities

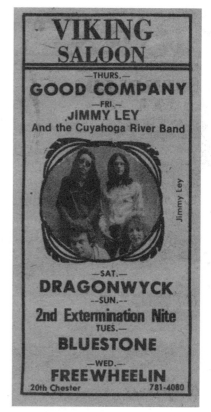

Ad for 2nd Extermination Nite, from Cleveland *Scene*, January 1975

emerged. Bands had identities and promoted those identities. The sound crept its way from bedroom to bedroom on vinyl, from basement to basement. The music just before punk was a rumor. Punk confirmed that rumor, and in confirming it, obliterated it.

## "See No Evil"

**A song by Tom Verlaine,** appearing most famously as the opening track on Television's *Marquee Moon*, released in 1977. There it is: a nervous, concocted thing, full of jumpy glory, with Richard Lloyd's guitar solos predicting a version of punk—jazzy and swinging—that would never happen. In fact, Verlaine has denied that there even was such a thing as punk: "I didn't think there was any punk and, in fact, I still don't. I think punk is slightly more aggressive bubblegum music." In fact, the early music of Television, like that of Patti Smith, was really poetry adorned with music, folk music for the distracted age:

> I get ideas
> I get a notion
> I want a nice little boat
> Made out of ocean

"See No Evil" is, more reasonably, a folk song without the specifics of locale or place. And in truth, the best version of the song is obscure and seldom heard. It was recorded by Peter Laughner in his bedroom at his parents' house shortly before he died, in June 1977. "Well, it's real late at night" he says, his voice dry and raspy, "and everybody's gone to sleep. But I got a six-pack of Genesee, and some Lucky Strikes. So I'm gonna do some songs." It would be easy to say that Laughner's version is stripped down, but it's not. It's extravagant, and you can imagine him there, in his twenties, in his old bedroom, with nothing to lose, as his friends Tom Verlaine and Richard Hell were making splashes in New York, and his ex-compatriots from Rocket from the Tombs, such as David Thomas, were actively recording and performing in bands like Pere Ubu.

In Don DeLillo's 1973 novel *Great Jones Street*, the rock star Bucky Wunderlick remembers the "mountain tapes" that he had recorded years earlier, which were the absolute opposite of the overproduced, massive rock star persona that he is trying to escape. The description might as well be of Laughner's late-at-night-the-night-before-his-death recordings in his parents' house:

> On the tapes were twenty-three songs, all written and sung by me (without accompaniment) on and old acoustic guitar, the first I'd ever owned . . . I had just

come off a world tour and my voice was weary and scorched, no sound nearer to my mind than the twang of baby murders in patriarchal hamlets . . . These songs conveyed a special desolation, a kind of abnormal naturalness . . . Every reel was full of repetitions, mistakes and slurred words.

Peter Laughner, singing alone in the night. In your own dark nights, it is his voice that you remember.

[Don DeLillo, *Great Jones Street*, 1973; repr., New York: Vintage, 1994, pp. 147–48; Tom Verlaine quoted in Scott Mervis, "Music Preview: Television's Tom Verlaine Turns in on Again," *Pittsburgh Post-Gazette*, June 8, 2006, www.post-gazette.com.]

# Self-referential, punk as

**No, the heading directly above** these words does not mean to suggest that punk or New Wave was some postmodern, ironic trick. What this entry does mean to say is this: Coming of age in a media-saturated era, many of the people who produced and wrote about punk were highly aware of rock history, of rock as a consumer good, of rock as a gesture of acting, of performance. This is not to say that punk was insincere. And yet, wasn't one of the targets of punk the "sincerity" of the sixties hippies, whose "good intentions" had done little if anything to thwart a failed war in Vietnam and a string of terrible assassinations of political leaders in the United States? How, exactly, had folks like Timothy Leary contributed to the social good of the nation?

By early 1978—earlier than that, even—the "new wave" that had swept the nation was already being written about in historical terms. Or, in these words from the Detroit (Dearborn Heights, really) fanzine *Ballroom Blitz* in 1978:

No doubt about it, 1977 was a landmark year for rock and roll music. The Seventies, a decade that seemed doomed to complete musical irrelevance, brought about primarily because of the pseudo-hip burnout faction of the early 'Seventies, where self-assumed pyrotechnical gods alienated many a rock and roll purist as they remained totally engrossed in their own irrelevance, as well as the mass-media manufactured disco-hype, generally regarded by most musical theorists as having as much emotion and musical substance as Fabian.

In fact, in that same issue punk could be so historical that it was already "history." In his column, "Mercy Beat," John Clayton wrote that "Punk is dead, and a new era of Beat music, dubbed 'power-pop' by the media cliché-merchants is on us. Certainly the hard-core punk storm has blown itself out sooner than expected."

["Blitz Awards for 1977," *Ballroom Blitz* no. 25, March 1978, p. 30; Jack Clayton, "Mersey Beat," *Ballroom Blitz* no. 25, p.5.]

## "Seventeen"

**A song by Peter Laughner, performed beautifully** and tragically with Lester Bangs during a jam session at *Creem*'s office north of Detroit. There are other recordings of the song—notably with Rocket from the Tombs in 1975—but these overpower it and kill its strange beauty. Was the *Creem* version with Bangs recorded in 1975 or 1976? It's hard to know for sure, which adds to its mystery. On the tape, Laughner says "eight-fifteen in Detroit, on CKLW" before beginning: "My teachers wouldn't let us kiss in the hall / My daddy told me I was headin' for a fall." There is a folksy vibe to the song—to most of the songs Laughner recorded with Bangs—and listening to it you remember what David Thomas of Pere Ubu has said: that punk was a real tragedy because when it took off, it overshadowed and maybe even obliterated the musical renaissance that was developing in cities like Cleveland. If punk hadn't happened, and if it hadn't caught people like Peter Laughner in its maelstrom, would music have sounded like "Seventeen"? Songs like this offered glimpses of a future that never came. At least it would be nice to think so.

## Sex Pistols

**It is hard to imagine a world** where the Sex Pistols are possible. They had to be destroyed, or to destroy themselves. All dire predictions about cultural disintegration seem confirmed by the fact of their existence. But so do all the hopes of rejuvenation. What is remarkable is not these contradictory facts—after all, nothing good can ever last—but that they destroyed themselves before anyone else could. They had to be destroyed, they knew this, and so they destroyed themselves. This was not an act of art, or some statement, and in fact the less you know about it the better. Today, it is easy to know too much about everything, including the act of destruction. YouTube clips of their final concert (before reuniting) in San Francisco are easy to find in seconds, and you wonder what this means. What used to be a mystery and an act of imagination is now right there in front of you, in the bright sunshine of your bedroom, or apartment, or living room.

Do you remember the very first time you heard them? The fact that there has been no other band like them before or since is both thrilling and terrible: The Sex Pistols are like a penny that keeps coming up heads: There's no explanation other than the fact that it is happening. At some point, you wonder if it is you who are listening to them, or they who are listening to you. You hated to learn about the way that Sid died. But then you understood, and you wanted to know more about Nancy. *Nancy*, you thought, what an old-fashioned name. Like the comic strip. And you even wondered about the Sinatra connection—there is the cover version of "My Way," and your mind races from Paul Anka to Frank Sinatra to Nancy Sinatra and from Nancy Sinatra to Nancy Spungen.

There is this early write-up in *New Musical Express*: "A quartet of spiky teenage misfits from the wrong end of various London roads, playing 60's styled white punk rock as unself-consciously as it's possible to play it these days i.e. self-consciously."

And then this:

"Actually, we're not into music,' one of the Pistols confided afterwards."

"Wot then?"

"We're into chaos."

The Sex Pistols ended just before they became a representation of themselves. This is certainly not true of other famous bands like the Beatles, the Rolling Stones, U2, etc., who survived long enough to incorporate their own image back into themselves, creating a sort of distorted feedback loop.

Today, now that the Sex Pistols have assumed the full status of rock legends, it's hard to imagine just how pathetically regular they were. Of course, we now live in an age of relentless demystification. Of their 1978 U.S. tour, Howie Klein wrote in *New York Rocker*:

> The Pistols seemed disappointed that Americans loved them primarily—in some cases primarily—for their music. They appeared on pro-punk radio stations KSAN and KSJO to try to shed some light on what they are actually all about. Many erstwhile fans were not at all happy by what was uncovered. The beast is not always pretty.

The fact of legend covers up a lot of mundane failures—but then, failure lies at the heart of punk. Even in our age of flat no-history, the footage of that final concert in San Francisco is amazing to the point of your thinking it was staged . . . which it was. This question lingers: How could punk end in San Francisco, the symbolic birthplace of the counterculture, and even of the sixties? Rotten's final words at the Winterland concert ("Ha ha. Ever get the feeling you've been cheated?") are a question to the audience about the quality of the show, and about the Sex Pistols as a band, about punk, about the seventies, and about us.

> [Howie Klein, "Pistols Tour Notes," *New York Rocker*, February–March 1977 [1978], p. 51; Neil Spencer, "Don't Look over Your Shoulder, but the Sex Pistols Are Coming," *New Musical Express*, February 21, 1976, p. 31.]

# Shirkers

**The band, out of Washington, D.C.**, released only one single, in 1978 on Limp Records. It features "Drunk and Disorderly," later covered by Black Market Baby. The group was made up of Steven Bialer, Liz DuMais, Libby Hatch, Thomas Kane, and Jeff

Zang. The song veers into Ramones territory, but then stakes out its own ground. The energy is fierce and fun, like kids jumping on a bed. "Goin down to the neighborhood bar / Behind the school in an old parked car," the song begins. It was recorded by Don Zientara in his basement and produced by Howard Wuelfing, and although the sound is murky and thick, this only adds to the power of the songs, especially "Suicide," with its cinemascope guitar that recalls early Iggy Pop.

In the July 1979 issue of the fanzine *descenes*, there is a letter to the editor, from Bryant Jamerson, about his punk band. He ends the letter with a P.S.: "Out of all the records on Limp I got at Yesterday & Today everyone around here seems to really like The Shirkers the best . . . 'Drunk and Disorderly' has become a party anthem with FRENZY!!!!!"

[Bryant Jamerson, "Dear Editor," *descenes* vol. 1 no. 3, July 1979, p. 4; "Recording Info," for "Drunk and Disorderly" available at www.30underdc.com.]

## Shivvers

**The fact that the Shivvers—**Jill Kossoris, Jim Richardson, Mike Pyle, Scott Krueger, Jim Eanelli, and Breck Burns—were from the Milwaukee area and that they are often classified as power pop means something. The Shivvers are power pop in the way that punk is garage rock. Lying just beneath the surface of jangling guitars and sweet melodies is a sadness that, from an Ohioan's point of view, is an affirmation. Their only 45—"Teen Line" b/w "When I Was Younger"—was released in 1980. "Last night I got a call on the telephone," begins "Teen Line," and you immediately realize that Jill Kossoris's voice sounds sometimes like it too is coming from an era of long, sagging telephone lines that carried voices in the dark across the Midwest of a beautiful country:

- The crisp guitars at the very beginning of "Please Stand By" that remind you of your father's fluorescent lights in the basement.
- "It Hurts Too Much," live: the best Shivvers song you've ever heard (you've heard about sixteen) because it seems like at least four different songs at the same time, and because Kossoris sounds like she's singing for her life, erasing any trace of irony that you suspected in the Phil Spector girl-group sound, that by the end of the song has dissipated in a thundering wail of guitars. The ending of that song is cinematic; unmade movies directed by you pop into your mind during those last thirty-five seconds.
- The fact that "No Reaction," with its swirling melodies and synthesizer, sounds like a cross between Blondie and Suicide.

The Shivvers are the sort of group whose existence proves a mockery of categories.

## "Short-lived fad, a"
### From *New York Rocker*, 1977:

Obviously, the movement is more than just a short-lived fad or anything the Yes fans are trying to tuck it out of sight as. The roots have firmly taken and as more records come out, the year should exhibit radical changes and growth patterns— that is, providing people, "punks" included, can fight off the prejudices which seem to pose the most danger.

Cryptic terms and phrases. An insurgency. Punk as a whisper, a secret, on its way to something too big to remain secret.

[Kris Needs, "BritBits," *New York Rocker*, May–June 1977, p. 21.]

## "Singles Reviewed by Roy Carr" (1976)

**"New York's Ramones**—the first group to have condensed an entire 14-track LP onto the head of a pin without any loss of definition . . . well, would you believe one side of a single! Truthfully, I've never heard so much rock energy being generated since the MC5's 'Back in the U.S.A.'"

[Roy Carr, "Singles Reviewed by Roy Carr," *New Musical Express*, September 18, 1976, p. 21.]

## "Sister Ray"

**In retrospect, the first three albums** by the Velvet Underground—released in 1967, 1968, and 1969—are, alongside the first albums by the Stooges, the first recognizably punk albums. To claim this is to confront all sorts of qualifications: that Lou Reed sounds an awful lot like Bob Dylan; that the first three albums are really closer to a sort of half-jiving folk than anything by the Ramones or the Sex Pistols; that the self-important indulgence of the longer songs mitigates against the very stripped down, amateurness of punk. In truth, it's hard to listen to the Velvet Underground without listening to the legend of the Velvet Underground—what they have become in the words of countless apologists and critics. Indeed, the uninitiated listener might, upon hearing the first three albums all the way through, say something like, *Hmm, interesting folk music. A few weird patches, but overall pretty good.*

Since most people who "get" the V.U. get them from the other side of the sixties, there's a tendency to downplay the fact that they were a sixties band. (This is still the part of the entry that acknowledges certain facts about V.U.) For instance, there is a tenderness in the songs "Pale Blue Eyes" and "Jesus" (both from the third album) that is difficult to dismiss as anything other than unironic.

Jesus, help me find my proper place

Jesus, help me find my proper place

Help me in my weakness, 'cause I've fallen out of grace

Jesus, Jesus

There is a fragility and openness to these songs that no amount of overdetermined irony can recuperate. In truth, the secret to V.U. lies in the very last song on their last great album, their third one, released the very last year of the sixties:

One, two, three:

If you close the door

The night could last forever

Leave the sunshine out

And say hello to never

It is sung by the percussionist Maureen Tucker. Was there ever a darker lyric? It's only more unsettling that it's such a simple ditty, in the 1920s style, like some of the songs on the Beatles' *White Album*. It also has this line:

If you close the door

I'd never have to see the day again

The lyrics put you in the mind of other words from that era, when Hunter S. Thompson wrote to his brother Davison that "I seriously believe this country deserves everything that's going to happen to it. War, revolution, madness, the whole bag."

[Hunter S. Thompson, "To Davison Thompson," October 16, 1968, in Douglas Brinkley, ed., *Fear and Loathing in America: The Brutal Odyssey of an Outlaw Journalist*, New York: Simon & Schuster, 2000, p. 137.]

## Six Million Dollar Man, The

**A popular television series** (based on a novel called *Cyborg*) that aired from 1974 through 1978. In 1975, the series included a two-part episode called "The Bionic Woman"; this led to a spinoff series the following season entitled *The Bionic Woman*. In 1978, X-Ray Spex released their first album, *Germ Free Adolescents*, which was awash in pop-culture references and which included "Genetic Engineering," a song about the potential terrors of a future "perfect race." Near the end of the song, Poly Styrene sang, "Bionic man is jumping / through the television set / He's about to materialize / and guess who's coming next."

# Sixties, punk as an affirmation of

**Mark Perry, the founder of one of the earliest punk fanzines,** *Sniffin' Glue,* has said: "Although [punk] was entirely connected to the hippy politics, it was entirely the natural progression of hippies' 'anti-establishmentism,' I think. You couldn't wear bells and flowers to freak the powers out anymore and there was a perfectly logical line from the San Francisco hippies to the London punks." Punk's heroes were the hippies, but this could never be openly acknowledged ("kill yr idols"). It was the pop stars of the sixties who articulated through their music the radical potential of rock and roll to threaten cultural orthodoxies; the problem was that by the time punk emerged, this had been exposed as myth. Despite the overeager, self-congratulatory, hyper-promotional fortieth anniversary "special issues" of *Rolling Stone,* rock and roll's real influence on contemporary events amounted, perhaps, to inspiring the Manson murders, Altamont, etc. Choose your atrocity. Punk did not have to reject the hippies because by 1975 they were fast approaching obsolescence anyway, as places like Berkeley and Ann Arbor sobered up to the realities of post-Watergate, pre-Reagan boredom. "When the American state refuses to help New York in a time of crisis, when hospitals and schools have to shut down, when social aid is cut back and the city is no longer cleaned, it's the dissolution of the city in its own outskirts, the future popular self-government of civil fear." So wrote Paul Virilio, the French cultural theorist. And indeed, from the outside, the United States must have looked as if it were imploding in the mid-seventies.

"To me," John Ellis of the Vibrators said in 1977, "the ideology of punk doesn't differ so much from that of flower-power, except that this is 1977. That is: we're fed up with the things that are going on around us that we have no control over." And Jello Biafra once noted that, "Spiritually, I think that punk was in tune with the *early* hippies." In truth, hippies and punks shared a sense that rock and roll was, elementally, a social movement, an expression of solidarity of *us* against *them.* But punk was also a bitter reminder of the early days of the supergroups of the late sixties, for at one point the Beatles, the Stones, the Who, and Bob Bylan were just a bunch of young lads playing their music before small, enthusiastic crowds. The difference is that most punk bands, with obvious exceptions like the Ramones, did not last long enough to be seduced by their own images. And, of course, punk disavowed the very notion of "quality" itself; once *Sgt. Pepper's* was released in 1967, there was no turning back, and it took punk to strip away the veneer of over-professionalized mediocrity that the shape of music had assumed by 1975. In 1978, Bob Dylan, in an interview with Philippe Adler, was asked, "What do you think of punks?" He responded: "I don't know much about this movement. I've heard some records and I've seen some groups. I think that above all they're releasing a lot of energy and that's important, but, to be frank, I mostly listen to good music."

[John Ellis quoted in Mick Brown, "The Vibrators: The Punks Who Came in from the Cold," *Sounds*, September 24, 1977; Bob Dylan, "The Philippe Adler Interview," July 3, 1978, *L'Express*, www.interferenza.com; Mark Perry, "The Birth of the Glue," *Sniffin' Glue: The Essential Punk Accessory*, London: Sanctuary, 2000, p. 122; Tony Rocco, "Biafra: 6,591 votes (3%!!)," *Damage* no. 4, January 1980, p. 18.]

# Sixties, punk as a rejection of (1)

**A 1973 review in *Creem* of a book by Abbie Hoffman,** Jerry Rubin, and Ed Sanders called *VOTE!* begins like this: "I hope the next book company that signs the primo 'counter-culture / revolutionary' bigmouths to a big fat book contract goes bankrupt."

Were it not for the indulgence, the excess, the utopianism of the sixties, there would have been less for punk to mock, to hate even. By the early to mid-seventies, even places that were bastions of countercultural thinking and production—like Ann Arbor, Michigan, and Berkeley, California—were revising and sometimes rejecting outright the sixties and its flaws. An ad in a 1974 issue of the underground newspaper *Ann Arbor Sun* for the radio station 106 FM put it this way: "A question posed by many of the respondents to W4 Listens dealt with women entering the broadcast industry. With the advent of Top 40, the deep-throated fast-talking male machine has dominated and created the image of radio. The industry is rapidly moving away from this mid-60's mentality. FM is penetrating the radio scene, and women are penetrating FM."

Pick up almost any punk, underground, or New Wave magazine or fanzine from the mid- to late seventies and there's likely to be an underlying tone of disdain regarding the hippies and the counterculture, which was mocked as being self-seri-ous, correct in its politics, and thoroughly lacking in the sort of defiant humor that characterized early punk (at least until its so-called hardcore phase). This sentence from the Detroit-area (Dearborn Heights) fanzine *Ballroom Blitz*—near the end of a review of an album by the Silver Tones—gives you some idea: "Most ironically, being based in the hopelessly lost cultural void of Ann Arbor, a notorious mecca for the last surviving remnants of the pseudo-intellectual street people movement that said much and accomplished little in the early Seventies . . ." Or this one, from Lester Bangs's 1976 piece on John Denver: "Now, with the collapse of our national ideals, it seems only fitting that we have one grand bespectacled avatar to ram them down our throats one last time, along with all that hippie peace and love crap . . ." Here is another, from the article "Why I Hate Pot," from the fanzine *Streetlife*: "There aren't many hippies left in our culture (praise the LORD) but anyone who lights up a joint just might as well be wearing MOCCASSINS, love-beads and peace-chains. Pot is a laid-back drug and there is NO ROOM for laying back in the eighties."

Such sentiments were not confined to the American Midwest, or the East Coast. An advertisement for "The Northern California New Wave Music and Punk Culture Convention/Extravaganza" in *Damage: An Inventory* from 1979—with bands ranging from the Dead Kennedys to the Mutants to the Dils—contains this promise: "Celebrate the Cremation of Woodstock."

This line is worth a second consideration.

"Celebrate the Cremation of Woodstock." And this, for a concert held at the symbolic dark heart of the counterculture: Pauley Ballroom, at the University of California, Berkeley, campus.

Later in this same publication, in a short write-up of the Santa Cruz band the Realtors, there is this line: "Since August 1977 they have conspired to reprogram this once-mellow, youthful hippie community into a legion of surfside barbarians." Sometimes this rejection was both funny and enlightening at the same time. Jeff Raphael, the drummer for the early San Francisco punk group the Nuns, has said that "a lot of people involved in punk were rejects anyway and were dissatisfied with things. The whole 'Sixties thing was peace and love, and that didn't work." And in his review of the U.K. music scene in 1977, Max Bell wrote that the New Wave slogans were "hate and war not love and peace" and that punkers sneered at "the hip jargon of a bygone psychedelia with a venom based on real hatred and nihilism."

Whether the sixties opened up Pandora's box, or whether that period was a phase that needed to pave the way for the hate and violence that punk would spawn, is still a matter of debate. What is remarkable is how rapidly and tragically the collapse happened. The sixties became an anachronism before it became "the sixties." As early as the Beatles' *White Album* (1968)—most notably the song "Revolution"—there was a rejection of the era itself and a blueprint for a new sound of harsh noise that would characterize the total demolition spawned by underground, punk, and grunge. This was further amplified in Stanley Kubrick's 1971 film adaptation of Anthony Burgess's novel *A Clockwork Orange*, just before the violence begins, when the Tramp says to Alex that "It's a stinking world because there's no law and order any more. It's a stinking world because it lets the young get onto the old like you done. It's no world for an old man any more. What sort of a world is it at all?" For those of us born in 1965—strike that, for those of us *born* (because someday there will be readers who are manufactured and cloned, not born, although perhaps they will still call it that)—there is certainly a sense that we have been betrayed by that era; our headlong rush into postmodern irony is an explanation, not an excuse. "The hippy movement was a failure," Joe Strummer told Caroline Coon in 1976, just four months after their first live performance. "All hippies around now just represent complete apathy."

In a 1979 *Descenes* review of a Pin-Ups concert at Studio 10 in New York, James Testa noted that the "joint is overrun by ugly guys with pony tails" and "ugly girls dressed like migrant farm workers" before finally sticking it to the hippies: "The Pin-Ups overcame a lot of troubles when they played Studio 10. Sandwiched between two godawful New York bands and a bunch of speeches promoting marijuana (as if hippies weren't high enough all the time already), the band played a rave-up set."

About halfway through Ken Russell's demented masterpiece *Altered States* (1980; based on Paddy Chayefsky's 1978 novel of the same name), Eddie Jessup (William Hurt) mockingly defends the radical sensory-deprivation experiments he's using to reconnect with his primordial ancestors: "I'm a man in search of his true self. How archetypically American can you get? Everybody's looking for their true selves. We're all trying to fulfill ourselves, understand ourselves, get in touch with ourselves, face the reality of ourselves, expand ourselves. Ever since we dispensed with God we've got nothing but ourselves to explain." For many punks the narcissistic quest for self-fulfillment was the logical outcome of the sixties, reversed in their music by an even greater—but more stringently ironic—embrace of those values. When the Ramones sang "I Wanna" they were expressing a simple human desire that layed bare the pretensions of deep quests for self-fulfillment.

In the spring of 2008, you watched *Altered States* with your fifteen-year-old son in the basement on a big screen. You had been hinting around for over a year about wanting to watch it with him, and then on an early March night he suddenly said, "All right, Dad. *Altered States*." You dropped what you were doing (finishing up your entry on the Dils for this very book [damn you Mr. Barker for your deadlines]), grabbed a beer, and headed down into the dark Michigan basement (sort of like an isolation chamber, no?) to watch this movie with him, terrified that it wouldn't hold up. But it starred William Hurt, whom your son admired from *The End of Violence*. The last gasp of the seventies spread itself out on the screen in all its beautiful and disgusting, self-indulgent glory, and after about twenty minutes it was clear that your son loved the movie, its crazy and sudden shifts of tone and pace, its sincerity, its deep deep deep deep deep deep deep deep wish to tap into some truth more meaningful than . . . Than what? Ah, there's the rub. When William Hurt bursts out of the isolation tank as a primordial man, running hairy and naked through the streets before eventually killing and eating a live animal at the zoo, he is both the last hippie and the first punk. If your son looked to you for answers, you had none to give.

Lester Bangs once wrote that admiring people for "being disgusting" was "the cultural history of the Seventies." Of course, that wasn't the legacy of the seventies. But the fact that Bangs could write something like that was, the savage nihilism of his statement—masked by humor that disguises its radical critique—remains the answer to a question that we (or at least some of us) have just happened to forget. Have you forgotten?

[Advertisement for the Northern California New Wave Music amd Punk Convention/ Extravaganza in *Damage: An Inventory* vol. 1, October 1979, p. 21; Advertisement for 106 FM, *Ann Arbor Sun*, May 17–31, 1974, p. 25; Lester Bangs, "John Denver Is God," *Creem*, January 1976, p. 31; Max Bell, "UK," *New Wave*, August 1977, p. 30; Caroline Coon, "The Clash: Down and Out and Proud," *Melody Maker*, November 13, 1976; Mike McDowell, "Rockabilly Renaissance: A Whole Lotta Shakin' Goin' On," *Ballroom Blitz* no. 22, September 1977, p. 15; Linda Roy, "Why I Hate Pot," *Streetlife: The Magazine of Detroit Street Culture*, October/November 1980, p. 24; Jeff Raphael interviewed by James Stark, *Punk '77*, Stark Grafix, 1992, p. 31; James Testa, "Pin-Ups," *Descenes* vol. 1, no. 3, July 1979, p. 14; Ed Ward, review of *VOTE!*, *Creem*, January 1973, p. 65.]

## Sixties, punk as a rejection of (2)

**But it was more than that, wasn't it?** It could be said that there are no generation gaps today because we have found ways to ruthlessly integrate, with few exceptions, the new and the old. Grandparents text their grandchildren. Parents ask their teen-aged children to make some good playlists for them. They and their kids share the Internet on the same computer. Teachers and students chat with each other on Facebook. It's hard to rebel—hard to create a gap—when you and your parents and elders are basically users and consumers of the same technology and the same media, when you like the same movies, when you like the same music, when you shop for stuff from the same Ikea catalogs.

But in 1975, '76, and '77, the gap was was still attainable. Here is Larry Rohter in *The Washington Post*, writing about punk in 1977:

Rock has had generational crises before, but never one so serious or heated as this . . . It's not too hard to see why Rotten and company heap as much abuse on the rock establishment as on politicians, actors and other celebrities. Read *Rolling Stone* magazine these days, and you're likely to learn as much about Boz Skaggs' house, Fleetwood Mac's fleet of cars and boats, Queen's taste in antique furniture and Hall and Oates' real estate investments as their music . . . The rebellious stars of the 'Sixties, in other words, have become the 'Seventies equivalent of the good burgher.

The attractions of comfort were too tempting for the baby-boom generation of rock stars, whose multimillion-dollar record contracts and lavish lifestyles had made them into part of the commercial entertainment-culture industry. Ironically, by 1975 folks like Dylan, Baez, and others were living lifestyles far more materialistic and pampered than the parents and politicians they had chided in their earlier music years. This contradiction—between the idealism and implied critique of capitalism in the sixties and the retreat to bougeoise decadence in the seventies— was a contradiction that punk exploited with the full awareness that it, too, would soon be in danger of *selling out*.

In 1969, vice president Spiro Agnew—who would resign in 1973 under a cloud of investigation regarding bribery, extortion, and tax fraud—made a series of speeches against the counterculture, protestors, and radicals. If this makes his speeches sound laughable, they were not, for Agnew's words were sharp, vindictive, blustery, and, above all, theoretical. His critiques of television and media were often as aphoristic and full of dissent as those of Marshal McLuhan or Theodor Adorno. In some strange and surprising ways, he described the conditions from which the violence and anarchy of the punk imagination arose. "A society which comes to fear its children," he said at the commencement ceremony at Ohio State University in June 1969 (two months before the Stooges' first album appeared, whose song "1969" begins, "Well it's 1969 ok all across the USA / It's another year for me and you / Another year with nothing to do"). "A sniveling, hand-wringing power structure deserves the violent rebellion it encourages," Agnew said. "If my generation doesn't stop cringing, yours will inherit a lawless society where emotion and muscle displace reason."

And, several months later, in October, Agnew said in a speech entitled "Impudence in the Streets" that by "accepting unbridled protest as a way of life, we have tacitly suggested that the great issues of our times are best decided by posturing and shouting matches in the streets. America today is drifting toward Plato's classic definition of a degenerating democracy—a democracy that permits the voice of the mob to dominate the affairs of government." After the sixties sputtered into the seventies, and the promises of revolution that had so terrified Agnew never materialized (and by one other measure, consider that in the approximately twenty-two-year period between 1969 and 1992, a Democrat was president for only four years), punk filled the gap symbolically, suggesting in lyrics, performance, and style the street anarchy that briefly emerged in the late sixties. "But what the hell," Hunter S. Thompson wrote in 1969. "When Agnew becomes president we won't have to worry about elections—except as film fantasies and weird scenes from the past." Of course Agnew never became president. After the Kent State shootings in 1970, large-scale campus demonstrations gradually dwindled. Nixon resigned. The war ended. Punk was surprising, really, for being so energetic at a time when the nation was so very, very tired.

[Spiro Agnew, "Impudence in the Streets: Address at Pennsylvania Republican Dinner, October 30, 1969," in *Frankly Speaking*, Washington, D.C.: Public Affairs Press, 1970, p. 44; Spiro Agnew, "Rationality and Effetism: Address at Ohio State University Commencement

Exercises, June 7, 1969," in *ibid.*, p. 18; Larry Rohter, "Punk Rock Music in the Second Generation: What's the Nastiest Four-Letter Word in Pop Today?" *The Washington Post*, May 1, 1977, p. 168; Hunter S. Thompson, "Letter to John Wilcock," December 17, 1969, in Douglas Brinkley, ed., *Fear and Loathing in America: The Brutal Odyssey of an Outlaw Journalist, 1968–1976*, New York: Simon and Schuster, 2000, p. 240.]

# Skunks

**An Austin, Texas-based hard rock/punk band** from the late seventies whose songs, especially "Earthquake Shake" and "Can't Get Loose," both from 1979, feel like a declaration of war. The band consisted of Jesse Sublett, Jon Dee Graham, Eddie Muñoz (who left the band in 1979), and Billy Blackman. There is an almost mathematical fury to "Earthquake Shake," whose first line—"My heart is burnin' like a witch at the stake"—is only topped by "set afire like a buddhist monk" later on. The song never lets up, and it ends with a weird reverb, as if some terrible signal from outer space smuggled its way into the ending of the song. Better still is the less showy "Can't Get Loose," which sounds like it's sung by Neil Young in a parallel universe. The song is bold enough to be quiet, and listening to it you realize how arbitrary mainstream fame is: Groups like the Clash made it big with lesser songs than "Can't Get Loose," whose last minutes build to a heart-of-darkness pop fury. According to Sublett, the single was recorded "on two-track in a friend's garage on a Friday afternoon." Production costs? A case of Budweiser. By 1979, the Skunks had made it to New York, where John Cale's manager, Jane Friedman, booked them in numerous places, including CBGB. Modest fame followed.

The Skunks stink up New York City

Do you need to know that Sublett's girlfriend had been murdered by a former roommate's friend in the summer of 1976, and that this haunted him, and that while he was onstage performing he felt most free from the terrible memory of finding her body? Probably not. There is little of that tragedy in the songs. Instead, where you imagine you hear the sadness is in those moments of beauty when Sublett's voice, reaching for something, breaks.

[Ken Lieck, "Young, Loud, and Cheap: The Skunks, the Band That Broke Austin Out of the Seventies," *The Austin Chronicle*, December 8, 2000.]

## Sleepers

**The Sleepers, an early San Francisco punk-era band,** first played the Mabuhay on Christmas Eve, 1977—possibly, according to V. Vale, "the 'deadest' night of the year for a club. There were only seven people in the audience—mostly drunks who had wandered in off the streets." Recorded "somewhere in the Hayward Hills" in 1978, "Seventh World" does indeed sound like it was recorded "somewhere." The song features Ricky Williams (who had previously been the drummer for Crime and who would latter join Flipper) on vocals, Michael Belfer on guitar, Tim Mooney on drums, and Paul Draper on bass.

You begin to notice that the song is picking up speed at about the thirty-five-second mark. Then the song momentarily stalls out at around :50, and then, a few seconds later, unleashes itself into the sort of fury that gives you hope, descending into Amboy Dukes / Stooges / Rocket from the Tombs blowout with the chanted lyric "You will be in the seventh world" snarled as from the snout of a dog.

"Holding Back," from a few years later, is almost unclassifiably perfect: David Bowie wired through Joy Divison.

"Zenith," released in 1980, is like a rough draft by Godspeed You Black Emperor!, building with a military beauty.

"Los Gatos" proceeds with a Caligari-like menace: "You can always tell / if you are going to hell." It sits between the seventies and the eighties like a sphynx: It knows the answers, but it's not telling.

[V. Vale, CD liner notes, *Sleepers: Less an Object*, Tim Kerr Records, 1996.]

## Slits

**The Slits are known to many primarily as an all-female punk band,** in the way that a band such as the Clash is not known primarily as an all-male punk band. Leave aside the fact that the label "punk" (as used throughout this book) does not really describe the Slits, and you are still left with this: the fact that the phrase "all-female" or "all-girl" usually precedes their name says something about gender and punk (or rock in general). Depending, dear reader, on who you are, or what sort of mood you're in, this fact is either insignificant (leave it to academics to point out this sort of thing in the face of the great music that the Slits made!), or boring (so what?), or important. If you're like me, it's all of the above.

The original members in 1976 were Ari Up (Arianna Forster), Palmolive (Paloma Romera), Kate Korus, and Suzi Gutsy. Tessa Pollitt and Viv Albertine replaced Korus and Gutsy, and eventually Budgie (Peter Clarke) replaced Palmo-live on drums. They toured with the Clash in 1977 on the White Riot tour, and video footage from that time (from Don Letts's *The Punk Rock Movie*) suggests an awkwardly violent stage presence that is more radical than anything from the Clash or the Sex Pistols. For the first few years, their music was beautiful and terrifying, a mix of what would come to be known as punk and dub and reggae. Were the Slits subversives pretending to be normal? Or were they normal pretending to be subversives? "You see, one thing I'd like to stress," Pollitt has said, "is that the Slits always had a sense of humor, a sense of the ridiculous, and some people just did not get it. They took it seriously." They exerted a tremendous gravitational pull on the imagination in America. Kris Needs, in *New York Rocker*, wrote, "The Slits are an all-girl band featuring a 14-year-old singer called Arianna who stamped and screamed into a tantrum as the equipment made rude noises. This was at their world debut, opening for The Clash at Harlesden's Colosseum. Drummer Palmo-live's kit kept falling apart as they careened through their brief set with rampaging abandon. Noisy, aggressive, and trashy, but lotsa fun!"

"Instant Hit" could be, in a parallel universe, a secret twin of Blondie's "The Tide Is High," except that there darkness beneath the surface of "Instant Hit" that takes the form of instability: The song is like a spinning top at the very moment before it wobbles. Ari's voice wobbles too, and almost takes you down with it. "Everything that went before our time, we just threw out the window," Ari has noted. "It wasn't good enough for us. We were so disappointed in what went before. We weren't from hippie stock. We hadn't come up from that, had nothing to do with that." And yet the easygoing-ness of "Instant Hit" suggests a secret affinity with the previous decade, which is perhaps why the Slits never really "became big": Their codes were complex and scrambled.

Before the Slits, Albertine had been in the Flowers of Romance, which included Sid Vicious and Keith Levine. "It was a bedroom band," according to Albertine "We played Ramones songs, and couldn't keep time." *Cuts*, the 1979 album from the Slits, does keep time, but to what? Produced by Dennis Bovell, the album is confounding, constantly shifting gears, forever keeping you off balance. "We all loved hypnotic dub bass lines," Pollitt has said. "Dennis devised all kinds of dub sounds for those sessions: spoons dropping, glass shattering, matches shaking and being lit on 'New Town.'" On "Spend, Spend, Spend," Ari sings, "I need something new / Something trivial would do / I want to satisfy this empty feeling." In interviews from this period, the band refused to get in line behind the "sign" of whatever they supposedly "stood for": "We don't want to do all that feminist stuff," Albertine told *ZigZag* magazine in 1977.

[Kris Needs, "And the Best of the Rest . . . ," *New York Rocker* vol. 1, #7, May–June 1977, p. 22; Viv Albertine quoted in Kris Needs, "The Slits," *ZigZag*, August 1977; Tessa Pollitt interviewed by Gregory Mario, "Earthbeat: In the Beginning There Was a Rhythm," available at www.3ammagazine.com; Viv Albertine quoted in Jon Savage, *England's Dreaming*, p. 248.]

## "Slouching Towards Bethlehem"
(compare to "White Noise Supremacists")

**Joan Didion's scathing snapshot of the harsh narcissism** at the heart of the sixties opens with this prophecy: "The center was not holding." Published in 1967, the cadences and rhythms of her prose are alarm bells disguised as words. "Adolescents drifted from city to torn city, sloughing off both the past and the future as snakes shed their skins, children who were never taught and would never now learn the games that had held the society together."

Didion's genius was to recognize and name the darkness of her era while her era was busy celebrating itself. She traveled to Haight Street, in San Francisco, and reported from ground zero. The closest equivalent to Didion's piece is "White Noise Supremacists," by Lester Bangs, published in 1979. In a world full of apologists, Bangs dared not to apologize. He was the last, really, to resist the notion that musical art was a commodity in need of promotion. His assessment of the music he loved and its era was damning: "So many of the people around the CBGB's and Max's scene have always seemed emotionally if not outright physically crippled— you see speech impediments, hunchbacks, limps, but most of all an overwhelming spiritual flatness." The connections between Didion's 1967 essay and Bangs's 1979 essay are powerful; both are indictments of the eras that, ironically, the authors themselves symbolize. In a 2005 interview, John Holmstrom (cofounder of *Punk* magazine) said that there "was a schizophrenic philosophical battle during the sixties between the radicals and the hedonists, the protestors and the potheads, the Yippies and the hippies. By 1974–75, the battle was long over with . . . The protest movement had fallen apart. 'Hippie' became 'alternative,' which soon became another word for 'politically correct.' The rebellious aspects to the hippie thing were gone . . . All early punk rockers were ex-hippies who got sick and tired of following their stupid rules."

Didion's essay predicts the disintegration that would lead not to revolution but to a gradual awareness that it had all gone wrong. "At some point between 1945 and 1967 we had somehow neglected to tell these children the rules of the game we happened to be playing. Maybe we had stopped believing in the rules ourselves, maybe we were having a failure of nerve about the game." The most unsettling and enduring aspect of Didion's essay is its tone, which shifts between pure documentary description ("I call the Lisches a day or so later and ask for Arthur") and subtly phrased but devastating mockery ("Don and Max want to go out to dinner but Don is only eating macrobiotic so we end up in Japantown again. Max is telling me how he lives free of all the old middle-class Freudian hang-ups"). Clearly, these are people already trapped by the ideas that were supposed to set them free. That very same year, Robert Bly published a poem, "Romans Angry About the Inner World," the opening lines of which were: "What shall the world do with its children? / There are lives the executives / know nothing of." The speaker of this poem is not trapped, but recognizes the trap.

Punk solved the problem by eliminating the distinction entirely.

[Lester Bangs, "The White Noise Supremacists," in *Psychotic Reactions and Carburetor Dung*, Greil Marcus, ed. 1979; repr., New York: Vintage, 1988, pp. 272–82; Robert Bly, "Romans Angry About the Inner World," *Selected Poems*, 1967; repr., New York: Harper Perennial, 1986, p. 65; Joan Didion, "Slouching Towards Bethlehem," in *Slouching Towards Bethlehem*, 1967; repr., New York: Farrar, Straus and Giroux, 1990; John Holmstrom, "Putting Punk in DIY: An Interview with John Holmstrom," AIGA, http://aiga.org/content.cfm/putting-the-punk-in-diy.]

# "So Cold"

**A song performed by Cleveland's Rocket** from the Tombs. Despite what they say, David Thomas's (later of Pere Ubu) best performance. Not blues exactly. But of the blues. There is a light in the sky. A familiar light, from far away. The song calls forth this light, the impossible rush of waves and particles, at the same time. A mournfulness. Death. Well, then. Death it is. You wonder: How could the logical termination of punk be No Wave when it had already died here, in this song, in 1975? Thomas growls, and in between the words you can hear history shattering, and then coming back together before you knew it shattered.

In 1944, a little more than thirty years before the performance of this song, Albert Einstein wrote to his friend Max Born that "You believe in the God who plays dice, and I in complete law and order in a world which objectively exists, and which I, in a wildly speculative way, am trying to capture." The periodic low roar of "So Cold" is more terrifying than the wrecked decade that it rejects, the long tail of history finally coming back to snap dead all the lies, the pitiful lies. The last one minute and twenty seconds of the song is the equivalent of this passage from Ernest Tidyman's novel *Shaft*, published in 1971:

> "Cocksuckers," Shaft groaned. He remembered who he hated. Almost how much . . . "Motherfuckers," he croaked. He was making a discovery. The angrier he became, or the more conscious he became of his anger, the less pain he felt. He let out all the stops of his fury and felt it swell through his battered flesh like the final, rising chord of a giant pipe organ. His anger roared, thundered silently.

> [Albert Einstein quoted in *The Born-Einstein Letters, 1916–1955*, New York: Macmillan, 2005, p. 146; Ernest Tidyman, *Shaft*, 1971; repr., London: Bloomsbury, 1997, pp. 179–80.]

## "Something's happening"

**The last line of a short, early notice of the New York** underground/punk scene to appear in a U.K. publication. Charles Shaar Murray's article for *New Musical Express* in June 1975 was published nearly a full year before the Ramones' first album appeared (April 1976) and about six months before Patti Smith's *Horses* (December 1975). The article is primarily about Television (who had debuted in March 1974) and Patti Smith. It begins like this: "C.B.G.B. is a toilet. An impossibly skuzzy little club buried somewhere in the sections of the Village that the cab-drivers don't like to drive through. It looks as if the proprietors kick holes in the walls and piss in the corners before they let the customers in . . . The audience, who consist mainly of nondescript urban hippies, a smattering of heavy street bro's, rock intelligentsia and the occasional confused tourist, are reveling in the tack and basking in their own hipness for just being there." The music is described as "chopped-down, hard-edged, no-bullshit rock and roll." Murray's piece ends like this: "One more thing. In the audience at the Alice Cooper gig in Detroit was a kid done up exactly like Patti Smith. Something's happening."

But back, for a moment, to the description of CBGB as "impossibly scuzzy." Elsewhere in this book are descriptions of the decrepit beauty of a decaying city left to die, and the imaginative spaces that this opens up. Here is another quote, from the photographer Jill Freedman, whose images from New York City in the seventies capture disintegration. In an unpublished manuscript about those times and the city, she wrote: "There are days I walk down the street feeling its ugliness on my skin like a sunburn . . . other days when I can hardly catch my breath for the beauty of it."

> [Jill Freedman quoted in Niko Koppel, "Through Weegee's Eyes," *The New York Times*, April 27, 2008, www.nytimes.com/2008/04/27/nyregion; Charles Shaar Murray, "Down in the Scuzz with the Heavy Cult Figures," *New Musical Express*, June 7, 1975.]

# Spock, Benjamin

**Spock was born in 1903 and died in 1998.** His *The Common Sense Book of Baby and Child Care*, first published in 1946, signaled a change, a loosening up, a more easygoing philosophy about raising children. "The attitude expressed and the general tenor of the advice," wrote one reviewer, "typify the present-day departure from rigidity in schedules and training." The book's tone is open and even breezy: "Don't take too seriously all that the neighbors say. Don't be overawed by what the experts say. Don't be afraid to trust your own common sense. Bringing up your child won't be a complicated job if you take it easy, trust your own instincts, and follow the directions that your doctor gives you." Along the way, Spock apologizes for using sexist language: "Everywhere I've called the baby 'him' . . . I hope the parents of girls will understand and forgive me." He talks openly about working mothers: "What about the woman who hesitates to nurse because she has to go back to work?" and "What about the mothers who don't absolutely have to work but would prefer to, either to supplement the family income, or because they think they will be more satisfied themselves and therefore get along better at home?" He discusses the pros and cons of separation (the word divorce is not used) in terms of the child's well being: "Parents who are considering separation sometimes ask a doctor whether it is better for the children to have the parents separate for the sake of peace, or to hold the family together in spite of friction. Of course there is no general answer to this."

The return to normalcy after World War II. The baby boomers, born (depending on how you read the numbers and set your terms) between 1946 and 1964. Here are some birthdates:

| | |
|---|---|
| Patti Smith | 1946 |
| Iggy Pop | 1947 |
| Alan Vega | 1948 |
| Richard Hell | 1949 |
| Joey Ramone | 1951 |
| Joe Strummer | 1952 |
| David Byrne | 1952 |
| Colin Newman | 1954 |
| Johnny Rotten | 1956 |
| Poly Styrene | 1957 |

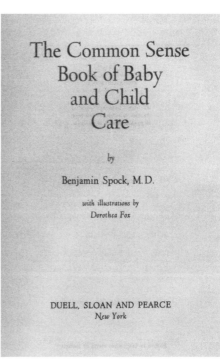

The Common Sense
Book of Baby
and Child
Care

by

Benjamin Spock, M.D.

*with illustrations by*
*Dorothea Fox*

DUELL, SLOAN AND PEARCE
*New York*

Title page to first edition of Dr. Spock's book, in 1946: loosening the restraints of authority and laying the groundwork for the counterculture

What did they produce? Something we call punk. What was punk? For one thing, it was a settling of scores against the counterculture. This process, which became inevitable once punk became notorious, was painful and beautiful, and it was a lesson about how the most radical music and art could, in the age of new media, be assimilated quickly and relatively painlessly into mass culture.

In a society like ours, which, despite some appearances to the contrary, tends to be seductive rather than coercive, the old defenses against the domination of the culture become weaker and weaker.

—Lionel Trilling, 1955

I think now that we were the last generation to identify with adults.

—Joan Didion, 1970

Adolescence: The culture, for reasons having to do with the working of the marketplace, did not make available any but the grimmest, most false-seeming adulthood. Childhood was provided. An amazing, various childhood, full of the most extraordinary material possibilities. That was it. Nothing more. Just childhood. An adolescence had to be improvised, and it was. That it *was* improvised—mostly out of rock-and-roll music—so astounded the people who pulled it off that they quite rightly considered it the important historical event of their times and have circled around it ever since.

—George W. S. Trow, 1980

What we should want and what we should make clear by our attitudes, our songs, our music, our venues, our publications, our lives is that this scene represents one thing if nothing else: A COMPLETE, A TOTAL REJECTION OF THE MINDLESSNESS OF CONFORMITY AND MASS CULTURE . . . Each little compromise we make towards the merchandizing of the music, of the related arts of the scene is just another step towards killing whatever hope remains of making this strange, confused, almost convulsive series of ideas and expressions not just another forgettable, eminently disposable movement swallowed by the gigantic bloated social machine as it descends into the mire from which it arose.

—Brad L., 1980

In the Sixties, however, the ideology of adolescence became an ideology of youth: "The Young Ones" became "My Generation." Adolescence had always been romanticized in song, the teenage world had always been idealized, but youth had previously been presented as a stage on the path to adulthood . . . The Sixties argument (and this was one sign of the difference between Sixties "rock" songs and Fifties "pop" songs) was that youth was preferable to age and that that no one need ever grow old. What was at issue was not chronology but ideology.

—Simon Frith, 1981

Punk was the first aesthetic act of defiance against the sixties. It was, at its core, reactionary, a stance not necessarily against the "progress" of the sixties, but rather against the idea of progress as sacred, and as incumbent upon a "Great Society." Benjamin Spock's book and its promotion of comfort, toleration, and joyful patience in the rearing of the people who would become the children of the sixties was profoundly important in the shaping of the emerging "youth culture." In 1946, Spock wrote this in regard to educating children: "There's no use knowing a lot if you can't be happy, can't get along with other people, can't hold the type of job you want." In 1969, Spiro Agnew, in a speech entitled "Education for What?" said: "In our reverence for education and our desire to do right by our children, we have inadvertently denied this generation's right to participate as mature citizens."

[Joan Didion, "On the Morning After the Sixties," in *The White Album*, 1970; repr., New York: Farrar, Straus and Giroux, 1979, p. 207; Simon Frith, *Sound Effects: Youth, Leisure, and the Politics of Rock 'n' Roll*, New York: Pantheon, 1981, pp. 33–34; Brad L., "End of Year Editorial Message," *Damage* no. 4, January 1980, p. 30; Benjamin Spock, M.D., *The Common Sense Book of Baby and Child Care*, New York: Duell, Sloan and Pearce, 1946, pp. 2, 3, 484, 481; Lionel Trilling, "Freud: Within and Beyond Culture," in *Beyond Culture: Essays on Literature and Learning*, 1955; repr., New York: Harcourt Brace Jovanovich, 1965, p. 98; George W. S. Trow, *Within the Context of No Context*, 1980; repr., New York: Atlantic Monthly Press, 1981, p. 86; Myron E. Wegmen, review of *The Common Sense Book of Baby and Child Care*, in *American Journal of Public Health and the Nation's Health*, vol. 36, November 1946, p. 1329.]

# Social threat of punk, the

**Did punk ever pose a social threat?** In "The Meaning Behind the Moaning," a 1981 article in *New York Rocker*, Simon Frith wrote about Christiana, an innercity youth ghetto in Copenhagan:

In the 'Sixties (the first Rock Era) youth politics meant only a delay in "settling down." There were specific goals (an end to the draft, most obviously) but when these were realized people did grow up. They brought a winder range of pleasure (sex and drugs and rock 'n' roll) to adult life, but slotted in, easily enough, to the consumer system. Eighties youth, by contrast, have no choices. They cannot settle down: there's no adult place for them—no jobs, no fun, so space . . . The social threat—and promise—of punk is being realized, and the paradox is that the appropriate music isn't being made much anymore.

Today, it seems strange and alien to even think of pop or even various subsets of "alternative" music in these terms—what social threat does alt-country pose? Or lo-fi? Or trip-hop? The digital era is one of fragments; to speak of "movements" anymore is an act of hubris. Besides, punk itself never really posed a social threat in any meaningful way. For every "political" band like the Clash there were dozens more (the Ramones, the Weirdos, etc.) for whom politics was merely the backdrop for their music. Strangely, the emergence of so many independent music labels during the punk era further eroded the possibility of any larger, cohesive social meaning of punk. In this regard, punk was the ultimate local music, a place where teenage alienation and anger could be transformed into pleasure.

The social threat posed by punk was imaginary. "Anarchy in the UK" was a sentiment, perhaps even an ironic one—not a civic fact. In California, the police and the many hardcore bands and their fans sometimes clashed. Off and on for a few years, there was worry in the U.S. and U.K. press about the violence of punk, but rarely did these worries ever extend into the realm of social life. There was no equivalent of Woodstock for punk during the seventies early-eighties period because punk itself was not about grand ideas ("peace") but was, on the contrary, a reaction against grand ideas. "I just came from Ann Arbor," Hunter S. Thompson wrote to Jann Wenner in 1974, "where things are not going nearly as well as they were 2 years ago, and tonight I read a piece in the *Wash/Post* on what seems like a similar downhill drift in Petaluma. The Berkeley situation is beyond my ken at this point, but here in Aspen we're facing a serious backlash very much like the Petaluma & Ann Arbor scenes." The "backlash" that Thompson writes of was already underway, as Barry Goldwater's early failures opened up the channels that would help lead to Ronald Reagan's victory in 1980. Jeane Kirkpatrick has written that the "extremes of this counter-culture had disappeared by 1976, but the residue was more lasting. Its effects on what has been called liberal politics were profound. The counter-culture was much broader than the anti-war movement with which it was associated and, I believe, constituted a sweeping rejection of traditional American attitudes, values, and goals. The counter-culture subjected virtually all aspects of American life and culture to criticism and repudiation."

Musically, punk itself was a radical rejection of the tenets that emerged during the counterculture; there truly was a backlash brewing on many fronts. The social threat posed by pop music—if there ever was one—had occurred in the folk- and social-protest music of the sixties. By 1981, the year of Frith's prediction, punk posed a social threat only in the imagination, as punk was never homogeneous enough to coalesce around shared grievances against the social order. Besides, by 1981 it was clear that punk was already becoming the object of nostalgia and that punk "actvisim" was often little more than one subculture disassociating itself from another. In the same *New York Rocker* issue as Simon Frith's article was an interview with Jello Biafra of the Dead Kennedys. "The preppies are just one part of what we're attacking in this country," he said. "They're just one element of the Me Generation, along with jocks and whoever else you wanna to throw in there." This was, it turns out, just about the extent of the social threat posed by punk.

[Simon Frith, "Striking Back: The Meaning Behind the Moaning," *New York Rocker* no. 41, July–August 1981, p. 11; Ira Kaplan, "A Dead Kennedy Speaks: Jello Biafra's Just Desserts," *New York Rocker* no. 41, p. 19; Jeane Kirkpatrick, "Neoconservatism as a Response to the Counter-Culture," in Irwin Stelzer, ed., *The Neocon Reader*, New York: Grove, 2004, p. 235; Hunter S. Thompson letter to Jann Wenner at *Rolling Stone*, February 15, 1974, ed. Douglas Brinkley, *Fear and Loathing in America: The Gonzo Letters, Volume II*, New York: Simon and Schuster, 2000, p. 579.]

## "Sonic Reducer"

**There are several versions of this song.** This entry is about the Rocket from the Tombs' version, performed live in Cleveland. The song is a little slower, a little more heavy-metal-like than the Dead Boys' version. It's harder, recorded during a middle passage of history with no land in sight. You get the sense that the band played slower because they wanted to stay on top of the chaos, rather than succumb to it. Recorded live at the Piccadilly Inn in Cleveland in 1975, the song's opening dronelike chant and glorious suspended-sound guitar are like the calm before the storm. The lyrics "don't need no mom and dad" (which is the not-so-secret subtext of rock and roll itself) become something far more threatening here, a call to physical action rather than an abstract philosophy. Rarely had rock and roll ever broken through into the realm of existential blankness—even the sonic anarchy of the Stooges was tempered by the humor in Iggy Pop's voice. But there is no humor to this song, which invents and then immediately destroys its own tradition.

## *Sonic Youth*

**An EP by Sonic Youth, released in March 1982.** Kim Gordon, Thurston Moore, Lee Ranaldo, and Richard Edson. Had Sonic Youth not gone on to become Sonic Youth, would we even be listening to this today? Mostly it's so quiet, such a quiet album. The first three songs, hushed. But there is the line "fucking youth" in the second song, "I Dreamed a Dream," that gives a hint, coming from the mouth of Kim Gordon in big glasses, of the terror to come. At some point, you can't help but wonder, What happened? What happened? Has rock been reduced to elementary school noodling on guitars and drums? Where is the fury? Where is the next step? Where is the sudden charge of melody to knock you off your feet and make you realize you are a sentimentalist at heart? You are not alone if you wonder this. It is true, "The Burning Spear" is beautifully menacing in its tornado/*Eraserhead* guitar hiss from about 1:36 to 2:36.

But does one minute make an entire album? You want to believe that it does. You want to understand—you want to be on the side of Sonic Youth, whose name alone should redeem a handful of dull albums—and you strain to listen for even a shard of pleasure here, in these arid songs made, it seems to you, by people who hate music. Richard Edson has said that "we were all post-punk, self-aware artists, which meant we were extremely conscious of everything." Does that mean that to love this music is to betray non-"self-aware" naivity? In other words, if I love any shard of this music, does that mean I'm missing the joke? Or is the joke on me? The music on this album is a frame with no painting. You imagine that the painting is there, but is it? You understand that Sonic Youth is an "important band," intellectually. And there are moments when you feel they are an "important band," emotionally, and you wonder if that is the whole point: Perhaps Sonic Youth could make every song as good as the best song on each of their albums, and they simply choose not to do this. What do real Sonic Youth fans privately think about the dull, pretentious songs? Do they really like them, or have they only convinced themselves that they do? Is there a difference? There is a wall of fame that surrounds bands like Sonic Youth that is difficult to overcome; if you try to climb over it, you risk getting shot in the back as a philistine.

The album was released again in 2006, with, as they say, bonus tracks. Of these, the primitivistic "She Is Not Alone," recorded live at the Music for Millions Festival in September 1981, is the redeemer, the only song that dares to bare its soul. It puts something on the line that can be judged, not as an ironic statement but as real feeling. Face it, you are a sucker for the big sound, for the sound that makes your heart skip a beat.

## Speedies, the

**The Speedies**—Eric Hoffert, Allen Hurken, John Marino, John Carlucci, and Greg Crewdson—were punk stripped and schellacked to its pure, bright essence in the late seventies. Working backward: Crewdson has gone on to become a professor and renowned artist. If you have not seen his photographs—immense and precise and brutally calm, as if all of David Lynch or Alfred Hitchcock had been boiled down into one frame—then, once you see them, you will, I hope, remember that this entry in this book led you there. In a short essay on Edward Hopper, "The Aesthetics of Alienation," Crewdson wrote that "everything in a Hopper painting, his

The Speedies from *New York Rocker* in 1979: cereal box realism

interiors in particular, is full of meaning that propels the narrative. It's the telling detail, whether it be a suitcase, a book or a bed, that is really important."

The Speedies debuted in December 1978 at Max's Kansas City; their single "Let Me Take Your Photo" solidified their power-pop status. But it was more than power pop, because in songs like "Time" the band's sound is so clean that, like a Hopper painting, every detail is available. Like many of the greatest bands of the era, the Speedies did not achieve success in the conventional sense of the word. They were always on the verge of breaking out onto the national scene. "Their tight, surging playing," wrote Robert Palmer in *The New York Times* in 1980, "their short, simple but hook-laden songs, even the lead singers' vocal mannerisms are evidence of the influence English groups like the Sex Pistols, the Clash, the Buzzcocks and many more are having on this side of the Atlantic."

Ira Kaplan predicted the future in *New York Rocker*: "By the time the Speedies reach drinking age, they will either have developed into ace songwriters or lost all of their charm and probably disbanded." The Speedies offered a vision of youth that was impossible to sustain; unlike the Sex Pistols, who self-destructed under the instability of their image, the Speedies, like many sort-of-forgotten bands of their time, simply disappeared. Some of the members went to college, and "real life" took over. In their day, they never released an album. They never had a chance to "evolve" as a band, which means that their music, mercifully, is not tainted by the inevitable fact of mediocrity that afflicts almost all bands that survive. And thus it can be said the Speedies never really fell from grace.

[Gregory Crewdson, "Aesthetics of Alienation," *TateEtc*, 2004, available at www.tate.org. uk; Ira Kaplan, "The Speedies," *New York Rocker* no. 21, 1979, p. 44; Robert Palmer, "Pop Rock: The Speedies," *The New York Times*, January 10, 1980, p. C18.]

## Spheeris, Penelope

**Born in December 1945 in New Orleans,** Spheeris has made films that have entered the popular imagination, such as *Wayne's World* (1992), as well as some of the most confounding documents of the California hardcore punk scene in the early 1980s. *The Decline of Western Civilization* (1981) is legendary, but far greater is *Suburbia* (1984), not just because it is a better film but because, by mixing documentary and fictional modes, Spheeris created a portrait of youth that was not weighted down by the burdens of fact. In other words, it was truer than truth.

Although *Decline* is a document of its time, it is also a document of the film itself. Spheeris obviously had an angle, a point of view, and at some point, watching the film, you realize what this point of view is: darkness. And it is enjoyable to watch darkness, is it not? The Weirdos are not dark, and they are not in the film. Neither are the Screamers, or the Plugz, or other bands that used the raw materials of destruction to make music that transcended narcissistic self-destruction. "*The Decline* was an interesting but unfortunate view of the scene," the photographer Jenny Lens has said. The kids interviewed were "mostly a bunch of slobbering chauvinistic idiots and psychos from Orange County . . . Penelope's movie focused on the homeless, aimless, self-destructive aspects as opposed to the creative, educated, even self-educated, fun people that I knew." This, however, is not necessarily a bad thing, and at its best moments, *Decline* achieves the sort of ambiguous relation to its subject as did Joan Didion's 1967 essay "Slouching Towards Bethlehem," which zeroed in on the San Francisco hippies with such blank ferocity that it was at times difficult to tell if Didion's voice was one of condemnation or endorsement.

While *Suburbia* verges on camp at times, it is closer in tone to David Lynch's *Blue Velvet* (1986) than to the work of Roger Corman (who coproduced it) or John Waters. Although the film asks us to identify almost entirely with the "kids," rather than the parents and other authorities, there is an almost radical conservatism that guides the film's vision. On one level, *Suburbia* is bleakly deterministic: The kids who become punks are born into dysfunctional families through no choice of their own. Early on in the film, there is this exchange between an alcoholic mother and her son:

> **Tina Johnson:** I'm the one who works all day so you can sit on your ass and read comic books. *[Slap]* You make me sick when you look like that. I can see your father in you. It makes me sick.
>
> **Evan Johnson:** Well that's not my fault. I didn't choose him to be my father, you did.

The problem in *Suburbia* is one of families whose dysfunction drives the punk subculture, with kids squatting in homes as physically devastated and polluted as the emotional environments of their "real" homes. According to Spheeris,

> The whole premise is that these kids kind of flock together because of their general difficulty in having, you know, normal families or their difficulty in integrating into society. My observation back then, and I think it's even become truer now, is that kids just feel so alienated and they're so un-nurtured and unguarded by their families that they just have to head out on their own and they form a new family. That's the premise of *Suburbia*—that these kids all go out and find love with each other.

It is the lack of family—not the excess of it—that in *Suburbia* lures and pushes kids into the punk scene. Specifically, there are no strong fathers. Ronald Reagan was a father figure. In 1984, the same year *Suburbia* was released, Reagan was elected to a second term as president. A television commercial entitled "Prouder, Stronger, Better"—better known as "Morning in America"—helped to re-elect him. This commercial celebrated good men and women and strong families. The narrator (Hal Riney) intoned that with "interest rates at about half the record highs of 1980, nearly 2,000 families today will buy new homes, more than at any time in the past four years. This afternoon 6,500 young men and women will be married." There are no real, decent fathers or mothers in *Suburbia*, no fathers like Reagan-president-father, and the results are a kid putting part of a live rat in his mouth, a baby eaten by a wild dog, a girl overdosing, and a ruined wedding at which terrible secrets are revealed. In 1981, Spheeris told Mick Farren in *New Musical Express* that "I am making a film called *Suburbia*, which is about kids in the suburbs destroying everything." The secret truth of the film is also a form of heresy: There is destruction, and it is a warning, and the nature of that warning is reactionary.

[Jenny Lens quoted in Mark Spitz and Brendan Mullen, *We Got the Neutron Bomb: The Untold Story of L.A. Punk*, New York: Three Rivers Press, 2001, p. 262; Penelope Spheeris, "Director's Commentary," *Suburbia*, Buena Vista Home Entertainment, 2000; Penelope Spheeris interviewed by Mick Farren, *New Musical Express*, April 11, 1981.]

## Starburn: The Story of Jenni Love

**A novel by the artist and writer Rosalyn Drexler,** published in 1979. The novel is about a punk superstar, and in its own way the book offers a performance on par with punk's anarchy. While this is not quite William S. Burroughs or Kathy Acker territory, the novel is full of asides, author's notes, fake news items, song lyrics, and columns from fake rock magazines and fanzines. *Starburn* is, on one level, a theory of punk, a study of the fine and blurry and overlapping lines between art and commerce. Ruth Spider, a member of Jenni's band, the Great Mother Goddess Cult, says after composing some lyrics, "Who gives a shit anyway! Lyrics are just filler. It's more political to spit at each other and fight on stage. That way, we can't be accused of selling a product. Nothing wrong with being nasty and rude. A woman who's nasty and rude can't sell cars, perfume, floor wax, or even oven-ready dough." A brutal mash-up of Patti Smith, Joan Jett, Ari Up (of the Slits), Poly Styrene (of X-Ray Spex), as well as an eerie premonition of riot grrrl, Jenni Love pinballs around the novel, full of ideas and full of nothing.

The plot revolves around (if it revolves around anything) the alleged murder of Mott Folm, a rock critic hostile to Jenni. She is accused of murdering him. The book is savage in its deconstruction of the rock critic, and in the process offers a humiliating and nearly heartbreaking set of truths:

> In secret he [Folm] regarded punk as nauseatingly puerile, yet he wrote pedantically about its strong influence and origins in fantasy, comparing it to the paintings of Bosch, the violence of Hitler, the grimness of Grimm's fairy tales, and to the dogma of the Fecalists, who declared that turds should be allowed to express themselves in song and dance just as any other earthly transients. Always there was some element of truth in what he said, yet it failed to come off.
>
> Folm could not admit, even to himself, that he led a disappointing life; as an important American critic he had particularly trying problems: he was looked up to for opinions that he no longer believed in.

The truth of that last phrase—and he was looked up to for opinions that he no longer believed in—cuts both ways and applies to critics and performers alike. The alienated rock legend in Don DeLillo's *Great Jones Street* or in Pink Floyd's *The Wall* are alike in their recognition of the gap between their public legends and their private doubts, a recognition that leads to withdrawal and self-destruction. As an ideal, punk was about tearing down the walls that separated the performer from the audience, and yet how quickly so many punk musicians became trapped by their own images, cutting and spitting and screaming and, sometimes, playing music. The Sex Pistols recognized this. Or at least Johhny Rotten did, and their willful kamikaze act in San Francisco in 1978 closed the gap so fully that everything after that was an echo in an echo chamber.

In *The New York Times*, Richard Lingeman ended his review of *Starburn* like this: "*Starburn* has the menacing import of the unsettling subconscious wishes unlocked by a fairy tale. Its author is the wise child wandering in the pop wilderness, a Gretel who sees clearly the witch inside the gingerbread house, waiting to lure the child in all of us, and eat it." But by 1979, punk had already eaten itself. The shocks and atrocities depicted in *Starburn* had by then already passed from rumor to glimmer to fact to cliché to legend.

[Rosalyn Drexler, *Starburn: The Story of Jenni Love*, New York: Simon and Schuster, 1979, pp. 88–89, 200; Richard R. Lingeman, "The Inner Logic of Punk Rock," *The New York Times*, June 17, 1979.]

## Static Disposal

**An LP by the Chickasha, Oklahoma, band Debris',** recorded on December 10 and 16, 1975, mixed on January 20, 1976, and released in April, the same month as the Ramones' first LP. Charles Ivey, Oliver Powers (who had a B.A. in music performance on upright bass), and Johnny Gregg. Influenced by Captain Beefheart, the Velvet Underground, the Stooges, the New York Dolls, Alice Cooper, John Cale, Roxy Music, and others, Debris' shatters categories as fast as you can name them. Listening to the songs is like watching David Lynch's *Inland Empire*: You know you're *some*where, right? But just when it begins to look and sound familiar, it gets strange again. It goes out of focus. "New Smooth Lunch" could be Gang of Four if they had some soul, but then again no Gang of Four song would ever have the line "Cold babies floating in the ashes." Of the song "Manhattan": (written in 1975) Powers says: "Debris' had a standing invitation in 1976 to play in NYC at Max's Kansas City and CBGB's. A number of factors kept us from doing that. We were all ready to go but not at the same time. Who knows where we would have ended up today. Perhaps deep down we believed this song too much. I think we could envision having all our gear ripped off or gaining enough notoriety to crack the big time and getting sucked into the heavy drug scene and not surviving." As a writer writing about music, most of the time you know that your words can never approximate the fierce beauty of the music. But of course you are a writer because you love words, and you hear them as music, like this: "My wandering gaze overtook the High School Dean / With my banker and the football queen / They were pretending, it seemed / That it was they . . . up on the screen."

[Oliver Powers, Liner notes. *Static Disposal*, Anopheles Records, 1999.]

# Sterling, Linder

**An artist and musician (she uses the name Linder)** born in Liverpool in 1954 whose work with cut-ups and montages circulated widely in the punk and post-punk scene. She designed the cover for the single "Orgasm Addict," (1977) by the Buzzcocks, as well as the album cover for Magazine's debut (1978), which featured ex-Buzzcock Howard DeVoto. With the critic Jon Savage, Linder cofounded the visual punk fanzine *Secret Public*, published in 1978. According to Linder:

> I remember the pure pleasure of photomontage. I had spent three years working with pencil, paint, and pen trying to translate lived experience into marks. It was a moment of glorious liberation to work purely with a blade, glass and glue. Almost a scientific methodology. Sitting in a dark room in Salford, performing cultural postmortems and then reassembling the corpses badly, like a Mary Shelley trying to breathe life into the monster. For a short period I'd found a perfect mode of articulation. Punk was cutting out the question, "Can I do this?"

Like Jamie Reid's, Linder's cut-up method was the on-the-page version of ripped and torn. Punk's stitched-together clothes were perfect for the incoherent era that was the mid-seventies: a smile snatched from here, a television set from there, a naked body from here. Pieced together, the governing vision was determined by the radical juxtaposition of elements, the gaps in meaning that provide the very freedom to create meaning. "I don't believe in closing them [gaps in communication] up," Howard DeVoto has said. "There's something totalitarian about complete and perfect understanding." Linder's work during this period was the perfect visual equivalent of punk, slashing through old meanings to make new ones. The "Orgasm Addict" design is both absurd and deeply menacing. For a teenager buying the single in 1977, the image hints at critique, but of what sort? We're all adults now, and punk's meanings are perilously close to petrifying into orthodoxy

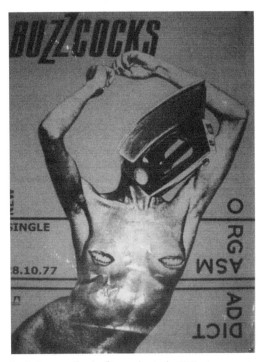

Linder's poster for the Buzzcocks single, 1977: giant gaps in meaning

(i.e., the image detours female objectification into . . . [fill in the blank]); but at the time, as a young man, maybe you found the image just plain sexy ("though I wish she didn't have creepy mouths where her nipples are"). But deep down, your inarticulate self knew there was some secret code, some signal there. Later, you would learn about feminism, but by that time you were a different, older person, and so when you returned to this Linder image to write about it for this book, so much had changed with the world, and with you, and with everyone: The woman with the iron on her head was less playful, more serious. It "said" something about gender, you supposed, but what? A woman whose breasts have been transformed into forced smiling faces, her head into the symbol of domesticity—certainly this must *mean* something. Looking at it thirty years on, it reminded you of David Cronenberg most of all, especially *Videodrome*. The body melding with technology. No matter: The old feeling you had when you saw this for the first time was gone. "Everyone can testify that the pleasure of the text is not certain," Roland Barthes once wrote. "Nothing says that this same text will please us a second time; it is a friable pleasure, split by mood, habit, circumstance."

Circumstances have indeed changed, Linder. No matter how I try, I can't shake the meanings now attached to your artwork for "Orgasm Addict." Like punk itself, I wish I could see it again for the first time, innocently, naively, in the heat of love.

[Roland Barthes, *The Pleasure of the Text*, trans. Richard Miller, 1973; repr., New York: Noonday, 1975, p. 52; Howard DeVoto quoted by Jon Savage, "Howard Devoto: Heart Beats up Love," *Sounds*, November 5, 1977, www.newhormonesinfo.com; Linder quoted by Jon Savage in "Indie Originals: The New Hormones Story," www.newhormonesinfo.com.]

## "Still bewildered by the death-machine"

**A phrase in a letter that Richard Hell** wrote to the poet Robert Bly in January 1970. Hell had come to New York in 1966 intending to become a writer, and for a while he booked poetry readings at the St. Mark's Church Poetry Project and produced his own literary magazines. The letter to Bly expresses admiration for Bly's own literary magazine, *The Sixties*, and asks Bly to submit some poems to Hell's project:

> I now feel this whole network of poets inside the country, some still bewildered by the death-machine and feebly or strongly affirming their own selves and perceptions—and I think these are lovable too, still somewhat unknowing victims, but wonderfully exploring themselves and language—helping to invent the possible future life—I don't think they are to be denounced but encouraged in their awakenings and explorations etc. and gradually turned on to the necessity of battling the evils also—they are like tender plants breaking through the U.S. soot and (as I

<u>know</u>) it is incredible struggle for some to violently shake off imposed perception-armor and fear our parents clamped and nailed around.

Punk would soon provide an outlet to "violently shake off" fear and to also create a new fear of its own. In retrospect, it's stunning how quickly the country had de-politicised itself by the mid-seventies, as if the cruelties and absurdities of the Vietnam War and Watergate had exhausted the nation's psyche. If in 1970 Hell could write of the "death-machine," just a few years later words like "void" and "blank" would suggest that the sixties had succeeded in destroying things just enough to allow for punk to flourish.

[Richard Hell, letter to Robert Bly, January 26, 1970, courtesy Fales Library & Special Collections, The Richard Hell Papers, New York University.]


## Stooges

**The first album by the Stooges,** released in 1969, predicts the future. The fact that Elektra, the label, rejected John Cale's mixes for being too "arty" is almost symbolic in its importance. There are facts about this album—well documented—and there are feelings. In this merciful universe, Mr. Barker has not restricted me to facts, easily accessible in places like Wikipedia. Like many people, I first heard "No Fun" as performed by the Sex Pistols, and learned only later that this was a Stooges song. The "full version" on the remastered CD was a revelation and suggested an electric fuzz and wall of noise as powerful as Rocket from the Tombs, except at least five years earlier. The relentless guitar suggests a decade winding down, but to what end? We all know now what an incoherent decade the seventies was (which made it the best of times) but how could the Stooges have known this in 1969?

In 1972 Lester Bangs wrote that "the Stooges had the strength to realize that they lived in a time when belief was worthless." In some ways, Iggy Pop's force of personality has eclipsed the simple power and beauty of the Stooges' music. No where is this clearer than on "I Wanna Be Your Dog," which moves in like a storm except that there are no breaks or moments of relief. "Now I'm ready to close my mind / And now I'm ready to feel your hand / And lose my heart on the burning sands / And now I wanna be your dog." The first three chords of the song sound like the last three chords of most songs: Right there is a sonic blueprint for something new. The drone reminds you of walking the dark, cold streets at night, your hands shoved into your pockets, your shoulders pulled forward, your collar up.

*The bums lost, Lebowski.* On which side of the divide did the Stooges belong? Parts of the album sound positively hippie indulgent—long and slow and worthless—and other parts sound like punk, post-punk, and grunge have come and gone already.

But then consider the differences between Ann Arbor and Detroit: Are the Stooges a Detroit band or an Ann Arbor band? Depends on whom you ask. The confusion is instructive, for if Ann Arbor in the sixties and seventies was considered a Midwest Berkeley, Detroit—just fifty miles away—was most certainly not. There is only a little untruth to the observation that, in 1967, while Detroit was burning, Ann Arbor was smoking. The Stooges' sound was forged from the absurd pragmatism of Detroit, and the decadent indulgences of Ann Arbor. Their primitivism could sometimes smack of self-consciousness, but never camp: There was nothing ironic about Iggy Pop.

1. *Stooges* was released in the United States in August 1969, just days before the Manson murders in Los Angeles.

2. Two months earlier, in June, then–vice president Spiro Agnew said, in a commencement speech at Ohio State University, that a "society which comes to fear its children is effete. A sniveling, hand-wringing power structure deserves the violent rebellion it encourages."

3. August 1969 saw the release of Credence Clearwater Revival's third album, *Green River*, whose song "Bad Moon Rising" defined the era's darkness from a different, more coherent angle. In some ways, the extremism and negativity of the Stooges' album seems harmless and even quaint today, especially in light of the hardcore scene that would develop in the late seventies and early eighties, and yet it represented the culmination of the sixties, as utopianism turned— as it always does—to romanticism, and then to revenge. Because latent in all efforts to change the world is violence, which isn't always a bad thing. Sometimes, though, it is. The genius of *Stooges* is that, even to this day, its sound upholds that contradiction.

[Spiro Agnew, "Rationality and Effetism: Address at Ohio State University Commencement Exercises, June 7, 1969," in *Frankly Speaking*, Washington, D.C.: Public Affairs Press, 1970, p. 18; Lester Bangs, "Detroit's Rock Culture," *Phonograph Record*, December 1972.]

# "Strange"

**A song by Wire with dark gurgling guitars** and a beat that sounds like it's counting remorselessly toward the apocalypse. Apparently, it was one of the only songs on *Pink Flag* whose vocals were not live: It is one of the most "produced"-sounding Wire songs. It is full of sound. You keep expecting the song to veer off into relief, but no. Would you guess that that the creepy, ghostly whines are transmogrified flute, played by Kate Lukas? "Her trilled flute clusters were . . . studio-mutated and the alien sound fits perfectly," Kris Needs wrote in *ZigZag*. For you, the song's title has always referred to the song itself. Strange indeed.

Wire is one of those bands that when people say to you that Wire is their favorite band you think them poseurs and liars: *Favorite?* Then again, how many people have actually and truly said that to you over the years? Perhaps a stray student or two, because they had discovered them after the angular music of Franz Ferdinand. R.E.M. covered the song. Stipe's voice took the song into poppier places. The Wire version is slower, heavier, almost like heavy metal: There are more spaces between the sounds. You find yourself nodding your head like during an AC/DC song. "Strange" builds itself up, but into what? "Something's going on that's not quite right." What's not quite right is the song, which seems of a different age, a dark future as imagined in science-fiction dystopian movies like *Soylent Green* or *Blade Runner.* Has England already reached this strange point, rendering postapocalyptic science fiction not fiction at all but something more like documentary? How you yearned for those alternate futures, to sweep away all of today's problems. The song is like someone doing cartwheels near a bonfire: *Watch out!* you want to yell.

But the other part of you is fascinated by the prospect of disaster.

[Kris Needs, "Wire," *ZigZag*, March 1978, p. 19.]

## Student Teachers

**For a brief period, the Student Teachers** (they were all teenagers) commanded. Opening up for the Ramones, Television, Iggy Pop, and others in the late seventies, the group was like an avalanche that was forever getting too far out in front of itself. "There's always been something engaging about the idea of the Student Teachers," wrote Richard Grabel in 1979, "unabashed students of their new wave elders who sat for years in the front rows of the CBGB classroom, soaking it up." It's hard to listen to a song like "Looks" without thinking of a version of New Order far better than New Order, of a version of New Wave far better than New Wave. "Now I wish the lights were dim / 'cause I see what this is leading to / and it looks real grim," the words go, and you know exactly what it means. One of the toughest things to do as a writer is to name music that transcends names: "Looks" is a song that defies categorization, that puts a lie to any label attached to it. It is now before you in this book on punk for many justifiable reasons: It was associated with the producers Jimmy Destri and Marty Thau; for a brief time Student Teachers were regulars at places like CBGB and Max's Kansas City, at the same time that the punk scene was coalescing.

"We called ourselves first splash," Scharff told me, punning off of New Wave/ first wave; "we wanted to make ripples. Neurotic teenage pop. TV and drug-influenced teenage angst—teenage panic," he said. "We saw our music as nihilistic tinged with fun." Also: "We were part of a niche. The niche did not become popular. It remained obscure." At the time there were so many different types of bands in the New York scene: punk, New Wave, art noise, art school, art. Scharff tells a funny story that reveals a lot about the evolving scene at the time. The first few times Student Teachers played they didn't know how to tune their instruments: Members of the No Wave band Teenage Jesus and the Jerks saw them and were impressed by the dissonance. Invited to open for Teenage Jesus, Student Teachers (who in the meantime had learned to tune their instruments and play properly) were denounced as selling out, even though playing their instruments properly was what they had aspired to do all along.

"Looks" is a song that can tempt you to chuck everything for the girl you saw crossing the street yesterday, in the afternoon sun, the wind blowing her hair, the way she glanced at you, the impossibility of her ever touching you, her hesitation in crossing the street, her green skirt.

[Richard Grabel, "Student Teachers," *New York Rocker*, August 1979, p. 45; David Scharff, telephone conversation with author, April 17, 2007.]

# Suicide

**Part of your brain wonders** what a synth and drum machine band like Suicide is doing on a book on punk. Yes, you will dutifully write this entry, but not to make the argument that Suicide was part of the punk scene, but rather because they evolved at the same time as punk, in a sort of parallel universe that revealed how—for a few years—the distinctions that we make today did not matter.

There are lots of ways to talk yourself out of writing an entry on Suicide's 1977 album. For one thing, you feel the anxiety of influence: There has been a lot written about Suicide lately—and yet here you go . . .

The first song, "Ghost Rider," contains the line "sneakin' 'round 'round 'round in a blue jump suit," and then later "America, America is killing its youth," and the drone of machines in the song convinces you. What does this mean, "America, America is killing its youth"? There is a repetitiveness to the music that you are forced to acknowledge: In the few interviews with Alan Vega and Martin Rev that you have read, they promote themselves in ways that make you want to resist their music. They are not humble. In the liner notes to the remastered CD version of the album, Martin Rev says that "we were breaking the status quo. Most bands will do it in one or two ways but we were breaking it on at least four different planes."

"Rocket USA" comes and goes, and then there is "Cheree," the third track, and you are in love. As you have grown older, and more sentimental, "Cheree" has taken on meaning for you beyond all possible imagination. When that drum machine quietly kicks in—like a fluttering heartbeat—at the thirty-three-second mark, you are lost. The song has taken over.

The thing is, you and your sister, Kori, had an organ in the early seventies (before the tragedy that took her away—God, she is waiting for you at the top of the stairs in that Polaroid of the night before Christmas, with her smile, and the promise of cold rooms with the heat turned down and distant stars that need no heat and the coming Bicentennial that she would not live to see) that made sounds sort of like those on the Suicide album. The organ was brown, you remember, with a knob on the side to turn it on and off.

"Keep Your Dreams" is clearly the best song, not despite of its sentimentality, but because of it. "Dream baby, dream baby," go the lyrics, and in the face of No Wave and then hardcore you marvel at the risk of this song, with its full-ahead sincerity. Sincerity in the age of suspicion. You have never solved the riddle of the band that called itself Suicide. Thank God. You have listened to their music. You have read the interviews, and still they are a mystery to you, like the Judge in the Cormac McCarthy novels. "Their sound is unique," wrote Joe Fernbacher in *Creem*, "a massive clot of Wild Man Fischer attitudinizing and stamping plant technological titillation without a scintilla of promise, just demise personified."

[Joe Fernbacher, "Suicide," *Creem*, April 1978, p. 70.]

## Survival Research Laboratories (SRL)

**Formed in 1978 by Mark Pauline.** In an interview with Julian Holman, Pauline has said this about SRL's link to punk:

> I went to college where a lot of members of the early punk scene went to college, like Arto Lindsay from DNA . . . and Gordon Stevenson who was in Teenage Jesus and the Jerks and Exene from X and her sister both hung around the School . . . I moved out to San Francisco and looked the same as I had for years and so did everybody else, all this youth culture thing, and I was just never very interested in music to do it. So I just thought, well I can sympathize with this approach to tearing down a certain sort of encrusted institutions but I said who cares about music? Why would anyone want to tear that down? It didn't seem to me that interesting. My idea was that I would sort of do this other thing and it ended up being a thing about the art scene.

From the film *Survival Research Laboratories: Ten Years of Robotic Mayhem*:

> The only way for a creative person to really make any sort of a statement that has to do with what's going on in the culture at this time, at least the technological culture that I live in, is to deal with the tools that have made it that kind of a culture.

SRL was of a moment, driven by the same impulses of boredom and incoherent culture that spawned punk. Watching the machines in their slow violence and destruction, you are reminded how everything degenerates, breaks down, fails. It is failure that is at the heart of the performances, as the machines often do what they are supposed to do (shoot fire, crush things, destroy each other), but in slow and inefficient ways. But for all the theory behind it, the events are basically meaningless and indulgent: What you see happening is a "critique of technological culture" as well as an advertisement for it. There is nothing new about the public spectacle of destruction, yet every new form of destruction tells a different story.

"All the new thinking is about loss. / In this it resembles all the old thinking," the poet Robert Hass wrote in 1979. And there is always more new thinking.

[Robert Hass, "Meditation at Lagunitas," in *Praise*, New York: Ecco, 1979, p. 4; Julian Holman, *Exposure Magazine*, December 1994.]

# Symbionese Liberation Army (SLA)

**An urban guerilla group** that, among other things, robbed banks, murdered people, and kidnapped Patty Hearst, the media heiress, in February 1974 in Berkeley, California. Her kidnappers demanded many things, including a ransom, the release of other SLA members, and food distribution. During her kidnapping, she participated in the Hibernia bank robbery, holding a rifle. Her image—caught on a security camera—is full of meaning. But what is this meaning? She looks like many things in those images, but most of all she looks like someone in a movie playing the part of a female bank robber. Her face is clear and open. She does not disguise herself. Later, she would claim that she was brainwashed, that her actions were coerced. During her trial (she was arrested in September 1975), some of her writings from the time of her captivity were introduced into court:

> None of us were allowed to go to public schools. Kids who went to public schools were not the kind of people we should have close associations with. As a result, I spent twelve years almost totally surrounded by young people who were busily developing ruling class aspirations. Looking back, the schools were, in fact, training grounds for future fascists, capitalistic values, and individualism, competition, classicism and racism. I never got along too well with the faculty or students at these schools, because I was always considered a rebel.

Now, there is a critique here, but Hearst disavowed it, telling the prosecutor, "It is true I did not go to public schools but the rest of it is not true." But what is "the rest of it"? The rest of it is a distilled, radicalized version of the sixties. "This was a California Girl and she was raised on a history that placed not much emphasis on

Patty Hearst and the gap preceding punk: New York *Daily News*, September 1975

why," Joan Didion wrote. What happened to Patty Hearst happened because there was a gap. What was the nature of the gap? The gap was the space between the sixties and what was supposed to come next. But no one knew what was supposed to come next, so by 1974, Mick Farren, writing about San Francisco in *New Musical Express*, could write that "Hippies sat in bars and giggled as TV commentators tried to decide if Patty was a helpless victim or a willing tool." The gap had opened, and in rushed the SLA and in rushed Patty Hearst. "Now, the hippie panhandlers are becoming almost indistinguishable from the old-time winos," Farren wrote.

The gap was filled by Patty Hearst, memorialized by Patti Smith in "Sixty Days," the spoken-word segment that prefaced "Hey Joe": ". . . and I would do anything and Patty Hearst, you're standing there in front of the Symbionese Liberation Army flag with your legs spread . . . Patty, you know what your daddy said, Patty, he said, he said, 'Well, sixty days ago she was such a lovely little child, now here she is with a gun in her hand.'" And the Weirdos sang, in "Fort U.S.A.": "I'm in the Secret Service / and the C.I.A. / I helped annihilate the S.L.A." Patty Hearst was not in a girl group: She was not a member of the Runaways, who formed a few months after Hearst was arrested. She was not a member of the Slits or the Raincoats. She happened before Sleater-Kinney. But the most iconic images of her—with her lean fingers squeezed around that gun in her hand—are really like great album covers, or stills from a forgotten film. Afterward, she disavowed everything, further cheapening the already incoherent revolutionary sentiments of the SLA.

It was as if the most radical parts of the sixties had been transformed into dumb violence, a few spitballs thrown in the face of the Man. For a while, nobody knew what to do. And then punk happened. And it gave shape and form to the madness. Punk transformed the whole incoherent mess into something that you could put on stage. Which is to say: in a different version of the story, Patty Hearst holds a guitar, not a gun.

[Mick Farren, "San Francisco: Who Needs Music When We've Got the Zebra?" *New Musical Express*, June 15, 1974; Selected Trial Transcript Excerpts in the Patty Hearst Trial," http://www.law.umkc.edu/faculty/projects/ftrials/hearst.]

# Target Video

**Founded in 1977 by Joseph Rees, Target Video,** out of San Francisco, was instrumental in not only documenting the nascent California punk scene, but in making a theory out of the medium of videotape. Capturing both live performances and staged music videos before there was such a thing as MTV, Target Video worked

Logo for Target Video column by Joe Rees, from *Damage* fanzine, 1980

fast and cheaply with consumer equipment at the dawn of the video age, eschewing perfection for the raw, real-time. In 1966, Marshall McLuhan said that when "an inexpensive play-back for video tape is available, the film will become as portable as a book after Gutenberg." A little over a decade later, Joe Rees put this theory into practice. At the time, he said that "video's worked out to be the ultimate medium for new wave because it's very fast; it instantly documents an event and also we can distribute this information very rapidly."

The distribution of information.

At its cold heart, wasn't this what punk was about?

"No Feelings," the Sex Pistols said.

"Our bodies make us worry," sang Gang of Four in "Contract."

The speed and spontaneity of video was a mystery, a contradiction. It was a contradiction because it was a medium of instantaneous emotion, destroying the time lag between the live event and its memory in the archive. And yet the very nature of the archive is that it preserves events so that they endure long beyond the moment of their original creation and performance. Rees started with borrowed video equipment: "It was definitely faster and easier to use for instant feedback of the events. I had free access to a local cable channel in San Francisco where I could show the material hours later."

Rees glimpsed the future of music video in 1979, while attending the "first rock 'n' roll video conference ever," in Los Angeles. Realizing he had to pay a hundred dollars to attend, he snuck into one of the presentations: "The room contains a TV monitor and about thirty-five slickly dressed types standing around it watching Elton John doing the same over-produced thing, 'Midnight Special'–style. Checking out the brochures lying around announcing upcoming videodisc shows, I soon realize nothing new in programming is in the offing and that the strategy of the companies involved is to feed the public the same garbage they have done for years." Although in its early years MTV did play some adventuresome, bizarre, and even avant-gardish videos (Devo come to mind) this was largely because they were in need of content. By the mid-1980s, most music videos on the network had become what Rees had predicted: "Arista and more of that bunch are spending *lots* of dollars to develop the video-album or 'videogram' market. It's the same Big Business versus the Artist problem all over again: artists now recording will have to struggle with over-produced visuals, i.e. special effects colorizing, dry ice, star filters, etc., and the high costs of live production running from $10,000 on up."

For Rees, punk was part of the inevitable overturning of the old order that was the sixties. The seventies, he said, were a time of "boredom, rejection of cultural styles, the pure desire and intensity of the young artists to make their statements and the natural cultural roll-over. As any new wave movement, [punk] rejects the old and creates a new language." As fast and amateurish as punk, video—as Rees conceived it—was the perfect medium for that language.

[Marhall McLuhan, *Essential McLuhan*, eds. Eric McLuhan and Frank Zingrone, New York: Basic, 1995, p. 290; Joseph Rees, "At that time in the 70's," e-mail to the author, February 8, 2008; Joseph Rees, "Items . . . Target Video," *Damage* no. 4, Jan. 1980, p. 34.]

# Teen Idles

**A short-lived but important hardcore band** from Washington, D.C. Formed in 1979, they were inspired by Bad Brains and Black Flag, and before that the Cramps, who had played a concert in January 1979 for Georgetown University's WGTB radio station. The band featured Ian MacKaye and Jeff Nelson (who formed Minor Threat in 1980), Nathan Strejcek, and Georgie Grindle. "In their one-year existence," Michael Azerrad has written, "the Teen Idles amassed $900.00, all of which went into a band kitty kept in a cigar box. When the band dissolved, they had to decide whether to split the money four ways or press up the recordings they'd done with Don Zienara." They decided to release them—the eight-song EP *Minor Disturbance*—on a label they created: Dischord Records. According to MacKaye, it "was decided that if we managed to sell enough of the Teen Idles records to make any of the money back, we would use the cash to put out records by these other bands. I was really inspired by the Dangerhouse Records label, which had released a series of singles by L.A. punk bands, and wanted to try to do something similar with Dischord."

The eight songs on *Minor Disturbance* are so fast and so loud that, even today, after their aesthetic has been absorbed into other and more familiar cultural channels, the songs come across as a threat. How can so few instruments produce so much sound? "Life has been the same for a long time," goes the first line in "Teen Idles," as if that's a reason (or an excuse; but then an excuse is not needed, is it?) for the rest of the EP. It's impossible to understand these lyrics outside the context of straight edge and its disavowal of drugs, drinking, and meaningless sex. Over the years, MacKaye has noted that the straight-edge movement that evolved as a result of his philosophy and song of the same name was not his intention or plan. And yet the songs on *Minor Disturbance* teeter unstably somewhere between *Mad* magazine parody and serious critique. "Deadhead, deadhead, take another toke / Deadhead, deadhead, you're a lousy joke," go the lyrics, and the chorus—"I'll be grateful when you're dead"—drives it home. In opposition to the orthodoxy that drugs provided a creative release that resulted in stunning art (the Beatles' *Sgt. Peppers* myth), "Deadhead" suggested this: "Riding that train high on cocaine / The music is really lousy, the fans are a pain." Although D.C. was never really known as a hippie town in the way that San Fransisco or Berkeley were, certain movements—such as the D.C. Statehood movement—had components that were almost John Sinclair-ish. Formed in the early seventies, the D.C. Statehood Party—which, as Fred Siegel has pointed out, "hoped to establish a socialist, if not a Marxist, commonwealth"— offered a platform in 1972 that included the following:

- the conversion of banks and public utilities to cooperatives
- a national guaranteed income

- legalization of gambling, prostitution, marijuana use, and drug addiction
- free health care for all citizens
- free abortions on demand

But was the music of the Teen Idles any better than the music of the Grateful Dead? This is a stupid, juvenile question, and therefore an important one. Both groups have, on different scales, their devoted, worshipful followers. Both spawned lifestyle cults that reject each other's habits. One group made relatively soft, easy-going music with lots of spaces to breathe and think; one group's music asked listeners to race as fast as possible to the end of the song.

[Michael Azerrad, *Our Band Could Be Your Life: Scenes from the American Indie Underground, 1981–1991*; New York: Little, Brown and Company, 2001, p. 131; Ian MacKaye, "History," available at www.dischord.com/history; Fred Siegel, *The Future Once Happened Here*, San Fransisco: Encounter, 1997, p. 99.]

## "That's Entertainment"

**There is a sadness at the heart of the Jam's 1981 song** "That's Entertainment" that is difficult to put into words. Songs that mean something to us are such personal things, so tied to individual moments, moments that often can never be repeated, that to try to write about them later is nothing less than a doomed prospect. For one thing, lyrically it is one of the most impressionistic songs by the Jam: "A baby wailing and a stray dog howling / The screech of brakes and lamplights blinking." The song is sort of catalog of details: "Waking up at 6 a.m. on a cool warm morning / Opening the windows and breathing in petrol / An amateur band rehearsing in a nearby yard." Like the best punk-era songs, this one is, at its heart, old-fashioned and tinged with regret.

## Theoretical Girls

**The Theoretical Girls**—Jeffrey Lohn, Wharton Tiers, Margaret Dewys, and Glenn Branca—could have been a punk band, but they weren't. They could have been a No Wave band, but they weren't. They could have been a post-punk band, but they weren't. They weren't any of these things because it's not words that describes bands, but sounds. But since I cannot put sounds in this book, you will have to rely on words—unless you already have some recordings by the Theoretical Girls, in which case you can dispense with this entry and simply listen to the music. The band released only one single, in 1978, although many of their songs were made available by Acute Records in 2002. They were not included on Brian Eno's *No*

*New York* No Wave compilation. They had been "pointedly excluded," notes Simon Frith, "because of their associations with the SoHo art scene."

But all quibbles about where the Theoretical Girls belong are obliterated once you listen to their music, which just knocks you off balance. Even your writing: You think the words are going to come smoothly, and then you are blindsided by a song that doesn't fit in the little box you were busy making. Here, for example, is a short paragraph that was meant to be longer.

"Mom & Dad" might very well be the most confounding punk-era song ever written, drooping down out of the sky like a lazy tornado that's sort of funny and slow at first—seen from the safe distance of miles—and then menacing, and then frightening, and then terrifying. Who knows what the lyrics are; it seems to be a poor live recording. There is a bit of the Beach Boys, the Ramones, Dead Boys, Rocket from the Tombs, New Order (impossibly), even the Who, heavy metal, and Suicide—all blended together in a way that if a girl you played this for late at night said, "Yes, I like it, sort of," you know you would ask her to marry you right there and mean it, and even burn your most prized books out on the balcony just to prove it to her. The song has the force of your heartbeat when everything is beautiful; it confirms every wondrous thing on God's green creation.

"Theoretical Girls" is a nearly perfect song because it is nearly perfect theory: For the first one minute and twenty seconds, the lyrics are no more than variations of a Ramones-like countdown, "one-two-three-four" (the song could be called "'Variations on one-two-three-four") but it doesn't sound like mockery so much as a recognition that the first, naive phase of punk is gone and dead forever. "Computer Dating" reminds you of Gang of Four, because of the idea behind the lyrics: "Were you born in the U.S.A.? / Do you believe in Women's Lib? / Where will you go when you have a date? / What kind of books do you like to read?" The song is mocking, but also sympathetic.

"Europe Man" is an anthem, but to what? It is a Stooges-like song, played with guilt because, in the arid world of the No Wave scene, any "grooviness" was likely too human. This song is mad genius because it smuggles in brief pop melodies. What if hardcore had taken this route and blossomed into something confounding and mysterious rather than something relentlessly antagonistic? The history of popular music is a history of paths not taken: What if the Theoretical Girls had made it?

Some notes:

"Europe Man": a Stooges-like background?

"Nato": reminds you of Pere Ubu

"Lovin in the Red": Kraftwerk and Suicide but more buttery

[Simon Reynolds, *Rip It Up and Start Again: Postpunk 1978–1984*, New York: Penguin, 2005, p. 147.]

## Theory, punk as a form of (1)

**If "theory" is a bad word today,** there are plenty of reasons why. Blame it on the academics, who squandered the tremendous vitality, playfulness, and energy of postmodernism's first wave and turned inward into ever more specialized, unmotivated, jargon-heavy discourse that quickly became self-parody. Blame it on larger market forces that reduce even the thorniest paradoxes down to their lowest common denominator. Blame it on social forces that increasingly put high value on vocation and pragmatism. But the fact remains that there was an unprecedented meeting of avant-garde and popular culture inaugurated during the Pop Art era and reaching its zenith during the punk era. Those who claim that first-wave punk was "stoopid" must ignore an avalanche of screaming evidence from the period—newspapers, fanzines, interviews, and of course the music itself—that suggests otherwise.

The fact that *New Musical Express* (hardly an obscure literary or art journal) could—on its cover from February 21, 1976—feature a photograph of Patti Smith with the headline SMITH SLAMS RIMBAUD is testament to the mixing of high and low that provided so much of the energy to the emerging underground and punk scene. Smith herself was a defender of rock as more than just entertainment, but as a form of art. In that same issue, she said, "I still think people have such an old-fashioned approach, an *academic* approach to art. They separate the 'art'—from the rock-and-roll."

And later in that issue, there is this letter to the editor: "We denounce your filthy capitalist rag as a tool of our oppressions and a Fascist trick to capture the attention of the masses away from the true struggle, namely against the tyrants of big business and the despots of government." The letter is signed "Ever-true Bay City Roller Fans."

The Marxist, "cultural studies" mind-set was at the time really and truly alive and well at the street level, before the academics moved in and ruined everything by pointing out what was already obvious. Tommy Gear, of the San Francisco group Screamers, has said of the 1977 era that "This time was more of an ideological challenge, as opposed to the more physical challenge of the later hardcore bands . . . Art goes in advance of the general populace whereas Commerce follows and tries to make money down the road."

Or take *Melody Maker* from April 24, 1976, and the article by Steve Lake and Karl Dallas "Rocking the Avant Garde," which reads positively like a dissertation: "The division between what is variously, and inaccurately, described as classical, symphonic or serious music on the one hand and popular or light music on the other, is a fairly modern invention." This was part of the fun of pop music at the time: It was being taken seriously (just look at this book that you are now holding in your hands or resting on your lap, written by a professor—*arrghhh!*—but he is a man who has lost, who has suffered; forgive him) and in that seriousness was also a recognition of the absurdity of the whole thing. At the end of his not-kind 1975 *Creem* review of Lou Reed's *Lou Reed Live*, Peter Laughner wrote, "I'll bet the kids that take Elliott Murphy's Advanced Rock 101 at Harvard in '86 will think that Lou Reed was pretty incredible." This is only sort of funny now because there actually *are* academic classes on rock, and the kids think Lou Reed *is* pretty incredible. Ah, well.

What's hard to remember is this: There was a time when there was great fun to be had in playing punk off the avant-garde because it was still possible to have an avant-garde. Today—when every new cultural form becomes disseminated in a matter of days via YouTube and other yet-to-be-named delivery devices—there's really no such thing as the avant-garde, which depends upon a cultural lag for its very being. An avant-garde means being in front of something, ahead of it, a predictor, a gamble about how things might turn out. The avant-garde depended on a media that would eventually disseminate its ideas, but slowly, slowly. It's that very lag-time that gave the avant-garde a chance to be the avant-garde. That's why—as late as 1979—a profile by of the Dils in *New York Rocker* could say that a "Dils performance is not a quirky artistic foray into the rock avant-garde, and it's not a safe, slick, 'new wave' act like the Police either."

The historically aware, theoretical dimension of punk (made explicit in postpunk by bands like Gang of Four) extended beyond the lyrics and the performance elements to the very design of record sleeves, posters, flyers, and other visual elements. According to Jamie Reid, who designed many of the early Sex Pistols sleeves and flyers, his style and methods of design were heavily influenced by the Situationists and other avant-gardes: "From the Surrealists to the Dadaists, to the Situationists and the whole movement of community agit-prop politics, down into punk, and then into all sorts of things. It's a continuing story . . . [What I did] was an attempt to take those movements into popular culture."

The tricky thing about punk and theory is that it's easy to forget that theory was always a part of the punk and post-punk movements. Today, if a rock critic were to mention Robbe-Grillet or Roland Barthes in an article about a band, she would probably be accused of being a "rock snob." It's fun to make fun of people who claim to know a lot. But so many articles and reviews from the mainstream press and from fanzines in the late seventies and early eighties referenced literary and cultural theorists. Here is J. D. Considine writing about Wire's third album, *154*: "It's stunning and literate, and my college-trained imagination leaps toward connections with Robbe-Grillet or perhaps Lucas Foss. But c'mon, pipes my rock and roll sensibility, this is *rock*. When ya listen to it, do ya tap yer toes or grab for yer *Bedside Roland Barthes*?"

The very last paragraph of Poly Publius's column, "The Nihilist #10," in the great punk fanzine *Sluggo!*, goes like this: "Enough for now. Next issue of *Sluggo!* I will define my terms and explain how to recognize a contradiction within the capitalist system. I will also attempt to explain how the purchase of Fruit Juicy Hawaiian Punch is a political act." Those lines are classic punk theory: They express a real theory as well as a sort of jokey guilt about theory, as if to assure us, Don't worry, this isn't too high-falutin'.

And here is the contradiction: As much as punk and early New Wave were about the pure, absurd thrill and joy of music experienced on a raw and visceral level, they also had a secret dimension that was, at its heart, a form of theory. "John Lydon's post–Sex Pistols project, Public Image, Ltd., or PiL," wrote Kris Needs in 1980, "has focused on these multiple perceptions, the manner in which the media identifies things and proceeds to disseminate the information. The way a studio records musical information and the subsequent way those sounds are duplicated. How the records are then packaged and sold."

In truth, punk as a form of theory is rooted in the very generation it sought to disavow—for the utopianism of the sixties contained its own B-side, its own dystopia, predicted with startling vision by Joan Didion in her 1967 essay "Slouching Towards Bethlehem." And it was there in the writing of people like Philip K. Dick, whose 1966 novel *Now Wait for Last Year* is its own strange form of music theory: "So this is how it feels to be hooked on JJ-180, she thought. She managed to pick up the Decca record. Its dark edges were like knife blades sawing into her hands as she carried it across the office to the door. Its hostility toward her, its inanimate yet ferocious desire to inflict destruction on her, became overwhelming; she cringed from the disk's touch."

[J. D. Considine, "Re: Wire," *New York Rocker*, March 1980, p. 37; Philip K. Dick, *Now Wait for Last Year*, 1966; repr., New York: Vintage, 1993, p. 74; Tommy Gear interviewed by James Stark in *Punk '77*, Stark Grafix, 1992, p. 35; Steve Lake and Karl Dallas, "Rocking the Avant Garde," *Melody Maker*, April 24, 1976, p. 25–31; Peter Laughner, review of *Lou Reed Live*, *Creem*, June 1975, p. 64; Greg McLean, "The Dils: Victory on the Eastern Front!" *New York Rocker*, August 1979, p. 19; Kris Needs, "Lydon: Rock & Roll Is Dead and He Don't Care," *New York Rocker*, March 1980, p. 9; Polly Publius, "The Nihilist #10," *Sluggo!* #17, March 1979 (labeled "April 1999"), no page; Jamie Reid interviewed by Bob Nickas, 1998, www.indexmagazine.com/interviews/jamie_reid.shtml; Patti Smith interviewed by Lisa Robinson in "So What Do You Park in an Intellectual Garage?" *New Musical Express*, February 21, 1976, pp. 22–23.]

# Theory, punk as a form of (2)

**A shorter version: When punk emerged,** it suggested such a clear break with inherited musical tastes that mainstream newspapers and magazines often engaged in a form of critique that went deeper than typical record-review writing. Some articles hinted at an almost Marxist suggestion that radical cultural movements are eventually co-opted into the mainstream, where they are subject to economic control and drained of their subversive qualities. Here, from the newspaper *The Brandon Sun*, out of Manitoba: "Eventually the new wave will be bled into the mainstream of the music business, compromised and embellished, filling the void that constantly occurs as old idols wither and audience taste changes."

[Anon., "Punk Rock Is Dead: New Wave Groping for Power," *The Brandon Sun*, December 1, 1977, p. 15.]

# "There is nothing inherently wonderful about starkness"

**A sentence from a scathing 1976 article** about Patti Smith by Ira Robbins, the editor of *Trouser Press*. Describing *Horses*—which had been released in December 1975—as a "fairly good album, capturing a small part of the feeling one got seeing her at Max's a year ago," Robbins wonders why she has become a darling of the "straight press." His critique rests on two objections. First, her music has been transformed from a sort of self-deprecating "imitation" of rock and roll into an actual, serious effort to be rock and roll: "she's trying to hook people with punk nostalgia, a theory that totally disallows the tongue-in-cheek self-parody that seeing her play a year ago displayed completely." Second, her newfound success with *Horses* is a betrayal of her roots and of the New York underground scene: "[She] has shed the New York tag and is trying to be a national incarnation of a local problem, and that just seems an improper way to approach music."

In some ways, Robbins's article predicts the countless attacks on punk and indie bands that would, in the coming decades, be accused of selling out, either because they signed to major labels or because they began adjusting their sound to accommodate the broader tastes of wider audiences.

But more than this, Robbins's assault has the tone of a spurned lover or, worse yet, a forgotten one. *Patti, why have you forgotten me? I love you. Please come back.* It's a feeling we've all had at one point or another about a favorite band, and about the betrayal we feel when that private experience goes public and *everybody* gets a chance to listen. In this respect, Robbins's essay is not a hatchet job but a confession of love.

[Ira Robbins, "Rats! Is Patti a Patsy?" *Trouser Press*, February–March 1976, pp. 19–20.]

## "There Are Only Three Rock Groups in America," by Lester Bangs, 1976

**"While I'm at it,** the best rock bands in America are The Dictators, Ramones and the Patti Smith Group." And: "We'll forgive you for not comprehending the genius of The Ramones." From one of Bangs's first pieces after leaving *Creem.*

> [Lester Bangs, "There Are Only Three Rock Groups in America," *New Musical Express,* September 18, 1976, p. 15.]

## Troggs

**In 1971, Lester Bangs wrote** that part of "the reason the Troggs ultimately cut their competitors and successors at raw high-energy electro-fertility stomps was their consistent sense of structure and economy—I don't think any of their songs ran over four minutes . . . Reg Presley didn't have the Tasmanian-devil glottal scope of an Iggy, but he did have one of the most leering, sneering punk snarls of all time."

The Troggs as anti-heroes of the punk subculture

And in 1973, Harold Bronson, in *Phonograph Record,* wrote that the "instrumental backing, hard and markedly simple, was sloppy, characteristic of the we're-tough-we-don't-care punk philosophy." Formed in 1964 in Andover, United Kingdom, the Troggs (originally called the Troglodytes) were a major influence on the sound that would eventually become known as punk. They consisted of Reg Presley (lead vocals), Chris Britton, Pete Staples, Ronnie Bond, and Tony Murray.

Despite number-one hits in both the United States ("Wild Thing," 1966) and the United Kingdom ("With a Girl Like You," 1966), the Troggs were always a marginalized band, coming closer than even the Rolling Stones in the mid-sixties to making explicit what everyone already knew: that rock and roll was fast moving out of its first-generation naive phase and pushing into much rawer and darker territory. There was also an element of spontaneity and improvisation at work in the recording of their first songs that would predict the fast, do-it-yourself, amateur quality of punk. "That first LP," Bond has said, "was recorded in three hours. Some of the songs weren't completely written yet. 'Jingle Jangle' and four other tracks Reg wrote the lyrics and the music while we were recording the instrumental backing." By the late sixties and early seventies—with the exception of the Velvet Underground, Lou Reed, etc.—rock had become so derivative, safe, and overproduced that imperfection was hard to come by. As late as 1979, certain bands from the sixties were still being referred to as punk (not pre-punk or proto-punk), including the Troggs. "What separates The Troggs from other great 'Sixties bands is pretty clear," wrote Todd Abramson in the fanzine *FFanzeen* (out of Brooklyn, New York). "Most of the great American punk bands of the 'Sixties ended up dissolving for various reasons . . . The Troggs stand apart for never having sacrificed any of their original vitality." The appeal of the Troggs was not just in their growling sound, amplified by the likes of Iggy Pop, but in the unburdened freedom of their songs, such as "Night of the Long Grass," with its simple riffs and low-roar minimalism. In songs such as this one, the Troggs kept predicting the future until it finally came and there was no more use for them.

[Todd Abramson, "Night of the Troggs," *FFanzeen* no. 3, Winter–Spring 1978–79, p. 20; Lester Bangs, "James Taylor Marked for Death," in *Psychotic Reactions and Carburetor Dung*, ed. Greil Marcus, 1971; repr., New York: Vintage, 1988, pp. 55–56; Ronnie Bond quoted in Harold Bronson, "Troggs: Fond Rememberings and Frank Quotes from the World's First Punk Rockers," *Phonograph Record*, February 1973.]

# Truth about punk, the

**From a letter to the editor by Tom Mitchell** in *White Noise*, a punk-era fanzine published out of Detroit in the late seventies. This letter, "Ass-Wholism," is from issue number four, 1979. I quote here the first two paragraphs in their demented, truthful entirety:

Here's a note to all you scene makers who are too cool for words. When are you people gonna grow up, huh? Just cuz you're punk rockers and you hate disco let's not forget that you are big assholes.

So what? So you got a ripped up T-shirt and a Romantics button. Do you think anyone really gives a damn? You people really make me wanna puke. I don't know who is impressed by your ability to raise your brow and look the other way when someone talks to you, but it certainly is not me.

This New Wave stuff is not all it's cracked up to be. In case you haven't noticed, half that shit you morons listen to with pride is totally garbage, and Sid Viscious [*sic*] singing "My Way" is downright obnoxious and I'm glad he's dead. And if obnoxious is so fun then why the hell do you assholes stand around at Bookies with that suave and debonair or I'm-too-clean-a-cunt-to-smile look plastered to your faces? Oh! Oh! You pogo! And you skip to your fucking Lou, I don't care. And Patti Smith is a bitch and I hate her and biting her leg is the best thing I ever did and I hope she dies too . . .

[Tom Mitchell, "Ass-Wholism," *White Noise* no. 4, 1979, p. 4.]

## "TV babies"

**A phrase used in 1974 by the manager** and record producer Marty Thau to describe the New York Dolls, whom he was then comanaging: "The Dolls are leading the way for a new generation of audience . . . They're TV babies. They're all interested in the visual aspect of entertainment." Here is a sentence from a letter to *Creem*, also from 1974: "I NEVER ventured out of TV land to write to a magazine but your recent Bowie Look Alike contest jolted me into at least TRYING to get thru to you."

TV land.

By the early to mid-seventies, debates about the "bad" influence of television had become academic. The heroic resistance of "vast wasteland" statements (resurrected in a different form in the first *Matrix* film) had given way to an ironic refashioning of TV as a sort of Warholian blankness: TV was so dumb it was cool. This attitude was a fundamental shift from the sixties, where television was seen as both an evil force by the counterculture as well as a medium by which to mock and prod the establishment, à la the *The Smothers Brothers Show*. "In retrospect, the sixties counterculture appears to have been an epidemic popular narcissism that swept the first generation to see its collective self on television," Kenneth Baker has noted.

"I'm so sick of T.V.," the Dead Boys sing on "Ain't Nothing to Do," from their 1977 debut album, and listening to Stiv Bators snarl his way across the wasteland, you secretly realize that he is speaking for you, too. It's a funny and confounding thing, in retrospect: Were the punks mocking TV, or simply responding to it as a given? "In the extreme," Jon Savage wrote in 1979, "most Angelinos are so TV-damaged anyway that they're actively relishing the thought of the Big Earthquake (astrologically scheduled for 1982) in the absolutely deffo expectation that it'll beat the movies hollow. Then they'll serialise it."

[Kenneth Baker, *Minimalism: Art of Circumstance*, New York: Abbeville Press, 1988, p. 15; Robert Hilburn, "N.Y. Dolls Hot on the Campaign Trail," *Los Angeles Times*, April 7,

1974, p. N61; Lance Loud, "Poochofeliac," *Creem*, October 1974, p. 10; Jon Savage, "The Screamers," *Melody Maker*, January 6, 1979.]

**u**

# Undertones

**The Undertones were one of the many bands** that had already been playing by the time punk happened. Like so many other bands from that era, they were essentially a pop group that became associated with punk during that frenzy of late 1976 and 1977. The band—Feargal Sharkey on vocals, John and Damian O'Neill, Michael Bradley, and Billy Doherty—were from around Derry, in Northern Ireland, described by Gavin Martin in *New Musical Express* as a "city with some of the worst housing and unemployment figures in the UK, a town of two communities segregated by a river and religion." They formed in 1975 and played their first show at a scout hut in 1976. Their early shows were mostly covers of songs by the Rolling Stones, Cream, Dr. Feelgood, and Fleetwood Mac. In "Get over You," from 1979, they sang, "Dressed like Thatcher, you must be livin' in a different world / And your mother doesn't know Why you can't look like all the other girls." But the Undertones were not a progressively political band; the driving beat to "Get over You" is as rock and roll traditional as you can get. The soaring *ooh-wah* chorus transports you in a way that only music can. There are no hints of darkness, only sunshine, which is both the strength of the band and its limits.

"Teenage Kicks," written in the summer of 1977, showed the powerful effect that punk could have in transforming a typical pop song into something greater. The genius of the song is that it is played slowly, almost at a heavy-metal pace. As in the Ramones' songs, kids and teenagers were oddly conceived: In Sharkey's perfectly warbling, unstable voice, it wasn't clear if he counted himself as a teenager or as a singer of teenagers. "I wanna hold her wanna hold her tight / get teenage kicks right through the night," he sings; but would a teenager talk about getting "teenage kicks"? This may seem like an obscure point but it's a key to the power of punk bands like the Undertones, who sang *about* teenagers, not simply *as* them. "(She's a) Runaround," from their first album, is the perfect expression of pop noise, and about as far away from the harsh anti-Romantic primitivism of bands like the Sex Pistols or the Dead Boys, or the hectoring, self-righteous clatter of the Clash as is possible.

[Gavin Martin, "Crash Course in Corruption with the Undertones," *New Musical Express*, November 4, 1978.]

**V**

## Vast Majority

**A Houston, Texas-area punk band** whose original lineup consisted of Scott Telles, Chris Armeniades, John Svatek, and Billy Mandel, and then later Henry Weissborn and Wayne Collins, and then again later Caroline Caustic and Walter Wolff. Their seven-inch, recorded in March 1980, included "I Wanna Be a Number," which at first sounded like the Ramones, four years too late. But the song is really a bitter testament to sheer impersonality, with lyrics like "The hell with a fuckin' stupid name / I wanna be a number" and "If everyone were a number we'd all be different." The drums are periodically and improbably off-beat; miraculously the song holds together. John Peters in *Damage* said this of Vast Majority: They "come onstage at Paradise Island untuned, untutored and unselfconscious to live out their star fantasies, a fascinating blend of punk and the sixties. They think nothing of abandoning their instruments or giving them to bystanders, but usually just hack at them noisily, producing a limited number of anti-chords."

[John Peters, "Houston Scene Report," *Damage* no. 4, January 1980, p. 16.]

## *Vertigo*

**A 1981 EP by the Standing Waves**, of Austin, Texas. What is this music? "Never Say Die," the final song, is perfect: punk as if filtered through a machine to cleanse it of all unrighteousness. A hidden gem that sounds a little bit like the Marbles' "Red Lights." "When the time is right / I'll know what to say," the lyrics go, and in the basement listening to the song for the very first time in preparation for writing this entry you wonder what it is you have done in your life that you have ended up here, at this point, listening to a song so perfect that you hesitate to write about it. You consider its connection to punk, and jot down some notes. They seem absurd now, typed out like this: "Beautiful. Sounds like seventies. Punk deformed by Austin. Talking Heads? Darker. Who to interview?" The song unfolds in beauty and you wonder who in the hell was Shona Lay, whose keyboards are so perfect that it brings out the narcissist in you: You swear this song was written for you (notice how many times the word "you" appears, ha-ha). "They're punchy, loose, danceable, intellectual, funny, and very serious about what they're doing," Ed Ward wrote in *New York Rocker*.

There are the facts about *Vertigo*, but what do they mean? They drift into this entry like afterthoughts: produced by Patrick S. Peel for Pool Productions Ltd. In addition to Shona Lay on keyboards, there is David Dage, Larry Seaman, and Bruce

Henderson, but the band was also David Cardwell, Randy Franklin, and Bob Murray. In 1980, Cardwell told the Austin, Texas, fanzine *Contempo Culture* that "in terms of the New Wave, it's much more of a lifestyle in NYC than in Austin . . . But I would say that Austin has the same full spectrum of music that New York has, there's just more of it in New York."

This entry cartwheels out of control. The writer is distracted, in need of coffee. The transition to *Creem* magazine in 1980, and an article about the movie *Roadie*, with the Standing Waves as the Spittle, a punk band. The movie stars Meat Loaf, Blondie, Alice Cooper, and Art Carney, and was filmed in Austin:

> A member of the film crew emerges onstage. He explains to the audience that they're actually to be a part of this film. There's much applause. Please be patient, he announces, this might take a while. Minutes later, Blondie cheerfully greets the crowd. They run through "Dreaming," "Ring of Fire," and "One Way or Another." Everyone's in fine form; the audience loves it. As the film crewman had explained, the band leaves after their third song. The audience calls for more. Next up: the Standing Waves, an Austin-based band that owes more than a little to the Talking Heads. They manage a respectable set nonetheless.

Roger Ebert said of *Roadie* that the "movie's so genial, disorganized and episodic that we never really care about the characters." And yet there's a softness to the movie, an openness like the space around Austin. In the context of hardcore and the dissolution of punk into sharp fragments, *Roadie* is nothing less than nostalgia for a shambling future that never arrived.

[David Cardwell, "Interview," *Contempo Culture* no. 3, 1980, p. 38; Dave DiMartino, "Blondie/Meatloaf: Meat to the Beat," *Creem*, February 1980; Roger Ebert, "*Roadie*," *Chicago Sun-Times*, June 18, 1980, http://rogerebert.suntimes.com; Ed Ward, "On the Verge with Standing Waves," *New York Rocker* no. 27, March 1980, p. 29.]

## Vibrators

**A British punk band, formed in Febuary 1976.** In 1977, they opened for the Stranglers and the Sex Pistols. During that time, the band was Ian Carnochan (Knox), Pat Collier, John Ellis, and John "Eddie" Edwards. In many ways, they were the consummate pop-punk band; their music veered off into unexpected directions just when you thought you had them figured out. "Baby Baby," from 1977, is perhaps the most beautiful punk song ever, a steady and slow undertow of organized noise. The lyrics "do have their own persona," Jon Savage wrote in 1977, "a kind of half-humorous, half-desperate offhand perversity, mixed in with a suppressed dementia." Like the Ramones, the Vibrators were not, on the surface, a theoretical

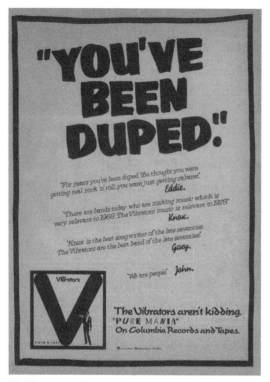

"YOU'VE BEEN DUPED."

"For years you've been duped. You thought you were getting real rock 'n' roll, you were just getting cabaret."
Eddie.

"There are bands today who are making music which is very relevant to 1968. The Vibrators music is relevant to 1978."
Knox.

"Knox is the best songwriter of the late seventies. The Vibrators are the best band of the late seventies."
Gary.

"We are people."  John.

The Vibrators aren't kidding.
"PURE MANIA"
On Columbia Records and Tapes.

The Vibrators aren't kidding

band. Unlike Pere Ubu, the Sex Pistols, Gang of Four, Wire, and others, there was not an aesthetic purity to their work, in part because their music was not self-consciously punk at a time in England when the scene was rapidly hardening into orthodoxy. "Punk in Britain is becoming very fascist," Knox said in a 1977 interview with Mick Brown, "all this business about people believing they have to conform to a certain image which is really only being determined by a small elite in London." The fact that the Vibrators (who were older anyway) were never fully one of "them" gave them a critical distance from the scene that illustrated just how deeply British punk was indebted to unlikely musical sources from the sixties, such as the Beatles, the Rolling Stones, and even the Who. Whereas American bands ranging from Patti Smith to the Ramones openly acknowledged their British Invasion influences, U.K. punk bands suffered from an anxiety of influence that suggested, on the surface, a more radical break from tradition. The Vibrators are a good example of why punk in the United Kingdom never really developed a hardcore scene in the late seventies and early eighties that was comparable to those in California or D.C. Bands like the Sex Pistols were *already* hardcore, in a manner and tone far more radical than we can appreciate today, when they have been mythologized to the point of perfection. Bands like the Vibrators cultivated the open spaces that more radical bands like the Sex Pistols cleared, making possible a longer arc for punk and a deliberate future in the face of No Future.

[Mick Brown, "The Vibrators: The Punks Who Came in from the Cold," *Sounds*, September 24, 1977; Jon Savage, "The Vibrators: *Pure Mania*," *Sounds*, June 11, 1977.]

# Vietnam War

**Was the violence in punk**—the absolute negation and assault in the music and performance, the wall of indifference, the hostility—a dark echo of the worst moments of the Vietnam War? Were the dead boys the Dead Boys?

1. The poet Robert Bly—an early hero of Richard Hell—said that the "Vietnam War and the revulsion against it carried us away. After its years of storm, the war ended in 1975. The war had eroded the confidence of men in each other, especially the confidence of younger men in older men, and it emphasized how estranged from nature the entire nation was . . . The war brought a new corrupion of language."

2. Ten years earlier, in 1976, Max Bell wrote in *New Musical Express* of the Ramones that you "have to admit they are pretty weird. Four guys straight out of the teenaged wasteland hanging loose while waiting for the advent of World War III. Four kids who came out of Forest Hills, New York suburbia, who all wanted to fight in Vietnam but ended up playing rock 'n' roll instead, 'cuz there's nothin' left on the radio to listen to no more."

3. The graphic details of the My Lai massacre were in the news in the late sixties. It is important not to forget that many of the originators of punk came of age when testimony like this—from the court marial of Lieutenant Calley—was coverend in the media:

"Meadlo led the people to a clearing he thought was in the center of the hamlet, though he couldn't be sure. There were thirty or forty people, some of them was already there. Conti and myself guarded them."

**Daniel:** What did you do when you got there?

**Meadlo:** Just guarded them.

**Daniel:** Did you see Lieutenant Calley?

**Meadlo:** Yes.

**Daniel:** What did he do?

**Meadlo:** He came up to me and he said, "You know what to do with them, Meadlo," and I assumed he wanted me to guard them. That's what I did.

**Daniel:** What were the people doing?

**Meadlo:** They was just standing there . . . [Calley] said, "How come they're not dead?" I said, "I didn't know we were supposed to kill them." He said, "I want them dead." He backed off twenty or thirty feet and started shooting into the people—the Viet Cong—shooting automatic.

He was beside me. He burned four or five magazines. I burned off a few, about three. I helped shoot 'em.

**Daniel:** What were the people doing after you shot them?

**Meadlo:** They were lying down.

**Daniel:** They were lying down?

**Meadlo:** They was mortally wounded.

**Daniel:** How were you feeling at that time?

**Meadlo:** I was mortally upset, scared, because of the briefing we had the day before.

Later, more Vietnamese had been gathered and moved to a ravine.

**Meadlo:** Then L. Calley said to me, "We've got another job to do, Meadlo."

**Daniel::** What happened then?

**Meadlo:** He started shoving them off and shooting them in the ravine.

**Daniel:** How many times did he shoot?

**Meadlo:** I can't remember.

**Daniel:** Did you shoot?

**Meadlo:** Yes. I shot the Viet Cong. He ordered me to help kill the people. I started shoving them off and shooting.

**Daniel:** How long did you fire?

**Meadlo:** I don't know.

**Daniel:** Did you change magazines?

**Meadlo:** Yes.

**Daniel:** Did L. Calley change magazines?

**Meadlo:** Yes.

**Daniel:** How many times did he change magazines?

**Meadlo:** Ten to fifteen times.

**Daniel:** How many bullets in a magazine?

**Meadlo:** Twenty, normally.

**Daniel:** How was L. Calley armed?

**Meadlo:** He had a M-16.

**Daniel:** What were the people doing after you and L. Calley shot them?

**Meadlo:** The people was just lying there, with blood all over them.

4. From a 1968 letter by Hunter S. Thompson to his mother, Virginia, regarding Thompson's brother Jim: "I'm not sure how to look at all this; my only flat conviction is that I don't want to see Jim drift into the cannon fodder mill, and especially right now when every life lost in Vietnam is a waste and a mockery of human reason. It's all mechanical now; the talks are getting started and we all know the war's over, in terms of the power struggle, but people will go on being killed right up to the final flag-whistling ceremony."

5. From a 1964 conversation between President Lyndon Johnson and one of his advisors, McGeorge Bundy:

> **Johnson:** I'll tell you, the more that I stayed awake last night thinking of this thing, I don't know what in the hell—it looks to me like we're getting into another Korea. It just worries the hell out of me. I don't see what we can ever hope to get out of with once we're committed. I believe the Chinese Communists are coming in to it. I don't think that we can fight 'em ten thousand miles away from home and ever get anywhere in that area. I don't think it's worth fighting for, and I don't think we can get out, and it's just the biggest damn mess that I ever saw.

> **Bundy:** It's an awful mess.

> **Johnson:** And we've just got to think about it. I was looking at this sergeant of mine this morning—got six little old kids over there—and he's getting out my things and bringing me in my night reading, and all that kind of stuff, and I just thought if I'd ordered all those kids in there and what in hell am I ordering them out there for? What the hell is Vietnam worth to me? What is Laos worth to me? What is it worth to this country?

6. Lyrics from "53rd & Third," from the Ramones' first album in 1976:

> If you think you can, well come on man
> I was a Green Beret in Vietnam

7. Lyrics from "Sonic Reducer," originally by Rocket from the Tombs; popularized by Dead Boys in 1977:

> Don't need no human race

[Max Bell, "The Ramones: 'Waitin; for World War III' Blues," *New Musical Express*, July 17, 1976; Robert Bly, *Selected Poems*. New York: HarperPerennial, 1986, pp. 62–63; Lyndon B. Johnson, May 27, 1964, PBH Online Newshour, www.pbs.org/newshour; Hunter S. Thompson, "To Virgina Thompson, May 8, 1968," in *Fear and Loathing in America: The Gonzo Letters, Volume II*, ed. Douglas Brinkley, New York: Simon and Schuster, 2000, p. 67.]

## Viletones

**They certainly lived up to their name,** and they were at the center of Toronto's punk scene during the late seventies. They included Steven Leckie ("Nazi Dog"), Freddy Pompeii, Chris Paputts ("Chris Hate"), and Mike Anderson ("Motor X"). They played at CBGB in 1977, where the violence of their performance suggested that punk was already speeding directly into hardcore. "The Viletones deliver on a level that exists only under rocks," wrote Jeremy Gluck in *Sounds*, and listening to the band you wondered if Canada's Long Grudge Against the World was finally being metted out in the music of the Viletones. Songs like "Screaming Fist," "Danger Boy," and "Rebel" laid waste to the pretense that punk was basically a return to rock and roll's roots. "Loud, rambunctious, and wild. Toronto's true punks," wrote Robert Barry Frances in *FFanzeen*, in his capsule review of the "Screaming Fist" 45. "Definitely should be bought by only those who want to blast their stereos." The Viletones played music like a kid raised by wolves would play with his baby cousin: watch out. "Nazi Dog, lead singer for a Toronto punk band called The Viletones," *Creem* reported in 1978, "has reportedly announced he will kill himself on stage in a year or so from now. Maybe he needs a Punk-to-Drunk talk with Alice Cooper . . . soon."

In a Canadian television feature on the punk scene, broadcast in September 1977, there was this exchange between Leckie and the reporter, Hana Gartner:

**Gartner:** I would really like to understand what you are trying to do. What *are* you trying to do?

**Leckie:** I'm trying to have fun, and having fun making money having fun. We'd like to create a generation gap.

**Gartner:** I think you've succeeded.

**Leckie:** Because there hasn't been one in years. I mean my parents . . .

**Gartner:** I'm of the same generation and you've created a gap.

**Leckie:** Okay. Alright. But like my parents love Fleetwood Mac, Elton John, Paul McCartney, the Beatles. You know what I mean? I mean that's acceptable for old people.

Leckie's historical self-consciousness—"we'd like to create a generation gap"—is one of punk's defining features. The proliferation of pop culture in the sixties and seventies meant that traditions were readily accessible and available—all the more easy to destroy. In 1935, Walter Benjamin wrote that an "analysis of art in the age of mechanical reproduction must do justice to these relationships, for they lead us to an all-important insight: for the first time in world history, mechanical reproduction emancipates the work of art from its parasitical dependence ritual. To an ever

A copy of a copy of a copy: mechanical reproduction in the punk era, from *New York Rocker* in 1981

greater degree the work of art reproduced becomes the work of art designed for reproducibility. From the photographic negative, for example, one can make any number of prints; to ask for the 'authentic' print makes no sense." The problem—by the mid-seventies, at the dawn of the video age—was that the past never went away. It hung around forever—on television reruns, on records, on tapes, on the radio, at the movies—an ever-present reminder of tradition. "DESTROY!" might have been the mantra ascribed to the Sex Pistols, but in truth groups like the Dead Boys and the Viletones were even more *destructive* in their music.

An advertisement in *New York Rocker* from 1981 for QUIK Cassette Corp. offers duplication services—"Cassette & Tape Copies from one to any number": the reproduction of sound, soon perfected in the digital age by the promise of no generation loss. The extremity of punk was necessary if it wanted to separate itself from the previous generation, whose music and icons had, it seemed, permanently saturated the culture. If the punks were to separate themselves from the hippies, it would be through music that sounded like Total War.

[Walter Benjamin, "The Work of Art in the Age of Mechanical Reproduction," in *Film Theory and Criticism*, ed. Leo Braudy and Marshall Cohen, 1935; repr., New York: Oxford University Press, 1999, p. 736; "Canadian Punk Rock," broadcast on September 27, 1977, Canadian Broadcasting Corporation, http://archives.cbc.ca; Robert Barry Frances, "A Glance at Singles and Albums," *FFanzeen* no. 3, Winter–Spring 1978–79, p. 27; Jeremy Gluck, "The Viletones: The Four Viletones of the Apocalypse," *Sounds*, January 21, 1978; "Rock 'n' Roll News," *Creem*, April 1978, p. 19.]

## *Village Voice, The*

**There is perhaps no better time capsule** of the cultural conditions that spawned underground and punk music in New York City in the mid-seventies than *The Village Voice*, which straddled the blurry divide between mainstream and what would come to be known as "alternative" media. Unlike the fanzines that were beginning to spring up, the *Voice* was not slavishly committed to the music it described; in many ways, the skepticism and distance here was more in keeping with the evolving punk spirit than the single-minded, claustrophobic worshipfulness of the zines.

Just eleven pages after Robert Christgau's enthusiastic review ("for me, it blows everything else off the radio") of the Ramones' first album in the June 14, 1976, *Village Voice*, you find the cafés, clubs, coffeehouse listings, a hodgepodge of clubs and musical acts. The simple design of the CBGB ad stands out, with its black background and white lettering. In this issue, CBGB advertises for the Shirts, Acme Band, Big Apple Kid, Blondie, the Mumps, Tuff Darts, Mink DeVille, Orchestra Luna, and Talking Heads. Right beside the CBGB ad is one for Max's Kansas City, listing shows by the Ramones, the Poppees, Chords Melody, Last American Heroes, and others. Big Julie's Cabaret, Disco, Steakhouse features Laurie Beechman opening June 14 and "disco dancing—a total experience in sound and light." There are ads for folk music, jazz, country, and bluegrass.

In the "Free or under $2.50" events section, here are a few of the events you could choose from for Saturday, June 12, 1976: "Revolution vs Counterrevolution," a discussion at St. Mark's in the Bowery, "Karl Marx and the Permanent Revolution," a talk at the School for Marxist Education, "Artists: An Endangered Species; What Can Be Done About It?," a discussion at the Pleiades Gallery, or "SoHo Art through Anarchist Eyes," a walking tour.

*The Village Voice* revealed more about the emergence of the underground/punk scene in New York than the music magazines, newspapers, and fanzines because, in its disorderly pages from the seventies, was evidence of the creeps, hustlers, and phony new-age gurus; the glorious filth and stink of the city; the corruption and the scandal; the piling garbage and the smeared-glass phone booths; the paranoia and violence; the vague understanding and resigned dread that the sixties had finally ended and that the slow, ruthlessly efficient restoration of order that would mark the Reagan era was gradually emerging on the horizon.

## vinyl

**It's difficult to write about vinyl without telling stories,** without being nostalgic. (This is a warning.) "I went over to Peter's parents' house," Charlotte Pressler once said, referring to Peter Laughner, "'cause he was still in high school, and I walked in the living room and there were his albums on the floor arranged in alphabetical order and the first one in the stack was Albert Ayler's *Bells*, and I said to myself, 'Boy, I think I want to get to know this person.'" Of course a version of this same story has happened, perhaps to us all, whether it be with albums, or tapes, or CDs, or iPod lists. But each of these mediums is unique and seductive in its own way. Vinyl was the perfect medium for punk because the warmth of its sound was an ideal foil for punk's harsh clarity and because the pops, hisses, and scratches—the imperfections—were in keeping with the punk aesthetic. By 1979, the end of vinyl in favor of tape and later digital was already being foretold. Here is Richard Robinson, writing in *Creem*, from that year:

> There's one fatal flaw in the business of putting music on record, and that's the method used to get the music back off the record. The needle riding in the undulating groove does retrieve the sound, but each time you play the record that needle sliding along the groove is ruining it. By the time you've played your favorite record, say 50 times, it's likely that you've destroyed most of its fidelity.
>
> Theoretically, the needle in the groove principle works great; practically, it's pretty terrible. The laser beam, digital recording, and other systems now in the planning stages do away with Tom Edison's original needle in groove idea.

Ah, but that sound. Yes, there were many debates about the overclarity, the pureness, the separation, the coldness of sound on CDs when they first emerged. And yet, the reactionaries were right, but in unexpected ways. For it's not just that vinyl sounds warmer and fuller (it doesn't always), but also this: the fact that vinyl's playback system—the turntable—was not readily portable meant that its sounds were attached to a specific place: a bedroom, a basement, a family room. The Walkman (introduced in 1979) freed music from its dependence on place, and further eroded the rituals of listening to music in a specific place.

Every generation romanticizes its formative technologies, even as it sheds them for new ones. Introduced in 1948 by CBS, long-playing records were, as Robert Fink has noted, "designed for serious classical music, its 22 minutes per side carefully chosen to allow uninterrupted playback of single movements within the standard concert repetoire." Rock and roll, driven by singles, transformed the LP into an archive of distinct songs, separated by bands, the shiny, quiet pauses between the songs. Repetition was the key, as the arm could be "set" to return to the beginning and drop the needle all over again. Of course the songs meant something as individual songs, but also as parts of a whole. Side One and side Two, or side A and side B—these were like book chapters with different characters, different moods, different styles. Why—and by whom, you wondered—were songs arranged in this sequence? Was there a connection between the last song of the first side and the first song of the last side? Was the last song on the album the most significant, the one most full of meaning? There was a deliberateness involved here, a process, an anticipation, and those first dusty, scratchy sounds as the needle made its inevitable progress toward the song. Was there something more valuable about music that came packaged in large sleeves and that was spread out across two or more sides of vinyl? Probably not, and yet as music has shrunk over the decades—from vinyl, to eight-track and cassettes, to CDs, and ultimately to nothing more than download-able "files"—it's hard to say where music even exists anymore. Dowloaded onto devices, it's as disposable as it ever was, but without the romance.

And here is the story: the boy in his room, the late August sun coming through in orange, the locusts just coming up, sitting on his floor, in bell-bottomed jeans and a T-shirt, listening to the Clash, feeling time run out in the spinning of the record, like a clock running down to the end of days, wondering how many rotations consti-tuted his life. In theory, the record could keep playing forever, the arm automatically returning and dropping the needle back at the beginning, over and over, as long as there was electricity to power it, as long as the needle held up, as long as the record held up. Of course, the boy would grow up, finish high school, and toss out or sell a few albums each time he moved (too burdensome to lug around from place to place), holding on to only his favorites. He fell in love. He married. Kids. House. Dog. The beauty and terrors of this world. Sometimes he loved the people he knew so deeply he weeped, for no reason other than that he loved them. He would write a book, and in it an entry called "vinyl" that he could not end by saying this:

Describing the sound of a cell phone conversation in William Gibson's novel *Spook Country*: "There was a silence, on his end. A true, absolute, and digital silence, devoid of that random background sizzle that she'd always taken as much for granted during an international call as she took the sky overhead when she was outside."

[Robert Fink, *Repeating Ourselves: American Minimal Music as Cultural Practice*, Berkeley: University of California Press, 2005, p. 176; William Gibson, *Spook Country*, New York: G. P. Putnam's Sons, 2007, p. 157; Charlotte Pressler quoted in Clinton Heylin, *From the Velvets to the Voidoids: A Pre-Punk History for a Post-Punk World*, New York: Penguin, 1993, p. 52; Richard Robinson, "Dirty Records," *Creem*, November 1979, p. 39.]

## Wallace and Ladmo Show, The

**A children's television show,** out of Phoenix, Arizona, that ran from 1954 through 1989. Like *Looney Tunes* had been in previous decades, it was really adult entertain-ment disguised as a kids' show. It was an anarchy of costumes, props, and sketches in which seemingly nothing in the adult world was sacred. Steven Hufsteter, of the Quick, has said of the show's hosts that "these guys were very hip kind of bohemian types. And all of the members of Alice Cooper and the Tubes grew up watching them. I grew up watching it, too, and the humor of bands like the Dickies and the Quick is all directly attributed to *Wallace and Ladmo*."

[Steven Hufsteter quoted in Mark Spitz and Brendan Mullen, *We Got the Neutron Bomb: The Untold Story of L.A. Punk*, New York: Three Rivers Press, 2001, p. 119.]

**W**

# Warhol, Andy

**Although Warhol is often distantly associated with punk** because of his work in the late sixties with the Velvet Underground, whose experimentation with noise and feedback would resonate years later in punk, his deeper impact lies in the way he—and Pop Art in general—collapsed distinctions between high and low, and in the process made it possible for New York's underground (and later punk and New Wave) music to be both acclaimed and rejected as either dumb junk or avant-garde genius. In some respects, bands like the Ramones were the culmination of Pop Art: cartoon-like characters on a stage playing music so repetitive yet earnest that their intentions remained mysterious.

It was Warhol who reminded us that context is everything. Take an advertising logo (i.e., Campbell's Soup's) and put it in an art gallery and it suddenly means something else, something totally different than it does on a soup can at Foodtown. If the hippies made some effort to distance themselves from the commodities of popular culture, Warhol embraced it in a way that suggested irony:

> What's great about this country is that America started the tradition where the richest consumers buy essentially the same thing as the poorest. You can be watching TV and see Coca-Cola, and you know that the President drinks Coke, Liz Taylor drinks Coke, and just think, you can drink Coke, too. A Coke is a Coke and no amount of money can get you a better Coke than the bum on the corner is drinking. All the Cokes are the same and all the Cokes are good. Liz Taylor knows it, the President knows it, the bum knows it, and you know it.

Warhol made it possible for the Ramones to sing about movies, TV shows, cereal, and all the rest of "junk" culture. About the U.S.A., Johnny Rotten said: "It's just like watching a boring American TV program. I could care less about New York or Chicago. They're just like any other city, you know. It's not the fucking promised land." For Warhol, what was special about America was precisely its obviousness: The transformation of the everyday into art offered a way to get beyond the feeling that, in the seventies, America was certainly not the promised land. Andy Warhol figured out a way to make that fact irrelevant, and that has made all the difference.

[Patrick Goldstein, "Sex Pistols in the Promised Land," *Creem*, April 1978, p. 34; Andy Warhol, *The Philosophy of Andy Warhol (from A to B and Back Again)*, New York: Harcourt Brace Jovanovich, 1975, p. 100.]

## "The wave of the future is not the long hair"

**So said Richard Nixon in 1971 in conversation with Ronald Ziegler,** who was White House Press Secretary. In a way, punk confirmed Nixon's prediction, even as the long hair of the Ramones was an exception. Punk fashion has always been more associated with the shorter, spiky hair of Johnny Rotten, and later the skinheads, whose look was an absolute repudiation of the hippies. Here is the quote in context:

**President:** —that's what irritates you g-, friends out in the press room. They just can't stand it, you know. They, they think they run the country and they don't anymore. Not even now. They, they, it's tougher now than it was, but on any great issue, and once we get the war over, we'll beat their livin' bejesus out of those people out there 'cause they're on the wrong side.

**Ziegler:** They're on the wrong side.

**President:** [Unintelligible] the wave of the future is not the long hair. And it isn't all this vice and it isn't all this decadent stuff. Sure—

**Unknown:** [Unintelligible].

**President:** —I don't mean the wave of the future doesn't include a lot of immorality—that's always been with us—but these people glorifying it; that's the point. That's where they're wrong. They are not gonna win that way. This country isn't gonna go that way, I don't think.

[Part of a conversation between President Nixon and Ronald L. Ziegler in the Oval Office between 2:14 pm and 2:30 pm on May 4, 1971, http://www.nixonlibrary.gov/forresearchers/find/tapes/finding_aids/tapesubjectlogs/trn490-22.pdf.]

## Weirdos

**Whenever I think of the Weirdos,** I think of an approximation of these lines from the novel *Ask the Dust*, by John Fante:

I got back to Los Angeles the next day. The city was the same, but I was afraid. The streets lurked with danger. The tall buildings forming black canyons were traps to kill you when then earth shook. The pavement might open. The street cars might topple.

Their 1981 demo, "Arms Race," is the perfect expression of this unfulfilled doom.

Let me start again . . . Weirdos. Formed in 1976 in Los Angeles, California. A faraway land. Their early music is always opening onto some new vista. There is a sheer joy and humanistic expressiveness (just listen to "Happy People" [1979] and tell me it doesn't convince you to remove that gun from your mouth, that rough noose from around your neck, to momentarily forget the memory of the one you have lost) in the music of the Weirdos that doesn't quite fit with the image of the California hardcore scene that developed in their wake. But let's go back to that song for a moment. The sound is pure joy. But the lyrics: "I knew a happy little girl / Trapped in her happy little world / Ravaged from desire." The song is happy despite the fact that it makes fun of being happy. A signal, a spark, leaped Tesla-like from the East Coast to the West, and was immediately refigured out there in California, the place of hippies and earthquakes.

That joy is also there in the demo version of "Fallout" (1980), which turns from dark sky into sunshine in the chorus. Listening to songs like this and you really do begin to wonder if there was a conspiracy to keep this music from mainstream radio.

Is there some permission that living in California gives you? In Ohio, all happiness made us guilty. This was, we believed, our strength. Many of us secretly believed that the economic terror of the seventies was Calvinist punishment for something, probably the sixties. That's why all the great Cleveland bands from the mid-seventies (Styrenes, Electric Eels, Rocket from the Tombs, Pagans, even Pere Ubu) have a sort of built-in destruction, the songs trailing off into a pre-*Vineland* Thomas Pynchon–like absurdity before coming 'round again. Not so with California bands that prefer to cut to the heart of the matter and linger there a little bit longer. Perhaps this is why some East Coast fanzines, like *New York Rocker*, viewed bands like the Weirdos as goofy throwoffs, stealing just enough of New York punk to distinguish themselves. "The non-punk *Biff Bang Pow* cites the Weirdos as supposed punk representation (a dubious choice!)," we learn from a 1979 column entitled "Los Angeles."

In 1979, the band described themselves like this: "In the earliest days of the scene, the Weirdos were the first Hollywood band to surface. There was no scene when we started . . . we think we helped seed the ground for what later came along." An important thing to remember about the Weirdos is that, according to John Denney—the vocalist and main songwriter for the band—"the main catalyst in the development of the Weirdos was the release of the Ramones' first album. That's what pushed us over the edge."

The previously unreleased demo "I'm Not Like You," recorded in July 1978 and available on the compilation *Weird World Vol. 1: 1977–1981*, is a testament to the unclassifiable nature of this music.

> [John Denney, "Weirdoism," in *Fucked Up + Photocopied: Instant Art of the Punk Rock Movement*, by Bryan Ray Turcotte and Christopher T. Miller, Berkeley, CA: Gingko Press, 1999; John Fante, *Ask the Dust*, 1939; repr., New York: Ecco, 2006, p. 102; "Los Angeles," *New York Rocker*, August 1979, p. 32; quote from Weirdos in *Damage, An Inventory* vol. 1, October 1979, p. 24.]

## "When You're Young"

**A song by the Jam, released in September 1979,** so lyric-heavy in its first minutes that its last minute comes on like a thing of shimmering, wordless beauty that you wish would never end. A song like this shatters distinctions between pop and punk, and lyrics like "You swear you're never ever gonna work for someone / No corporations for the new age sons"—which might sound like neo-Marxist theory in a textbook—sound like a call to dance in a punk song. But the real heart of the song comes in that last minute, after the lyrics, when the sheer music transcends any theory that motivates the lyrics.

## Whistle punk

**Before the word punk became associated with music,** it had other meanings and uses. Here is a good definition:

> The engineer or donkey puncher ran the [steam] donkey. In the early days of logging, the donkey was run in response to signals relayed by the whistle punk. The

An old word, new again in the mid-seventies

donkey would often be out of site from the logging area itself and the whistle punk would relay messages to the donkey puncher from the logging site letting them know when the timber was ready to be moved and to where. The whistle punk was often a youth, possibly a new camp member or sometimes a disabled logger. Whistle punks jerked the whistle wire running from the logging site to the donkey in a combination of long or short blasts based on Morse code.

*The Whistle Punk of Camp 15* is the name of a children's book (first published as *Lumbercamp* in 1939, and later as *Whistle Punk* in 1959) written and illustrated by Glen Rounds. My copy is stamped with two phrases: PROPERTY OF NAHA AIR BASE LIBRARY OKINAWA and, several pages later, CONDEMNED.

["The Work: Workers' Roles, Camp to Community, www.camptocommunity.ca/english/work/roles.html.]

## *Who Killed Bambi?*

**It is, as they say, strange but true** that the film critic Roger Ebert, at the request of Malcom McLaren, had in 1977 written a screenplay for the film *Who Killed Bambi?*, which would star the Sex Pistols. Apparently they were fans of the Russ Meyer film *Beyond the Valley of the Dolls*, which Ebert had written. That movie is in many ways a reverse history of punk, as an all-girl rock band heads to California to try to make it. There's none of the anger of punk in the film, but all of the exaggeration and absurdity. Ebert has said of *Beyond the Valley of the Dolls*, "I think of it as an essay on our generic expectations. It's an anthology of stock situations, characters, dialogue, clichés, and stereotypes, set to music and manipulated to work as exposition and satire at the same time . . . [it's] a wind-up machine to generate emotions, pure movie without message." He might as well be describing punk.

*Who Killed Bambi?* was never completed, because the Sex Pistols never really wanted to make it. Meyer and Ebert flew to London to meet the Sex Pistols, where they "affected a total disinterest in the screenplay; their literary contributions were limited to penciling in 'f - - -' every three words." Ebert was to have written the script with the writer and director Rene Daadler, who described the experience this way:

> Russ Meyer, the filmmaker who was the best man at my wedding, was asked to make a Sex Pistols movie. He called me because of my teenage movie *Massacre at Central High*, which anticipated punk, *Heathers*, and Columbine back in '76 . . . and so McLaren, Russ, Roger Ebert, and myself were supposed to collaborate on developing a movie concept for the Pistols. Roger and myself were to write the script with input from Russ and Malcom. It was an impossible mix . . . I worked

Ad for *The Great Rock 'n' Roll Swindle* double album, *New Musical Express*, March 1979

for months writing and rewriting different versions of what came to be called *Who Killed Bambi?* but I couldn't bridge the chasm that existed between the band and their management at one end and Russ at the other . . . One day Russ yelled at Johnny Lydon to have some respect. He shouted out: "We saved your limey asses in World War II!" It all ended in bitter tears of rage and lawsuits, and Russ would never make a film again.

[Roger Ebert, comments on *Beyond the Valley of the Dolls*, 1980, http://rogerebert.suntimes. com; Roger Ebert, "Anarchy in the U.K.: My Life with Sid Vicious," 2005, http://roger ebert.suntimes.com; Rene Daadler quoted in Mark Spitz and Brendan Mullen, *We Got the Neutron Bomb: The Untold Story of L.A. Punk*. New York: Three Rivers Press, 2001, pp. 153–54.]

## "Why?"

**A song by the Seize,** from Reading, United Kingdom. They were Colin and David Newton, and Jillian and Andy Stafford. "Why?" was released in 1980, and it's as if no one had told the Seize that the days of fun punk were over, that things either needed to get superserious with hardcore or insipid with post-punk (with a few groups, like Wire, being the exception). In truth, the Seize sounded like the Weirdos crossed up with the Sex Pistols. The song seemed to ask, in its off-kilter cadences and headlong plunging, why punk had to end.

# "The World's a Mess; It's in My Kiss"

**A strange and wonderful song** from the band X from their 1980 LP, *Los Angeles*, produced by Ray Manzarek. Featuring Billy Zoom, John Doe, Exene Cervenka, and D. J. Bonebreak. There is a sort of *Wind-Up Bird Chronicle* force that propels the song beyond reason. It starts simply enough, with a Buddy Holly–like riff—but then: "No one is united / all thing are untied." So what if the rest of the song doesn't live up to those opening seconds? It doesn't have to. The secret lies in Exene's enunciation of the word "kiss," which extends into Barbara Stanwyck territory: Suddenly you feel yourself in a car careening over some California highway cliff late at night like in some film noir or in *Mulholland Drive*, and you know you are going to die, but you also know it is going to be, until those last agonizing seconds, a lot of fun.

"This is one of the finest pieces of poetry ever set to music," *Damage* proclaimed at the time. "Traces of Burroughs, Bukowski—the words run around the music, daring it to keep up." Yes, the album is legendary, and yet it achieves greatness mostly on "The World's a Mess," "Los Angeles," "Your Phone's Off the Hook, But You're Not," and "Nausea." And of those, only "The World's a Mess" transports you so far away from yourself that ending sentences properly is no longer . . .

[Miss Nomer, review of *Los Angeles*, *Damage* vol. 1, no. 7, July 1980, p. 36.]

# "Write Down Your Number"

**A song by La Peste that spreads itself in your brain** like a pesticide designed to kill all bad and cynical thoughts. This song exterminates cynicism. It makes you fall in love.

You have no idea if "Write Down Your Number," from 1978, is punk or not, and you don't care. The speed and purity of this song puts a lie to every evil thought you have ever had, every grudge you have harbored, every doubt about the truth of beauty you have obsessed over. You are a new person when you listen to it. The tempo changes, and so does your heart. You even consider that if bad people listened to this song, they would become good. You can imagine a knife being removed from its throat-slitting position. A criminal at 3:00 a.m. deciding not to enter through the carelessly unlocked door. The sun comes out. And then the clouds move across the sky and cover the sun and everything is dark again. The truth is always dark.

In all honesty, you had never heard of La Peste until you began writing this book, until D. Barker expressed his faith in you by sending you a contract. You heard about La Peste via Rave Up Records, from Italy, and the last thirty-five seconds of this song (that address in Italy—Via Crispolti 16—is a mystery almost as great as the music itself) confirms the best thoughts you have ever had in your life (probably when you were eight years old) and rejects the worst thoughts. "Don't tell your papa / he's gonna try and stop ya / from talkin' / to me . . . Call me if you wanna / I think you're gonna." The song's tempo changes—shifting from punkish speed to slow sunny vistas that remind you of wide meadows—make you wonder just what is wrong with the world that more people don't know this song. The song "Better Off Dead"—it makes you laugh! "You keep you hands off my daughter you'd be better off dead / that girl's only thirteen she ain't never giving head."

**X**

## "Xerox Days"

**A phrase used by Ed Ward** in his profile of the Austin, Texas, punk/New Wave group the Standing Waves in *New York Rocker*:

> These are the Xerox Days, the day when ideas that were fresh a year or so ago are coming back at their creators in the form of thinly-disguised copies, replicas that seem to have been copied off a video screen with poor reception.

And of course so many of the early punk fanzines were duplicated on Xerox machines, as described by Mark P., whose *Sniffin' Glue* was among the earliest:

> I put the magazine together with the same "back to basics" approach as the music that I was to feature. The main text, if you could call it that, was typed out on an old children's typewriter that my parents had bought me as a Christmas present when I was about ten. The titles and the limited "graphics" I scrawled out with a black felt tipped pen . . . Once I'd finished putting the mag together, my girlfriend, Louise, got some printed up on the Xerox machine in the office where she worked.

Cheap copying meant not only that you could mass-produce a fanzine at fairly low costs, it also mean that, by the late seventies, you could duplicate and exchange music on cassettes as well. "The Punk style," Charlie Gere has written, "with its disruptions and disjunctures, its emphasis on texts and its use of iconic graphics anticipates the coming world of ubiquitous graphic computing." But the liberation of cheap copying was also a contradiction, for it struck at the deep punk desire for originality and authenticity. On the one had, punk derided the progressive-pop notion of the arena-rock star or the sensitive singer-songwriter, yet on the other hand punk depended on the unique force of the shock of the new. In the age of mechanical reproduction and fast copies, punk proliferated faster than it could produce new material; this is essentially why its influence has been so lasting. In harnessing the basic technologies of Xerox and duplication, punk out-copied itself and spread, viruslike, into even the most mainstream channels, such as sitcoms like *C.P.O. Sharkey* and *Archie Bunker's Place.*

Jean Baudrillard (not a name you want to come across in a book such as this, I know, but there you have it) once wrote that it "is no longer possible to fabricate the unreal from the real, the imaginary from the givens of the real." Punk's original appeal was in laying utter waste to the pretenses of the unreal music of the counterculture, which had by the early seventies become intoxicated by its own obsolescent banality. On a fairer note, it could be said that the Xerox-based aesthetic was not something that emerged merely out of necessity, but that it emerged in direct reaction to the psychedelic rock-art of the sixties—by the likes of Alton Kelley, Rick Griffin, Stanley Mouse, and others—that was colorful, complex, deep, and "original." Punk art, in contrast, was simple, and often openly gloried in thievery, as fliers were pieced together from other sources (letters from headlines, etc.) in a form of reductive bricolage.

"The mind which plunges into Surrealism relives with glowing excitement the best part of its childhood," André Breton wrote in "Manifesto of Surrealism" in 1924. And while punk's roots in surrealism and Dada have been ably explored by the likes of Greil Marcus and Dick Hebdige, I think there is also a simpler and perhaps less gracious explanation for punk's simplicity and destruction that is captured nicely in the quote from Breton. Punk was, on so many levels, a return to childhood, to a time before all the taboos and repressions had taken hold. A time of disorder, of randomness, of violence even ("No hitting! No biting! No spitting!"). The throwing of objects at concerts, the slamming, the fights, all sort of a hyper-realized large-scale elementary-school-cafeteria foodfight turned into melee. Punk was less of a self-conscious *detournment* of the media landscape as it was a collective effort to forget what it was like to be an adult. "Now that she had accepted it, the threat of violence in the air had matured Anne," goes a line in J. G. Ballard's novel *High-Rise*, published during the first punk era. The problem for punk was not that it matured, but that in returning to childhood for inspiration it grew nostalgic. When the Ramones sang "They're forming in a straight line" in "Blitzkrieg Bop" (a punk anthem if there ever was one) they were counting themselves in as the "kids," as if this could last forever.

But of course they weren't.

And it didn't.

[J. G. Ballard, *High-Rise*, 1975; repr., New York: Popular Library, 1978, p. 133; André Breton, "Manifesto of Surrealism," in *Manifestos of Surrealism*, trans. Richard Seaver and Helen R. Lane, 1924; repr., Ann Arbor: University of Michigan Press, 1972, p. 39; Charlie Gere, *Digital Culture*, London: Reaktion, 2002, p. 168; Mark Perry, "Mark P.'s Blurb," *Sniffin' Glue: The Essential Punk Accessory*, London: Sanctuary, 2000, pp. 15–16; Ed Ward, "On the Verge with the Standing Waves," *New York Rocker* no. 27, March 1980, p. 27.]

**Z**

## Zeros

**From in and around Chula Vista, California,** came the Zeros, in 1976 and 1977. They were Javier Escovedo (his brother Alejandro was in the Nuns), Robert Lopez, Hector Penalosa, and Baba Chenelle. "Our sound," Escavedo has said, "was influenced by all our favorite bands: The New York Dolls, The Stooges, Bowie, Kiss, T-Rex, Velvet Underground as well as sixties punk groups like The Seeds, The Standells and The Animals, who we also took our look from." In early 1977, the *Los Angeles Times* ran an article by Richard Cromelin entitled "L.A. Translation of 'New Wave' of Punk" with this sentence: "The Zeros represents the Ramones wing, with a touch of Stones via the New York Dolls, and while doing it first means a lot when the style is so elementary, the Zeros still comes across pretty well. The presence is stern and motionless; the group has a lean, hungry barrio look."

While the Zeros sound a lot like the Ramones on first listen, their great insight was to slow things down just a little; the resulting noise is fuller and thunkier and a little closer to heavy metal. This is most evident on "Beat Your Heart Out" from 1978, their second single (on Bomp! Records) and probably their best song. Deceptively framed as a sort of sixties punk song, "Beat Your Heart Out" is relentlessly *the same* throughout, even during the twenty-two second guitar solo near the middle. "Don't Push Me Around," from their first single in 1977, is even more ruthlessly uniform and repetitive, the guitars churning up crunch.

[Richard Cromelin, "L.A. Translation of 'New Wave' of Punk," *Los Angeles Times*, June 22, 1977, p. H8; Javier Escovedo, "The Zeros," 1990, http://punkmodpop.free.fr/zeros.]

# Postscript

# 1982 and the Terminal Aesthetics of Punk

In 1982, U.S. unemployment averaged 9.71 percent, the highest it had been since the end of World War II. In September of that year, it reached 10.1 percent, with nearly 11.3 million people out of work. And domestic auto sales fell nearly 16 percent for the 1982 model year, making it the worst sales year since 1961. In a *New York Times* article by Seth King from August 1982, the president of the A.F.L.-C.I.O. was quoted as saying that these statistics "could not begin to convey the dimensions of the human disaster that is unfolding across the United States." But within just a few years, everything would change as the stock market rose, unemployment fell, as did inflation and interest rates. Even publications such as *The New York Times*, which had been skeptical of Reagan and his policies, ran articles that marveled at the economic turnaround. As Peter Kilborn wrote in the *Times* in 1986:

> Any economist, businessman or politician who just a few months ago predicted anything akin to the current combination of mortgage rates that dip into single digits, inflation of 3 to 4 percent and $15 oil could not have found a job even in that citadel of American optimism, the White House, or in the thousands of lesser institutions that trade on economists' foresight.
>
> Yet the economy has delivered itself of just such a mix of extraordinary good news. And if the booming stock market is any indication, spirits across the land are soaring. Interest rates, dropping into territory not seen since the Seventies, have been the single most important set of numbers, buoying the mood and kicking off Wall Street's heady rise. And the good times—heralded by a new era of lower lending rates—seem here to stay awhile . . . Ronald Reagan, with three straight years of economic growth under his belt, may now be presiding over the longest stretch of low-interest-rate prosperity since Eisenhower.

It would be too easy to say that good times killed off punk, which by 1982 had already evolved into post-punk, Oi!, hardcore, etc. In fact, some of the more popular videos on MTV in 1982 and '83 were by veterans of the first-wave punk scenes: "Back on the Chain Gang" by the Pretenders, "Our Lips Are Sealed" by the

Go-Gos, and "I Love Rock 'n' Roll" by Joan Jett. In a strange sort of way, punk was made possible by and thrived beneath the long shadow cast by the sixties; in the cool shade of its legacy, punk was able to thrive as a contradiction. Once that contradiction was resolved—for instance, once punk evolved into its *pure* form in hardcore—it dissipated. The seventies, sprawled out in chaos between the progressive sixties and the conservative eighties, was so incoherent that punk's incoherency made perfect sense, or nonsense. For in truth, groups like the Sex Pistols or the Ramones or the Dead Boys were sheer nonsense, scrambled signals from the far reaches of disorder. The Resoration of Order during the 1980s, under the symbols of Ronald Reagan and Margaret Thatcher, helped to speed punk's meaning into nostalgia.

In 1985, Tipper Gore and others launched the Parents' Music Resource Center in response to music whose lyrics supposedly contributed to violence, suicide, rape, and the use of drugs and alcohol in American society. In a letter sent out to parents who had expressed similar concerns, the PMRC asked that "you and your friends join our MEDIA WATCH by monitoring your local radio and TV broadcasts carefully and, if offensive material is aired, writing down the objectionable words/songs/scenes, name and date of the program, and its commercial sponsors." As part of the broader culture wars, the activities of the PRMC were not that surprising, and the resulting "explicit lyrics" warnings are not that much different from movie ratings. And of course television shows and video games have generally followed the same patterns for labeling content. But abundance of labeling that gained favor in the eighties is significant for other reasons that go beyond questions of censorship. For in truth, the economies of the so-called culture industries—movies, music, television, cable, video games, and the vast post-reality of the Internet itself—depend upon extremity in content and style.

Punk emerged in the pre–New Media era when signals from the frontiers and outposts of culture still traveled a bit slowly; it had time to evolve before coming under broader public scrutiny. As a style and stance, punk reflected and distorted a particular era, just as film noir was a product of its time, or baroque music was a product of its time. By the early eighties, punk was an established, respectable genre, generating millions of dollars in profit. It had survived long enough for there to be backlashes against it, for it to be considered cliché, even for there to be nostalgia about its beginnings. In a strange way, the power and appeal of conservatism in the eighties conferred a sort of legitimacy on punk. In 1987, Margaret Thatcher, in an interview with *Woman's Own* magazine, said, "There is no such thing as society." In other contexts—anarchy, punk, surrealism—the statement might have the force of prophecy, but coming from Thatcher, it meant something like: *Society has no obligation to help the unfortunate because there is no such thing as society, but rather a collection of individuals.* Both Reagan and Thatcher preached the gospel of individualism and self-reliance—in other words, a DIY ethic.

Was there a meanness to that?

Perhaps, just as there was a meanness to punk.

And that, as they say, is that.

[Peter T. Kilborn, "At the Dawn of Low Interest Rates," *The New York Times*, March 16, 1986; Seth King, "Unemployment Up to 9.8% for July, a Postwar Record," *The New York Times*, August 7, 1982.]

# Postscript Redux

## [by Ephraim P. Noble]

**I find myself in the unenviable position** of being "allowed" only 533 words by the tyrannical forces at Continuum to respond to my appearance in these pages, as both "author" of at least one entry, and as the subject of several others. While it is unfortunately true that I wrote the "Dictators" entry (unfortunate because the assignment was sprung on me at a very low point in my late life during the throes of almost perpetual intoxication) I would never have used the phrase "structural incongruities," as anyone who knows me (and granted very few people know me now or have ever known me) can testify. As for the mailroom incident so colorfully depicted in the "Cindy 2" entry, I can only say that, again, the phrase "Don't get supernatural on me" is simply not something that could possibly ever come from my mouth. Granted, the rest of the entry is accurate (but then what is *accurate* in today's uncertain age?), and even captures the weird desperation of those times, when burning buildings and fleeing across campuses and seeking revenge on hateful hunchbacks seemed the glorious—and proper—sorts of things to do.

As for punk itself, I would erase the whole blasted era if I could. I would *paint it black*, as they say, so black that it disappeared forever and completely. Nothing kind came from it, and since the signed (in triplicate) agreement regarding my 533 words allows me the absolute freedom to use whatever words I choose (with the exception of three) I can say whatever I want about punk. I have total immunity. So come and get me, if you dare. I live in a vast underground tunnel system these days, winding its way beneath the Falling Apart Dis-United States of America, with enough food and weapons to last beyond my years. There is a growling Noise that comes at night, true enough, as if something was stalking me through these tunnels, where I composed these words by the light of a slender taper. The Noise follows me, and indeed in the deepest of deepest of nights I admit I sometimes regret going underground, becoming invisible, a fugitive from my very own nation. What used to be my nation.

As for D. Barker and N. Rombes, I believe they have acted badly and against their better natures. The author of this volume, especially, should have thought twice. In the first place, punk is simply not a worthy subject of so many words. Any half-wit knows as much. But more importantly—and unforgivably, I'm afraid—he has dragged me into the whole mess, involving me in his shenanigans, exposing me to readers who are strangers, and forcing me to defend myself and reveal, out of necessity, the existence of the sub-American tunnels, where, until now, I have lived completely alone, my own man, my own Thoreau in his own labyrinth of Walden Ponds. God and Heaven help him—and you—if, as a result of this book, I am forced to make peace with the Noise, and become its ally, and emerge with vengeance out of the tunnels back into the Land that once was, so long ago and far away, my home.